心灵鸡汤全集

（英汉对照）

青　闰⊙主　编

程　爽⊙副主编

台海出版社

图书在版编目(CIP)数据

英汉双语心灵鸡汤全集 / 青闰主编 . -- 北京 : 台
海出版社 , 2018.5
ISBN 978-7-5168-1882-4

Ⅰ . ①英… Ⅱ . ①青… Ⅲ . ①英语—汉语—对照读物
②故事—作品集—世界 Ⅳ . ① H319.4:Ⅰ

中国版本图书馆 CIP 数据核字 (2018) 第 092501 号

英汉双语心灵鸡汤全集

主　　编：青　闰			
责任编辑：高惠娟　赵旭雯		装帧设计：同人阁文化传媒·书装设计	
版式设计：同人阁文化传媒·书装设计		责任印制：蔡　旭	

出版发行：台海出版社

地　　址：北京市东城区景山东街 20 号　　邮政编码：100009

电　　话：010 — 64041652（发行，邮购）

传　　真：010 — 84045799（总编室）

网　　址：www.taimeng.org.cn/thcbs/default.htm

E－mail：thcbs@126.com

经　　销：全国各地新华书店

印　　刷：香河利华文化发展有限公司

本书如有破损、缺页、装订错误，请与本社联系调换

开　　本：710mm×1000mm		1/16	
字　　数：352 千字		印　　张：20.25	
版　　次：2018年9月第1版		印　　次：2018年9月第1次印刷	
书　　号：ISBN 978-7-5168-1882-4			

定　　价：39.80 元

前　　言

　　《心灵鸡汤全集》是让人获得成功的心灵密码，是按摩情感的心灵圣经，也是温暖千万心灵、改变千万人生的传世宝典。本书所选篇章以英汉对照形式编排，原汁原味，新颖独特，系统全面，贴近实际，贴近时代，贴近生活，所选内容发人深省、引人入胜、耐人寻味、励人奋进。

　　《心灵鸡汤全集》分为点亮生命的航灯、永不放弃、通向成功的神秘之门、生命的加减法、幸福的旅程、春天的乐章、坚持你的梦想、看不见的小奇迹和飞向我的爱等九卷，涉及心态、宽容、尊重、亲情、爱情、友谊、善良、感恩、幸福、做人、做事、挫折、成功等一系列人生课题。这些文章既可以使读者感到心灵震撼，又可以从容自信，端正人生态度，找到生活方向，成就美满人生。

　　朋友，每当华灯初上，白天的喧哗与骚动渐渐平息，伴着明月清风，和着舒缓旋律，携一卷美文，品一杯香茗，坐在属于自己的空间，体验文字带给你的优美、睿智、灵动与流畅，感受时间从指缝间飘然而去，体味一种纯净、充实和有趣的生活，是何等美妙和惬意！

　　我们奉献给你的正是这样一种精神享受。她们像一只只神奇灵动的手拨动着你的心弦，使你如沐春风、如逢甘霖。她们就像鲜花一样芬芳，月色一样柔和，微风一样清新，春雨一样滋润。

　　朋友，请走进我们营造的精神家园，这里有你的青春，有你的记忆，有你的梦想，还有你的爱情和希望。让我们在此相会，让我们的人生得到心灵的滋润，提升人生的品位。

  本书由焦作大学青闺主编、翻译和统稿，焦作大学外语学院程爽副主编并参与部分翻译。

目　　录

第一卷　点亮生命的航灯

第二卷　永不放弃

第三卷　通向成功的神秘之门

第四卷　生命的加减法

第五卷　幸福的旅程

第六卷　春天的乐章

第七卷　坚持你的梦想

第八卷　看不见的小奇迹

第九卷　飞向我的爱

第一卷

点亮生命的航灯

The Light Lit up in My Life

Some of my sisters work in Australia. On a reservation, among the Aborigines, there was an elderly man. I can assure you that you have never seen a situation as difficult as that poor old man's. He was completely ignored by everyone. His home was disordered anddirty.

I told him, "Please let me clean your house, wash your clothes and make your bed."

He answered, "I'm okay like this. Let it be."

I said again, "You will be still better if you allow me to do it."

He finally agreed. So I was able to clean his house and wash his clothes. I discovered a beautiful lamp, covered with dust. Only God knows how many years had passed since he last lit it.

I asked him, "Don't you light your lamp? Don't you ever use it?"

He answered, "No. Nobody comes to see me. I have no need to light it. Who would I light it for?"

I asked, "Would you light it every night if my sisters came?"

He replied, "Of course."

From that day on my sisters committed themselves to visiting him every evening. We cleaned the lamp and my sisters would light it every evening.

Two years passed. I had completely forgotten that man. He sent this message, "Tell my friend that the light she lit in my life continues to shine still."

I thought it was a very small thing. We often neglect the small things.

在我生命中点亮的那盏灯

我的几个姊妹在澳洲工作。在一片保留地的土著居民中有一位上了年纪的人。我可以向你保证，你从未见过有比这个可怜老人处境更艰难的人，大家都对他熟视无睹，他的家又脏又乱。

我告诉他："请让我帮你打扫房子、洗洗衣服、铺铺床吧。"

他应道："我这样很好，随它去吧。"

我又说道："如果你允许我这么做，你会觉得更好。"

他最终表示同意。于是，我才能帮他收拾房子、洗衣服。我发现一盏漂亮的灯，上面积满了灰尘。只有上帝晓得他最后一次点亮是多少年前的事儿。

我问他："你不点这盏灯吗？你从没用过它吗？"

他回答说："没有。谁都不来看我，我没必要点亮它，我为谁点亮呢？"

　　我问："如果我的姊妹们来，你愿意每天夜里点亮它吗？"

　　他答道："当然愿意。"

　　从那天起，我的姊妹们每天晚上都来看望他。我们把灯擦净，姊妹们每天晚上都把它点亮。

　　两年过去了，我已经完全忘记了那个人。他捎口信说："告诉我的朋友，她在我生命中点亮的那盏灯仍在继续闪耀。"

　　我原以为这是一件区区小事，我们常常会忽视那些小事。

Life Is like a Cafeteria

　　A friend's grandfather came to America from Eastern Europe. After staying at Ellis Island, he went into a cafeteria in lower Manhattan to get something to eat. He sat down at an empty table and waited for someone to take his order. Of course nobody did. Finally, a woman with a tray full of food sat down opposite him and informed him how a cafeteria worked.

　　"Start out at the end," she said. "Just go along the line and pick out what you want. At the other end they'll tell you how much you have to pay."

　　"I soon learned that's how everything works in America," the grandfather told a friend. "Life's a cafeteria here. You can get anything you want as long as you are willing to pay. You can even get success, but you'll never get it if you wait for someone to bring it to you. You have to get up and get it yourself."

　　We can't change the inevitable. The only thing we can do is to dominate our attitudes. Once you reach that point in life, contentment and happiness cannot be too far away. And that will give you success.

人生就像自助餐厅

　　一位朋友的祖父从东欧来到美国。在埃利斯岛逗留后，他走进曼哈顿岛一家自助餐厅想吃点什么。他在一张空桌边坐下，等人来让自己点菜。当然不会有人来。最后，有一个端着盛满食物托盘的女人在他对面坐下来，告诉他自助餐厅是怎么经营的。

　　"从这头开始，"她说，"请顺着这排走，挑选你想吃的。到了另一头，他们会告诉你要付多少钱。"

　　"我马上明白美国的一切都是怎样运作的，"祖父告诉一个朋友，"在这里，人生就像自助餐厅，只要愿意付出，你就能得到自己想要的任何东西，你甚至能得到成功。但是如果等待别人带给你，你绝不会得到，你要起来自己去拿。"

我们无法改变命运，我们唯一能做的就是支配自己的态度。一旦你达到人生的那种境界，幸福和满足就不会太远，而且它会带给你成功。

It's All Good

I heard the story told recently about a king in Africa who had a close friend he grew up with. The friend had a habit of looking at every situation that ever occurred in his life (positive or negative) and remarking, "This is good!"

One day the king and his friend were out on a hunting expedition. The friend would load and prepare the guns for the king. The friend had apparently done something wrong in preparing one of the guns, for after taking the gun from his friend, the king fired it and his thumb was blown off. Examining the situation the friend remarked as usual, "This is good!" To which the king replied, "No, this is NOT good!" and proceeded to send his friend to jail.

About a year later, the king was hunting in an area that he should have known to stay clear of. Cannibals captured him and took them to their village. They tied his hands, stacked some wood, set up a stake and bound him to the stake.

As they came near to set fire to the wood, they noticed that the king was missing a thumb. Being superstitious, they never ate anyone that was less than whole. So untying the king, they sent him on his way.

As he returned home, he was reminded of the event that had taken his thumb and felt remorseful for his treatment of his friend. He went immediately to the jail to speak with his friend. "You were right," he said, "It was good that my thumb was blown off." And he proceeded to tell the friend all that had just happened. "And so I am sorry for sending you to jail for so long. It was bad for me to do this."

"No," his friend replied, "this is good!"

"What do you mean? How could it be good that I sent my friend to jail for a year?"

"If I had NOT been in jail, I would have been with you."

万 事 皆 宜

我听到最近有人讲非洲一位国王的故事。国王有一位一起长大的亲密朋友，这个朋友习惯审视自己生活中发生的各种情况，无论正面的还是负面的，他都会说："这是好事！"

有一天，国王和他的朋友外出打猎。这个朋友为国王装好弹药，准备好枪支。他显然在准备其中一支枪时出了差错，因为国王从朋友这里拿过枪开火后，大拇指被炸飞了。研究分析了情况后，国王的朋友像往常一样说："这是好事！"国王回答说："不，这不是好事！"接着就把朋友送进了牢房。

大约一年后，国王在一片他应该知道要避开的地区打猎。食人族抓住了他，把他带到村子里，捆住他的双手，堆起一些木柴，竖起木桩，把他绑在木桩上。

正当他们靠近并放火点燃木柴时，他们注意到国王少了一根大拇指。因为迷信，他们从不吃不完整的人，于是就松开国王，又送他上路。

回家时，别人的提醒让国王想起了自己失去大拇指这件事，那样对待朋友使他感到懊悔。他马上去牢房和朋友交谈。"你是对的，"他说，"我的大拇指被炸飞是好事。"接着，他把发生的一切告诉了朋友。"因此，我很抱歉让你坐了这么久的牢。我这样做真糟糕。"

"不，"他的朋友回答说，"这是好事！"

"你这话什么意思？我让朋友坐了一年牢，这怎么能是好事呢？"

"如果不坐牢，我就会跟你在一起。"

Gift of Insults

There once lived a great Samurai warrior. Though quite old, he was still able to defeat any challenger. His reputation extended far and wide throughout the land and many students gathered to study Zen under him.

One day an infamous young warrior arrived at the village. He was determined to be the first man to defeat the great master. Along with his strength, he had an uncanny ability to spot and exploit any weakness in an opponent. He would wait for his opponent to make the first move, thus revealing a weakness, and then would strike with merciless force and lightning speed. No one had ever lasted with him in a match beyond the first move.

Much against the advice of his students, the old master accepted the young warrior's challenge. As the two squared off for battle, the young warrior began to insult the master. But the old warrior stood there, motionless and calm. Finally, the young warrior exhausted himself. Knowing he was defeated, he left ashamed of himself.

Somewhat disappointed that he did not fight the insolent youth, the students gathered around the master and asked him, "How could you endure such an indignity? How did you drive him away?"

"If someone comes to you with a gift, and you do not accept it, to whom does the gift belong?" asked the Samurai.

"To the one who tried to deliver it," replied one of his students.

"The same goes for envy, anger and insults," said the master.

自 取 其 辱

曾经在一个村子里住着一位杰出的日本武士，尽管他年事已高，但仍能打败任何挑战者。他名扬全国，许多学徒都聚到他门下学习禅宗。

有一天，一个声名狼藉的年轻武士来到大师所居住的村子。他下定决心要成为第一个击败大师的人。除了实力，他还有发现和利用对手弱点的神秘本领。他急切地等待对手先出招，这样对手就会露出破绽，然后他会毫不留情地以闪电般的速度给予还击。从来没有人能在与他的较量中顶得住第一招。

大师力排徒弟们的建议，欣然接受了年轻武士的挑战。二人摆开阵势，年轻武士开始辱骂大师。但是，大师一动不动，镇定自若。最后，年轻武士精疲力竭，自知已败，羞愧而去。

徒弟们见大师并没有和这个无礼小辈交手，略感失望，就围住大师，问道："你怎么能忍受这样的侮辱？你是怎么把他赶走的呢？"

"如果有人携礼物来见你，你不接受，礼物会属于谁呢？"大师问道。

"属于想设法送礼的人。"其中一个徒弟回答。

"嫉妒、愤怒和谩骂也一样。"大师说。

Just Five More Minutes

While at the park one day, a woman sat down next to a man on a bench near a playground. "That's my son over there," she said, pointing to a little boy in a red sweater who was gliding down the slide.

"He's a fine-looking boy," the man said. "That's my son on the swing in the blue sweater." Then, looking at his watch, he called to his son. "What do you say we go, Todd?"

Todd pleaded, "Just five more minutes, Dad. Please just five more minutes." The man nodded and Todd continued to swing to his heart's content.

Minutes passed and the father stood and called again to his son, "Time to go now." Again Todd pleaded, "Five more minutes, Dad. Just five more minutes."

The man smiled and said, "OK."

"My, you certainly are a patient father," the woman responded.

The man smiled and then said, "My older son Tommy was killed by a drunk driver last year while he was riding his bike near here. I never spent much time with Tommy. I've vowed not to make the same mistake with Todd. He thinks he has five more minutes to swing. The truth is that I get five more minutes to watch."

Life is all about making priorities. What are your priorities? Give someone you love five more minutes of your time today!

就　五　分　钟

有一天，公园里一个女人挨着一个男人在游乐场旁边的一条长椅上坐下来。"那边那个是我的儿子。"她指着一个身穿红色厚运动衫正在滑滑梯的小男孩说。

"他是一个漂亮的男孩，"男人说，"那个穿蓝色厚运动衫荡秋千的是我的儿子。"说着，他看了看手表，朝自己儿子喊道："我们走，你说怎么样，托德？"

托德央求道："就等五分钟，爸爸，就再等五分钟。"男人点点头，托德继续尽情地荡着秋千。

时间一分钟一分钟地过去了。这位父亲站在那里，又朝儿子喊道："现在该走了吧。"托德又央求道："再有五分钟，爸爸，就再等五分钟。"

男士微微一笑说："好吧。"

"哎呀，你的确是一位有耐心的父亲。"那位女士说。

男士微微一笑，然后说道："我的大儿子汤米去年在附近骑自行车时被一个醉酒司机撞死了。我从来没有花多少时间陪伴汤米，我发过誓不在托德身上犯同样的错误。"

生活中的任何事都有轻重缓急。你会优先考虑什么事情呢？把你今天的时间多给你爱的人五分钟吧！

The Most Important Part of My Busy Day

"Mommy, look!" cried my daughter, Darla, pointing to a hawk soaring through the air.

"Uh huh," I murmured, driving, lost in thought about the tight schedule of my day.

Disappointment filled her face. "What's the matter, sweetheart?" I asked.

"Nothing," my seven-year-old said. The moment was gone. Near home, we slowed to search for the albino deer that came out from behind the thick mass of trees in the early evening. She was nowhere to be seen.

Dinner, baths and phone calls filled the hours until bedtime.

"Come on, Darla, time for bed!" She raced past me up the stairs. Tired, I kissed her on the cheek, said prayers and tucked her in.

"Mom, I forgot to give you something!" she said.

My patience was gone. "Give it to me in the morning," I said, but she shook her head.

"You won't have time in the morning!" she retorted.

"I'll take time," I answered. Sometimes no matter how hard I tried, time flowed through my fingers like sand in an hourglass, never enough. Not enough for her, for my husband, and definitely not enough for me.

She wasn't ready to give up yet. She wrinkled her little nose in anger and tossed away her chestnut brown hair.

"No, you won't! It will be just like today when I told you to look at the hawk. You didn't even listen to what I said."

I was too tired to argue. "Good night!" I shut her door with a resounding thud.

My husband asked, "Why so glum?" I told him.

"Maybe she's not asleep yet. Why don't you check?" he said.

I opened her door, and the moonlight from the window spilled over her sleeping form. In her hand I could see the remains of a crumpled paper. Slowly, I opened her palm to see what the item of our disagreement had been.

Tears filled my eyes. She had torn into small pieces a big red heart with a poem she had written, "Why I Love My Mother?"

I carefully removed the pieces. Once the puzzle was put back into place, I read what she had written:

"Why I Love My Mother? Although you're busy, and you work so hard, you always take time to play with me. I love you Mommy, because I am the biggest part of your busy day!"

The words were an arrow straight to the heart.

Ten minutes later I carried a tray to her room, with two cups of hot chocolate and two peanut butter and jelly sandwiches. When I softly touched her smooth cheek, I could feel my heart filled with love.

She woke from the sleep. "What is that for?" she asked.

"This is for you, because you are the most important part of my busy day!"

She cracked a sweet smile.

一天中最重要的部分

"妈咪，快看！"女儿达拉指着一只在空中翱翔的鹰喊道。

"嗯，呃。"我一边开车，一边咕哝道，想着排得满满的日程。

她一脸失望。"怎么了，宝贝？"我问。

"没什么。"7岁的女儿说。那个时刻转瞬即逝。快到家时，我们放慢速度寻找那只患白化病的鹿。傍晚时分，它会从茂密的树丛后面走出来。但是今天哪里都不见它的踪影。

晚饭、沐浴和电话占满了就寝前的所有时间。

"快点，达拉，该睡觉了！"她跑过我，上了楼梯。我疲惫不堪，吻了吻她的脸颊，祈祷，给她掖好被子。

"妈妈，我忘记给你一件东西！"她说。

我没有了耐心。"明天早上给我吧。"我说，但她摇了摇头。

"明天早上你不会有时间！"她反驳。

"我会抽时间。"我回答。有时无论我如何努力，时间还是像沙漏中的沙粒一样从指间流过，总是不够用，不够用来陪她，不够用来陪丈夫，当然对自己也不够用。

她还不准备放弃。她气呼呼地皱起小鼻子，把红棕色的头发甩到了一边。

"不，你不会！就像今天我让你看那只鹰时一样，你连我说什么都不听。"

我太累了，不想辩解。"晚安！"我砰的一声关上她的房门。

我的丈夫问道："为什么闷闷不乐？"我告诉了他。

"可能她还没睡着，你为什么不去看看呢？"他说。

我打开她的门，窗外的月光洒在她熟睡的身上。我可以看到她手里有一些揉皱的纸片。我慢慢地掰开她的手掌，想看看我们的分歧到底是什么。

泪水溢满了我的眼眶。她撕成碎片的原是一颗大大的红心，上面是她写的一首诗："为什么我爱我的妈妈？"

我仔细移动那些纸片。纸片一拼回原样，我就读出了她写的那首诗：

"为什么我爱我的妈妈？尽管你很忙，工作很辛苦，但你总是抽时间陪我玩。我爱你妈咪，因为我是你忙忙碌碌一天中最重要的部分！"

这些话像箭一样直射我的心脏。

十分钟后，我端着一只托盘来到她的房间，托盘上放着两杯热巧克力饮料和两块花生酱果冻三明治。我温柔地抚摸着她光洁的脸蛋，能感觉到自己心里充满了浓浓爱意。

她从睡梦中醒来。"这是干什么？"她问。

"这是送给你的，因为你是我忙忙碌碌一天中最重要的部分！"

她露出了甜蜜的微笑。

23 to 4

An 80-year-old man was sitting on the sofa with his 45-year-old son. Suddenly a cove perched on their windowsill.

The father asked his son, "What is this?"

The son replied, "It is a dove."

After a few minutes, the father asked his son for the second time, "What is this?"

The son said, "Father, I have just told you. It's a dove."

After a little while, the old father asked his son for the third time, "What is this?"

This time the son told his father crudely, "It's a dove, a dove."

After a moment, the father asked his son for the fourth time, "What is this?"

This time the son shouted at his father, "Why do you keep asking me the same question again and again? I have told you so many times 'IT IS A DOVE!' Don't you understand this?"

A little later the father went to his room and came back with an old tattered diary. On opening a page, he asked his son to read that page.

"Today my little son aged three was sitting with me on the sofa, when a dove sat on the windowsill. My son asked me 23 times what it was, and I replied to him all 23 times that it was a dove. I hugged him lovingly for 23 times each time he asked me the same question. I did not at all feel irritated. Instead, I felt affection for my innocent child."

When the little child asked him 23 times "What is this", the father only felt affection for his son. But when today the father asked his son the same question for just 4 times, the son felt irritated.

So if your parents attain old age, do not repulse them or look at them as a burden, but speak to them a gracious word, be obedient and considerate to them. From today on, say this aloud, "I want to be kind to my parents, for they have always showered their selfless love on me."

23 比 4

一位80岁的老人和他45岁的儿子一起坐在沙发上。突然，一只鸽子落在了窗台上。

父亲问儿子："这是什么？"

儿子回答："这是一只鸽子。"

过了几分钟，父亲第二次问儿子："这是什么？"

儿子说："爸爸，我刚刚告诉过你，这是一只鸽子。"

过了一小会儿，老父亲第三次问儿子："这是什么？"

这次，儿子生硬地告诉父亲："这是一只鸽子，一只鸽子。"

又过了一会儿，父亲第四次问儿子："这是什么？"

这次儿子冲父亲大声喊道："为什么你一直反复问我同样的问题？'这是一只鸽子！'我已经告诉你许多次了，你听不明白吗？"

片刻之后，父亲走进他的房间，拿回来一本破旧的日记。他翻开一页，让儿子读。

"今天我和3岁的小儿子坐在沙发上，这时有一只鸽子卧在窗台上。儿子问了我23次那是什么，我共回答了他23次，说那是一只鸽子。每一次他问同样的问题，我都亲切地拥抱他，共拥抱了他23次，我一点儿也不感到恼火。相反，我感受到了我对天真孩子的慈爱之情。"

小孩子问了23次"这是什么"，父亲只是感到了对儿子的慈爱之情。但是，如今父亲只问了4次相同的问题，儿子就感到恼火。

所以，如果你的父母上了年纪，不要排斥他们，也不要把他们视为负担，而要对他们言语亲切、孝顺体贴。从今天起，要大声这样说："我会善待父母，因为他们总是给予我大量无私的爱。"

The Embassy of Hope

When Mark was five years old, his parents divorced. He stayed with his mother, while his father enlisted in the armed forces. As Mark grew up, he occasionally had recollections of the brief time he had with his father and longed to see him again. But as Mark became an adult, the thoughts of his father began to subside. He was now more into girls, motorcycles, and parties.

After Mark graduated from college, he married his high-school sweetheart. A year later she gave birth to a healthy baby boy.

One day when Mark's son was five years old and as Mark was preparing to shave his face, his son looked up at him and laughed, "Daddy, you look like a clown with that whipped cream on your face."

Mark laughed, looked into the mirror and realized how much his son looked like him at that age. Later he remembered a story his mother had told him of him telling his father the same thing.

Mark began thinking about his father and started asking his mother. It had been a long time since Mark spoke of his father and his mother told him that she had not spoken to his father in over twenty years and all her knowledge of his whereabouts stopped when Mark became eighteen.

Mark looked deep into his mother's eyes and said, "I need to find my father." His mother commented that his relatives had all passed away and she had no idea where to begin searching for him but added, "Maybe, just maybe, if you contact the United States Embassy in England, they might be able to help you."

Even though the chances seemed slim, Mark was determined. He called the Embassy.

"U. S. Embassy, how may we help you?"

"My name is Mark Sullivan and I am hoping to find my father."

After a long pause, the receiver asked, "Is this a Mr. Mark Joseph Sullivan?"

"Yes," Mark said anxiously.

"And you were born in Vincennes, Indiana, at the Good Samaritan Hospital on October 19, 1970?"

"Yes."

"Mark, please don't hang up," the man made an announcement at the embassy. "Everyone listen! ...I have terrific news...Lieutenant Ronald L. Sullivan's son is on the phone...he found us!"

On this instant, Mark heard a roar of a crowd clapping, cheering and laughing.

The man returned to the telephone and said, "Mark, we're so glad you have called. Your father has been coming here in person or calling almost every day for the past nine years, checking to see if we found you."

希望大使馆

马克5岁时，他的父母分道扬镳。他和母亲一起住，父亲应征参军。马克逐渐长大，他偶尔会想起与父亲一起度过的那段短暂岁月，渴望再见到父亲。但是，马克成人后，他对父亲的思念开始淡去。他现在关注更多的是姑娘、摩托车和各种聚会。

大学毕业后，马克娶了中学时那位情人。一年后，她生了一个健康的男婴。

马克的儿子5岁那年，有一天，马克正准备刮脸，儿子抬起头看着他笑道："爸爸，你脸上涂着生奶油像个小丑。"

马克哈哈大笑，望着镜子，意识到儿子看上去多么像那个年纪的自己。稍后，他记起了母亲曾对他讲过他也对父亲这样说过。

马克开始想自己的父亲，也开始询问自己的母亲。马克很久没有说起自己的父亲了，母亲告诉他，她有二十多年没有跟他父亲联系了，她对他父亲行踪的了解还停留在马克18岁那年。

马克凝视着母亲的眼睛说："我要找到父亲。"母亲说父亲的亲戚都已经去世了，她不知道该去哪里寻找他，但又补充说："也许，只是也许，如果你联系一下美国驻英国大使馆，他们说不定能帮助你。"

即使希望渺茫，马克还是下定决心，给大使馆打去了电话。

"美国大使馆，你需要我们如何帮你？"

"我叫马克·沙利文，我希望找到我的父亲。"

过了好一阵子，接电话的人问道："是马克·约瑟夫·沙利文吗？"

"是。"马克不安地说。

"那你是1970年10月19日出生在印第安纳州温森尼斯市乐善好施医院吗？"

"是。"

"马克，请不要挂断，"那个人在大使馆宣布，"大家听着……我有惊人的消息……罗纳德·L. 沙文中尉的儿子正在与我通话……他找到了我们！"

顷刻间，马克听到了电话里响起了众人的掌声、欢呼声和笑声。

那个人回话说："马克，我们非常高兴你打来电话。你的父亲在过去9年里几乎每天不是亲自来这里，就是打电话来，询问我们是否找到了你。"

A Little Piece of Me

When he told me he was leaving, I felt like a vase which has just smashed. There were pieces of me all over the tidy floor. He kept talking, telling me why he was leaving, explaining it was for the best. I could do better. It was his fault and not mine. I had heard it before many times and yet somehow was still not immune; perhaps one did not become immune to such felony.

He left and I tried to get on with my life. I filled the kettle and put it on to boil. I took out my old red mug and filled it with coffee, watching as each coffee granule slipped into the china. That was what my life had been like, endless coffee granules, somehow never managing to make that cup of coffee.

Somehow when the kettle piped its finishing warning I pretended not to hear it. That's what Mike's leaving had been like, sudden and with an awful finality. I would rather just wallow in uncertainty than have things finished. I laughed at myself. Imagine getting philosophical and sentimental about a mug of coffee. I must be getting old.

And yet it was a young woman who stared back at me from the mirror. A young woman full of hope, a young woman with bright eyes and full lips, just waiting to take on the world. I never loved Mike anyway. Besides, there are more important things. More important than love, I insist to myself firmly. The lid goes back on the coffee just like closure on the whole Mike experience.

He doesn't haunt my dreams as I feared that night. Instead I am flying far across fields and woods, looking down on those below me. Suddenly I fall to the ground and it is only when I wake up that I realize I was shot by a hunter, brought down by the burden of not the bullet but the soul of the man who shot it. I realize later, with some degree of understanding, that Mike was the hunter holding me down and I am the bird that longs to fly. The next night my dream is similar to the previous night's, but without the hunter. I fly free until I meet another bird who flies with me in perfect harmony. I realize with some relief that there is a bird out there for me, and there is another person, not necessarily a lover perhaps just a friend, but there is someone out there who is my soul mate.

I think about being a broken vase again and realize that I have glued myself back together. What Mike has is merely a little part of my time, a little understanding of my physical being. He has only a little piece of me.

我生命历程的一段记忆

他告诉我他要离开时，我就像只刚摔碎的花瓶，支离破碎的我散落在洁净的地面上。他不停地劝说着，告诉我他离开的原因，解释说这会是最好的结局。我本可以表现得更好些，毕竟，错在他不在我。这些话我已经听了很多次了，但莫名其妙的是，我仍不能冷静面对；或许如此痛苦，谁都无法冷静面对。

他走了，而我要尽力把自己的生活支撑下去。我把水壶灌满并打开火烧水。我取出那只红色的旧杯子，倒满咖啡，注视着每一粒咖啡滑落进陶瓷杯内。我的生活就如同这咖啡，一粒又一粒的咖啡却怎么也冲泡不成一杯咖啡。

不知何故，水壶尖厉地发出警报声，我假装没有听到。这就是迈克离开的情形，那么突然，带着极度的痛苦。我宁愿陷入将信将疑之中，也不愿将事情做一了结。我嘲笑自己，我对一杯咖啡的遐想竟然理性而感伤，我一定是老了。

然而，的确有一个女人从镜子里注视着我。一个满怀希望的青年女子，双眸闪烁，嘴唇丰盈，蠢蠢欲动正准备驾驭这个世界。毕竟，我从未爱过迈克。而且，还有其他更重要的事情，比爱情更重要，我向自己强调着。杯盖回到咖啡杯上，好似给了迈克这段经历一个终结。

那天晚上，他并没有像我担心的那样萦绕在我的梦里。相反，我飞得很远，飞过片片田野和丛林，俯瞰身下的一切。突然，我掉在地面上。就在我醒来的那一刻，我发觉我被猎人射中，击倒我的不是子弹，而是射出子弹的那个人的灵魂。随即，我带着几分醒悟，意识到，迈克正是那个掠我下来的猎人，而我就是那只渴望飞翔的鸟。第二天晚上，我的梦与前夜的梦差不多，但没有猎人出现。我自由飞翔，直至遇到另一只鸟，它与我飞得是那样和谐平静。我稍稍释然，毕竟有只鸟为我出现在梦里，会有另一个人，不见得是情人，或许仅仅是朋友，但会有某个人在那里成为我灵魂的伴侣。

我又一次想象自己成了一只碎花瓶，感觉到我已把自己黏合完整。迈克呢，只是我生命的一小段历程，是我对自己的一点认识。他占据的只是我生命的一小段记忆。

Thanks for Your Time

It had been some time since Jack had seen the old man. College, girls, career, and life itself got in the way. In fact, Jack moved across the country in pursuit of his dreams. There, in the rush of his busy life, Jack had little time to think about the past and stay with his wife and son. He was working on his future, and nothing could stop him.

Over the phone, his mother told him, "Mr. Belser died last night. The funeral is on Wednesday."

Memories flashed through his mind like an old newsreel as he sat quietly remembering his childhood days.

"Jack, did you hear me?"

"Sorry, Mom. Yes, I heard you. It's been so long since I thought of him. I'm sorry, but I honestly thought he died years ago," Jack said.

"Well, he didn't forget you. Every time I saw him he'd ask how you were doing. He'd reminisce about the many days you spent over 'his side of the fence' as he put it," Mom told him.

"I loved that old house he lived in," Jack said.

"You know, Jack, after your father died, Mr. Belser stepped in to make sure you had a man's influence in your life," she said.

"He's the one who taught me carpentry," he said. "I wouldn't be in this business without him. He spent a lot of time teaching me things he thought were important… Mom, I'll be there for the funeral," Jack said.

As busy as he was, he kept his word. Jack caught the next flight to his hometown. Mr. Belser's funeral was small and uneventful. He had no children of his own, and most of his relatives had passed away.

The night before he had to return home, Jack and his Mom stopped by to see the old house next door one more time.

Standing in the doorway, Jack paused for a moment. It was like crossing over into another dimension, a leap through space and time.

The house was exactly as he remembered. Every step held memories. Every picture, every piece of furniture…Jack stopped suddenly.

"What's wrong, Jack?" his Mom asked.

"The box is gone," he said.

"What box?" Mom asked.

"There was a small gold box that he kept locked on top of his desk. I must have asked him a thousand times what was inside. All he'd ever tell me was 'the thing I value most'," Jack said.

It was gone. Everything about the house was exactly how Jack remembered it, except for the box. He figured someone from the Belser family had taken it.

"Now I'll never know what was so valuable to him," Jack said. "I'd better get some sleep. I have an early flight home, Mom."

It had been about two weeks since Mr. Belser died. Returning home from work one day Jack discovered a note in his mailbox. "Signature required on a package. Please stop by the main post office within the next three days," the note read.

Early the next day jack got the package. The small box was old and looked like it had been mailed a hundred years ago. The handwriting was difficult to read, but the return address 'Mr. Harold Belser' caught his attention.

Jack took the box out to his car and opened the package. Inside there was the gold box and an envelope. Jack's hands shook as he read the note inside.

"Upon my death, please forward this box and its contents to Jack Bennett. It's the thing I valued most in my life." A small key was taped to the letter. His heart racing, tears filling his eyes, Jack carefully unlocked the box. There inside he found a beautiful gold pocket watch.

Running his fingers slowly over the beautiful casing, he unlatched the cover. Inside he found these words engraved: "Jack, thanks for your time!—Harold Belser"

"The thing he valued most was my time!" Jack held the watch for a few minutes, and then called his office to cancel his appointments for the next two days. "Why?" Janet, his assistant asked.

"I need some time to spend with my son," he said. "Oh, by the way, Janet, thanks for your time!"

Life is not measured by the number of breaths we take, but by the moments that take our breath away.

感谢你的陪伴

距离杰克上次见那位老人已有段日子了。学业、女友、事业和生活琐事使杰克无暇去看望老人。他为了追逐自己的梦想游走在全国各地，如此一来，为了生活奔波的杰克少有时间去思索过去、陪伴妻儿。他忙于前途，什么也阻挡不了他。

电话里，杰克的母亲告诉他："贝尔瑟先生昨晚去世了，葬礼周三举行。"

回忆不断闪过杰克的脑海，就像一部老新闻片，他静静地坐在那里追忆自己的童年时光。

"杰克，你在听吗？"

"抱歉，妈妈。是的，我在听。上次想起他已是很早以前了。我很抱歉，但说实话我原以为他几年前就去世了。"杰克说。

"噢，他可没有忘记你。每次我见到他，他都会问你的情况。他总会提到那些你在'篱笆那边他家'度过的日子，他是这么说的。"母亲告诉他。

"我喜欢他住的那栋老房子。"杰克说。

"杰克，你要知道，你爸爸去世之后，贝尔瑟先生走进了我们的生活，确保你能够受到成年男性的影响。"母亲说。

"他正是那个教会我做木工活的人。"杰克说，"没有他，我不会进入这个行业。他花了很多时间教我他认为重要的事情……妈妈，我会去参加葬礼的。"

他依旧繁忙，但他遵守了承诺。杰克乘坐最近的一个航班回到自己的家乡。贝尔瑟先生的葬礼规模很小，平淡冷清，他自己没有儿女，亲戚大多已不在人世了。

回家的前一天晚上，杰克和他母亲顺道又一次去看看那栋老房子。

站在门廊里，杰克踟蹰了一会儿。他仿佛跨越了时空，进入了一个异度空间。

这栋房子正如他记忆中的那样，每个台阶都饱藏着回忆，每幅画，每件家具……杰克突然站住了。

"怎么了，杰克？"母亲问道。

"盒子不见了。"他回答。

"什么盒子？"母亲问。

"他锁着放在书桌上的一只小金盒。我问过他一千次里面放的是什么，每次他告诉我的只是'我最珍视的东西'。"杰克说。

盒子不见了。房子里的每件东西都一如杰克记忆中的样子，除了那个盒子。他推测是贝尔瑟先生家里的人拿走了。

"好了，我永远都不会知道是什么对他那么重要了，"杰克说，"我最好睡一会儿。我是凌晨的飞机，妈妈。"

贝尔瑟先生去世大约两周后，有一天杰克下班回家，发现邮箱里有个纸条。"包裹需要签收。请于三日内到邮政总局取。"纸条上写道。

次日清晨，杰克取了包裹。那个小盒子旧迹斑斑，如同一百年前邮寄的一般。字迹难以辨认，但寄件人"哈罗德·贝尔瑟先生"引起了他的注意。

杰克拿上盒子，走出邮局，来到车上，打开包裹。里面装着那只金盒和一个封信。杰克读着里面的信，手颤抖着。

"我死的时候，请把这个盒子和里面的东西转寄给杰克·班尼特。这是我这一生最珍视的东西。"一把小钥匙附在信上，杰克的心怦怦直跳，泪水盈眶。他小心翼翼打开盒子，在盒子里面，他看到一块漂亮的金怀表。

杰克手指摩挲着漂亮的表盒，打开表盖，注意到里面几个刻下的文字："杰克，谢谢你的陪伴！——哈罗德·贝尔瑟。"

"他最珍视的东西是我陪伴他的时间！"杰克握着怀表好几分钟，然后打电话到办公室取消了接下来两天的预约。"为什么呢？"他的助手珍妮特问道。

"我需要点时间来陪儿子，"他说，"噢，顺便说一句，珍妮特，谢谢你的陪伴！"

生命不取决于我们呼吸的次数，而取决于那些带走我们呼吸的时光。

God Has Been Good to Me

This is a heart-warming story. I guess we never view life in such a way. We all complain when life seems unfair to us. We have never thought about how much we are blessed.

For 25 years, I watched him fight cancer of the face. First just a small speck that begin to grow larger. Year after year I watch him go to hospital to have a bit cut out each time. As the years went by, more and more of his face was cut away. When he returned with what is left of his face, he tried to smile. He never complained or was downhearted.

He was a skilful mechanic and carpenter. In fact, he was one of the best. Whenever he does his job, he stands back to see if there is anything left out that could be added to make it perfect. Then he would see some little place that the average person would neglect. He would then touch it up.

I suspect he said this to himself "My work will be my face and my life." I doubt if he open looked in the mirror at his damaged face where the cancer ate into every day. No matter how small the job was or how crude the other workers seemed, it never bothered him. This was his work and it had to be done right. He never glanced at the work of others. A shoddy work done by others was not his concern. Nevertheless, I suspect when the job was done, he had a sense of inner pride and joy when he saw how outstanding it was. But he never boasted about it.

As the years went by, he became weaker and weaker. His hands did not move with confidence and speed that so characterized him. He was unable to do many things. However, no matter what the work or pay was he always had the insatiable desire to do a good job.

The helpers he got were not able to impress him. They thought he was cranky, trying so hard to complete every detail. So he worked alone. He did not complain. He would just appear the next morning by himself with no explanation of the absence of his helpers.

During the latter day, he had only the shambles of a face. He would wrap it up in a red handkerchief, leaving only his eyes. When you met him on the streets, he would always give a cheerful greeting. As time went on, it was more and more difficult for him to speak. Often he would move his walking stick. This stick, too, was a thing of beauty, carved out by his skilful hands.

His life seemed to be filled with contentment and peace. I suspect that he thanked God for those hands and the fact that they was not marred in any way.

He would often be missed about his usual haunts for weeks or months. He would make his journey to the hospital for the surgeon to cut away more of his face. Then you would see him again, a bit more gruesome. There would be no complaint, no telling of his operation and pain. He would just quietly go to work that was awaiting him.

In all his time, I never knew him to come back with any complaints about the pain. You would think there was nothing the matter if you did not see his face. When the days of his labors seemed to come to an end, his chief concern was that his tools might be in good hands. He sent for me one day and told me he wished someone would appreciate the tools and use them properly.

When I took a young man to see him about the tools, there came a look of contentment and satisfaction. His work was finished and he was ready to cash in. A few days before he died he was walking in the yard. His face was nearly completely covered with bandages. Only his eyes were uncovered. As he hobbled about the yard, he said, "I am going to keep young just as long as I can."

The day he died, I went to see him again. The smell was so offensive you could hardly stay there. What was left of his face was a mass of scars and there was really nothing to cut away. You could tell he was in great pain and had many sleepless nights. But still there were no words of complaints.

I shall never forget his last words. Even afterwards they have made me ashamed whenever I feel like complaining. Still day after day, they are vivid in my mind.

The words are, "God has been good to me. I have never had any reason to complain."

上帝善待我

这是一个感人的故事。我想我从未以这样的方式来审视人生。生活看起来好像对我们不公正时，我们往往去抱怨，从不考虑我们是多么幸福。

25年来，我看着他与面部的癌症抗争。起初只是一个小小的斑点，后来越长越大。一年又一年，我目睹他上医院每次切除一点。年复一年，他的脸部一点点被切除掉。每次带着他那张剩下的脸回来，他都试图微笑着。他从不抱怨，也不垂头丧气。

他是一个技艺娴熟的木工技师。实事求是地讲，他是一流的。只要是做活，他总会退后察看有没有任何疏忽可以加以完善的地方。他总会瞅见某处会被常人忽视的小细节，然后他就会把它细细修缮。

我猜想他对自己说过这样的话，"我的活儿就是我的脸面和人生"。我寻思他是否对着镜子正视过他那张被癌每天侵蚀、形容已毁的脸。无论活计多小，无论其他工匠看起来多么拙劣，这都不会影响他。这就是他的工作，他的工作必须尽职尽责完成。他从不搭眼看其他人做的活，别人干的蹩脚活与他毫无关系。不过，我猜想当活儿干完时，当他注意到自己的手艺是多么卓绝不凡时，他会由衷骄傲与欣喜，但他绝不会据此自吹自擂。

年复一年，他越来越虚弱，双手无法像人们描述的那样自信麻利地移动，许多活儿他都做不动了。但是，无论活大活小，报酬如何，他总是怀着义无反顾之心做得令人满意。

他的助手往往不能让他满意，而他们认为他性情古怪，苛求成就每个细节。为此，他独自一人工作。他没有抱怨，只是在次日清晨只身而来，对于助手缺席也不多言。

工作之余，他仅有一张扭曲怪异的脸。他把脸裹进红色手帕里，只露出眼睛来。街上相遇，他总是热情打招呼。随着时间的推移，他说话越来越困难。他往往动动手杖，这根手杖也是个精美物件，精美的刻工出自他这双灵巧的手。

他的生活似乎洋溢着满足平和的气氛。我想他感谢上帝赋予他这双灵巧的手，感谢上帝它们未曾受到任何损伤。

他常常几周或数月杳无音讯。他去医院找外科医生切除他脸部的其他一些部分。事后，你会重新看到他，他的面目更加狰狞。他没有怨言，也不提及他的手术和痛苦，只是默默地去做等候着他的工作。

他这一辈子，我从未见他回来对疼痛抱怨过。你会以为什么情况也没有，要是你没有看到他的脸的话。他的劳动时代似乎要结束了，他最担心的是他的工具能否落到能工巧匠之手。有一天他派人找来我，跟我说他希望有个赏识他这些工具的人能妥善使用它们。

我带了个年轻人去他那看那些工具时，他脸上露出了安然称心的神色。工作结束了，他等着收货款。他去世前几天总是在院子里散步，脸几乎完全被绷带覆盖，只有两只眼睛还露在外面。他在院子里蹒跚而行，说："我要尽力保持年轻。"

他去世那天，我又去看望他。气味刺鼻难闻让人待不下去，他的脸只剩下一片疤痕，脸上也确实没有什么可以切除的了。你可以想到他所受的痛苦有多么巨大，他度过了多少不眠之夜，但他仍然没有留下任何抱怨的话。

我不会忘记他的临终遗言。甚至是后来在我想抱怨时，这些话总会让我羞愧不已。即便是经年累月，这些话仍然鲜活于我的脑海。

这些话就是："上帝已经善待了我，我从来没有任何理由去抱怨。"

Climb Every Mountain in Life

I'm actually the first (and only) cancer survivor to summit the world's highest mountain, Mt. Everest. When I was only 13, I was diagnosed with Hodgkin's disease and given three months to live. When I was 15, I was diagnosed with Askin's tumor. The prognosis was much worse as the doctors gave me only two weeks to live. Again, I survived.

Being the only person in the world to have ever had these two cancers, I really felt I should share my story to help motivate others and influence lives. On May 16th, 2002, at 9: 32 a. m. , I became the first cancer survivor to summit Mt. Everest.

Since then, I have been lucky enough to reach the summits of three more of the world's seven highest peaks and have spoken internationally about my life and adventures to countless people and organizations. On the summit of Everest I brought a flag adorned with names of people who have been affected by cancer and left it on the top of the world forever, commemorating the struggle of cancer patients worldwide.

I did the same to the highest point in Africa, Europe and just recently returned from 23,000-foot Aconcagua in South America! My ultimate goal is to climb the highest mountain on each continent and trek to the North and South poles.

I am covering the globe with inspiration. There are plans for live chat shows during the expeditions as well as TV spots and live summit bids from a number of the mountains! The reason for these expeditions is to inspire those affected by cancer (as well as anyone with a pulse!) to dream big and never give up.

攀登人生的每一座山峰

我居然成为第一个也是唯一登顶世界最高峰——珠穆朗玛峰的癌症幸存者。13岁时，我被确诊患有霍奇金病（淋巴肉芽肿病），只剩下三个月的生命。15岁时，我被确诊患有阿斯金瘤。诊断结果更糟糕，医生说我只能活两个星期了。又一次，我存活了下来。

身为世界上唯一曾患过这两种癌症的人，我确实感到我应该分享自己的故事，来激励他人，影响他们的生活。2003年5月16日，清晨9点32分，我成为第一个登顶珠穆朗玛峰的癌症幸存者。

从那以后，我有幸登临了世界七座最高山峰中的三座峰顶，向世界无数人和组织讲述了有关我生活和探险的故事。在珠穆朗玛峰顶，我带上一面饰有曾经得过癌症的人名字的旗子，把它永远留在了世界的顶峰，以纪念世界各地癌症患者与癌症的抗争。

在非洲、欧洲，以及最近刚从那里返回的南美23000英尺（1英尺约合0.3米）的阿空加瓜山的最高峰上，我做了相同的事情！我的终极目标是攀登各洲的最高峰，徒步抵达北极和南极。

我满怀激情，足迹遍布全球。我计划在探险期间做现场访谈节目、电视直播节目以及现场登顶邀请！这些探险活动是为了鼓舞那些经受癌症磨难的人（还有那些一息尚存的人们）要敢于梦想，决不放弃！

What Goes around, Comes around

His name was Fleming, and he was a poor Scottish farmer.

One day, while trying to make a living for his family, he heard a cry for help coming from a nearby bog. He dropped his tools and ran to the bog. There, mired to his waist in black muck, was a terrified boy, screaming and struggling to free himself. Farmer Fleming saved the boy from what could have been a slow and terrifying death.

The next day, a fancy carriage pulled up to the Scotsman's sparse surroundings. An elegantly dressed nobleman stepped out and introduced himself as the father of the boy Farmer Fleming had saved.

"I want to repay you," said the nobleman. "You saved my son's life."

"No, I can't accept payment for what I did," the Scottish farmer replied, declining the offer.

At that moment, the farmer's own son came to the door of the family hovel. "Is that your son?" the nobleman asked.

"Yes," the farmer replied proudly.

"I'll make you a deal. Let me provide him with the level of education my own son will enjoy. If the lad is anything like his father, he'll no doubt grow to be a man we both will be proud of."

And that he did. Farmer Fleming's son attended the very best schools and in time, he graduated from St. Mary's Hospital Medical School in London, and went on to become known throughout the world as the noted Sir Alexander Fleming, the discoverer of Penicillin.

Years afterward, the same nobleman's son who was saved from the bog was stricken with pneumonia. What saved his life this time? Penicillin.

The name of the nobleman? Lord Randolph Churchill.

His son's name? Sir Winston Churchill.

付出终有回报

他叫弗莱明，是个贫苦的苏格兰农夫。

一天，弗莱明正为一家人的生计努力劳作时，听到附近沼泽地里传来呼救的声音。他扔下农具，奔向沼泽地。黑乎乎的烂泥已没到了腰部，是一个受惊的男孩，他尖叫着、挣扎着想挣脱出来。农夫弗莱明把这个男孩从一场缓慢煎熬、恐怖窒息的死亡中拯救了出来。

第二天，一辆豪华马车驶入这个苏格兰男人那片荒凉的土地。一位穿着雅致的贵族步下车来，介绍自己是农夫弗莱明救的那个男孩的父亲。

"我想报答你，"贵族说，"你挽救了我儿子的性命。"

"不，我不能因为我做的事情而接受报酬。"这个苏格兰农夫回答，谢绝了好意。

就在此时，农夫自己的儿子从一家人居住的小屋里出来了。"这是你的儿子吗？"贵族问道。

"是的。"农夫骄傲地回答。

"我向你提一个建议。请让我为他提供我儿子将会享受的教育水准。如果这个小家伙能像他父亲一样品德高尚，他肯定会成长为我们都会为之骄傲的男人。"

他兑现了承诺。农夫弗莱明的儿子在各个一流的学校就读，按时从伦敦圣玛丽医学院毕业，继而享誉全球，成为著名的亚历山大·弗莱明爵士——盘尼西林的发现者。

数年后，还是那个被人从沼泽里救下的贵族的儿子患上了肺炎。这次是什么挽救了他的性命呢？盘尼西林。

这个贵族的名字是？伦道夫·丘吉尔勋爵。

他的儿子呢？是温斯顿·丘吉尔爵士。

Father's White Ribbons

On a train to Smithville, a man happened to sit down next to the young man no more than 17 years old. Because the boy was tense, the man wondered what could be worrying him. Whatever it was, the boy's tension was clear.

The boy kept staring out of the window, paying no attention to anyone else on the train. The man opened up a book and started reading. Now and then, he would look up and see the boy's face pressed against the window. He sensed that the boy was fighting to keep from crying. This was how they traveled through the night—the man attempting to read and the boy staring out of the window.

Finally, the boy asked the man, "Do you know what time it is? And do you know when we are to arrive at Smithville?"

The man gave the boy the time, and went on to say, "Smithville, that's a very small town, isn't it? I didn't know the train stopped there." "It usually doesn't," said the boy, "But they said that they would stop there for me so that I could get off—If I decide to. I used to live there."

The boy returned to the window and the man to his book. It was quite a while before conversation began once again. But when it did, the boy told the man the whole story of his life. "Four years ago," he said, "I did something very bad, so bad that I had to run away from home. I couldn't face my father. So I left without even saying goodbye to him. Since then, I have worked here and there. I never stayed very long in one place. I've been pretty lonely. Until finally, I decided that I want to go back to my father's house."

The man went on to ask, "Does your father know you're coming? And the boy responded, "He knows I'm coming, but I don't know if he will be there. I sent him a letter. I didn't know if he would still want me back. I wasn't sure if he would forgive me. So in my letter, I said that I would come home if he wanted me to. I told him that if he wanted me to come home, he could put a sign on a tree which is a few hundred yards before the railroad station in Smithville. I told him that I would look for a white ribbon on one of the branches of that tree as the train passes. If there is a white ribbon on the tree, then I'll get off. If not, then I'll just keep on riding to wherever this train goes."

The two of them were now waiting for Smithville. Suddenly, the boy asked, "Will you do me a favor? Will you please look for me? I'm scared to look for that ribbon on the tree." Now involved, the man agreed and took a turn staring out the window for a ribbon on a tree.

A few moments later, the conductor came down the aisle and called out, "Next stop—Smithville." The boy could not move. The man, however, looked as hard as could. And then he saw it! He shouted so loud that all the people in the train turned around. "It's there! Look! The tree is covered with white ribbons! Not just one— there's a whole bunch!"

The father had every reason not to put up a white ribbon—and yet he did. Only a father whose love is real could blanket the tree with white ribbons, each one of them proclaiming reconciliation.

父亲的白丝带

在驶往史密斯维尔的列车上，一位男士碰巧在一个不满17岁的年轻小伙旁边坐下来。男孩紧张不安，男士不知道是什么使他焦虑不安。无论是什么，男孩的紧张显而易见。

男孩一直盯着窗外，对列车上其他人毫不关注。男士打开本书开始阅读。时不时地，他会抬起头看看男孩紧贴在窗户上的脸。他感到男孩正在努力忍着不哭出来。他们就是这样彻夜旅行的——男士试图阅读，男孩则注视着窗外。

后来，男孩问男士："你知道几点了吗？你知不知道我们什么时候能到史密斯维尔呢？"

　　男士告诉男孩时间，继续说道："史密斯维尔，那是个很小的城镇，是吗？我不知道列车会在那儿停。""一般不停，"男孩说，"可是，他们说他们会为我在那儿停车，这样我就能下去了——如果我决定的话。我过去住那里。"

　　男孩转向窗户，男士继续看书，过了好一会儿才又开始交谈。但话题一开，男孩给男士讲述了他全部的生活。"四年前，"他说，"我干了些很糟糕的事情，实在是太糟糕了，我只能逃离家乡，无法面对父亲。因此，我甚至都没有跟他道别就离开了。从那以后，我到处干活，从来没有在一个地方待很久。我非常孤独，直到后来，我决定要返回父亲的家。"

　　男士接着问道："你父亲知道你来了吗？"男孩答道："他知道我来了，但我不知道他会不会在那里，我托人给他捎了封信，我不知道他是否还愿意我回来，我也不确定他会不会原谅我。所以，在信里，我说我会回家，如果他想让我回来，他可以在史密斯维尔列车站台前一百码外的一棵树上做个标记。我告诉他火车经过时我会在那棵树的枝头寻找一条白色丝带。如果树上有白丝带，我就下车。如果没有，我就继续乘车到这列火车驶往的任何地方。"

　　他们两个现在等待着史密斯维尔。突然，男孩问道："您能帮我个忙吗？您能帮我找找吗？我不敢在树上寻找丝带。"已经牵连进来，男士答应下来，两人轮流盯着窗外寻找树上的丝带。

　　过了一会儿，乘务员走下过道喊道："下一站——史密斯维尔。"男孩动弹不得。那个男士仍然尽力寻找着。接着，他看到了！他声音那么高，列车里所有的人都转过头来。"在那里！瞧！那棵树满是白色丝带！不仅是一条——满枝都是！"

　　那位父亲有足够的理由不去挂白丝带——但他挂了。只有胸怀真爱的父亲才会用白丝带将树覆盖，每条白丝带都表达了和解之意。

The Secret of the Outer Ears

"Can I see my baby?" the happy new mother asked. When the bundle was nestled in her arms and she moved the fold of cloth to look upon his tiny face, she gasped. The doctor turned quickly and looked out the tall hospital window. The baby had been born without ears. Time proved that the baby's hearing was perfect. It was only his appearance that was marred.

When he rushed home from school one day and flung himself into his mother's arms, she sighed, knowing that his life was to be a succession of heartbreak.

He blurted out, "A boy, a big boy…called me a freak." He grew up, handsome for his misfortune. A favorite with his classmates, he might have been class president, but for that. He developed a gift, a talent for literature and music. "But you might mingle with other young people," his mother reproved him, but felt a kindness in her heart.

The boy's father talked with the family physician. Could nothing be done? "I believe I could graft on a pair of outer ears, if we could get them," the doctor decided. So the search began for a person who would make such a sacrifice for a young man. Two years went by. Then, "You are going to the hospital, son. Mother and I have someone who will donate the ears you need. But it's a secret," said the father.

The operation was a brilliant success, and a new person appeared. His talents blossomed into genius, and school and college became a series of success. Later he married and entered the diplomatic service. "But I must know!" He urged his father. "Who gave so much for me? I could never do enough for him."

"I do not believe you could," said the father, "but the agreement was that you are not to know…not yet." The years kept their secret, but the day did come…one of the darkest days that ever passed through a son. He stood with his father over his mother's casket. Slowly, tenderly, the father stretch forth a hand and raised the thick, reddish-brown hair to reveal the mother had no outer ears.

"Mother said she was glad she never let her hair be cut," he whispered gently, "and nobody ever thought mother less beautiful, did they?"

外耳的秘密

"我能看看宝宝吗？"一位满心欢喜的新妈妈询问，包裹被她环抱在双臂里，她拨开折在一起的包布，抬眼瞧他那娇小的脸庞，一下子屏住了呼吸。医生迅速转过头，从医院高大的窗户外望出去。这个婴儿生下来就没有耳朵。后来证明婴儿的听力完好，仅仅是他的相貌受到了损伤。

一天，他从学校飞奔回家，一头扑进母亲的怀里。她叹了口气，明白他的一生会心碎不断。

他脱口而出："一个男孩，一个大男孩……叫我畸形。"他长大了，他因自己的不幸而慷慨无私。他受同学喜爱，要不是因为那个缺陷，他本可以成为班长。他显示出了天赋，对文学和音乐的才能。"可你有可能和其他年轻人混在一起。"他母亲责备他，但她是一片好心。

男孩的父亲与家庭医生商讨。难道什么也做不了吗？"我想我能移植上一对外耳，如果我们能得到的话。"医生做出决定。于是他们开始搜寻一个能为一个年轻人做此捐献的人。两年过去了。"你要去医院，儿子。妈妈和我已经找到为你捐献耳朵的人了，但这个人是保密的。"父亲说。

手术非常成功，一个崭新的人出现了。他的才能脱颖而出，他在中学和大学不断成功。后来他结婚了，进入外交部门工作。"但我必须知道！"他敦促父亲，"谁为我付出这么多？我永远都报答不了他。"

"我想你不能，"父亲说，"但约定规定你不能知道……还不能。"岁月尘封了这个秘密，但这一天还是到来了……这是儿子经历的最黑暗的那几天中的一天。他和父亲站在母亲的棺椁旁，缓缓地，父亲轻柔地伸出一只手，撩开赭红色的浓密头发，揭开母亲早已没有了外耳的秘密。

"妈妈说她很高兴从没剪掉过自己的头发，"他柔声低语道，"而且也没有人认为妈妈不漂亮，是吗？"

The Only Memory That Lingers

I have many memories about my father and about growing up with him in our apartment next to the elevated train tracks. For 20 years, we listened to the roar of the train as it passed by his bedroom window. Late at night, he waited alone on the tracks for the train that took him to his job at a factory, where he worked the midnight shift.

On this particular night, I waited with him in the dark to say good-bye. His face was grim. His youngest son had been drafted. I would be sworn in at six the next morning, while he stood at his paper-cutting machine in the factory.

My father had talked about his anger. He didn't want them to take his child, only 19 years old, who had never had a drink or smoked a cigarette, to fight a war in Europe. He placed his hands on my slim shoulders. "You should be careful, Srulic, and if you ever need anything, write to me and I'll see that you get it."

Suddenly, he heard the roar of the approaching train. He held me tightly in his arms and gently kissed me on the cheek. With tear-filled eyes, he murmured, "I love you, my son." Then the train arrived, the doors closed him inside, and he disappeared into the night.

One month later, at age 46, my father died. I am 76 as I sit and write this. I once heard Pete Hamill, the New York reporter, say that memories are man's greatest inheritance and I have to agree. I've lived through four invasions in World War II. I've had a life full of all kinds of experiences. But the only memory that lingers is of the night when my dad said, "I love you, my son."

萦绕心间的唯一记忆

我有许多回忆是有关父亲和我在我们临近高架轻轨的公寓里那段日子的。20年里，我们听着列车经过他卧室窗口时的轰鸣声。深夜，他独自一人在轻轨上等待那列载他去工厂上班的列车，因为他在那里上零点班。

在那个特殊的夜晚，我与他在黑暗中一起等候着道别的时刻。他的脸色阴沉，他最小的儿子被征入伍。第二天早晨六点钟，我将被宣布入伍，而他却站在工厂自己那台切纸机前。

父亲曾表达过他的愤怒。他不愿让他们带走自己的孩子，让那个才19岁，还从未喝过酒抽过烟的孩子去欧洲打仗。他把手放在我单薄的双肩上。"你要小心，斯鲁里克，要是你需要什么的话，写信给我，我保证你会得到的。"

突然，他听到了列车驶来的轰鸣声，紧紧把我抱在怀里，温柔地亲吻我的脸颊，眼含着泪水，低声地说："我爱你，我的儿子。"接着，列车就到了，列车门把他关在里面，他消失在夜色中。

一个月后，46岁的父亲去世了。如今，76岁的我坐着写下这些。我曾听《纽约时报》记者皮特·哈米尔说记忆中的往事是男人最宝贵的遗产，我必须认同。我在第二次世界大战中经历了四次侵略战争，我的一生饱经风霜。但是，萦绕在我心间的回忆只有父亲说"我爱你，我的儿子"的那个夜晚。

The Legacy

When my husband, Bob, died very suddenly in January 1994, I received condolences from people I hadn't heard from in years: letters, cards, flowers, visits. I was overwhelmed with grief, yet uplifted by this outpouring of love from family, friends and even mere acquaintances.

One message touched me profoundly. I received a letter from my best friend from sixth grade through high school. We had drifted apart since graduation in 1949, as she stayed in our home town and I had not. But it was the kind of friendship that could quickly resume even if we lost touch for five or ten years.

Her husband, Pete, had died perhaps 20 years ago at a young age, leaving her with deep sorrow and heavy responsibilities: finding a job and raising three young children. She and Pete, like Bob and I, had shared one of those rare, close and "love-of-your-life-you-can-never-forget" relationships.

In her letter she shared an anecdote about my mother (now long deceased). She wrote, "When Pete died, your dear mother hugged me and said, 'Trudy, I don't know what to say…So I'll just say I love you.'"

She closed her letter to me repeating my mother's words of so long ago, "Bonnie, I don't know what to say…So I'll just say I love you."

I felt I could almost hear my mother speaking to me now. What a powerful message of sympathy! How dear of my friend to cherish it all those years and then pass it on to me. I love you—perfect words, a gift, a legacy.

隔世的馈赠

1994年1月，我的丈夫鲍勃突然去世。我收到多年没有书信往来的人们的吊唁：书信、卡片、鲜花、拜访。我悲痛欲绝，而这来自家人、朋友，甚至是泛泛之交对我倾注的爱使我振作了起来。

有一个问候深深触动了我。我收到中学六年级我最好朋友的一封信。我们从1949年毕业开始渐渐疏远，因为她留在了我们家乡，而我却没有。但是，我们的友谊正是那种能够迅速恢复的友谊，不论我们失去联系已是五年还是十载。

她的丈夫皮特大概20年前年纪轻轻就去世了，留给她深深的悲痛和沉重的负担：找工作还要抚养三个年幼的孩子。她和皮特，跟鲍勃和我一样，拥有的是一份那种珍贵亲密、永世难忘的爱情。

信中，她告诉我一段有关我母亲的故事，我母亲现在早已不在了。她写道："皮特去世时，你善良的妈妈抱着我说：'特鲁迪，我不知道该说些什么……那我就说句我爱你吧。'"

她在信的结尾处不停重复我母亲很久以前说的话："特鲁迪，我不知道该说些什么……那我就说句我爱你吧。"

我觉得我几乎能够听到母亲此时此刻正在对我讲话。这是多么富有同情心的问候啊！我的朋友是多么善良，她将这句话珍藏这么多年，然后将它传递给我。我爱你——这至善至美的言语，是一份礼物，是一份隔世的馈赠。

Perseverance

"Will you give my kite a lift?" said my little nephew to his sister, after trying in vain to make it fly by dragging it along the ground. Lucy very kindly took it up and threw it into the air, but, her brother neglecting to run off at the same moment, the kite fell down again.

"Ah! now, how awkward you are!" said the little fellow. "It was your fault entirely," answered his sister. "Try again, children," said I.

Lucy once more took up the kite. But now John was in too great a hurry; he ran off so suddenly that he twitched the kite out of her hand, and it fell flat as before. "Well, who is to blame now?" asked Lucy. "Try again," said I.

They did, and with more care; but a side wind coming suddenly, as Lucy let go the kite, it was blown against some shrubs, and the tail became entangled in a moment, leaving the poor kite hanging with its head downward.

"There, there!" exclaimed John, "that comes of your throwing it all to one side." "As if I could make the wind blow straight," said Lucy. In the meantime, I went to the kite's assistance; and having disengaged the long tail, I rolled it up, saying, "Come, children, there are too many trees here; let us find a more open space, and then try again."

We presently found a nice grassplot, at one side of which I took my stand; and all things being prepared, I tossed the kite up just as little John ran off. It rose with all the dignity of a balloon, and promised a lofty flight; but John, delighted to find it pulling so hard at the string, stopped short to look upward and admire. The string slackened, the kite wavered, and, the wind not being very favorable, down came the kite to the grass. "O John, you should not have stopped," said I. "However, try again."

"I won't try any more," replied he, rather sullenly. "It is of no use, you see. The kite won't fly, and I don't want to be plagued with it any longer." "Oh, fie, my little man! would you give up the sport, after all the pains we have taken both to make and to fly the kite?A few disappointments ought not to discourage us. Come, I have wound up your string, and now try again."

And he did try, and succeeded, for the kite was carried upward on the breeze as lightly as a feather; and when the string was all out, John stood in great delight, holding fast the stick and gazing on the kite, which now seemed like a little white speck in the blue sky. "Look, look, aunt, how high it flies! and it pulls like a team of horses, so that I can hardly hold it. I wish I had a mile of string: I am sure it would go to the end of it."

After enjoying the sight as long as he pleased, little John proceeded to roll up the string slowly; and when the kite fell, he took it up with great glee, saying that it was not at all hurt, and that it had behaved very well. "Shall we come out to-morrow, aunt, after lessons, and try again?"

"I have no objection, my dear, if the weather is fine. And now, as we walk home, tell me what you have learned from your morning's sport." "I have learned to fly my kite properly." "You may thank aunt for it, brother," said Lucy, "for you would have given it up long ago, if she had not persuaded you to try again."

"Yes, dear children, I wish to teach you the value of perseverance, even when nothing more depends upon it than the flying of a kite. Whenever you fail in your attempts to do any good thing, let your motto be, —try again."

坚 持 不 懈

"你能帮我放风筝吗？"我的小侄子对他姐姐说，他在之前把风筝拖在地上，试过好几次，可每一次都失败了。好心的露西把掉在地上的风筝捡起来，把它抛向空中，但是她的弟弟配合得不好，他并没有跟风筝同时跑出去，结果风筝又掉了下来。

"哎呀！你真笨！"小家伙说。"这完全是你的错。"他姐姐反驳道。我说："孩子们，再试一次。"

于是，露西再一次捡起掉在地上的风筝。但是，约翰太急了，他跑得太突然，结果风筝还是和刚才一样，一头栽在了地上。"看看吧！这到底是谁的错？"露西说。"再试一次。"我说。

他们又试了一次，而且更谨慎了，但是，就在露西抛出风筝的时候，刮来一阵大风，把风筝吹到灌木丛中去了，风筝的尾巴缠在一起，可怜的风筝头朝下挂在了那里。

"哎呀！哎呀！"约翰大叫道，"你到底会不会放啊！""我又不能决定风的方向！"露西说。与此同时，我决定帮助他们。我把缠在风筝上的线解掉，对他们说："孩子们，这里的树太多了，我们不妨找一个空旷的地方，然后再试一次。"

我们来到一片广阔的草地，我手里拿着风筝，一切准备就绪，当小约翰跑出去之后，我迅速抛起风筝。只见风筝像气球一样飞上了天，似乎能飞成功。但是，当约翰高兴地发现他拉紧了风筝线时，他停下来抬头朝天上看。风筝线松了，风筝在摇晃，由于风速不够，风筝又掉到了草地上。"啊！约翰，你不应该停下来。"我说，"我们再试一次！"

"我不想再试了，"约翰耷拉着脸说，"再怎么试也没用，你都看见了，无论怎么试，风筝就是飞不起来，况且我累了，不想再试了。""噢！我的好孩子，我们克服重重困难，为的就是把风筝放上天，你要在这个关头放弃吗？我们不能因为几次小小的失败就垂头丧气。快过来，我帮你把风筝线绑上，现在再试一次。"

他再试了一次，这回成功了，风筝飞在天上，看起来就像羽毛一样轻。

当风筝线完全放完之后，约翰高兴地站在那儿，紧握线柄，看着风筝，风筝已经成为蓝天中的一个小白点。"看呀！看呀！姑妈，看它飞得多高啊！它拉风筝线的劲头可真足，我快拽不住了，我希望有一英里（1英里约合1.6千米）的风筝线，我保证也能用完。"

约翰玩得尽兴之后，开始缓慢地往回收风筝线。当风筝落到地上时，他欢快地把风筝捡起来，说风筝没有破损，而且风筝刚才飞得棒极了。约翰说："姑妈，明天放学之后，我们还能出来放风筝吗？"

"亲爱的孩子，我不反对，只要天气好就行。现在，我们该回家了。告诉我，你从今天早上的运动中学到了什么？""我学会了如何放风筝。"约翰说。"你应该感谢姑妈，"露西说，"要不是姑妈劝你再试一次，你早就放弃了。"

"对，孩子们，我希望教会你们做事情坚持不懈，尽管有些事情不需要像放风筝这样的坚持。任何时候，尝试做任何事情失败了，都不要气馁，只需记住一句座右铭——再试一次！"

Harry's Riches

One day, our little Harry spent the morning with his young playmate, Johnny Crane, who lived in a fine house, and on Sundays rode to church in the grandest carriage to be seen in all the country round.

When Harry returned home, he said, "Mother, Johnny has money in both pockets!"

"Has he, dear?"

"Yes, ma'am; and he says he could get ever so much more if he wanted it."

"Well, now, that's very pleasant for him," I returned, cheerfully, as a reply was plainly expected. "Very pleasant; don't you think so?"

"Yes, ma'am; only—"

"Only what, Harry?"

"Why, he has a big popgun, and a watch, and a hobbyhorse, and lots of things." And Harry looked up at my face with a disconsolate stare.

"Well, my boy, what of that?"

"Nothing, mother," and the telltale tears sprang to his eyes, "only I guess we are very poor, aren't we?"

"No, indeed, Harry, we are very far from being poor. We are not so rich as Mr. Crane's family, if that is what you mean."

"O mother!" insisted the little fellow, "I do think we are very poor; anyhow, I am!”

“O Harry!” I exclaimed, reproachfully.

“Yes, ma'am I am,” he sobbed; “I have scarcely any thing—I mean anything that's worth money—except things to eat and wear, and I'd have to have them anyway.”

“Have to have them?” I echoed, at the same time laying my sewing upon the table, so that I might reason with him on that point; “do you not know, my son—”

Just then Uncle Ben looked up from the paper he had been reading: “Harry,” said he, “I want to find out something about eyes; so, if you will let me have yours, I will give you a dollar apiece for them.”

“For my eyes!” exclaimed Harry, very much astonished.

“Yes,” resumed Uncle Ben, quietly, “for your eyes. I will give you chloroform, so it will not hurt you in the least, and you shall have a beautiful glass pair for nothing, to wear in their place. Come, a dollar apiece, cash down! What do you say?I will take them out as quick as a wink.”

“Give you my eyes, uncle!” cried Harry, looking wild at the very thought, “I think not.” And the startled little fellow shook his head defiantly.

“Well, five, ten, twenty dollars, then.” Harry shook his head at every offer.

“No, sir! I wouldn't let you have them for a thousand dollars! What could I do without my eyes?I couldn't see mother, nor the baby, nor the flowers, nor the horses, nor anything,” added Harry, growing warmer and warmer.

“I will give you two thousand,” urged Uncle Ben, taking a roll of bank notes out of his pocket. Harry, standing at a respectful distance, shouted that he never would do any such thing.

“Very well,” continued the uncle, with a serious air, at the same time writing something in his notebook, “I can't afford to give you more than two thousand dollars, so I shall have to do without your eyes; but,” he added, “I will tell you what I will do, I will give you twenty dollars if you will let me put a few drops from this bottle in your ears. It will not hurt, but it will make you deaf. I want to try some experiments with deafness, you see. Come quickly, now! Here are the twenty dollars all ready for you.”

“Make me deaf!” shouted Harry, without even looking at the gold pieces temptingly displayed upon the table. “I guess you will not do that, either. Why, I couldn't hear a single word if I were deaf, could I?”

“Probably not,” replied Uncle Ben. So, of course, Harry refused again. He would never give up his hearing, he said, “no, not for three thousand dollars.”

Uncle Ben made another note in his book, and then came out with large bids for “a right arm,” then “left arm,” “hands,” “feet,” “nose,” finally ending with an offer of ten thousand dollars for “mother,” and five thousand for “the baby.”

To all of these offers Harry shook his head, his eyes flashing, and exclamations of surprise and indignation bursting from his lips. At last, Uncle Ben said he must give up his experiments, for Harry's prices were entirely too high.

"Ha! ha!" laughed the boy, exultingly, and he folded his dimpled arms and looked as if to say, "I'd like to see the man who could pay them!"

"Why, Harry, look here!" exclaimed Uncle Ben, peeping into his notebook, "here is a big addition sum, I tell you!" He added the numbers, and they amounted to thirty-two thousand dollars.

"There, Harry," said Uncle Ben, "don't you think you are foolish not to accept some of my offers?" "No, sir, I don't," answered Harry, resolutely. "Then," said Uncle Ben, "you talk of being poor, and by your own showing you have treasures for which you will not take thirty-two thousand dollars. What do you say to that?"

Harry didn't know exactly what to say. So he blushed for a second, and just then tears came rolling down his cheeks, and he threw his chubby arms around my neck. "Mother," he whispered, "isn't God good to make everybody so rich?"

哈利的财富

一天，小哈利和他的伙伴约翰尼·克莱恩一起玩了一上午。约翰尼住在一幢漂亮的大房子里，星期天他总会坐着气派的马车去教堂，全镇的人都能看见。

哈利回到家后说："妈妈，约翰尼的两个口袋里都有钱。"

"是吗，亲爱的？"

"是的，妈妈。他还说，只要他想要，他还可以有更多的钱。"

"噢，是吗？那很好。"妈妈随便回答说，"非常好，你说呢？"

"是的，妈妈，可是——"

"可是什么，哈利？"

"为什么他有一把大大的玩具枪、一块手表、一个木马，还有好多好多东西？"哈利抬起头闷闷不乐地看着妈妈。

"怎么了，我的孩子？"

"没什么，妈妈。"可此时泄露秘密的眼泪涌了出来，"只是，我想我们很穷，对吗？"

"不，不是的，哈利，我们并不穷，但我们也不像克莱恩家里那样富有，如果这就是你所说的穷的话。"

"噢，妈妈，"小家伙还在难过，"我还是觉得我们很穷，不管怎么样，我很穷。"

"哈利！"妈妈带着责备的口气说。

"是的，妈妈，我就是太穷，"他抽泣着，"我几乎什么都没有——我指那些值钱的东西——除了吃的和穿的，那些必须拥有的东西我都没有。"

"必须拥有的东西？"妈妈重复着他的话，把手中的织物放在桌上，这样她可以就这个问题和哈利好好谈谈，"你不知道吗，我的孩子——"

就在这时，正在读报纸的本叔叔抬起头来，"哈利，"他说，"我想研究一下人的眼睛，如果你愿意给我你的眼睛，那么我会给你2美元。"

"要我的眼睛？"哈利大声喊道，他对此很是吃惊。

"是的，"本叔叔平静地说，"要你的眼睛。我可以给你麻醉，这样你就不会感到疼了，你可以戴一对漂亮的玻璃眼球。快点，一美元一只，否则要降价了。你觉得怎么样？我会很快把它们取出来的。"

"给你我的眼睛，叔叔？"哈利像是无法相信自己的耳朵，"我想不行。"

受惊的小家伙坚决地摇着头。

"那么，5美元、10美元、20美元，怎么样？"每一次哈利都不停地摇着头。

"不，先生，就算你给100美元，我也不会让你取走我的眼睛。没有了眼睛我怎么办？我将不会再看见妈妈，看不见小孩，看不见花，也看不见马了，什么也看不见了。"哈利说着，越来越激动。

"我给你2000美元。"本叔叔继续说，并从口袋里掏出一叠钱。哈利站得远远的，他永远不会做这样的事情。

"那么，好吧。"本叔叔说。此时，他的表情十分严肃，一边在本子上写着什么，一边说："我不能给你高过2000美元的价格，所以，我只能放弃你的眼睛了。但是，"他又说，"我要告诉你我还会怎么做，如果你让我把这瓶子里的东西滴几滴到你的耳朵里的话，我会给你20美元。你并不会感觉到疼，但会让你变聋。你知道，我想做一个关于耳聋的实验。快，现在就做决定吧，这20美元是给你的。"

"会让我变聋！"哈利已经快气疯了，他看也不看放在桌上的钱，大声喊道："我想你不会那样做的，如果我聋了，我就再也听不见了，不是吗？"

"可能吧。"本叔叔说。当然了，哈利还是拒绝了，他说："不，哪怕给我3000美元，我也不答应。"

本叔叔在本子上又记下了一条。之后，他又出更多的钱要"哈利的右手"，然后是"左手""双手""双脚""鼻子"，最后出价10万要他的"妈妈"，5000美元要"小孩"。

哈利拒绝了所有的建议，他的眼睛闪着光，不停地表达着自己的震惊和愤怒。最后本叔叔说他必须放弃他的实验，因为哈利的价格实在太高了。

"哈哈！"哈利高兴地笑了，他架着胳膊，似乎在说："我倒要看看谁能买得起！"

"来，哈利，看这儿！"本叔叔看着笔记本里的东西，"这儿有一大笔钱呢！"他把所有的数目加起来，一共是32000美元。

"现在，哈利，"本叔叔说，"你不觉得放弃这么一大笔钱太愚蠢了吗？"

"不，先生，我不要。"哈利坚决地说。

"那么，"本叔叔说，"你说你很穷，但又不肯拿你所有的东西来换取32000美元，这是为什么呢？"

哈利不知道怎么回答，他涨红了脸，泪水顺着脸颊流了下来，他用胖乎乎的手搂着妈妈的脖子。"妈妈，"他在妈妈的耳旁轻声说，"上帝实在太好了，他让我们每个人都那么富有。"

Harry and his Dog

"Beg, Frisk, beg," said little Harry, as he sat on an inverted basket, at his grandmother's door, eating, with great satisfaction, a porringer of bread and milk. His little sister Annie, who had already dispatched her breakfast, sat on the ground opposite to him, now twisting her flowers into garlands, and now throwing them away.

"Beg, Frisk, beg!" repeated Harry, holding a bit of bread just out of the dog's reach; and the obedient Frisk squatted himself on his hind legs, and held up his fore paws, waiting for master Harry to give him the tempting morsel.

The little boy and the little dog were great friends. Frisk loved him dearly, much better than he did anyone else; perhaps, because he recollected that Harry was his earliest and firmest friend during a time of great trouble.

Poor Frisk had come as a stray dog to Milton, the place where Harry lived. If he could have told his own story, it would probably have been a very pitiful one, of kicks and cuffs, of hunger and foul weather.

Certain it is, he made his appearance at the very door where Harry was now sitting, in miserable plight, wet, dirty, and half starved; and that there he met Harry, who took a fancy to him, and Harry's grandmother, who drove him off with a broom.

Harry, at length, obtained permission for the little dog to remain as a sort of outdoor pensioner, and fed him with stray bones and cold potatoes, and such things as he could get for him. He also provided him with a little basket to sleep in, the very same which, turned up, afterward served Harry for a seat.

After a while, having proved his good qualities by barking away a set of pilferers, who were making an attack on the great pear tree, he was admitted into the house, and became one of its most vigilant and valued inmates. He could fetch or carry either by land or water; would pick up a thimble or a ball of cotton, if little Annie should happen to drop them; or take Harry's dinner to school for him with perfect honesty.

"Beg, Frisk, beg!" said Harry, and gave him, after long waiting, the expected morsel. Frisk was satisfied, but Harry was not. The little boy, though a good-humored fellow in the main, had turns of naughtiness, which were apt to last him all day, and this promised to prove one of his worst. It was a holiday, and in the afternoon his cousins, Jane and William, were to come and see him and Annie; and the pears were to be gathered, and the children were to have a treat.

Harry, in his impatience, thought the morning would never be over. He played such pranks—buffeting Frisk, cutting the curls off of Annie's doll, and finally breaking his grandmother's spectacles—that before his visitors arrived, indeed, almost immediately after dinner, he contrived to be sent to bed in disgrace.

Poor Harry! there he lay, rolling and kicking, while Jane, and William, and Annie were busy about the fine, mellow Windsor pears. William was up in the tree, gathering and shaking; Annie and Jane catching them in their aprons, and picking them up from the ground; now piling them in baskets, and now eating the nicest and ripest; while Frisk was barking gayly among them, as if he were catching Windsor pears, too!

Poor Harry! He could hear all this glee and merriment through the open window as he lay in bed. The storm of passion having subsided, there he lay weeping and disconsolate, a grievous sob bursting forth every now and then, as he heard the loud peals of childish laughter, and as he thought how he should have laughed, and how happy he should have been, had he not forfeited all this pleasure by his own bad conduct.

He wondered if Annie would not be so good-natured as to bring him a pear. All on a sudden, he heard a little foot on the stair, pitapat, and he thought she was coming. Pitapat came the foot, nearer and nearer, and at last a small head peeped, half afraid, through the half-open door.

But it was not Annie's head; it was Frisk's—poor Frisk, whom Harry had been teasing and tormenting all the morning, and who came into the room wagging his tail, with a great pear in his mouth; and, jumping upon the bed, He laid it in the little boy's hand.

　　Is not Frisk a fine, grateful fellow?and does he not deserve a share of Harry's breakfast, whether he begs for it or not?And little Harry will remember from the events of this day that kindness, even though shown to a dog, will always be rewarded; and that ill nature and bad temper are connected with nothing but pain and disgrace.

哈利和他的狗

　　"作揖，弗里斯克，作揖！"小哈利说，他坐在奶奶门前一个倒扣着的篮子上，心满意足地吃着面包和牛奶。他的妹妹安妮坐在他对面的地上，她把花朵编成花环，然后再扔掉。

　　"作揖，弗里斯克，作揖！"哈利重复道，他在离狗不远的地方拿了一小块面包，听话的弗里斯克后腿蹲下来，举起前爪，等待主人哈利给它一顿诱人的美餐。

　　小男孩和小狗是好朋友。弗里斯克十分喜欢哈利，并且比任何人对他都好，也许，因为当它回忆起自己深陷困境的时候，只有哈利是它最坚定的朋友。

　　可怜的弗里斯克是作为一只流浪狗来到哈利住的米尔顿的。如果它能有机会讲述自己的故事，那么这一定是关于被殴打、忍受饥饿和恶劣天气的悲惨故事。

　　可以肯定的是，它就在哈利现在坐的位置，出现在他的眼前。它那时处境悲惨，全身潮湿、肮脏并且处于半饥饿的状态，它正是在这里遇到了哈利，哈利很喜欢它，但是哈利的奶奶却用扫帚轰它走。

　　最后，哈利获得家人的许可，让弗里斯克在家门口住下，并且用吃剩的骨头、凉土豆和他能弄到的其他食物喂它。他给弗里斯克准备了一个睡觉的小篮子，就是现在哈利倒扣着当椅子的篮子。

　　过了一段时间，小狗用吼叫赶跑了那些上树偷梨的小偷，以此证明它是一条好狗。当它被准许进入哈利的家之后，弗里斯克便成为家里最警觉、最有价值的伙伴。它会跑很多路去拿东西或送东西；如果小安妮不小心弄掉顶针或棉花球的话，它会叼起来，或者忠诚地去学校给哈利送饭。

　　"作揖，弗里斯克，作揖！"哈利说经过漫长的等待之后，它如愿以偿地得到了那顿大餐。弗里斯克感到很满意，但哈利却没有。这个小男孩尽管是个好脾气的人，但是他也很顽皮，有时他可能一整天都这样，并且希望证明这是他最坏的一方面。在假期的一天下午，表妹简和表弟威廉来他家做客，他和安妮把梨拿出来款待这两个孩子。

哈利不耐烦地想，今天的早晨太漫长了，于是他便做了一些恶作剧——殴打弗里斯克、把安妮的洋娃娃的卷发剪下来，最后打坏了奶奶的眼镜。在他的客人到来之前，事实上，他是在吃过晚饭之后，被毫无颜面地赶回自己卧室的。

可怜的哈利！他躺在那里，又滚又踢，而简、威廉和安妮则忙着采摘熟透的温莎梨。威廉爬到树上采摘和摇晃，安妮和简用她们的裙子接住被摇下来的梨，并把地上的梨捡起来，放进篮子里；她们现在吃到的梨都是最好、最熟的，而弗里斯克在他们中间欢快地叫着，好像它也捡到了温莎梨！

可怜的哈利！他躺在床上，透过开着的窗户，他可以听到他们的欢声笑语。当他们的欢笑消失之后，哈利开始躺在床上哭泣，时不时地啜泣。当他听到那些稚嫩的笑声之后，他就想，要不是因为自己的行为葬送了自己的快乐的话，他也能这么开心地笑。

哈利想，安妮会不会好心地给自己一个梨呢？突然，他听到楼梯上传来脚步声，他以为是妹妹来了，脚步声越来越近，最后一个小脑袋伸进了半开的门。

但是伸头进来的不是安妮，而是弗里斯克——可怜的弗里斯克，那个已经被哈利戏弄和折磨了一上午的弗里斯克。此时，它摇着尾巴走进哈利的房间，嘴里叼着一个梨，然后跳上床，把梨放在了小男孩的手里。

这不就是哈利那懂得感恩的好伙伴吗？不论它是否作揖，难道它不该得到哈利的那份早餐吗？小哈利会永远记住今天发生的事，给予别人善意，即使是狗，也会得到回报，但是恶毒和坏脾气只能给人带来痛苦和懊悔。

The Noblest Revenge

"I will have revenge on him, that I will, and make him heartily repent it," said Philip to himself, with a countenance quite red with anger. His mind was so engaged that he did not see Stephen, who happened at that instant to meet him.

"Who is that," said Stephen, "on whom you intend to be revenged?" Philip, as if awakened from a dream, stopped short, and looking at his friend, soon resumed a smile that was natural to his countenance. "Ah," said he, "you remember my bamboo, a very pretty cane which was given me by my father, do you not?Look! there it is in pieces. It was farmer Robinson's son who reduced it to this worthless state."

Stephen very coolly asked him what had induced young Robinson to break it. "I was walking peaceably along," replied he, "and was playing with my cane by twisting it round my body. By accident, one of the ends slipped out of my hand, when I was opposite the gate, just by the wooden bridge, where the ill natured fellow had put down a pitcher of water, which he was taking home from the well.

"It so happened that my cane, in springing back, upset the pitcher, but did not break it. He came up close to me, and began to call me names, when I assured him that what I had done had happened by accident, and that I was sorry for it. Without regarding what I said, he instantly seized my cane, and twisted it, as you see; but I will make him repent of it."

"To be sure," said Stephen, "he is a very wicked boy, and is already very properly punished for being such, since nobody likes him or will have anything to do with him. He can scarcely find a companion to play with him; and is often at a loss for amusement, as he deserves to be. This, properly considered, I think will appear sufficient revenge for you."

"All this is true," replied Philip, "but he has broken my cane. It was a present from my father, and a very pretty cane it was. I offered to fill his pitcher for him again, as I knocked it down by accident. I will be revenged."

"Now, Philip;" said Stephen, "I think you will act better in not minding him, as your contempt will be the best punishment you can inflict upon him. Be assured, he will always be able to do more mischief to you than you choose to do to him. And, now I think of it, I will tell you what happened to him not long since.

"Very unluckily for him, he chanced to see a bee hovering about a flower which he caught, and was going to pull off its wings out of sport, when the animal stung him, and flew away in safety to the hive. The pain put him into a furious passion, and, like you, he vowed revenge. He accordingly procured a stick, and thrust it into the beehive.

"In an instant the whole swarm flew out, and alighting upon him stung him in a hundred different places. He uttered the most piercing cries, and rolled upon the ground in the excess of his agony. His father immediately ran to him, but could not put the bees to flight until they had stung him so severely that he was confined several days to his bed.

"Thus, you see, he was not very successful in his pursuit of revenge. I would advise you, therefore, to pass over his insult. He is a wicked boy, and much stronger than you; so that your ability to obtain this revenge may be doubtful."

"I must own," replied Philip, "that your advice seems very good. So come along with me, and I will tell my father the whole matter, and I think he will not be angry with me." They went, and Philip told his father what had happened. He thanked Stephen for the good advice he had given his son, and promised Philip to give him another cane exactly like the first.

A few days afterward, Philip saw this ill-natured boy fall as he was carrying home a heavy log of wood, which he could not lift up again. Philip ran to him, and helped him to replace it on his shoulder. Young Robinson was quite ashamed at the thought of this unmerited kindness, and heartily repented of his behavior. Philip went home quite satisfied. "This," said he, "is the noblest vengeance I could take, in returning good for evil. It is impossible I should repent of it."

最高尚的复仇

"我要报仇，让他对自己的所作所为感到悔恨。"菲利普对自己说，他的脸气得通红。此时的他太过专注，完全没有看到这时遇到的史蒂芬。

"他是谁？"史蒂芬问，"你想要报复谁？"菲利普好似从梦中惊醒，他看着他的朋友，停顿片刻，很快脸上浮现出自然的微笑。"嗯，"他说，"你还记得我父亲送给我的竹手杖吧？看！农夫罗宾逊的儿子把它弄成了好几截，这下可好，这手杖一文钱都不值了。"

史蒂芬脸色凝重地问菲利普，小罗宾逊是怎么弄坏手杖的。"有一天，我安静地在路上走着，"菲利普答道，"我把手杖挎在身上。但是，发生了意外，手杖的一头脱离了我的手，当时我站在木桥入口的对面，这个坏家伙来到木桥上，并且扔下一个水壶，他从这儿打完水，打算带水回家。

"碰巧我的手杖弹了回来，打翻了他的水壶，但是手杖并没有坏。当我说这一切都是个意外，并且对他表示歉意的时候，他向我走来，开始叫我的名字。他毫不理会我说的话，而是迅速拿起我的手杖，把它折断了，然后我的手杖就成这样了。你也看到了，不过我会让他付出代价的。"

"确切地说，"史蒂芬说，"他是个招人烦的孩子，而且他也受到了应有的惩罚，因为没人喜欢他，没人愿意跟他在一起，他连个玩伴都没有，对于他来说没有快乐可言，这是他自作自受。我认为，这就足够他受的了。"

"你说的这些都很对，"菲利普答道，"但是他折断了我的手杖，这是我父亲给我的礼物，这手杖很珍贵。我答应帮他重新灌一次水，因为我不小心碰掉了他的水壶，但是他不领情，所以我一定要报复。"

"菲利普，"史蒂芬说，"我认为你不理他更好，你对他的蔑视是对他最好的惩罚，记住，他永远都有数不完的恶作剧去整你。我给你讲不久前发生在他身上的一件事吧。

"那次他很不走运，他发现他摘的花上有一只蜜蜂，它展开双翅把他蛰了，然后安全地飞回蜂巢。他感到疼痛难忍，就像你一样，他发誓要复仇。于是，他拿起一根木棍，捅进了蜂箱。

"就在捅进去的一瞬间，所有的蜜蜂都飞了出来，它们飞到他身旁，把他全身蛰了个遍。他声嘶力竭地吼叫起来，痛苦地在地上打滚。他父亲立刻跑过来，但是那些蜜蜂直到把他蛰得很严重才罢休，以至于他在家里躺了好几天。

"你看，他的复仇并没有成功，因此，我建议你，无视他对你的侮辱，他是个坏孩子，而且他比你更强壮，所以我很担心，以你的能力，很难实现你的复仇。"

"我必须这样做，"菲利普说，"不过，你的建议听起来不错，跟我一起去吧，我会把这件事告诉我父亲，他听了之后，或许就不会像我这样生气了。"之后，他们一起去了，菲利普把这件事向父亲说了，他父亲十分感谢史蒂芬，因为史蒂芬给自己的儿子提了一个好建议。然后，他给了菲利普一根一模一样的手杖。

几天之后，菲利普又看到了那个坏小孩，他正扛着木头走在回家的路上，但是他摔倒了，而且站不起来。菲利普连忙跑过去把他扶起来，并帮他摆好肩膀上的木头。小罗宾逊对他的一番好意感到十分羞愧，他对自己之前的行为感到后悔。然后，菲利普心满意足地回了家，他说："这是我所做过的最高尚的复仇，以德报怨，而且我绝不后悔这么做。"

第二卷

永不放弃

The Wolves within

An old Indian grandfather said to his grandson, who came to him with anger at a friend who had done him an injustice. "Let me tell you a story."

"I too, at times, have felt great hatred for those who have taken so much, with no sorrow for what they do. But hate wears you down, and does not hurt your enemy. It's like taking poison and wishing your enemy would die. I have struggled with these feelings many times."

"It is as if there are two wolves inside me. One is good and does no harm. He lives in harmony with all around him and does not take offense when no offense is intended. He will only fight when it is right to do so, and in the right way."

"But the other wolf…ah! The smallest thing will send him into a fit of temper. He fights against everyone, all of the time, for no reason. He cannot think because his anger and hatred are so great. It is helpless anger, for his anger will change nothing."

"Sometimes it is hard to live with these two wolves inside me, for both of them try to dominate my spirit."

The boy looked intently into his grandfather's eyes and asked, "Which one wins, Grandfather?"

The grandfather smiled and quietly said, "The one I feed."

Whether you are angry or not is totally up to you.

心中的两只狼

一位印第安老爷爷对他的孙子说："让我给你讲个故事吧。"他的孙子来找他是因为被朋友欺负而生气。

"我有时也觉得非常憎恨那些索取太多而对自己的行径毫不悔恨的人。但是，仇恨会使你萎靡不振，却于你的敌人无妨。这就如同服用毒药，却希望你的敌人死去一样。有很多次我都挣扎在这种感觉中。

"这种感觉就像我心里有两只狼。一只善良无害，他与周边的一切和睦相处，做到人不犯我、我不犯人。他师出有名，有理有节。

"可是，另一只狼……啊！最微不足道的事情也会使他大为光火。他跟所有的人争斗，自始至终，毫无理由。他无法理性思考，因为他的愤怒和仇恨太大、太深。那是无用之火，因为他的愤怒无济于事。

"有时与我心里的这两只狼相处很难，因为他们两个都试图控制我的情绪。"

男孩目不转睛地看着爷爷的眼睛问道："哪一只赢了呢，爷爷？"

爷爷笑了笑，平静地说："我饲养的那只。"

你生气与否，都完全取决于你自己。

Cut the Rope and Let Go

They tell the story of a mountain climber who, desperate to conquer the Aconcagua, initiated his climb after years of preparation. But he wanted the glory all to himself, therefore, he went up alone. He started climbing and it was becoming late. He did not prepare the camping, and decided to keep on going.

Soon it got dark. Night fell with heaviness at a very high altitude. Visibility was zero. Everything was black. There was no moon, and the stars were covered by clouds.

As he was climbing a ridge at about 100 meters from the top, he slipped and fell. Falling rapidly he could only see blotches of darkness that passed. He felt a terrible sensation of being sucked in by gravity. He kept falling and in those anguishing moments, good and bad memories passed through his mind. He thought certainly he would die.

But then he felt a jolt that almost tore him in half. Yes! Like any good mountain climber he had staked himself with a long rope tied to his waist. In those moments of stillness, suspended in the air he had no other choice but to shout: "Help me, Help me!"

All of a sudden he heard a deep voice from heaven, "What do you want me to do?"

"Save me."

"Do you REALLY think that I can save you?"

"Of course."

"Then cut the rope that is holding you up."

There was another moment of silence and stillness. The man just held tighter to the rope. The rescue team says that the next day they found a frozen mountain climber hanging strongly to a rope…TWO Feet OFF THE GROUND.

Sometimes you have to have some faith, cut the rope and let go. The results might be out of your expectation.

割断绳索，然后放手

人们讲述了一个登山者的故事，他不顾一切要征服阿空加瓜山，经过数年的准备，他开始了攀爬。可是，他希望荣耀光环都只属于自己，因此他只身前往，开始攀爬。天色已经渐晚，他并没有准备宿营，仍然决意继续前进。

很快天黑了，海拔高的地方夜幕阴沉黑寂，能见度为零，一切都黑黢黢的，没有月亮，星星也被云遮蔽了。

他在攀登一道距离峰顶大约有100米的山脊时，脚下一滑摔了下来。下落的速度快得让他只能看到所经之处是一片片的黑暗。他异常惊恐，觉得要被地球重力吞噬了。他继续下落，在这种痛苦煎熬的时刻，美好和痛苦的回忆都划过他的脑海。他笃信自己必死无疑。

但是，他感到一震，有股力道几乎要把自己断成两半。对！正如任何优秀的登山者一样，他用一条长绳索系住腰部把自己拴住了。在沉寂下来的时间里，他悬在空中，别无选择，只是呼喊着："救救我，救救我！"

突然，他听到天空中传来一个低沉的声音："你想让我为你做什么呢？"

"救我。"

"你的的确确认为我能救你吗？"

"当然。"

"那就割断支撑你的绳索吧。"

又是一阵沉寂无声。那个男人只是紧紧附在绳索之上。营救队说，第二天他们发现一个冻僵的登山者牢牢地吊在绳索之上……离地两尺。

有时，人们需要一定的信念，割断绳索，然后放手，结局或许会出乎你的意料。

Earn Respect with the Truth

The crowd cheered as the young man walked across the stage to claim his award as the company's top producer. He received the microphone, looked over the audience and faltered. I watched him confront his fear, wrestle with the doubt. It took him a moment to start again.

"The last three months hit me pretty hard," he began. "And I feel the need to share a piece of my story—though I'm not sure why."

"About four months ago, one of my colleagues called me about this new marketing system, an outbound fax blaster that could reach thousands of potential customers at very little cost." He paused. "I checked it out, got excited and signed up. Long story short—after thousands of faxes, a process server showed up to deliver some papers. It seems that what I did was illegal. One of the companies that received a blast complained to the attorney general who filed a lawsuit against me—not just for that fax, but with a dollar punishment for every one sent out."

The crowd gasped.

"I failed to do proper research, didn't pay attention to the details and now face prosecution with enormous potential liability."

Two hundred people sat riveted to their chairs.

"As some of you know, I recently moved up here from down south." He ran his fingers through his hair.

"I stored my stuff in my old office, which we closed down. When I drove back to pick it all up, I found that everything except my computer and the clothes I brought with me, was gone. Every memento, every memory and every possession had been stolen."

No one moved. "It gets better. As some of you know, I drive a sports car—black on black convertible, my pride and joy. I love that car." His voice cracked a little. "No more," he added. A memory flooded his mind.

"As it sometimes happens, a guy cut my car off. Instead off letting it go, my ego kicked in. coming up on a ramp, I stomped on the accelerator, missed the final turn, lost control at 85 miles an hour, spun across three lanes, hit the guard rail and bounced back across two—in the middle of rush hour. I wrecked the car and by some weird fate, walked away without a scratch."

The room sighed with relief. "Because I had been on the road, I didn't open my mail and missed an insurance payment. I don't know what's going to happen."

Heads shook in dismay.

"In three months, I got sued, lost everything I owned, and wrecked my car."

He gathered himself. "We all face challenges," he smiled, "Some tougher than others. I guess I wanted to share mine with you. Thanks for listening." He then left to a standing ovation.

Standing in the back of the room, I realized how much respect that young man earned. He confronted his fear, publicly admitted his mistakes and never quit, despite the obstacles. That day, he won much more than a trophy.

真诚赢得尊重

写年轻人走上台来领取他作为公司一流销售员的奖品时，听众一片喝彩。年轻人接过麦克风，看了看听众，颤抖起来。我看到他克服了胆怯，消除了顾虑。他花费了一点时间重新开始。

"过去的3个月对我的打击很沉重，"他开始说，"我认为有必要分享一段我的故事——尽管我不清楚为什么。"

"大概4个月前，一个同事给我打电话告诉我这种新的销售系统，这种传真外联机能以非常低的成本联系到成千上万的潜在客户。"他顿了一下，"我检验之后很兴奋，随即注册使用。长话短说——发送了数千封传真之后，程序服务器跳出来，发送一些文件。看起来我所做的事情是违法的。收到群发传真的其中一家公司向首席检察官提出控诉，他对我提出了诉讼——不仅针对那封传真，还针对发送出去的所有传真进行现金处罚。"

听众都屏住了呼吸。

"我没有进行正当的调研，没有注重细节，如今要面对负有重大责任的起诉程序。"

两百人牢牢地坐在椅子上。

"正如你们有些人所了解的，我最近刚从南部升职到这里。"他用手指捋捋头发。

"我在原来的办公室里存放了我的物品，那里已经被我们关闭了。我开车回去想都取走时，发现除了我随身携带的电脑和衣物，其他所有东西都不见了。每个纪念品、每段记忆和所有物品都失窃了。"

谁也没有动。"它会转好的。你们有人知道，我开的是一辆跑车——黑色车身黑色敞篷，它是我的骄傲，也是我的乐趣，我爱那辆车。"他的声音有些轻微嘶哑了，"它不再是我的了。"他补充道。回忆在他的脑海里潮水般翻涌。

"就像有时发生的那样，一个家伙夺走了我的车。我没有放手，我的自尊突然蹦出来，无法按捺，我猛踩加速器，错过了最后一个转弯，车以每小时85英里的速度失控了，在三条巷子里不停打转，撞上护栏，在两个护栏间被弹回来——当时正值高峰期。我毁了那辆车，凭着一点诡异的运气，我皮都没擦破就离开了。"

房间里，人们松了口气。"因为我在公路上无法打开邮箱，所以错过了一份保险赔付金。我不清楚会发生什么事情。"

大家沮丧摇头。

"3个月里，我被起诉，失去了拥有的一切，还毁了我的车。"

他打起精神。"我们都会面临挑战，"他笑着说，"有些比其他挑战更棘手。我觉得我需要与你们分享我面临的挑战，谢谢倾听。"于是，他立刻迎来一阵长时间的起立鼓掌。

站立在房间后面，我认识到这个青年赢得了很多的尊重。他战胜了自己的胆怯，公开承认自己的过失，决不言弃，无视困境。那天，他赢得的远不止一份奖品。

Never Give up

You are never given a wish without also having been given the power to make it come true. —Richard Bach

Just imagine a young girl who learned dancing when she was three years old and whose greatest passion remains dancing. She loses one of her legs in an accident. Read on this true incident that took place almost 20 years ago and find out whether she gives up dancing or fights back to realize what she believes in:

Sudha Chandran, a classical dancer from India, was cut off in the prime of her career—quite literally—when her right leg had to be amputated after a car accident. Though the incident brought her bright career to a halt, she didn't give up.

In the painful months that followed, she met a doctor who developed an artificial limb made from vulcanized rubber filled with sponge. So strong was her desire that she decided to go back to dancing after she had been fitted with an artificial leg. Knowing that she believed in herself and could fulfill her dream, Sudha began her courageous journey back to the world of dancing—learning to balance, bend, stretch, walk, turn, twist, twirl and finally dance.

After every public recital, she would ask her dad about her performance. "You still have a long way to go" was the answer she used to get in return.

In January 1948, Sudha made a historic comeback by giving a public recital in Bombay. She performed in such a marvelous manner that it moved everyone to tears while pushing her to the Number One position again. That evening when she asked her dad the usual question, he didn't say anything. He just touched her feet as a tribute to a great artist.

Sudha's comeback was such heart-warming that a film producer was inspired to capture the incident into a box office hit, 'Mayuri. '

When someone asked Sudha how she managed to dance again, she said quite simply, "YOU DON'T NEED FEET TO DANCE."

If you have fallen down, get up and brush the dust off your knees and move on. A temporary setback is not a defeat. For that matter, there's no such thing as defeat. Nothing is impossible in this world. If you have the will to win, you can achieve anything. And always remember that the whole world will help you when you want to achieve something.

永 不 放 弃

只要有梦想，也就有让梦想成真的力量。

——理查德·巴哈

设想一下，有一个3岁开始学跳舞的小姑娘，她把全部激情都倾注在了舞蹈上。在一次意外事故中，她失去了一条腿。请读读这个大约20年前发生的真实故事，看看她是放弃了舞蹈，还是不断抗争成就了她的信念：

苏哈·占德让，一个印度古典舞舞蹈家，正值事业鼎盛时期——确切地讲——是她的右腿在车祸后必须被截肢时，被剥夺了跳舞的权利。尽管这次事故中断了她辉煌的事业，她却没有放弃。

在接下来痛苦不堪的几个月里，她结识了一位医生，他发明了一种用硫化橡胶制成、内部填充海绵体的假肢。安装上假腿后，她决意重新开始跳舞的欲望是那么强烈。苏哈清楚她对自己有信心也笃信她能够实现自己的梦想，苏哈重新返回舞蹈世界，开始她的勇敢之旅——学习平衡、弯腰、伸展、行走、转身、旋转，直到最后舞动起来。

每一场公开表演，她都会问父亲她的表演如何。"你仍有很长一段路要走"是她通常得到的回答。

1948年1月，苏哈在孟买举行了一次公演，取得了历史性的回归。她的表演形式非凡绝伦，使每一位观众都感动得潸然泪下，也把她再次推到头号人物的宝座。那天晚上，她又向父亲问起那个老问题，父亲什么也没说。他只是抚摸着她的双脚，这是对一位伟大艺术家的礼赞。

苏哈的再次辉煌感人至深，一位制片人获得灵感，将她曲折动人的经历拍成了一部票房轰动一时的影片——《孔雀女》。

当有人询问苏哈是怎样设法重新跳舞时，她讲得特别简单："你不需要脚来跳舞。"

摔倒了，起身掸掉膝盖上的尘土再继续前行，暂时的挫折并不是失败。正因为如此，我们才能够虽败犹荣。这个世界上没有什么事情是不可能的。只要你想赢，你可以得到任何东西。要永远牢记，只要你想得到什么，整个世界都会帮助你。

Blind Ambition

Charlie Boswell has always been one of my heroes. He has inspired me and thousands of others to rise above circumstances and live with our true passion.

Charlie was blinded during World War II while rescuing his friend from a tank that was under fire. He was a great athlete before his accident and in a testimony to his talent and determination he decided to try a brand new sport, a sport he had never imagined playing, even with his eyesight—golf!

Through determination and a deep love for the game, he became the National Blind Golf Champion! He won that honor 13 times. One of his heroes was the great golfer Ben Hogan, so it truly was an honor for Charlie to win the Ben Hogan Award in 1958.

Upon meeting Ben Hogan, Charlie was awestruck and stated that he had one wish and it was to have one round of golf with the great Ben Hogan.

Mr. Hogan agreed that playing a round together would be an honor for him as well, as he had heard about all of Charlie's accomplishments and truly admired his skills.

"Would you like to play for money, Mr. Hogan?" blurted out Charlie.

"I can't play you for money, it wouldn't be fair!" said Mr. Hogan.

"Aw, come on, Mr. Hogan…$1,000 per hole!"

"I can't, what would people think of me, taking advantage of you and your circumstance," replied the sighted golfer.

"Chicken, Mr. Hogan?"

"Okay," blurted a frustrated Hogan, "but I am going to play my best!"

"I wouldn't expect anything else," said the confident Boswell.

"You're on, Mr. Boswell. You name the time and the place!"

A very self-assured Boswell responded, "10 o'clock…tonight!"

盲人的雄心

查理·博斯韦尔一直以来都是我崇拜的英雄中的一个。他鼓舞着我，也鼓舞着其他成千上万的人走出逆境，怀着炽热的真情生活。

"二战"期间，查理在从一辆被炮火攻击的坦克里营救自己的朋友时失明了。出事之前，他是一名卓越的运动员。在一段对他才华和毅力的陈述中，这样叙述他决定尝试一项全新的运动，一项他从未设想参与的运动，他甚至没有亲眼见过——高尔夫！

凭借坚韧的毅力和对这项运动的喜爱，他成为全国盲人高尔夫冠军！这一奖项他赢得了13次。他的偶像之一是杰出的高尔夫选手本·霍根，因此对查理而言，1958年获得本·霍根奖项实属荣幸。

见到本·霍根，查理敬慕不已，并说他有一个愿望，希望与这位杰出的本·霍根竞技一个回合。

霍根先生表示同意并说一起竞技一个回合也是他的荣幸，因为他早已听闻查理所有的成就，而且真心钦佩查理的技艺。

"你愿意玩赌钱的吗，霍根先生？"查理突然冒出一句。

"我不能跟你玩赌钱的，这不公平！"霍根先生说。

"噢，快点，霍根先生……1000美元一杆！"

"不行，人们会怎么看我，恃强凌弱，乘人之危。"目清神明的高尔夫手回应道。

"懦夫，霍根先生？"

"那好，"窘迫的霍根脱口而出，"可我会打出我的最高水平！"

"我别无他求。"信心十足的博斯韦尔说道。

"你接受了，博斯韦尔先生。你来定时间和地点！"

意气满满的博斯韦尔回道："10点钟……今晚！"

Saying Your Thank-yous

One year ago, at a get-together of a dozen girlfriends from college, I saw my old friend, Therese Gibson. When I told her I was writing a book called Happy for No Reason, which focuses on the 21 core habits of unconditionally happy people, she told me about the daily gratitude ritual she practices with her 95-year-old father Charlie that keeps them smiling and feeling good.

Therese moved in with Charlie during a bad time in both their lives. Charlie's wife had just died, Therese was at the tail end of a painful divorce, and money was tight. They were as glum as any two people could be. But both had heard that gratitude was a great way to feel better, so they decided to sit together for a few minutes each morning before Therese went off to work and tell each other three things they were grateful for in their lives.

"It was slow going in the beginning," Therese told me. "The first time we did it, I had a hard time thinking of even one thing I was grateful for." Finally, she looked around the room and saw a vase she liked. She told Charlie, "I'm grateful for how pretty that vase is." It sounded silly, but it was the best she could do. Charlie wasn't any better at it, often waiting for Therese to give him a clue about what to say. But she and Charlie both noticed that even a thank-you for something superficial had a good effect.

Soon, their decision to focus on what was right in their lives began to pay off. Both Therese and Charlie started to feel happier, and to notice that more and more things were going their way. Even their money situation was improved. Three thank-yous became five, then ten, and soon they had to stop listing the good things in their lives long before they ran out of things to say—or Therese would be late for work.

One day, they were feeling so light and happy after finishing their lists that

Charlie, who'd always liked the musical Oklahoma, started singing "Oh, What a Beautiful Morning." Therese joined it. It was the perfect expression of how being grateful made them feel. They added this song to their ritual and now "saying their thank-yous" and singing together has become one of the highlights of their day.

I've experienced myself just how powerful gratitude is. Once, after going through a heartbreak, a friend told me to write down five things I was grateful for each night before I went to bed for three weeks straight. I knew that psychologists say it takes 21 days to change a habit, so I agreed. At first I struggled to come up with anything, but I continued doing it every night and over time the pain in my heart eased.

Try doing the gratitude exercise yourself. Every night before you go to sleep, list five things that you're grateful for that day, and notice how you feel when you wake up the next morning. A grateful heart can send your happiness level soaring.

常怀感恩之心

一年前，在有十几个大学女朋友参加的一次聚会上，我见到了老朋友特丽萨·吉布森。我告诉她我正在写一本名为《幸福不需要理由》的书，它关注的是百分百幸福人群的21个重要的生活习惯，她对我提起她与95岁的父亲查理每天一起做的感恩仪式，这种仪式使他们心情愉悦，感觉良好。

特丽萨在他俩生活消沉的日子里搬去与查理同住。查理的太太刚刚去世，特丽萨还处于痛苦不堪的离婚过程的尾声，而且过得捉襟见肘。他们愁眉不展，困苦不已。然而，他俩都听闻怀有感恩之心是一种能感觉好些的途径，于是决定，每天早晨在特丽萨去上班前的几分钟坐在一起，给对方讲3件生活中要感恩的事情。

"开始会很耗时，"特丽萨告诉我，"我们第一次做时，我即便是想出一件要感恩的事情都很伤脑筋。"后来，她环顾房间看到她喜欢的一只花瓶。她对查理说："我要感谢这只花瓶是如此美丽。"这听起来无聊可笑，但她已经尽力而为了。查理根本好不到哪里去，常常等着特丽萨提示他该说些什么。可是，她和查理都发现，即便是对微乎其微的事物道一声感谢，都会产生愉快的效果。

不久，他们关注生活中积极向上方面的决定开始回报他们。特丽萨和查理开始觉得更开心了，开始发现越来越多的事情走入正轨。他们的资金状况也得到改善。3个感恩变成5个，接着是10个，很快他们不得不终止列出生活中的好事，他们要说的事情需要太长时间——否则特丽萨上班就会迟到。

一天，他们感恩过所列出的内容后，感觉非常轻松愉快，查理一直喜爱音乐之乡的俄克拉何马州，开始高歌起来："噢，多么美丽的清晨。"特丽萨跟着唱起来。这首歌完美地抒发了感恩之心带给他们的感受。他们把这首歌附在感恩仪式之后，现在"说出他们的感恩之心"和一起颂唱已成为他们每天重要的一部分。

我自己也体会了感恩之心的巨大力量。有一次，经历痛苦心碎之后，一个朋友告诉我，在我每晚睡觉前写下5件我要感恩的事情，坚持3周。我记得心理学家说过改变一个习惯需要21天，就同意了。开始我很难想到什么，可我仍然坚持每天晚上都做，随着时间的流逝，我内心的伤痛平息了下来。

尝试去做这种感恩活动。每天晚上你睡觉之前，列出当天所要感谢的5件事情，感受一下第二天清晨醒来时的心情，一颗感恩的心会使你的幸福程度剧增。

The Most Fitting Finish Line

In December of 1992, I was a happy husband and father of two young children. A month later, I was diagnosed with Acute Lymphoblastic Leukemia.

After two years of chemo that helped me into remission, my body was weak and lifeless. I felt as if I were a puppet who needed help to lift his arms or hold up his head.

I began to run. Six months later my strength came back. On one of my runs, one where I felt I could run forever, I decided that I was going to try to run a marathon.

After telling my dad about my plan, he told me of a program that trains people to ran a marathon, while raising funds for Leukemia research at the same time. So that summer, through the Leukemia Society's Team In Training program, I started to train for the Marine Corps Marathon. During mile after mile of uncertainty, the day finally came to run the marathon.

On October 27, 1996, at 8 A. M. , the cannon went off and so did I. Along with 19000 other brave souls I started on a 26. 2-mile journey that I will never forget.

I first saw my wife Patty at the six mile mark. She seemed happy that I was still looking as if I knew what I was doing, and having a good time doing it. At mile 17, my mind was going back to those two horrible years that tried to bring my family and me down. I saw her again. The concern in her face told me she knew I was starting to struggle. I felt as if we were thinking the same, nine more miles and these last few years would be behind us.

That thought alone pulled me forward. Mile 22, 23, slowing but going, 24, 25, then there it was. The Iwo Jima War Memorial. I have seen nothing so grand and inspiring in my life. Three hours and forty one minutes after I started, I crossed what I think has to be the most fitting finish line in all of road racing!

That night the Leukemia Society gave me a pin at a post-race party that simply says, "Leukemia 26. 2."

If God wills, and I relapse, my cancer may once again take away my hair and my strength, maybe even my life. But it can never take away my pin, or the fact that I am a marathoner.

最完美的终点线

1992年12月，我还是一位幸福的丈夫、两个孩子的父亲。一个月后，我被诊断患有急性淋巴细胞性白血病。

经过两年促使我恢复健康的化疗之后，我的身体变得虚弱无力，毫无生气。我觉得自己如同一只木偶，需要有人牵动手臂才能支起头部。

我开始跑步，6个月后体力开始复原。有一次跑步时，我决心尝试跑马拉松，因为那次跑步经历使我觉得自己可以一直跑下去。

跟父亲讲了我的打算后，他告诉我一个组织机构，它培训人如何跑马拉松，同时为白血病研究募集资金。于是，那个夏季，通过白血病社团训练队机构，我开始为参加海军陆战队马拉松而训练。在绵绵无尽的半信半疑中，跑马拉松的这一天终于到来了。

1996年11月27日，早晨8点，子弹射出，我也出发了。和其他一万九千个勇敢之躯一起，我开始了那段26.2英里长的永远难忘的马拉松之旅。

我先是在6英里标记处看到妻子帕蒂。她好像很开心，因为我看起来好像还清楚自己的状态，而且感觉良好地进行着。在17英里处，我的思绪回到了将家人和我击垮的那痛苦不堪的两年。我又看到了她，她脸上焦虑的神情告诉我，她清楚我开始挣扎了。我觉得好像我们在想着同样的事情，还有9英里，然后过去的这几年就被我甩在身后了。

这样的念头支撑着我继续向前。22……23英里，虽然缓慢，但仍在继续，24……25，马上就到了。硫黄岛战斗纪念碑，我一生再没有见过有比它更雄伟更令人鼓舞的事物。从开始跑历时3小时41分钟，我跨过了我认为应当是所有公路赛跑中最完美的终点线！

那天晚上，白血病社团在赛后聚会上奖励我一枚胸针，上面文字简洁地写着："白血病26.2。"

如果上帝执意如此，我白血病复发，那么我体内的癌会再次夺走我的毛发和气力，甚至我的生命。但是，它永远夺不走我的胸针，也无法更改我是一名马拉松运动员的事实。

Great Expectations

Pete Rose, the famous baseball player, and I have never met, but he taught me something so valuable that it changed my life. Pete was being interviewed in the spring training, the year he was about to break Ty Cobb's all time hits record. One reporter blurted out, "Pete, you only need 78 hits to break the record. How many at-bats do you think you'll need to get the 78 hits?" Without hesitation, Pete just stared at the reporter and said very matter-of-factly, "78." The reporter yelled back, "Ah, come on, Pete, you don't expect to get 78 hits in 78 at-bats, do you?"

Mr. Rose calmly shared his philosophy with the throngs of reporters who were anxiously awaiting his reply to this seemingly boastful claim. "Every time I step up to the place, I expect to get a hit! If I don't expect to get a hit, I have no right to step in the batter's box in the first place!" "If I go up hoping to get a hit," he continued, "then I probably don't have a prayer to get a hit. It is a positive expectation that has got me all of the hits in the first place."

When I thought about Pete Rose's philosophy and how it applied to everyday life, I felt a little embarrassed. As a father, I was hoping to be a good dad. As a married man, I was hoping to be a good husband.

The truth was that I was an adequate salesperson, I was not so bad of a father, and I was an okay husband. I immediately decided that being okay was not enough! I wanted to be a great salesperson, a great father and a great husband. I changed my attitude to one of positive expectation, and the results were amazing. I was fortunate enough to win a few sales trips, I won Coach of the Year in my son's baseball league, and I share a loving relationship with my wife, Karen, to whom I expect to be married for the rest of my life! Thanks, Mr. Rose!

雄 心 壮 志

皮特·罗斯是著名棒球运动员，虽然我从未与他谋面，但他教给我的一些有价值的事情改变了我的生活。皮特在春季训练期间接受采访，那年他计划打破泰·科布的全垒打纪录。记者脱口就问："皮特，你只要再有78个全垒打就能破这项纪录。你认为你需要多少个击球才能得这78个全垒打呢？"皮特直视着记者，实事求是地说："78个。"记者嚷嚷着回应："啊，得了，皮特，你并不指望这78个击球每次都是全垒打吧？"

拥挤成团的记者们迫切等待看罗斯先生如何回应这句似乎傲慢自负的

话，罗斯先生平静地向他们道出了他的人生哲学。"每次踏入击球区，我都准备打出全垒打！如果不准备击球，我就没有资格踏入击球区一垒！如果我只是希望获胜，那我可能毫无希望获胜。正是这种乐观预期使我在一垒成功击出所有的球。"

当我认真思考皮特·罗斯的人生哲学，并思考如何将它付诸日常生活时，我感到一丝羞愧。身为人父，我希望自己是个好爸爸；身为人夫，我希望自己是个好丈夫。

然而现实生活中我是一名差强人意的销售员，一个还算不赖的父亲，一个说得过去的丈夫。我随即下定决心不能流于一般！我要成为一名杰出的销售员、一位伟大的父亲、一个大丈夫。我改变了对乐观预期所持的态度，结果出乎意料。我很幸运地赢得了几次销售旅行，我赢得了儿子棒球队年度教练荣誉，我和太太克伦夫妻恩爱，我希望在有生之年与她永结连理之好！感谢你，罗斯先生！

Control Your Attention and Mind

A disciple and his master were walking through the forest. The disciple was disturbed by the fact that his mind was in constant unrest.

He asked his master, "Why most people's minds are restless, and only a few possess a calm mind? What can one do to still the mind?"

The master looked at the disciple, smiled and said, "I will tell you a story. An elephant was standing and picking leaves from a tree. A family fly came, flying and buzzing near his ear. The elephant waved it away with his long ears. Then the fly came again, and the elephant waved it away once more.

"This was repeated several times. Then the elephant asked the fly, 'Why are you so restless and noisy? Why can't you stay for a while in one place?'

"The fly answered, 'I am attracted to whatever I see, hear or smell. My five senses pull me constantly in all directions and I cannot resist them. What is your secret? How can you stay so calm and still?'

"The elephant stopped eating and said, 'My five senses do not rule my attention. Whatever I do, I get immersed in it. Now that I am eating, I am completely immersed in eating. In this way I can enjoy my food and chew it better. I rule and control my attention, and not the other way around.'"

Upon hearing these words, the disciple's eyes opened wide and a smile appeared on his face. He looked at his master and said, "I understand! If my five senses are in control of my mind and attention, then my mind is in constant unrest. If

I am in charge of my five senses and attention, then my mind becomes calm."

"Yes, that's right," answered the master, "The mind is restless and goes wherever the attention is. Control your attention and mind."

神聚则心收

一对师徒步行穿过森林，徒弟因自己心神不宁而烦恼。

他问师父："为什么大多数人的内心都躁动不安，而只有少数人能保持沉静之心？如何才能静心呢？"

师父看看徒弟，笑着说："我给你讲个故事。有一只大象站着从树上采叶子吃，一只苍蝇飞来，在它耳畔又飞又哼。大象用长耳朵把苍蝇扇跑。可是，苍蝇又飞过来，大象再次把苍蝇扇跑。

"这种情形重复了几次。大象问苍蝇：'你怎么这么烦、这么吵呢？你就不能在哪里待一会儿吗？'

"苍蝇回答：'不论什么东西，只要是见到、听到、闻到，我都会被吸引住。五官不停地把我趋向各个方向，我无法抗拒。你有什么秘诀？你怎么能保持这么平静安详呢？'

"大象停止进食，说道：'我的五官并不掌控注意力。无论做什么，我都沉浸其中。既然我在进食，我就完全沉浸于进食，这样我就能享用食物，把它咀嚼得更好。我掌握控制注意力，别无他法。'"

听了这些话，徒弟双目圆睁，笑容展现在他脸上。他看着师父说道："我明白了！如果我的五官受制于心神，内心就不得安宁。如果我控制五官和注意力，内心就平静下来了。"

"对，说得对。"师父答道，"心无宁则神不定，神聚则心收。"

Time Your Actions

Whatever your career is, you will accomplish twice as much in half the time when you learn to time your actions.

All of us are, in a sense, sales people who are trying to sell our way through life successfully.

But only a relatively few of us manage to become master Salesmen. The secret lies largely in learning to time your words and deeds to the most opportune moment.

A southern lumberman wanted a large loan from a bank in Big Stone Gap, Virginia, owned by General Rufus A. Ayers. Fearing that his modest credit rating by itself would never convince the bank to take such a large risk, he decided to take a different approach to overcome this hurdle.

He knew that Mrs. Ayers was a lover of flower gardens. With the help of his wife, the lumberman learned the particular flowers for which Mrs. Ayers had the greatest fondness. He procured some very rare specimens and presented them to her.

Nothing was said about bank loans or business of any nature because the approach was being conducted by an expert salesman who kept it strictly on a social, neighborly basis. After three different presentations of flowers to Mrs. Ayers, she reciprocated by inviting the lumberman and his wife for dinner.

After dinner, General Ayers and his guest went into the library to visit while their wives had a talk in the flower garden. That was a perfect setting for the lumberman to get over to General Ayers the story of his lumber business and describe a large tract of timber, for which he was negotiating if he could get some additional financing.

The General wanted to know how much he needed. When told the amount he said, "Go down to the Bank tomorrow and I'll tell the Cashier to make you a loan of the amount you need."

By proper timing, the lumberman got his loan without actually having to ask for it. If he had gone into the Bank without the preparation, and had asked for the loan he probably would have been refused by the Cashier.

It has been said that a man who can sell himself successfully to people can also sell his goods and wares successfully, a fact which strongly indicates that buyers often buy the salesman first or they don't buy his wares.

It is estimated that not one person in a million who buys insurance ever takes the trouble to find out what is in the policy. What he actually buys is the personality of the salesman who did such a good job that reading the policy seemed unnecessary.

In public speaking and in ordinary conversation, timing plays an important part as to the impression the speaker makes upon his listener. This writer once paid Professor William Hawn, a distinguished teacher of public speaking, a fee of $100 for a single lesson in speaking which consisted of only thirteen words: get up, have something to say worth hearing, say it and sit down. The lesson was worth every dollar of its cost.

When asked the secret of his success as a criminal lawyer the great Clarence Darrow replied, I usually win by letting the other lawyer talk his case to death.

There's only one way to assure yourself that your words and actions are properly timed. Think and plan before you speak or act.

把握行动时机

无论从事什么职业，只要学会把握行动时机，你就能做到事半功倍。

从某种意义上说，我们都是推销员，我们都在尽力使自己成功销售人生。

但是，我们中只有少数人能够成为销售大师。成功的秘诀很大程度上在于要学会在最恰当的时刻去表现你的言行。

一个南方的木材商想要从弗吉尼亚大石峡的一家银行贷一大笔款，这家银行的老总是鲁弗斯·埃尔斯行长。但是，木材商担心他的信用等级不高，银行不会冒这么大风险把款贷给他，于是他决定另辟蹊径解决这个难题。

他得知埃尔斯夫人爱好花卉，并在妻子的帮助下知道了埃尔斯夫人最喜欢的那几种花卉。他就设法弄到了一些非常稀有的品种送给了她。

在送给埃尔斯夫人花卉时，他没有提到任何有关贷款和生意之类的话题，因为这是一个老练的销售员在掌控着事情的进展，他严格把这种往来控制在睦邻友好的基础上。送了3次花后，埃尔斯夫人为了答谢他，邀请他和他的妻子共赴晚餐。

晚餐后，妻子们在花园里聊天，埃尔斯行长领着他去参观书房，这是一个绝佳的场合，于是他就向行长谈起了自己的生意情况，说他正在和别人谈判要买下一大片林地，但需要得到一些资金支持。

行长问他需要多少钱，他告诉了行长后，对方就说："明天你就去银行，我会让出纳员贷给你需要的钱。"

通过把握合适的时机，这个木材商不求而得，获得了他需要的贷款。如果他毫无准备径直去银行要求那笔贷款，他可能已经被出纳员拒绝了。

只有一个能把自己成功销售出去的人才能成功卖掉他的商品。事实表明，买方总是要先接受销售员，然后才会买他的东西。

据估计，在买保险的人中，不到百万分之一的人会仔细看保险单上的说明。事实上，他买的是销售员的人品，销售员工作如果认真，就会为他阅读看起来并不重要的保险单的条款说明。

无论是公共场合的讲话还是平时的普通谈话，把握时机对给听者留下印象起着关键作用。本文作者曾付给一位杰出的公共演讲老师威廉·霍恩教授100美元听他的一堂课，这堂课只由13个字组成：起立说值得一听的话，说完坐下。这堂课物有所值。

当被问到成功的秘密时，伟大的刑事辩护律师克拉伦斯·达罗答道："通常我会让另一个律师滔滔不绝地说下去，然后我就赢了。"

你要想把握好你言行的时机，只有一种方法，那就是在言行之前要仔细思考、周密计划。

Go for It!

While watching the Olympics the other night, I came across an incredible sight. It was not a gold medal, or a world record broken, but a show of sheer determination and guts.

The event was swimming and started with only three men on the blocks. For one reason or another, two of them false started, so they were disqualified. That left only one to compete. That would have been difficult enough, not having anyone to race against, even though the time on the clock is what's important.

I watched the man dive off the blocks and knew right away that something was wrong. Now I'm not an expert swimmer, but I can tell a good dive from a poor one, and this was not exactly medal quality. When he resurfaced, it was evident that the man was not out for gold—his arms were flailing in an attempt at freestyle. The crowd started to titter. Clearly this man was not a medal contender.

I heard to the crowd begin to laugh at this poor man that was clearly having a hard time. Finally he made his turn to start back. It was pitiful. He made a few desperate strokes and you could tell he was exhausted.

But in those few awkward strokes, the crowd had changed. No longer were they laughing, but beginning to cheer. Some even began to stand and yell things like, "Come on, you can do it!" and, "Go for it!" He did.

A clear minute past the average swimmer, this young man finally finished his race. The crowd went wild. You would have thought that he had won the gold, and he should have. Even though he recorded one of the slowest times in Olympic history, this man gave more heart than any of the other competitors.

Just a short years ago, he had never even swum, let alone raced. His country had been asked to Sydney as a courtesy.

In a competition where athletes remove their silver medals, feeling they have somehow been cheated out of gold, or when they act so arrogantly in front of their rivals, it is nice to watch an underdog, a man that gave his all—knowing that he had no chance, but still competed because of the spirit of the games.

加油，你行！

前几天夜里，我正在观看奥运会比赛时，看到了让人难以置信的一幕。那一幕不是谁夺取了金牌，也不是谁打破了世界纪录，而是一场不折不扣的决心和意志的展现。

那是一场游泳比赛，开始时只有3个选手在跳台上。由于种种原因，两个选手都在起跳时因出现错误而被取消了比赛资格，因此只剩下一名选手来完成比赛。虽然计时器上的时间非常重要，但因为没有人和他比赛，那将会很难。

我看着那个人跳入水中，马上就知道他有些不对劲。虽然我不是游泳专家，但我能够判断出什么是优秀的跳水，什么是蹩脚的跳水。他的跳水完全拿不了奖。当他再次露出水面时，显然他是得不到金牌的。他摆动胳膊，试图采用自由泳方式。人们开始偷笑，显而易见，这个人拿不了奖牌。

我听到人们开始嘲笑那个蹩脚的选手了，显然他游得艰难。最后，他游到池壁开始转身。真遗憾，他拼命划了几下水，看得出他已是筋疲力尽了。

但在他笨拙地划水时，人们的反应变了。大家不再嘲笑他了，而是开始为他加油呐喊。有的人甚至站起来大声喊："加油，你行！加油！"他奋力拼搏。

几分钟过去了，这个年轻选手最终完成了比赛，人们为他疯狂。你会认为他得了金牌，而且他也该得。虽然他创造了奥运会历史上最慢的纪录，但他比其他任何选手更让人激动。

就在几年前，他还从未游过泳，更别说参加比赛了。他的国家是出于礼节才被邀请来悉尼参加奥运会的。

在比赛中，那些因为觉得被欺骗而没有获得金牌就摘下银牌的选手，或者那些在对手面前表现得狂妄自大的选手，应该来看看这场比赛，看看一个输了的选手是怎样全力以赴的——在知道他没有丝毫机会取胜时仍奋力拼搏，他是在为体育精神进行比赛。

Hang in There

Nicolo Paganini was a well-known and gifted nineteenth century violinist. He was also well-known as a great showman with a quick sense of humor. His most memorable concert was in Italy with a full orchestra. He was performing before a packed house and his technique was incredible, his tone was fantastic, and his audience dearly loved him.

Toward the end of his concert, Paganini was astounding his audience with an unbelievable composition when suddenly one string on his violin snapped and hung limply from his instrument. Paganini frowned briefly, shook his head, and continued to play, improvising beautifully.

Then to everyone's surprise, a second string broke. And shortly after that, a third one. Almost like a slapstick comedy, Paganini stood there with three strings dangling from his Stradivarius. But instead of leaving the stage, Paganini stood his ground and calmly completed the difficult number on the one remaining string.

坚 持 下 去

尼科罗·帕格尼尼不仅是19世纪很有才华的著名小提琴家，还是一个颇具幽默感的伟大表演家，他最让人难忘的一次演奏是在意大利的管弦音乐会上。音乐厅里坐满了人，他的演奏技巧非常出色，他演奏的音乐美妙无比，听众们都非常喜欢他。

在音乐会接近尾声时，帕格尼尼演奏起一段乐曲，给观众带来了阵阵惊喜，突然小提琴的一根弦断了，断弦从小提琴上松松垮垮地垂下来。帕格尼尼微微皱了皱眉，摇摇头，继续演奏下去，他的即兴表演非常精彩。

接着让人吃惊的是，第二根弦也断了，紧接着第三根也断了，简直就像一场闹剧。帕格尼尼站在那里，他的小提琴上的三根弦都垂了下来。可是，帕格尼尼并没有离开舞台，而是站在自己的位置上，在仅存的最后一根弦上完成了最难演奏的一段曲子。

A Boy Named Sparky

The late Earl Nightingale, writer and publisher of inspirational and motivational material, once told a story about a boy named Sparky.

For Sparky, school was all but impossible. He failed every subject in the eighth grade. He flunked physics in high school, getting a grade of zero.

Sparky also flunked Latin, algebra, and English. He didn't do much better in sports. Although he did manage to make the school's golf team, he promptly lost the only important match of the season. There was a consolation match—he lost that too.

Throughout his youth, Sparky was awkward, socially. He was not actually disliked by the other students; no one cared that much. He was astonished if a classmate ever said hello to him outside of school hours.

There's no way to tell how he might have done at dating. Sparky never asked a girl out in high school. He was too afraid of being turned down.

Sparky was a loser. He, his classmates, everyone knew it. So he went with it. Sparky had made up his mind early in life that if things were meant to work out they would. Otherwise, he would content himself with what appeared to be his inevitable mediocrity.

However, one thing was important to Sparky—drawing. He was proud of his artwork. Of course, no one else appreciated it. In his senior year of high school, he submitted some cartoons to the editors of the yearbook. The cartoons were turned down. Despite this, Sparky was so convinced of his ability that he decided to become a professional artist.

After completing high school, he wrote a letter to Walt Disney Studios. He was told to send some samples of his artwork, and the subject for a cartoon was suggested. Sparky drew the proposed cartoon. He spent a great deal of time on it and on all the other drawings he submitted. Finally, the reply came from Disney Studios. He had been rejected once again. Another loss for the loser.

So Sparky decided to write his own autobiography in cartoons. He described his childhood self—a little boy loser and chronic underachiever.

The cartoon character would soon become famous worldwide. For Sparky, the boy who had such lack of success in school and whose work was rejected again and again, was Charles Schulz.

He created the "Peanuts" comic strip and the little cartoon character whose kite would never fly and who never succeeded in kicking a football—Charlie Brown.

一个名叫斯帕奇的男孩

厄尔·南丁格尔——启迪和励志作品的作家和出版家——曾经讲过一个叫斯帕奇的男孩的故事。

对斯帕奇来说，上学是他最不可能做好的事情。八年级时，他门门功课都不及格。上高中时，他物理不及格，得了个零分。

斯帕奇的拉丁文、代数和英语也都不及格，体育运动方面也不是太好，尽管他勉强进入了学校的高尔夫球队，还是很快就输掉了赛季中唯一的一场重要比赛，就连随后的安慰赛也输掉了。

整个青年时期，斯帕奇都拙于交际。其他人并不是讨厌他，而是没有人在乎他。如果有同学在课余时间和他打招呼，他会感到非常吃惊。人们也无从得知他约会时是什么样子，因为上高中时，他从来没有和女孩约会过。他害怕被拒绝。

斯帕奇是个失败者，他自己、他的同学，每个人都清楚这一点。所以，他也安然接受。斯帕奇很小时就认为，如果事情会有好结果，那它迟早总会有的。否则的话，他就对自己注定的平庸自我满足。

但是，有一件事对斯帕奇很重要，就是绘画。他为自己的绘画作品感到自豪。当然，没有人欣赏他的作品。高中的最后一年，他把自己画的一些卡通画提交给学校年刊的编辑，却遭到拒绝。尽管这样，斯帕奇对自己的能力依然深信不疑，他决心成为一名职业画家。

高中毕业后，他给沃特·迪士尼工作室写了一封信。迪士尼工作室让他寄一些绘画样本过去，并给他提供了一幅卡通画的主题。斯帕奇完成了指定的卡通画。他花了大量时间来画这幅卡通画和他要提交的其他画。最后，迪士尼工作室的答复是：拒绝。一个失败者的又一次失败。

于是，斯帕奇决定用卡通画来写自传。他描绘了自己的童年——一个失败的小男孩、永远的落后生。

这个卡通人物很快就风靡全球。那个在学校里处处失败，作品被再三拒绝的男孩斯帕奇，就是查尔斯·舒尔茨。

他创作了连环漫画"花生"，还塑造了一个小卡通人物查理·布朗——他的风筝永远飞不起来，他永远也踢不到足球。

Sharpen Your Axe

A young man approached the foreman of a logging crew and asked for a job. "That depends," replied the foreman. "Let's see you fell this tree." The young man stepped forward, and skillfully felled a great tree. Impressed, the foreman exclaimed, "You can start Monday."

Monday, Tuesday, Wednesday, Thursday went by—and Thursday afternoon the foreman approached the young man and said, "You can pick up your paycheck on the way out today."

Startled, the young man replied, "I thought you paid on Friday."

"Normally we do," said the foreman. "But we're letting you go today because you've fallen behind. Our daily felling charts show that you've dropped from first place on Monday to last place today."

"But I'm a hard worker," the young man objected. "I arrive first, leave last, and even have worked through my coffee breaks!"

The foreman, sensing the young man's integrity, thought for a minute and then asked, "Have you been sharpening your ax?"

The young man replied, "No sir, I've been working too hard to take time for that!"

Our lives are like that. We sometimes get so busy that we don't take time to "sharpen the ax." In today's world, it seems that everyone is busier than ever, but less than ever. Why is that? Could it be that we have forgotten how to stay sharp?

There's nothing wrong with activity and hard work. But we shouldn't get so busy that we neglect the truly important things in life. We all need time to relax, to think and meditate, to learn and grow. If we don't take time to sharpen the axe, we will become dull and lose our effectiveness.

打 磨 斧 头

一位年轻人找到一个伐木队的工头，想讨份工作，"那得视情况而定，"工头答道，"你把这棵树砍倒让我看看。"年轻人走上前，娴熟地砍倒了一棵大树。工头很振奋，大声说："周一你就能来上班了。"

周一、周二、周三、周四，时间一天天过去了。到了周四下午，工头来到年轻人跟前说："你今天就可以领走薪水回去了。"

年轻人吃惊地回答："我想周五才会发薪水。"

"通常是这样的，"工头说，"但我们今天就要解雇你，因为你已经落后了。我们的每日砍伐图显示，你已经从周一的第一名落到了今天的最后一名。"

"可我工作很努力，"年轻人辩解道，"我来得最早，走得最晚，甚至连休息时间也在工作。"

工头觉得这个年轻人很诚实，思索了一会儿问道："你有没有磨过你的斧头？"

年轻人回答："没磨过，先生，我一直在努力伐木，没有时间去磨斧头。"

生活中也是如此，有时我们太忙了，顾不上去"磨斧头"。在当今社会，似乎大家都比以前更忙了，却比以前拥有更少的快乐。为什么会这样？难道我们已经忘记了如何使自己保持敏锐？

积极行动、努力工作本没有错。但是，我们不应该太忙碌而忽视了生活中真正重要的东西。我们都需要时间放松，需要时间深思，并需要时间不断学习和成长。如果我们不花时间来打磨斧头，就会变得愚钝而失去效率。

The Competitive Spirit

This speech is delivered by Scott W. Biehl, General Manager of Mercedes Benz of Fresno.

While growing up I spent a lot of time at my Grandparents' home. Yes, they would spoil my sister and me like most loving grandparents with gifts and treats but the things I loved most was playing catch, having putting contests in the living room, and playing basketball with my Grandpa.

My Grandfather had a basketball hoop set up in his backyard and when I would come over we would always play a game of 21. The way it was scored was if you made a basket it was worth 2 points and then you could shoot free throws for 1 point a piece until you missed. My Grandfather who was a professional boxer in his younger days always stayed fit and was in great shape. As I got older, the basketball games became more competitive but he would never just let me win.

Then one day when I was about 12 years old I finally did it! I beat him at a game of 21. After all those years of playing, I finally won. Then a couple of days later I called to see if he would be home so I could come by and visit and then took the bus across town to his house to see him. I couldn't wait to play him again at 21. All those years of losing to him and now I know I can beat him.

I arrived at his house and was greeted by my Grandmother and asked, "Where's Grandpa?" As she turned to point out in the backyard I could see my Grandfather. He was practicing shooting free throws. My 70-year-old Grandfather was practicing shooting free throws. I then went out in the backyard with my confidence of just winning a few days before, to play a game of 21 with Grandpa.

So, we started to play our usual game of 21 and I made the first basket for 2 points and then made only 1 free throw. My Grandfather then made a basket and proceeded to make 19 free throws in a row and beat me 21-3. Game over!

I learned a lot of lessons from my Grandfather over the years but none of them stands out like the lesson I received in his backyard that day. While he was since passed on, his competitive spirit still lives on through me today. Now I have a 6-year-old son of my own and I know that there is a game of 21 in our future and many of life's lessons to be learned while playing it.

竞 争 精 神

这是弗雷斯诺的梅赛德斯奔驰公司的总经理斯科特·W. 贝希尔做的一次演讲。

小时候，我经常住在祖父母家里。的确，他们也像大多数慈爱的祖父母一样，总是给我们好吃的好玩儿的，对我和妹妹百般溺爱，但我最喜欢的却是玩传球，就在客厅里玩，还喜欢和祖父一起打篮球。

祖父的后院里有个篮球框架，每次我到那里去，总是会和祖父打一场21分制的篮球赛。它得分的规则是投进一个球得两分，接着你可以进行罚球，罚球进一个得一分，直到你没投进为止。祖父年轻时是一名职业拳击手，他身体很棒，十分健壮。随着我渐渐长大，我们的篮球赛的竞争性更强了，但祖父从未输给我。

后来，大约12岁时，我终于打赢了！我在一场比赛中击败了他。经过这些年的比赛，我终于赢了。过了几天，我给他打电话，看他在不在家；在家的话，我就到他家去。打过电话后，我坐公交车穿过整个市区来到了他的家，迫不及待地想要和他再打一场比赛。这些年总是输给他，而现在我知道我能打败他了。

到了他的家，祖母出来迎接我，我就问她："祖父呢？"她转过身，指了指后院，我就看到了祖父，他正在练习罚球。70岁高龄的祖父正在练习罚球。我满怀着前几天获胜的信心，跑到院子里，和他进行比赛。

就这样，我们开始像往常那样进行比赛，我第一个球投进了，得了两分，接着罚球时只进了一个，得了一分。然后我祖父投进了一个球，接着罚球时，他连续进了19个球。最后以21比3打败了我。比赛结束了！

多年来，我从祖父那里学到了许多经验教训，但最重要的却是那天在他家后院学到的东西。虽然他已经去世了，但他的竞争精神如今却能通过我继续延续下去。现在我有了一个6岁的儿子，我知道我们将来也会有一场21分制的比赛，许多人生经验将会在这样的比赛中获得。

Weakness or Strength

Sometimes your biggest weakness can become your biggest strength. Take, for example, the story of one 10-year-old boy who decided to study judo despite the fact that he had lost his left arm in a devastating car accident.

The boy began lessons with an old Japanese judo master. The boy was doing well, so he couldn't understand why, after three months of training, the master had taught him only one move.

"Sensei," the boy finally said, "shouldn't I be learning more moves?"

"This is the only move you know, but this is the only move you'll ever need to know," the sensei replied.

Not quite understanding, but believing in his teacher, the boy kept training. Several months later, the sensei took the boy to his first tournament. Surprising himself, the boy easily won his first two matches. The third match proved to be more difficult, but after some time, his opponent became impatient and charged; the boy deftly used his one move to win the match. Still amazed by his success, the boy was now in the finals.

This time, his opponent was bigger, stronger, and more experienced. For a while, the boy appeared to be overmatched. Concerned that the boy might get hurt, the referee called a time-out. He was about to stop the match when the sensei intervened.

"No," the sensei insisted, "Let him continue."

Soon after the match resumed, his opponent made a critical mistake: he dropped his guard. Instantly, the boy used his move to pin him. The boy had won the match and the tournament. He was the champion.

On the way home, the boy and sensei reviewed every move in each and every match. Then the boy summoned up the courage to ask what was really on his mind.

"Sensei, how did I win the tournament with only one move?"

"You won for two reasons," the sensei answered. "First, you've almost mastered one of the most difficult throws in all of judo. Second, the only known defense for that move is for your opponent to grasp your left arm."

The boy's biggest weakness had become his biggest strength.

是弱项还是强项

有时，你的弱项能变成你的强项。例如一个10岁小男孩的故事。小男孩在一次悲惨的车祸中失去了左臂，尽管这样，他还是决心学习柔道。

男孩开始跟着一个年长的柔道大师学习。男孩学得非常棒，但他不明白，训练3个月了，老师却只教给他一个动作。

"老师，"男孩终于说道，"我不该学习更多的招数吗？"

"你只知道这一招，但这也是你需要知道的唯一一招。"

男孩虽然相当不解，但他相信老师，于是继续训练着。几个月后，老师带着男孩去参加他的第一次比赛。男孩自己也感到惊讶，他居然轻而易举地赢了前两场比赛。第三场比赛更为艰难，但过了一会儿，对手就沉不住气了，向他猛冲过来。男孩非常敏捷地用他学过的一招赢得了比赛。男孩对自己的成功感到不可思议，他就这样进入了决赛。

这次，他的对手更高、更强，也更有经验。很快，男孩似乎就招架不住了。裁判担心男孩可能受伤，就叫了暂停。当他正要停止比赛时，那位老师阻止了他。

"不，"老师坚持道，"让他继续比下去。"

比赛继续进行，不久，男孩的对手就犯了一个致命的错误：他放松了警惕。男孩立刻用那一招将他扳倒。他赢得了比赛，成了冠军。

在回家的路上，男孩和他的老师回顾了每场比赛里的每个动作。男孩鼓起勇气问老师他心中的不解。

"老师，我是怎么一招制胜赢得比赛的？"

"你能获胜有两个原因，"老师答道，"首先，你已经基本掌握了柔道里最难的一个动作。其次，对付那个动作的唯一防御方法就是对手要抓住你的左臂。"

男孩最大的弱项成了他最大的强项。

A Seed

Once upon a time, there was a seed and because it was only a seed, nobody cared to notice it. Thus, seized by a sense of inferiority, the seed gave no importance to his existence.

Then one day, a wind picked him up—randomly or otherwise he didn't know—and threw him on an open field under the sweltering sun. He was confused. Why would anything do such a thing? But instead of any copasetic answers, he was provided with rain (in addition to sunlight) sometimes in drizzles and sometimes in torrents.

Meanwhile time flew and years later he saw a traveler sitting by his side. "Thank God for this. I really needed some rest," he heard the traveler say.

"What are you talking about?" The seed promptly asked. He thought the man was making fun of him. Sure, he had witnessed many people sitting by his side—more so in recent years—but no one ever spoke to him like that.

"Who is this?" The man was startled.

"This is me. The seed."

"The seed?" The man looked at the giant tree. "Are you kidding me? You are no seed. You are a tree. A goliath of tree!"

"Really?"

"Yes! Why else do you think people come here?"

"What do they come here for anyway?"

"To feel your shade! Don't tell me you didn't know you had grown over time."

A moment passed before the traveler's words struck the chord of realization within him.

The seed, now a flourishing tree, thought and smiled for the first time in his life. The years of relentless tortures by the sun and the rain finally made sense to him.

"Oh! That means I'm not a flimsy seed anymore! I wasn't destined to die unnoticed but was actually born to drive away people's lassitude. Wow! Now that's life worth a thousand gems!"

一 粒 种 子

从前有一粒种子，因为它只不过是一粒种子，没有人在意它，所以这粒种子总是自惭形秽，妄自菲薄。

有一天，一阵风把它吹起来——也许风只是随意为之或是它并不知道的什么原因——把它吹到烈日照射下的田野里。它被搞糊涂了，为什么有人做这样的事儿？它想不出什么好的理由，却得到了雨水的滋润（除了阳光外），有时是毛毛细雨，有时是倾盆大雨。

时光飞逝，几年之后，它看到一个旅行者正坐在他旁边。"谢天谢地，我的确需要休息休息了。"它听到旅行者说道。

"你在说什么呀？"这粒种子急切地问。它以为这个人在取笑它，当然它已经看到过很多人都曾坐在它旁边——近几年更是如此——但从来没有人对它那样说过。

"是谁？"那个人吃惊地问道。

"是我，一粒种子。"

"种子？"那个人看着这棵参天大树说，"你在跟我开玩笑吗？你不是一粒种子，你是一棵树，一棵参天大树！"

"真的吗？"

"是啊！你认为人们到这来是为别的什么原因吗？"

"他们来这里到底做什么？"

"来乘凉啊！不要告诉我你还不知道自己已经长大了。"

过了好一会儿，它才明白了旅行者说的话。

那粒种子现在已是一棵枝繁叶茂的大树了，它平生第一次想了想，笑了起来。多年不断的日晒雨淋最后对它产生了重大意义。

"噢！那就是说我不再是一粒无足轻重的种子了！我不会悄然死去了，而是生来要为人们赶走疲劳的。哇！现在这是价值千金的生活！"

See Yourself Winning

Do you believe our imagination has much to do with success?

Arnold Schwarzenegger won the title of Mr. Universe seven times. But he didn't keep his title by only pumping iron. As part of his workout routine, he would frequently to into the corner of the gym and visualize himself winning the title again.

Jack Nicklaus, the great professional golfer, explained his imaging technique. He said, "First I 'see' the ball where I want it to finish—nice and white and sitting up high on the bright green grass. Then the scene quickly changes, and I 'see' the ball going there, its path, trajectory and shape, even its behavior on the landing. Then," says Nicklaus, "There's sort of a fade-out, and the next scene shows me making the kind of swing that will turn the previous images into reality."

I recall hearing the story of a prisoner of war who spent his years of solitary confinement playing gold—on the course of his mind. When he was released and returned to California, one of his first desires was to head for the nearest golfing facility. He was totally shocked at how his game had improved. Without question, his imagination had greatly enhanced his physical skills.

Today, practice "seeing" yourself winning.

想象自己胜利

你相信成功和我们的想象力密切相关吗?

阿诺德·施瓦辛格曾7次赢得世界先生的称号。但是,他并非只是靠举重来享有这个称号的。作为训练的一部分,他经常去健身房锻炼,想象着自己再一次获此殊荣。

伟大的职业高尔夫球手杰克·尼克劳斯曾这样描述他的想象技巧。他说:"首先,我假设球的落点——漂亮的白球在明媚的绿地上弹起。接着情况发生了变化,我想象着球到达目的地,想象着它通过的路线和轨迹以及形状,甚至还要想象它落地时的样子。然后,"尼克劳斯说,"球就会出现那种想象中运动的样子,这样就会把我先前的假设变为现实。"

我记得听过这样一个故事,一名战犯在被单独监禁期间练习打高尔夫——是在脑子里想象着打。他刑满释放,回到加州后,他最先做的事情就是直奔最近的高尔夫球场。他对自己球技大长感到震惊。毫无疑问,他的想象力已经极大地提高了他的球技。

如今,要练习"想象"你自己的胜利。

Don't Sit on Your Talent

There was a man who played piano in a bar. He was good piano player. People came out just to hear him play. But one night, a patron told him he didn't want to hear him play anymore. He wanted him to sing a song.

The man said, "I don't sing."

But the customer was persistent. He told the bartender, "I'm tired of listening to the piano. I want that guy to sing!"

The bartender shouted across the room, "Hey, buddy! If you want to get paid, sing a song. The patrons are asking you to sing!"

So he did. He sang a song. A piano player who had never sung in public did so for the very first time. And nobody had ever heard the song, Mona Lisa sung the way it was sung that night by Nat King Cole!

He had talent he was sitting on! He may have lived the rest of his life as a no-name piano player in a no-name bar, but because he HAD to sing, he went on to become one of the best-known entertainers in America.

You, too, have skills and abilities. You may not feel as if your "talent" is particularly great, but it may be better than you think! And with persistence, most skills can be improved. Besides, you may as well have no ability at all if you sit on whatever talent you possess! The better question is not "What ability do I have that is useful?" It is rather "How will I use whatever ability I have?"

发挥你的才能

一个人在酒吧里弹琴，弹得非常好。人们到这里来就是为了听他弹琴。但一天晚上，一个老顾客说他不想再听他弹琴，想听他唱歌。

这个人说："我不会唱歌。"

但这位顾客坚持让他唱。顾客告诉酒吧服务员："我听烦了钢琴弹奏，想让那个人唱歌！"

服务员喊道："嗨，老兄！如果想拿到钱就唱首歌吧，这位顾客要你唱歌！"

那个人照做了，他唱了一首歌。一个从没有在公众面前唱过歌的钢琴演奏者第一次唱歌。人们从没有听过像纳特·金·柯尔那样唱出来的《蒙娜丽莎》这首歌！

他有唱歌的天赋却不知利用。也许他余生只会是一个普通酒吧不知名的钢琴演奏者。但由于被逼着唱歌，他成了美国著名的歌手之一。

你也许同样有才能和天赋，也许你并不觉得你的"才能"有多了不起，但它可能比你想的要好！只要坚持下去，大多数才能都能得到施展。可是，如果你怀有才能却不知利用，那你就会毫无才能！最好的问题不是"我有什么有用的才能"，而是"我该如何利用自己的才能"。

I Have a Dream

I am happy to join with you today in what will go down in history as the greatest demonstration for freedom in the history of our nation.

Five score years ago, a great American, in whose symbolic shadow we stand today, signed the Emancipation Proclamation. This momentous decree came as a great beacon light of hope to millions of Negro slaves who had been seared in the flames of withering injustice. It came as a joyous daybreak to end the long night of their captivity.

But one hundred years later, the Negro still is not free. One hundred years later, the life of the Negro is still sadly crippled by the manacles of segregation and the chains of discrimination. One hundred years later, the Negro lives on a lonely island of poverty in the midst of a vast ocean of material prosperity. One hundred years later, the Negro is still languished in the corners of American society and finds himself an exile in his own land. And so we've come here today to dramatize a shameful condition.

In a sense we've come to our nation's capital to cash a check. When the architects of our republic wrote the magnificent words of the Constitution and the Declaration of Independence, they were signing a promissory note to which every American was to fall heir. This note was a promise that all men, yes, black men as well as white men, would be guaranteed the "unalienable Rights" of "Life, Liberty and the pursuit of Happiness." It is obvious today that America has defaulted on this promissory note, insofar as her citizens of color are concerned. Instead of honoring this sacred obligation, America has given the Negro people a bad check, a check which has come back marked "insufficient funds."

But we refuse to believe that the bank of justice is bankrupt. We refuse to believe that there are insufficient funds in the great vaults of opportunity of this nation. And so, we've come to cash this check, a check that will give us upon demand the riches of freedom and the security of justice.

We have also come to this hallowed spot to remind America of the fierce urgency of Now. This is no time to engage in the luxury of cooling off or to take the tranquilizing drug of gradualism. Now is the time to make real the promises of democracy. Now is the time to rise from the dark and desolate valley of segregation to the sunlit path of racial justice. Now is the time to lift our nation from the quicksands of racial injustice to the solid rock of brotherhood. Now is the time to make justice a reality for all of God's children.

It would be fatal for the nation to overlook the urgency of the moment. This sweltering summer of the Negro's legitimate discontent will not pass until there is an invigorating autumn of freedom and equality. Nineteen sixty-three is not an end, but a beginning. And those who hope that the Negro needed to blow off steam and will now be content will have a rude awakening if the nation returns to business as usual. And there will be neither rest nor tranquility in America until the Negro is granted his citizenship rights. The whirlwinds of revolt will continue to shake the foundations of our nation until the bright day of justice emerges.

But there is something that I must say to my people, who stand on the warm threshold which leads into the palace of justice: In the process of gaining our rightful place, we must not be guilty of wrongful deeds. Let us not seek to satisfy our thirst for freedom by drinking from the cup of bitterness and hatred. We must forever conduct our struggle on the high plane of dignity and discipline. We must not allow our creative protest to degenerate into physical violence. Again and again, we must rise to the majestic heights of meeting physical force with soul force.

The marvelous new militancy which has engulfed the Negro community must not lead us to a distrust of all white people, for many of our white brothers, as evidenced by their presence here today, have come to realize that their destiny is tied up with our destiny. And they have come to realize that their freedom is inextricably bound to our freedom.

We cannot walk alone.

And as we walk, we must make the pledge that we shall always march ahead.

We cannot turn back.

There are those who are asking the devotees of civil rights, "When will you be satisfied?" We can never be satisfied as long as the Negro is the victim of the unspeakable horrors of police brutality. We can never be satisfied as long as our bodies, heavy with the fatigue of travel, cannot gain lodging in the motels of the highways and the hotels of the cities. We cannot be satisfied as long as a Negro in Mississippi cannot vote and a Negro in New York believes he has nothing for which to vote. No, no, we are not satisfied, and we will not be satisfied until "justice rolls down like waters, and righteousness like a mighty stream."

I am not unmindful that some of you have come here out of great trials and tribulations. Some of you have come fresh from narrow jail cells. And some of you have come from areas where your quest —quest for freedom left you battered by the storms of persecution and staggered by the winds of police brutality. You have been the veterans of creative suffering. Continue to work with the faith that unearned suffering is redemptive. Go back to Mississippi, go back to Alabama, go back to South Carolina, go back to Georgia, go back to Louisiana, go back to the slums and ghettos of our northern cities, knowing that somehow this situation can and will be changed.

Let us not wallow in the valley of despair, I say to you today, my friends.

And so even though we face the difficulties of today and tomorrow, I still have a dream. It is a dream deeply rooted in the American dream.

I have a dream that one day this nation will rise up and live out the true meaning of its creed: "We hold these truths to be self-evident, that all men are created equal."

I have a dream that one day on the red hills of Georgia, the sons of former slaves and the sons of former slave owners will be able to sit down together at the table of brotherhood.

I have a dream that one day even the state of Mississippi, a state sweltering with the heat of injustice, sweltering with the heat of oppression, will be transformed into an oasis of freedom and justice.

I have a dream that my four little children will one day live in a nation where they will not be judged by the color of their skin but by the content of their character.

I have a dream today!

I have a dream that one day, down in Alabama, with its vicious racists, with its governor having his lips dripping with the words of "interposition" and "nullification" —one day right there in Alabama little black boys and black girls will be able to join hands with little white boys and white girls as sisters and brothers.

I have a dream today!

I have a dream that one day every valley shall be exalted, and every hill and mountain shall be made low, the rough places will be made plain, and the crooked places will be made straight; "and the glory of the Lord shall be revealed and all flesh shall see it together." ?

This is our hope, and this is the faith that I go back to the South with.

With this faith, we will be able to hew out of the mountain of despair a stone of hope. With this faith, we will be able to transform the jangling discords of our nation into a beautiful symphony of brotherhood. With this faith, we will be able to work together, to pray together, to struggle together, to go to jail together, to stand up for freedom together, knowing that we will be free one day.

And this will be the day — this will be the day when all of God's children will be able to sing with new meaning:

My country 'tis of thee, sweet land of liberty, of thee I sing.

Land where my fathers died, land of the Pilgrim's pride,

From every mountainside, let freedom ring!

And if America is to be a great nation, this must become true.

And so let freedom ring from the prodigious hilltops of New Hampshire.

Let freedom ring from the mighty mountains of New York.

Let freedom ring from the heightening Alleghenies of

Pennsylvania.

Let freedom ring from the snow-capped Rockies of Colorado.

Let freedom ring from the curvaceous slopes of California.

But not only that:

Let freedom ring from Stone Mountain of Georgia.

Let freedom ring from Lookout Mountain of Tennessee.

Let freedom ring from every hill and molehill of Mississippi.

From every mountainside, let freedom ring.

And when this happens, when we allow freedom ring, when we let it ring from every village and every hamlet, from every state and every city, we will be able to speed up that day when all of God's children, black men and white men, Jews and Gentiles, Protestants and Catholics, will be able to join hands and sing in the words of the old Negro spiritual, "Free at last! free at last! Thank God Almighty, we are free at last!"

我有一个梦想

今天，我很高兴跟大家一道参加这次将成为我国历史上为争取自由而举行的最伟大的示威集会。

100年前，一位伟大的美国人签署了解放黑奴宣言，今天我们就是在他的雕像前集会。这一庄严宣言犹如灯塔的光芒，给千百万在那摧残生命的不义之火中受煎熬的黑人带来了希望。它的到来犹如欢乐的黎明，结束了束缚黑人的漫漫长夜。

然而，100年后的今天，我们必须正视黑人还没有得到自由这一悲惨事实。100年后的今天，在种族隔离的镣铐和种族歧视的枷锁下，黑人的生活备受压榨。100年后的今天，黑人仍生活在物质充裕的海洋中一个穷困的孤岛上。100年后的今天，黑人仍畏缩在美国社会的角落里，并且意识到自己是故土家园中的流亡者。今天我们在这里集会，就是要把这种骇人听闻的情况公之于众。

就某种意义而言，今天我们是为了要求兑现诺言而汇集到我们国家的首都来的。我们共和国的缔造者在草拟宪法和独立宣言的气壮山河的词句时，曾向每个美国人许下了诺言，他们承诺给予所有人以生存、自由和追求幸福的不可剥夺的权利。

就有色公民而论，美国显然没有实践她的诺言。美国没有履行这项神圣义务，只是给黑人开了一张空头支票，支票上盖着"资金不足"的戳子后便被退了回来。但是，我们不相信正义的银行已经破产，我们不相信这个国家巨大的机会之库里已经没有足够的储备。因此，今天我们要求将支票兑现——这张支票将给予我们宝贵的自由和正义的保障。

我们来到这个圣地也是为了提醒美国，现在是非常急迫的时刻。现在绝不是侈谈冷静下来或服用渐进主义的镇静剂的时候。现在是实现民主的诺言的时候。现在是从种族隔离的荒凉阴暗的深谷攀登种族平等的光明大道的时候，现在是向上帝所有的儿女开放机会之门的时候，现在是把我们的国家从种族不平等的流沙中拯救出来，置于兄弟情谊的磐石上的时候。

如果美国忽视时间的迫切性和低估黑人的决心，那么，这对美国来说，将是致命伤。自由和平等的凉爽秋天如不到来，黑人义愤填膺的酷暑就不会过去。1963年并不意味着斗争的结束，而是开始。有人希望，黑人只要撒撒气就会满足；如果国家安之若素，毫无反应，这些人必会大失所望。黑人得不到公民的权利，美国就不可能有安宁或平静，正义的光明一天不到来，叛乱的旋风就会继续动摇这个国家的基础。

但对等候在正义之宫门口的心急如焚的人们，有些话我必须要说。在争取合法地位的过程中，我们不要采取错误的做法。我们不要为了满足对自由的渴望而抱着敌对和仇恨之杯痛饮。我们斗争时必须永远举止得体，纪律严明。我们不能允许我们的具有崭新内容的抗议蜕变为暴力行动。我们要不断升华到以精神力量对付物质力量的崇高境界中去。

现在黑人社会充满着了不起的新的战斗精神，但不能因此不信任所有的白人。因为我们的许多白人兄弟已经认识到，他们的命运与我们的命运紧密相连，他们今天参加游行集会就是明证。他们的自由与我们的自由是息息相关的。我们不能单独行动。

我们行动时，必须保证向前进，我们不能倒退。现在有人问热心民权运动的人："你们什么时候才能满足？"

只要黑人仍遭受警察难以形容的野蛮迫害，我们就绝不会满足。

只要我们在外奔波而疲乏的身躯不能在公路旁的汽车旅馆和城里的旅馆找到住宿之所，我们就绝不会满足。

只要黑人的基本活动范围只是从少数民族聚居的小贫民区转移到大贫民区，我们就绝不会满足。

只要密西西比仍有一个黑人不能参加选举，只要纽约有一个黑人认为他投票无济于事，我们就绝不会满足。

不！我们现在并不满足，我们将来也不满足，除非正义和公正犹如江海波涛，汹涌澎湃，滚滚而来。

我并非没有注意到参加今天集会的人中，有些受尽苦难和折磨，有些刚刚走出窄小的牢房，有些因寻求自由曾在居住地惨遭疯狂迫害和打击，并在警察暴行的旋风中摇摇欲坠。你们是人为痛苦的长期受难者。坚持下去吧，要坚信，忍受不应得的痛苦是一种赎罪。

让我们回到密西西比去，回到亚拉巴马去，回到南卡罗来纳去，回到佐治亚去，回到路易斯安那去，回到我们北方城市中的贫民区和少数民族居住区去，要心中有数，这种状况是能够也必将改变的。我们不要陷入绝望而不可自拔。

朋友们，今天我对你们说，此时此刻，我们虽然遭受种种困难和挫折，我仍有一个梦想，这个梦想深深扎根于美国的梦想之中。

我梦想有一天，这个国家会站立起来，真正实现其信条的真谛："我们认为这些真理不言而喻，人人生而平等。"

我梦想有一天，在佐治亚的红山上，从前奴隶的后嗣将能和奴隶主的后嗣坐在一起，共叙兄弟情谊。

我梦想有一天，甚至连密西西比州这个正义匿迹、压迫成风，如同沙漠般的地方，也将变成自由和正义的绿洲。

我梦想有一天，我的四个孩子将在一个不是以他们的肤色，而是以他们的品格优劣来评价他们的国度里生活。

我今天有一个梦想。我梦想有一天，亚拉巴马州能有所转变，尽管该州州长现在仍满口异议，反对联邦法令，但有朝一日，那里的黑人男孩和女孩将能与白人男孩和女孩情同骨肉，携手并进。

我今天有一个梦想。

我梦想有一天，幽谷上升，高山下降；坎坷曲折之路成坦途，圣光披露，满照人间。

这就是我们的希望。我怀着这种信念回到南方。有了这个信念，我们将能从绝望之岭劈出一块希望之石。有了这个信念，我们将能把这个国家刺耳的争吵声，改变成为一支洋溢手足之情的优美交响曲。

有了这个信念，我们将能一起工作，一起祈祷，一起斗争，一起坐牢，一起维护自由，因为我们知道，终有一天，我们会自由。

在自由到来的那一天，上帝的所有儿女们将以新的含义高唱这首歌：

"我的祖国，美丽的自由之乡，我为您歌唱。您是父辈逝去的地方，您是最初移民的骄傲，让自由之声响彻每个山岗。"

如果美国要成为一个伟大的国家，这个梦想就必须实现。让自由之声从新罕布什尔州巍峨的崇山峻岭响起来！让自由之声从纽约州的崇山峻岭响起来！

让自由之声从科罗拉多州冰雪覆盖的落基山响起来！让自由之声从加利福尼亚州蜿蜒的群峰响起来！不仅如此，还要让自由之声从佐治亚州的石岭响起来！让自由之声从田纳西州的瞭望山响起来！

让自由之声从密西西比的每座丘陵响起来！让自由之声从每片山坡响起来。

当我们让自由之声响起来，让自由之声从每个大小村庄、每个州和每个城市响起来时，我们将能加速这一天的到来，那时上帝的所有儿女，黑人和白人，犹太教徒和非犹太教徒，耶稣教徒和天主教徒，都将手携手，合唱一首古老的黑人灵歌："终于自由啦！终于自由啦！感谢全能天父，我们终于自由啦！"

Waste not, Want not

Mr. Jones. Boys, if you have nothing to do, will you unpack these parcels for me?

The two parcels were exactly alike, both of them well tied up with good whipcord. Ben took his parcel to the table, and began to examine the knot, and then to untie it.

John took the other parcel, and tried first at one corner, and then at the other, to pull off the string. But the cord had been too well secured, and he only drew the knots tighter.

John. I wish these people would not tie up their parcels so tightly, as if they were never to be undone. Why, Ben, how did you get yours undone?What is in your parcel?I wonder what is in mine! I wish I could get the string off. I will cut it.

Ben. Oh, no, do not cut it, John! Look, what a nice cord this is, and yours is the same. It is a pity to cut it.

John. Pooh! what signifies a bit of pack thread?

Ben. It is whipcord.

John. Well, whipcord then! what signifies a bit of whipcord?You can get a piece of whipcord twice as long as that for three cents; and who cares for three cents?Not I, for one. So, here it goes.

So he took out his knife, and cut it in several places.

Mr. Jones. Well, my boys, have you undone the parcels for me?

John. Yes, sir; here is the parcel.

Ben. And here is my parcel, father, and here is also the string.

Mr. Jones. You may keep the string, Ben.

Ben. Thank you, sir. What excellent whipcord it is!

Mr. Jones. And you, John, may keep your string, too, if it will be of any use to you.

John. It will be of no use to me, thank you, sir.

Mr. Jones. No, I am afraid not, if this is it.

A few weeks after this, Mr. Jones gave each of his sons a new top.

John. How is this, Ben? These tops have no strings. What shall we do for strings?

Ben. I have a string that will do very well for mine. And he pulled it out of his pocket.

John. Why, if that is not the whipcord! I wish I had saved mine.

A few days afterward, there was a shooting match, with bows and arrows, among the lads. The prize was a fine bow and arrows, to be given to the best marksman. "Come, come," said Master Sharp, "I am within one inch of the mark. I should like to see who will go nearer."

John drew his bow, and shot. The arrow struck within a quarter of an inch of Master Sharp's. "Shoot away," said Sharp; "but you must understand the rules. We settled them before you came. You are to have three shots with your own arrows. Nobody is to borrow or lend. So shoot away."

John seized his second arrow; "If I have any luck," said he;—but just as he pronounced the word "luck," the string broke, and the arrow fell from his hands.

Master Sharp. There! It is all over with you.

Ben. Here is my bow for him, and welcome.

Master Sharp. No, no, sir; that is not fair. Did you not hear the rules? There is to be no lending.

It was now Ben's turn to make his trial. His first arrow missed the mark; the second was exactly as near as John's first. Before venturing the last arrow, Ben very prudently examined the string of his bow; and, as he pulled it to try its strength, it snapped.

Master Sharp clapped his hands and danced for joy. But his dancing suddenly ceased, when careful Ben drew out of his pocket an excellent piece of cord, and began to tie it to the bow.

"The everlasting whipcord, I declare!" cried John. "Yes," said Ben, "I put it in my pocket today, because I thought I might want it."

Ben's last arrow won the prize; and when the bow and arrows were handed to him, John said, "How valuable that whipcord has been to you, Ben. I'll take care how I waste anything hereafter."

俭 以 防 匮

琼斯先生说："孩子们，如果你们无事可做，能帮我打开这些包裹吗？"

这两个包裹从外面看一模一样，都是用上好的绳子系着的。本把他的包裹拿到桌子上，检查绳子上面的结，然后开始解绳子。

约翰拿了另一个包裹，他用了各种方法解绳子，但绳子系得太结实，他那样做只能让绳子勒得更紧。

约翰说："我真希望这些人不要把绳子系得这么紧，好像这包裹再也不用打开似的。本，你是怎么把它解开的？你的包裹里面都有什么？我很好奇我的包裹里面装的是什么！我真希望我能把绳子解开，我还是把它剪掉算了。"

本说："噢，不，别剪，约翰！看看这绳子多好啊，你的绳子也是一样的。就这么剪了，实在太可惜了。"

约翰说："一根破绳子有什么可惜的？"

本说："那可是鞭绳。"

约翰说："好吧，鞭绳就鞭绳吧！谁会在乎三美分的鞭绳呢？至少我不会，所以我要剪了它。"

于是他拿起刀子，把鞭绳剪成了好几段。

琼斯先生说："好了，孩子们，你们都帮我解开包裹了吗？"

约翰说："是的，先生。在这儿呢。"

本说："这是我解开的包裹，这是鞭绳。"

琼斯先生说："你还留着鞭绳啊，本！"

本说："是的，先生，你看这鞭绳多好啊！"

琼斯先生说："约翰，你也留着鞭绳呢，对吧！这绳子或许有什么用处呢！"

约翰说："那绳子对于我来说没什么用，先生。"

琼斯先生说："如果剪成这样，恐怕是没什么用处了。"

在这之后的几个月，琼斯先生给他的两个儿子每人买了一个陀螺。"

约翰说："这是怎么回事，本？这些陀螺没有鞭绳，该怎么玩啊？"

本说："我有绳子，和我的陀螺正适合。"然后他从口袋里拿出了绳子。

约翰说："为什么，如果当时那鞭绳我还留着，也有绳子用了。"

又过去几天，一群小伙子举行射箭比赛。冠军的奖品是一副质地精良的弓箭。夏普大师说："看！我射的箭离靶心不到一英寸，看看谁射的箭离靶心更近。"

约翰拉开他的弓，把箭射出去，箭射在了离夏普大师四分之一英寸的地方。

"歪靶，"夏普说，"你要知道比赛的规则，这些规则在你来之前就已经定好了。你有三次射箭的机会，没有人会借给你箭。"

约翰拿起第二支箭，"但愿我好运。"他说。不过，就在他刚说到运气的时候，他弓上的绳子断了，箭从他手里掉了下去。

夏普说："好啦！你的比赛结束了。"

本说："我把我的弓借给他。"

夏普说："不行，这样不公平，你不知道比赛规则吗？比赛中你不能把自己的弓或箭借给别的选手。"

现在轮到本了。他第一箭射偏了，第二箭又射到了约翰第一箭的位置附近。在本射出最后一箭之前，他仔细地检查了弓上的绳子。他拉了一下绳子，想看看那绳子的力道，结果绳子断了。

夏普大师拍起了手，并且欢快地跳起舞来。不过他很快就停了下来，因为本小心翼翼地从口袋里拿出了一条精致的绳子，然后把这段绳子绑在弓上。

"这不就是之前那条鞭绳吗！"约翰叫道，"是的，"本说，"我今天把它放在了口袋里，因为我觉得没准会用上。"

本正是通过这最后一箭拿到了奖品，当夏普把那副弓箭交到本手上的时候，约翰说："那段鞭绳对你来说真是太有价值了，本。我从今以后再也不浪费了。"

Emulation

Frank's father was speaking to a friend, one day, on the subject of competition at school. He said that he could answer for it that envy is not always connected with it.

He had been excelled by many, but did not recollect ever having felt envious of his successful rivals; "nor did my winning many a prize from my friend Birch," said he, "ever lessen his friendship for me."

In support of the truth of this, a friend who was present related an anecdote which had fallen under his own notice in a school in his neighborhood.

At this school the sons of several wealthy farmers, and others, who were poorer, received instruction. Frank listened with great attention while the gentleman gave the following account of the two rivals:

It happened that the son of a rich farmer and the son of a poor widow came in competition for the head of their class. They were so nearly equal that the teacher could scarcely decide between them; some days one, and some days the other, gained the head of the class. It was determined by seeing who should be at the head of the class for the greater number of days in the week.

The widow's son, by the last day's trial, gained the victory, and kept his place the following week, till the school was dismissed for the holidays.

When they met again the widow's son did not appear, and the farmer's son, being next to him, might now have been at the head of his class. Instead of seizing the vacant place, however, he went to the widow's house to inquire what could be the cause of her son's absence.

Poverty was the cause; the poor woman found that she was not able, with her utmost efforts, to continue to pay for the tuition and books of her son, and so he, poor fellow! had been compelled to give up his schooling, and to return to labor for her support.

The farmer's son, out of the allowance of pocket money which his father gave him, bought all the necessary books and paid for the tuition of his rival. He also permitted him to be brought back again to the head of his class, where he continued for some time, at the expense of his generous rival.

竞　争

一天，弗兰克的父亲正在和一位朋友谈论在学校里竞争的话题，他说他敢负责任地说，嫉妒并不总是和竞争联系在一起的。

他曾经被很多人超越过，但是他不记得自己嫉妒过竞争对手。"即使我和我的朋友博奇竞争，并且我获胜，"他说，"也不会破坏我们之间的友谊。"

他的朋友也支持他的观点，并且讲了一个故事，这是发生在他家社区学校里的故事。

在这所学校里，有一些学生来自富裕家庭，其他人则来自贫穷家庭，他们一同接受教育。这位绅士讲这个故事的时候，弗兰克非常认真地听着。

"事情是这样的，一个有钱人家的孩子和一个穷寡妇的儿子为了争夺班里的头名而展开激烈的竞争。他们的成绩相当，就连老师也无法判断谁的成绩更好。有时候有钱人家的孩子拿第一，有时候穷寡妇的儿子拿第一。于是，大家只能通过一周内谁得第一的次数最多来决定谁是班里的头名。

"最后，寡妇的儿子获得了胜利，并且在接下来的一周保住了第一的位置，直到学校开始放假。

"但是，开学之后，那个寡妇的孩子没来上学，这回有钱人家的孩子可以拿第一了。然而，他并没有占这个便宜，而是来到寡妇家，问她为什么她的儿子没有来上学。

"那个寡妇说，因为她家太穷，而且她发现自己无法再继续支付儿子的学费和书费，因此，儿子只好辍学在家，通过干活挣钱，来照料母亲。

"于是，有钱人家的孩子拿出父亲给他的零花钱，用这笔钱把对手的学费和书费都交了，而且他还允许对手回去之后继续当班长。寡妇的儿子继续坐回班长的位置，而学费却是他慷慨大方的对手支付的。"

第三卷

通向成功的神秘之门

First Step to Success

Think back to a time in your life when you felt inspired and excited to make a significant change. Did you go for it or did your inner obstacles get in the way?

Your thoughts and beliefs are the foundation on which you build your success. You can't build a solid house on a foundation of clay and debris, and the same truth holds for your success.

If your thoughts and beliefs are shaky, these internal obstacles will hold you back unless you eliminate them.

Learning to handle obstacles is the best way to stand your ground and succeed while evasion only undermines your self-esteem.

Nature presents you with these challenges in order to learn to weather the storm and grow stronger.

To succeed in overcoming obstacles you need to have the guts not to quit, but to see things through, to have the strong faith to believe in yourself than in the obstacles and to have the willingness to do what it takes to turn the obstacles around.

This means you need to stand up to your obstacles and believe you can overcome them. When you attack your obstacles and do something about them, you will find that they are not as threatening as they appeared to be at first.

Decide that you will not give up and if something has to give, it will have to be the obstacles and not you.

Standing up to your obstacles imparts you with a sense of accomplishment and reinforces the sense of your inner power. By developing a habit of facing resistance, you instill into your psyche a strong message of endurance and success. This strengthens the faith and the belief in yourself, which helps remind you of the responsibility to yourself.

Sometimes you may have to resort to some other measures to overcome obstacles. If you can't get through the problem, try going around it, and if you can't go around it, try getting under it, and if you can't get under it, try going over it, and if you can't go over it, just dive straight into it.

In your path to a successful life, you are the only real obstacle.

走向成功的第一步

回想一下你生命中某个时刻得到灵感，兴奋地做出一个重大改变，你是会去努力争取，还是内心的障碍会阻止你的脚步呢？

你的思想和信仰是你成功的基础。你在泥土和残骸的地基上无法建造坚固的房子，对对你的成功也是基于同样的道理。

如果你的思想和信仰摇摆不定，如果你不清除内心的障碍，它们就会阻止你前进。

学会清理障碍是你站稳脚跟、获得成功的最佳途径，而逃避只会伤害你的自尊。

大自然将这些挑战呈现在你面前，是为了让你经受风吹雨打，更加茁壮成长。

要成功越过障碍，你需要有永不放弃的勇气，但也要看清事物，具有相信自己战胜那些障碍的坚强信念，还要有绕过那些障碍所采取的自愿行动。

这意味着你必须勇敢面对自己的障碍，相信自己能战胜它们。当你向自己的障碍发起进攻、采取行动时，就会发现它们并不像开始时的那样岌岌可危。

做出决定，永不放弃。如果有什么要让步的话，那一定会是障碍，而不是你。

勇敢面对自己的障碍，会使你有一种成就感，会使你内在的力量变得强大。培养直面阻力的习惯，你就会慢慢地给自己的心灵灌输一种忍耐与成功的坚强信念。这会增加你对自身的信仰与信心，有助于提醒你对自己的责任感。

要战胜这些障碍，有时你也许还要采取其他方法。如果你不能克服这个问题，就试着绕过去；如果你无法绕过去，那就试着控制它；如果无法控制它，那就试着越过去；如果无法越过去，那就直接冲向它。

在通向成功人生的道路上，你是唯一真正的障碍。

The Watchman of Your Mind

We must all have a watchman at the gate of our thoughts. The watchman at the gate is our subconsciousness.

We have the power to choose our thoughts.

For thousands of years, it seems almost impossible for us to control them. They rush through our minds like stampeding cattle or sheep.

But a single sheepdog can control the frightened sheep and guide them into the sheep pen.

I saw a picture in the newsreels of a shepherd dog. He had rounded up all but three. These three baaed and lifted their front hooves in protest, but the dog simply sat down in front and never took his eyes off them. He didn't bark or threaten. He just sat and looked at the three sheep with his determination. In a little while the sheep went into the pen.

We can learn to control our thoughts in the same way, by determination, not by force.

While our thoughts are on the rampage, we take an affirmation, keep repeating it and help us retrieve the inner quietude.

We cannot always control our thoughts, but we can control our words; repetition impresses the subconscious and we are master of the situation.

Your success and happiness in life depend upon the watchman at the gate of your thoughts. Sooner or later its function will show through your words and deeds.

You will form the habit of giving attention to every thought and word when you realize their importance.

Our subconsciousness is our watchman of our thoughts; it will, like a pair of scissors, cut out all the trivialities of our life so that we can go to success with our body and mind.

思想的守门人

我们的思想都必须有一个守门人，这个守门人就是我们的潜意识。

我们有权选择自己的思想。

几千年来，我们好像几乎不可能来控制它们，它们像受惊的牛羊一样闯过我们的思想。

但是，一只牧羊犬能把受惊的羊群赶回羊圈。

我看过一部有关牧羊犬的新闻影片。除了3只羊，牧羊犬把所有的羊都聚拢了起来。这3只羊咩咩叫着，抬起前蹄，以示反抗。牧羊犬没有叫，也没有威胁，只是卧在那里意志坚定地盯着3只羊。过了一小会儿，那些羊就进了羊圈。

我们同样可以学会这样来控制自己的思想，凭的是坚定的意志，而不是武力。

我们思想狂野时，要坚定意志，不断重复，帮助自己重新找回内心的平静。

尽管我们总是无法控制自己的思想，但我们可以控制自己的言语；不断向潜意识施加影响，我们就会控制局势。

你一生的成功和幸福取决于你思想的守门人，其作用迟早会通过你的言行表现出来。

当你认识到每个言行的重要性时，就会养成注意它们的习惯。

我们的潜意识就是我们思想的守门人，它会像一把剪刀，会剪掉我们生活中的所有琐事，以便我们能全心全意地走向成功。

My Definition of Success

Today I'm very glad to be here to share with you my ideas of success. What is success? It is what everyone is longing for. Sometimes success would be rather simple. Winning a game is success; getting a high grade in the exam is success; making a new friend is a success; even now I'm standing here giving my speech is also a success.

However, as a person's whole life is concerned, success becomes very complicated. Is fortune success? Is fame success? Is high social status success? No, I don't think so. I believe it is the realization of people's hopes and ideals. In the modern society there're many people who are regarded as the successful. And the most obvious characteristics of them are money, high position and luxurious life. So most people believe that is success and all that they do is for this purpose. But the problem is whether it is real success. We all know there are always more money, higher position and better condition in front of us. If we keep chasing them, where is the end? What will satisfy us at last? Therefore, we can see, to get the real success we need something inside, which is the realization of people's hopes and ideals.

Different people have different ideas about success because their hopes and ideas vary from one another. But I'm sure every success is dear to everybody because it is not easy to come by, because in the process of our striving for success we got both our body and soul tempted while we are enlightened by the most valuable qualities of human beings: love, patience, courage and sense of responsibility. These are the best treasures. So now I'm very proud that I have this opportunity to stand here speaking to all of you. It is my success because I rise up to challenge my hope.

What is success? Everyone has his own interpretation as I do. But I'm sure every success leads to a brighter future. So believe in our hopes; believe in ourselves. We, every one of us, can make a successful life!

成功的定义

今天，我很高兴在这里和你们一起分享我对成功的想法。成功是什么？每个人都渴望成功。有时成功会相当简单：赢得一场比赛是成功，考一次高分是成功，交一位新朋友是成功，甚至现在我站在这里演讲也是成功。

然而，就一个人的一生来说，成功变得非常复杂。财富是成功吗？名声是成功吗？出人头地是成功吗？不，我不这样认为。我认为成功是人们实现了自己的希望和理想。在现代社会中，很多人被认为是成功人士，他们最明显的特点就是有金钱、有地位，生活舒适。所以，大多数人认为这就是成功，他们所做的都是为了这个目的。但是，问题是这是否真的就是成功。我们都知道我们面前总会有更多的金钱、更高的地位和更好的条件。如果我们一味追求这些，哪里是尽头呢？什么会最终满足我们呢？所以，我们要明白，要想获得真正的成功，我们需要内在的一些东西，那就是实现人们的希望和理想。

不同的人对成功有不同的看法，因为他们的希望和想法彼此不同。但是，我相信每一次成功对每个人都非常珍贵，因为它来之不易，因为在争取成功的过程中我们的身心都受到过诱惑，同时我们也会受到人类最高贵的品质——爱、耐心、勇气和责任感的启迪。这些是最好的财富。所以，现在我很自豪有机会站在这里对大家演讲。这就是我的成功，因为我奋起挑战自己的希望。

成功是什么？每个人都和我一样有自己的解释。但是，我确信每次成功都会让我们走向更加光明的未来。所以，相信我们的希望，相信我们自己，我们每个人都能取得成功！

The Definite Goal

A father went to hunt for hares with his three sons to the grassland.

Upon arrival at the destination, all well prepared, before they took action, their father asked three sons a question, "What do you see?"

The eldest son replied, "I saw the shotguns in our hands, the hares running on the prairie and the endless stretch of grassland."

His father shook his head and said, "You're wrong."

The second son answered, "I saw our father, eldest brother, younger brother, shotguns, hares and the boundless grassland."

The father again shook his head and said, "You're wrong."

The youngest only answered, "I can only see hares."

Then their father said, "You're right."

Only can a definite goal point out the right direction of action and less detour on the road to achieving the objective. In fact, the indiscriminate or excessive goals will impede our progress, so in order to achieve what we have in our mind, if unrealistic, we may ultimately accomplish nothing.

明确的目标

父亲带着3个儿子到草原上猎杀野兔。

在到达目的地、一切准备得当、开始行动之前，父亲向3个儿子提出了一个问题："你们看到了什么？"

老大回答道："我看到了我们手里的猎枪、在草原上奔跑的野兔，还有一望无际的草原。"

父亲摇摇头说："不对。"

老二回答："我看到了爸爸、大哥、弟弟、猎枪、野兔，还有茫茫无际的草原。"

父亲又摇摇头说："不对。"

而老三的回答只有一句话："我只看到了野兔。"

这时，父亲才说："你答对了。"

只有明确的目标，才会为行动指出正确的方向，才会让我们在实现目标的道路上少走弯路。事实上，漫无目标或目标过多都会阻碍我们前进，要实现自己的心中所想，如果不切实际，那么最终可能会一事无成。

Ford's Principle of Success

When he decided to produce his V-8 motor, Henry Ford chose to make an engine with the entire eight cylinders cast in one block. The engineers said that it was simply impossible to cast an eight-cylinder engine-block in one piece.

Ford said, "Produce it anyway."

"But," they replied, "it is impossible."

"Go ahead," Ford commanded, "and stay on the job until you succeed, no matter how much time is required."

Six months passed and nothing happened. Another six months passed, and still nothing happened. The engineers tried every conceivable plan to carry out the orders, but the thing seemed out of the question.

At the end of the year the engineers again informed Ford they had found no way to carry out his orders.

"Go right ahead," said Ford. "I want it, and I'll have it."

They went ahead, and then, as if by a stroke of magic, the secret was discovered.

Ford's determination had won once more!

Henry Ford was successful because he understood and applied the principles of success. One of these is desire: knowing what one wants. If you can do this, you can equal his achievements in any calling for which you are suited.

福特成功的法则

亨利·福特决定生产V-8汽车时，想造一台8个汽缸合在一块的发动机。

工程师们说要把8个汽缸全浇铸在一起根本不可能。

福特说："无论如何要生产出来。"

"可是，"他们回答说，"那是不可能的。"

"只管做就是了，"福特命令道，"无论需要多少时间，直到做成为止。"

6个月过去了，没有做成。又过了6个月，还是没有做成。工程师们试过了每一种想得出来的计划去执行命令，但事情好像仍不可能。

一年后，工程师们再次告诉福特，他们找不到什么办法来执行他的命令。

"继续做，"福特说，"我要的东西，就一定会得到。"

他们继续努力，随后，像是得到魔力一般，终于发现了其中的奥秘。

福特的决心让他又一次取得了胜利！

亨利·福特之所以成功，是因为他了解并运用了这些成功法则。其中一个法则就是渴望：知道自己想要什么。如果你能做到这一点，就可以在适合自己的任何行业取得像他那样的成就。

Be Yourself

As a little boy, there was nothing I liked better than Sunday afternoons at my grandfather's farm in western Pennsylvania. Surrounded by miles of winding stonewalls, the house and barn provided endless hours of fun for a city kid like me. I was used to parlors neat as a pin that seemed to whisper, "Not to be touched!"

I can still remember one afternoon when I was eight years old. Since my first visit to the farm, I'd wanted more than anything to be allowed to climb the stonewalls surrounding the property. My parents would never approve. The walls were old; some stones were missing, others loose and crumbling. Still, my yearning to scramble across those walls grew so strong. One spring afternoon, I summoned all my courage and entered the living room, where the adults had gathered after dinner.

"I, uh, I want to climb the stonewalls," I said hesitantly. Everyone looked up. "Can I climb the stonewalls?" Instantly a chorus went up from the women in the room. "Heavens, no!" they cried in dismay. "You'll hurt yourself!" I wasn't too disappointed; the response was just as I'd expected. But before I could leave the room, I was stopped by my grandfather's booming voice. "Hold on just a minute," I heard him say, "Let the boy climb the stonewalls. He has to learn to do things for himself."

"Scoot," he said to me with a wink, "and come and see me when you get back."

For the next two and a half hours I climbed those old walls and had the time of my life. Later I met with my grandfather to tell him about my adventure. I'll never forget what he said. "Fred," he said, grinning, "you made this day a special day just by being yourself. Always remember, there's only one person in this whole world like you, and I like you exactly as you are."

Many years have passed since then, and today I host the television program *Mister Rogers' Neighborhood,* seen by millions of children throughout America. There have been changes over the years, but one thing remains the same: my message to children at the end of almost every visit, "There's only one person in this whole world like you, and people can like you exactly as you are."

做 你 自 己

我小时候最喜欢在爷爷的农场度过每个星期天的下午。爷爷的农场在宾州西部。农场四周都围上了绵延几英里的石墙。房子和谷仓给我这个城市男孩带来了无穷的快乐时光。我习惯了城里非常整洁的客厅似乎在低声说："不要摸！"

我仍能记得我8岁那年的一天下午的情景。因为我第一次去农场，所以我很想爬上农场四周的那些石墙。父母绝不会同意。这些墙年深日久，有的石头不见了，有的石头松动倒塌。然而，我渴望爬这些墙的欲望非常强烈。一个春天的下午，我鼓足勇气，走进客厅。午饭后，大人们都聚在这里。

"我，呃，我想爬那些石墙。"我犹豫地说。大家都抬起头。"我能去爬那些石墙吗？"屋里的女人们马上齐声叫了起来："天哪，不能！"她们惊慌地叫道，"你会伤着自己的！"我并没有太失望，我早就预料到会是这样的回答。但还没等我离开客厅，爷爷低沉的声音拦住了我。"等一会儿，"我听到他说，"让孩子爬那些石墙吧。他必须学会自己做事。"

"快走吧，"他对我眨眨眼说，"你回来后找我。"接下来的两个半小时，我爬起了这些古老的石墙，别提有多开心了。后来，我把自己的冒险经历告诉了爷爷。我永远也不会忘记他说过的话。"弗雷德，"他咧嘴笑道，"你做了一回自己，让这个日子不同凡响。永远记住，整个世界只有一个你，而且我喜欢真实的你。"

许多年过去了，现在我主持电视节目《罗杰斯先生的街坊四邻》，全美国几百万儿童收看。几年过后，节目已经发生了一些变化，但有一点没变，几乎每期节目后我都会传递给孩子们这样一个信息："这个世界上只有一个你，人们都喜欢真实的你。"

The Millet of Life

When the two brothers were old enough to marry, their father was not gratified because their family wasn't so rich that the brothers were often in discord with each other for some small interests and he really didn't know how they would dispute when they broke up the family and lived apart.

One day, their father was sick, lying in bed and staring blankly, when the elder son came over to wish him good health. His father said, "Ask your brother to come here, and I have something to say."

The younger brother arrived. Their father sat up and said, "I don't know how the disease hit. I'm feeling terribly unwell." The brothers persuaded their father not to worry about it, but he shook his head, "In fact I don't worry about this disease because I can manage it; but if you are in discord with each other in future, it will be our family's 'disease' and no one can cope with it." The brothers felt ashamed.

The father got out of the bed, pointed to some chickens in the courtyard and said, "Look at them squatting there in peace with each other, isn't it good?" Then their father brought out a bowl of millet, went quietly behind the house and scattered most of them on the ground. Then he went back to the courtyard with only a few grains left and flung at the chickens. At the sight of the millet, the chickens jumped up, scrabbled for it, quacked and brandished their wings. The formerly tranquil world was filled with "smoke of gunpowder" for some grains of millet.

The brothers smiled and understood what their father was driving at.

Their father added, "Both of you saw more millet is behind the house…"

Virtually, aren't many troubles in life because God scattered some grains of millet before us?

人生的谷子

兄弟俩大了，到了结婚的年龄，他们的父亲并不感到欣慰，因为家庭不那么富裕，兄弟俩时常为一些小利不和，一旦到分家那天，还真不知道会发生怎样的争执。

有一天，父亲病了，躺在床上发呆。这时，老大过来问安。父亲说："叫你弟弟来，我有话说。"

老二到了，父亲坐起身来，说："我自己也不知道这病如何来的，难受得很。"兄弟俩劝父亲别担心，父亲摇摇头："其实这病我也不担心，因为我自己能应付过去，但如果你们将来不和，那就是我们家庭的'病'了，谁都难应付。"兄弟俩很惭愧。

父亲下床，指着院子里的几只鸡，说："看看它们，蹲在那里相安无事，这不是很好吗？"然后，父亲到屋子里端出了一碗谷子，悄悄走到屋后，将大部分谷子撒在地上，仅留了几粒回到院子里，扔向那些鸡。那些鸡看见来了谷子，腾地跳起身，一起上前争夺，翅膀挥舞，嘎嘎乱叫，原本清静的世界，因为这几粒谷子而"硝烟弥漫"。

兄弟俩笑了，他们明白了父亲的意思。

父亲又说："你们都看见了，更多的谷子在屋后……"

其实，人生中的许多麻烦，又何尝不是因为上帝在我们眼前撒了几粒谷子呢？

We Never Told Him He Couldn't Do It

My son Joey was born with club feet. The doctors assured us that with treatment he would be able to walk normally—but would never run very well. The first three years of his life were spent in surgery, casts and braces. By the time he was eight, you wouldn't know he had a problem when you saw him walk. The children in our neighborhood ran around as most children do during play, and Joey would jump right in and run and play, too. We never told him that he probably wouldn't be able to run as well as the other children. So he didn't know. In seventh grade he decided to go out for the cross-country team. Every day he trained with the team. He worked harder and ran more than any of the others—perhaps he sensed that the abilities that seemed to come naturally to so many others did not come naturally to him. Although the entire team runs, only the top seven runners have the potential to score points for the school.

He continued to run four to five miles a day, every day—even the day he had a 103-degree fever. I was worried, so I went to look for him after school. I found him running all alone. I asked him how he felt. "Okay," he said. He had two more miles to go. The sweat ran down his face and his eyes were glassy from his fever. Yet he looked straight ahead and kept running. We never told him he couldn't run four miles with a 103-degree fever. So he didn't know. Two weeks later, the names of the team runners were called. Joey was number six on the list. Joey had made the team. He was in seventh grade—the other six members were all eighth-graders. We never told him he shouldn't expect to make the team. We never told him he couldn't do it. We never told him he couldn't do it…so he didn't know. He just did it.

无知者无畏

儿子乔伊出生时双脚畸形。医生向我们保证，经过治疗，他能像常人一样走路，但绝不会跑得很好。他人生的前3年是在手术、石膏和吊带中度过的。到他8岁时，你看他走路不会知道他的脚曾有过毛病。我们附近的小孩子们做游戏时总是跑来跑去。乔伊也会马上加入跑和玩。我们从不说他不可能像别的孩子那样跑。所以，他不知道。七年级时，乔伊决定参加越野队。每天他和大家一起训练，他训练得比任何人都更努力、跑得更多，也许是他意识到自己先天条件好像不如其他许多人吧。虽然是全队参加，但只有前7名有可能为学校得分。

他继续每天跑四五英里，甚至在烧到了40℃那天，仍坚持跑步。我为他担心，于是他放学后我去学校看他。我发现他正一个人在跑步。我问他感觉怎么样。"还好。"他说。他还要跑两英里。他满脸是汗，眼睛因发烧而呆滞。然而，他直视前方，继续跑着。我们从来没有告诉他高烧40℃不能跑4英里，所以他不知道。两周后，学校公布了赛跑队员的名字，乔伊名列第6，入选赛跑队。他才上七年级，其余6人都是八年级学生。我们从来没有告诉他不会有希望入选赛跑队，我们从来没说过他不行。我们从来没有说他不行……所以他不知道。他就这样做到了。

Think with the Few and Speak with the Many

Swimming against the stream makes it impossible to remove error and easy to fall into danger—only a Socrates can undertake it. To dissent from others' views is regarded as an insult, because it is a condemnation of their judgment. The offense is doubled on account of the judgment condemned and of the person who championed it. Truth is for the few, error is both common and vulgar. The wise person is not known by what he says on the public square, for there he speaks not with his own voice but with that of common folly, however much his inmost thoughts may deny it. The prudent person avoids being contradicted as much as he avoids contradicting others—though they have their judgment ready they are not ready to publish it. Thought is free, force cannot and should not be used on it. The wise person therefore retires into silence and if he allows himself to come out of it, he does so in the shade and before few and fit persons.

与少数人一起思考，与多数人一起交谈

逆流而上，不可能不犯错误，会很容易让人落入险境——只有苏格拉底才能挑战这种危险。不赞同别人的观点被看成一种侮辱，因为这是对他们判断

的一种谴责。这种冒犯具有双重性，因为既冒犯了受到谴责的判断，又冒犯了主张这种判断的人。真理属于少数人，谬误属于平民百姓。智者不是凭他在大庭广众之下说的话被认出来的，因为他不是用自己的声音说话，而是用普通百姓的声音说话，无论他内心是多么不愿接受。谨慎者避免被人反驳，也避免反驳他人——尽管他们早有看法，但不准备公之于众。思想是自由的，我们不能也不该对它使用武力。因此，智者陷入沉默，即使允许自己走出沉默，他也只会在暗处、在少数合适的人面前那样做。

Avoid Outshining Your Superiors

All victories breed hate, and that over your superior is foolish or fatal. Preeminence is always detested, especially over those who are in high positions. Caution can gloss over common advantages. For example, good looks may be cloaked by careless attire. There are some that will grant you superiority in good luck or in good temper, but none in good sense, least of all a prince—for good sense is a royal prerogative and any claim of superiority in that is a crime against majesty. They are princes, and wish to be so in that most princely of qualities. They will allow someone to help them but not to surpass them. So make any advice given to them appear like a recollection of something they have only forgotten rather than as a guide to something they cannot find. The stars teach us this finesse with happy tact: though they are his children and brilliant like him, they never rival the brilliance of the sun.

不要让你的上司相形见绌

所有胜利都会引起仇恨，所以胜过上司，要么愚蠢，要么致命。出类拔萃总是遭人憎恨，尤其是超越那些身居高位的人。小心谨慎能够掩饰常见的优点。比如，美貌可以通过不修边幅加以掩盖。有的人愿意承认你在好运气或好脾气上的优势，但没有人愿意承认你机智，君王尤其不愿承认，因为机智是君王的特权，任何声称自己机智超人都是对王权的犯罪。他们是君王，希望自己具有这种最高贵的品质。他们允许有人辅佐自己，但不愿有人超过自己。所以，对他们提出任何忠告，都要像是在提醒他只是忘了某件事，而不是为他求之不得的事情指点迷津。那些星星巧妙机智地教给了我们这个策略：尽管它们是太阳的孩子，并像它一样闪耀，但从来不和它一争高低。

Know How to Withdraw

If it is a great lesson in life to know how to deny, it is still greater to know how to deny oneself as regards both affairs and persons. There are extraneous occupations that eat away precious time. To be occupied in what does not concern you is worse than doing nothing. It is not enough for a careful person not to interfere with others, he must see that they do not interfere with him. One is not obliged to belong so much to others as not to belong at all to oneself. So with friends, their help should not be abused or more demanded from them than they themselves will grant. All excess is a failing, but above all in personal relationships. A wise moderation in this best preserves the goodwill and esteem for all, for by this means that precious boon of courtesy is not gradually worn away. Thus you preserve your genius and freedom to select the best and never sin against the unwritten laws of good taste.

知道如何退出

如果人生中懂得如何拒绝是一大功课的话，那么无论人还是事，更重要的是懂得如何舍弃。有些无关的职业常常侵蚀宝贵的时间。从事与自己无关之事比无所事事还要糟糕。对谨慎者来说，他不干涉别人还不够，他必须明白，也不要让他们来干涉他。一个人不必过分归属别人，以免自己不属于自己。所以，不应该滥用朋友的帮助，也不应该向朋友要求他们不同意给的东西。过犹不及是一种过失，尤其在个人关系上更是这样。对所有人来说，在这方面适可而止，可以最好地保持善意与尊重，因为用这种方法，那种善意的宝贵恩惠才不会逐渐消退。因此，你要保护好自己的天赋和自由，做出最佳选择，绝不要违反优雅品位的不成文法。

Know How to Show Your Strength

Even hares can pull the mane of a dead lion. Courage is no joking matter. Give way to the first and you must yield to the second, and so on till the last, and to gain your point in the end costs as much trouble as it would have a first. Moral courage exceeds physical courage; it should be like a sword kept ready for use in the scabbard of caution. It is your shield. Moral cowardice degrades one more than physical weakness. Many have had eminent qualities yet, for want of a stout heart, they passed inanimate lives and found a tomb in their own sloth. Wise nature has thoughtfully combined in the bee the sweetness of its honey with the sharpness of its sting.

懂得如何显示自己的力量

即使是兔子，也能拔死狮的鬃毛。勇气绝不是开玩笑。第一次让步，第二次你肯定也会屈服，如此这般，到最后，要想最终胜人一筹，付出的艰辛会和当初一样多。道德上的勇气常常超过身体上的勇气，它应该像时刻准备出鞘的剑一样，这也是你的盾。道德上的怯懦会比身体上的虚弱更降低一个人的品格。许多人虽然声名显赫，但因为缺乏一颗勇敢的心，所以他们过着死气沉沉的生活，在懒惰中找到了自己的归宿。英明的大自然富有创见地将蜜的甜美和刺的锋利结合在了蜜蜂身上。

Make Use of Your Friends

This requires all the art of discretion. Some are good far off, some when near. Many are no good at conversation but excellent as correspondents, for distance removes some failings which are unbearable in close proximity to them. Friends are for use even more than for pleasure, for they have the three qualities of the good, or, as some say, of being in general: unity, goodness, and truth. For a friend is all in all. Few are worthy to be good friends, and even these become fewer because people do not know how to pick them out. Keeping friends is more important than making them. Select those that will wear well—if they are new at first it is some consolation that they will become old. Absolutely the best are those well salted, though they may require soaking in the testing. There is no desert like leaving without friends. Friendship multiplies the good of life and divides the evil. It is the sole remedy against misfortune, like fresh air to the soul.

善用你的朋友

这需要所有的判断技巧。有些朋友宜远交，有些朋友须近交。许多朋友不善交谈而善通信，因为距离会消除亲近时无法忍受的一些缺点。朋友是为了应用，而不是为了快乐，因为他们具有三种美好品质，这就像一些人所说的具有普遍存在的品质：团结、善良和真诚。因此，一个朋友就是所有的一切。配得上做好友者寥寥无几，这些人之所以会变得越来越少，是因为人们不懂得如何选择朋友。保住朋友比结交朋友更重要。选择那些久经考验的人做朋友——即使他们起初是新朋友，他们也会成为老朋友，这多少让人感到安慰。尽管最好的朋友也许需要在考验中浸泡，但绝对是那些饱经风霜的朋友。再没有像离去时没有朋友那样的沙漠了。友谊增加生活的美好，分担生活的不幸，它是治疗不幸的唯一妙方，就像新鲜空气对灵魂一样。

Never Share the Secrets of Your Superiors

You may think you will share pears, but you will only share parings. Many have been ruined by being confidants: they are like sops of bread used like spoons, they run the same risk of being eaten up afterwards. It is no favor to a prince to share a secret—it is only a relief. Many break the mirror that reminds them of their ugliness. We do not like seeing those who have seen us as we are, nor is he seen in a favorable light who has seen us in an unfavorable one. No one ought to be too much beholden to us, least of all one of the great, unless it is for favors done for him rather than for favors received. Especially dangerous are secrets entrusted to friends. When you communicate a secret to someone you make yourself his slave. With a prince this is an intolerable position that cannot last; he will desire to recover his lost liberty, and to gain he will overturn everything, including right and reason. Accordingly, neither tell secrets nor listen to them.

绝不要和你的上司分享秘密

你也许认为自己会分到梨，但你只能分到削掉的皮。许多人因为成了他人的心腹而毁了自己：他们就像面包片做的匙子，同样冒着随后被吞吃的危险。分享一位君王的秘密绝不是恩宠——只是一种消遣。许多人打碎镜子，是因为镜子让他们想起了自己的丑陋。我们不喜欢看到那些曾经看到过我们本来面貌的人；如果他曾经看到过我们不利的一面，他就不会以赞许的眼光看我们。谁也不应该对我们过分感谢，尤其是伟人更不应该，除非你曾经给过他帮助，而不是接受他的帮助。尤其危险的是，把秘密托付给朋友们。你把秘密传给某个人，就会使自己成为他的奴隶。对君王来说，这是一个无法忍受、难以长久的位置，他一定会期望恢复失去的自由；为了获得自由，他一定会颠覆一切，包括正义和理性。因此，既不要泄露秘密，也不要去听秘密。

Two Ways of Telling a Story

In one of the most populous cities of New England, a few years ago, a party of lads, all members of the same school, got up a grand sleigh ride. The sleigh was a very large one, drawn by six gray horses.

On the following day, as the teacher entered the schoolroom, he found his pupils in high glee, as they chattered about the fun and frolic of their excursion. In answer to some inquiries, one of the lads gave him an account of their trip and its various incidents.

As he drew near the end of his story, he exclaimed:" Oh, sir! there was one thing I had almost forgotten. As we were coming home, we saw ahead of us a queer looking affair in the road. It proved to be a rusty old sleigh, fastened behind a covered wagon, proceeding at a very slow rate, and taking up the whole road.

"Finding that the owner was not disposed to turn out, we determined upon a volley of snowballs and a good hurrah. They produced the right effect, for the crazy machine turned out into the deep snow, and the skinny old pony started on a full trot.

"As we passed, some one gave the horse a good crack, which made him run faster than he ever did before, I'll warrant.

"With that, an old fellow in the wagon, who was buried up under an old hat, bawled out, 'Why do you frighten my horse?' 'Why don't you turn out, then?' says the driver. So we gave him three rousing cheers more. His horse was frightened again, and ran up against a loaded wagon, and, I believe, almost capsized the old creature—and so we left him."

"Well, boys," replied the teacher, "take your seat, and I will tell you a story, and all about a sleigh ride, too. Yesterday afternoon a very venerable old clergyman was on his way from Boston to Salem, to pass the rest of the winter at the house of his son. That he might be prepared for journeying in the following spring he took with him his wagon, and for the winter his sleigh, which he fastened behind the wagon.

"His sight and hearing were somewhat blunted by age, and he was proceeding very slowly; for his horse was old and feeble, like his owner. He was suddenly disturbed by loud hurrahs from behind, and by a furious pelting of balls of snow and ice upon the top of his wagon.

"In his alarm he dropped his reins, and his horse began to run away. In the midst of the old man's trouble, there rushed by him, with loud shouts, a large party of boys, in a sleigh drawn by six horses. 'Turn out! turn out, old fellow!' 'Give us the road!' 'What will you take for your pony?' 'What's the price of oats, old man?' were the various cries that met his ears.

"'Pray, do not frighten my horse!' exclaimed the infirm driver. 'turn out, then! turn out!' was the answer, which was followed by repeated cracks and blows from the long whip of the 'grand sleigh,' with showers of snowballs, and three tremendous hurrahs from the boys.

"The terror of the old man and his horse was increased, and the latter ran away with him, to the great danger of his life. He contrived, however, to stop his horse just in season to prevent his being dashed against a loaded wagon. A short distance brought him to the house of his son. That son, boys, is your instructor, and that 'old fellow, 'was your teacher's father!"

When the boys perceived how rude and unkind their conduct appeared from another point of view, they were very much ashamed of their thoughtlessness, and most of them had the manliness to apologize to their teacher for what they had done.

By HENRY K. OLIVER.

讲故事的两种方法

很多年前，在新英格兰人口最多的城市里，年轻小伙以及同一学校的所有学生都拥有高贵、华丽的雪橇，这种雪橇非常大，需要6匹马才能拉动。

在这之后的一天，当老师走进教室的时候，他发现学生们的情绪都很高涨，他们之间相互分享雪橇探险中碰到的趣闻。他们中的一个学生开始详细叙述他们的旅行和旅行中层出不穷的滑稽事。

就在他快要说完的时候，他大叫道："噢，先生！有一件事我差点忘了，当我们快要到家的时候，我们发现在路的前方有什么奇怪的东西，走近看才知道是一个生了锈的旧雪橇，被绑在马车后面，并以非常慢的速度前进，把整条大路都占了。

"我们发现这辆马车的车主并不打算现身，于是我们把许多雪球扔到他的马车上，并且欢呼起来。这样做有了效果，因为那辆马车被陷在雪里，而那匹枯瘦如柴的小马则全速奔跑起来。

"当我们从马车身边经过的时候，我们中有些人抽鞭子去吓唬那匹马。我敢保证，那匹马跑得比之前还要快。

"就在这时，马车里那个戴着一顶帽子的老家伙大叫起来：'你们为什么要吓唬我的马？你们管什么闲事！'我们开始起哄，他的马再一次受到惊吓，撞上了一辆满载货物的马车，我相信，那一下撞击几乎把那破车弄翻了。然后，我们就离开了。"

"好吧，孩子们，"老师回答，"都坐下吧。我给你们讲个故事，也是一个关于雪橇的故事。昨天下午，一位德高望重的老牧师走在从波士顿到塞勒姆的路上，他要在儿子家度过整个冬天；然后到第二年春天，他会乘马车去旅行，而在冬天，他会把雪橇绑在他的马车后面。

"随着年龄的增长，他的视力和听力都有所下降，他之所以走得这么慢，是因为他的马也老了、虚弱了，就像它的主人一样。他突然被从后面传来的欢呼声所惊扰，并且许多掉落的雪球和冰块砸中车顶。

"由于惊慌，他弄掉了缰绳，他的马也开始失控。就在老人麻烦不断时，一群大嚷大叫的孩子驾驶着由6匹马拉的雪橇，大声嚷嚷道：'闪开，闪开，老家伙！快把路给我们让开！你带你的小马要去哪里？知道惹我们是什么下场吗？老家伙！'

"'求求你们，不要吓坏我的马！'那个虚弱的老人高喊，然而他得到的回答却是'闪开，闪开！'然后从大雪橇上传来鞭打声和口哨声，雪球不停地砸过来，男孩们还不停地起哄。

"老人和他的马更害怕了，那匹马带着老人猛跑起来，这对老人非常危险。然而，老人想尽一切办法让马停了下来，这样才没有撞上那辆满载货物的马车。还有那么一小段路就到他的儿子家了。孩子们，他的儿子就是你们的老师，而那个你们口中的'老家伙'，就是你们老师的父亲！"

当学生们从不同的角度去看他们的做法，他们才意识到自己的所作所为是多么粗鲁和恶劣，他们为自己的轻率感到羞耻，他们中大多数都勇敢地向他们的老师道了歉。

亨利·K.奥利弗

The Best Capital

One would have said that modest John Brooke, in his busy, quiet, humble life, had had little time to make friends; but now they seemed to start up everywhere, — old and young, rich and poor, high and low; for all unconsciously his influence had made itself widely felt, his virtues were remembered, and his hidden charities rose up to bless him.

The group about his coffin was a far more eloquent eulogy than any that man could utter. There were the rich men whom he had served faithfully for years; the poor old women whom he cherished with his little store, in memory of his mother; the wife to whom he had given such happiness that death could not mar it utterly; the brothers and sisters in whose hearts he had made a place forever; the little son and daughter who already felt the loss of his strong arm and tender voice; the young children, sobbing for their kindest playmate, and the tall lads, watching with softened faces a scene which they never could forget.

That evening, as the Plumfield boys sat on the steps, as usual, in the mild September moonlight, they naturally fell to talking of the event of the day.

Emil began by breaking out in his impetuous way, "Uncle Fritz is the wisest, and Uncle Laurie the jolliest, but Uncle John was the best; and I'd rather be like him than any man I ever saw."

"So would I. Did you hear what those gentlemen said to Grandpa to-day? I would like to have that said of me when I was dead;" and Franz felt with regret that he had not appreciated Uncle John enough.

"What did they say?" asked Jack, who had been much impressed by the scenes of the day.

"Why, one of the partners of Mr. Laurence, where Uncle John has been ever so long, was saying that he was conscientious almost to a fault as a business man, and above reproach in all things. Another gentleman said no money could repay the fidelity and honesty with which Uncle John had served him, and then Grandpa told them the best of all.

"Uncle John once had a place in the office of a man who cheated, and when this man wanted uncle to help him do it, uncle wouldn't, though he was offered a big salary. The man was angry, and said, 'You will never get on in business with such strict principles;'and uncle answered back, 'I never will try to get on without them, 'and left the place for a much harder and poorer one."

"Good !" cried several of the boys warmly, for they were in the mood to understand and value the little story as never before.

"He wasn't rich, was he?" asked Jack.

"No."

"He never did anything to make a stir in the world, did he?"

"No."

"He was only good?"

"That's all;" and Franz found himself wishing that Uncle John had done something to boast of, for it was evident that Jack was disappointed by his replies.

"Only good. That is all and everything," said Uncle Fritz, who had overheard the last few words, and guessed what was going on in the minds of the lads.

"Let me tell you a little about John Brooke, and you will see why men honor him, and why he was satisfied to be good rather than rich or famous. He simply did his duty in all things, and did it so cheerfully, so faithfully, that it kept him patient, brave, and happy, through poverty and loneliness and years of hard work.

"He was a good son, and gave up his own plans to stay and live with his mother while she needed him. He was a good friend, and taught your Uncle Laurie much beside his Greek and Latin, did it unconsciously, perhaps, by showing him an example of an upright man.

"He was a faithful servant, and made himself so valuable to those who employed him that they will find it hard to fill his place. He was a good husband and father, so tender, wise, and thoughtful, that Laurie and I learned much of him, and only knew how well he loved his family when we discovered all he had done for them, unsuspected and unassisted."

Uncle Fritz stopped a minute, and the boys sat like statues in the moonlight until he went on again, in a subdued and earnest voice: "As he lay dying, I said to him, 'Have no care for your wife and the little ones; I will see that they never want. 'then he smiled and pressed my hand, and answered, in his cheerful way, 'no need of that; I have cared for them. '

"And so he had, for when we looked among his papers, all was in order, —not a debt remained; and safely put away was enough to keep his wife comfortable and independent. Then we knew why he had lived so plainly, denied himself so many pleasures, except that of charity, and worked so hard that I fear he shortened his good life.

"He never asked help for himself, though often for others, but bore his own burden and worked out his own task bravely and quietly. No one can say a word of complaint against him, so just and generous and kind was he; and now, when he is gone, all find so much to love and praise and honor, that I am proud to have been his friend, and would rather leave my children the legacy he leaves his than the largest fortune ever made.

"Yes! simple, genuine goodness is the best capital to found the business of this life upon. It lasts when fame and money fail, and is the only riches we can take out of this world with us. Remember that, my boys; and, if you want to earn respect and confidence and love, follow in the footsteps of John Brooke."

最好的资本

人们可能会说，诚挚的约翰·布鲁克，在忙忙碌碌、卑微且平庸的一生中，几乎没有时间交朋友，但是，现在他的朋友从各地涌现了出来——老人、年轻人、富人、穷人、高个子和矮个子——因为人们受到了他的潜移默化的影响，他的道德观念被人们铭记，而且他默默的善举也给自己带来了祝福。

围在他棺材周围的人流比任何人朗诵的颂词都更顺畅。有他忠诚服务了数年的有钱人；有他用自己的店铺照顾的可怜的老妇人，以此纪念自己的母亲；有他的妻子，他给她带来的快乐就算是死亡也无法损毁；有他的兄弟姐妹，他们把他永久地留在了自己心中；有他的儿女，他们已然失去了爸爸宽厚的臂膀和慈爱的声音；有小孩子们，他们为仁慈友善的玩伴而啜泣，年龄稍长的孩子们则用柔和的目光注视着这永远无法忘怀的场景。

那天傍晚，在9月明亮的月光下，梅园的孩子们像往常一样走上台阶，讲述这一整天所发生的事情。

埃米尔开始用他那鲁莽的腔调第一个发言："弗里兹叔叔最聪明，劳里叔叔最快乐，但是约翰叔叔是最棒的，在我见过的所有人里面，我最愿意成为约翰叔叔那样的人。"

"我也是。你们知道今天那些绅士们都是怎么跟祖父说话的吗？如果我死了，我也希望别人能够那样说我。"弗朗兹觉得有些后悔，因为他以前对约翰叔叔崇敬得还不够。

"他们都是怎么说约翰叔叔的？"杰克问道，今天的场景深深地触动了他。

"劳伦斯先生的合伙人之一跟约翰叔叔共事过很久，他说，约翰叔叔作为一个生意人，做事认真负责，任何人都无法挑出责备他的理由。另一位绅士说，多少金钱也无法买来约翰叔叔的忠诚和诚信，然后爷爷讲了约翰叔叔的一件最牛气的事。

"有一次，约翰叔叔在某个人的公司工作，那个人曾经说过谎话，然后那个人想要约翰叔叔帮他骗人，尽管那人答应付给约翰叔叔一大笔钱，约翰叔叔还是没有答应。结果那个人很生气，说道：'你的态度要是这么强硬的话，就永远也别想在生意上有什么进展。'然后约翰叔叔答道：'我不会为了成功而抛弃原则。'于是约翰叔叔辞掉了工作，找了一份更困难、收入更低的工作。"

"太牛了！"几个小男孩喊道，因为他们从这个故事中受到了启迪。

"他一点也不富有，不是吗？"杰克问道。

"是的，一点都不富有。"

"他也没做过什么轰轰烈烈的大事，不是吗？"

"是的。"

"但他是个好人。"

"这就足够了。"弗朗兹希望自己能够找到一些约翰叔叔做过的可以炫耀的事迹，因为，很明显杰克对他的答复很失望。

"他只是个好人，这是他做的所有的事。"弗里兹叔叔说道，他听到了孩子们说的话，能猜出来那些孩子到底在想什么。

"让我给你们讲讲约翰·布鲁克的故事吧，你们会发现为什么人们会尊敬他，为什么他宁愿选择当好人，而不是富人或者有名气的人。他做任何事都会负起责任来，在他多年的贫穷和寂寞中，他依旧能够保持耐心、勇敢和快乐的心境。

"他是个好人，他为了留下来照顾自己的母亲而放弃了自己的事业。他是个好伙伴，不仅教劳里叔叔希腊语和拉丁语，而且不知不觉间教了劳里叔叔不少东西，还以自身为榜样，教会劳里叔叔如何做一个正直的人。

　　"他还是个忠诚的仆人，那些雇用他的人都认为他非常有价值，几乎无人能及。他也是个好丈夫、好父亲，他温柔、智慧、考虑周全，我和劳里从他身上学到了许多东西，当我们发现他为家人所做的一切之后，我们才发现他多么爱自己的家人。"

　　弗里兹叔叔停顿了一下，在月光的照射下，孩子们像雕像一样坐在月光下，直到他继续用低沉的声音说："就在他快死的时候，我对他说：'不要担心你的妻子和你的孩子们，我会照顾好他们，让他们什么都不缺。'他微笑着握住我的手，用惯用的热情的口吻答道：'不用了，我已经照顾好他们了。'

　　"他确实已经照顾好了，因为看到他的遗嘱时，我们发现一切都安排得井井有条，没有留下任何负债，而且他的积蓄足够让他的妻子过上舒服、自在的生活。我们这才知道，为什么他活得这么节俭，除了慈善，他拒绝了很多的娱乐活动，我担心正是他那么拼命地工作，才缩短了他的寿命！

　　"他从来没有求过别人，而且还常常替他人着想，他总是把重担扛在自己肩上，勇敢、默默地做完自己的工作。没有人会抱怨他，现在他去世了，人们都发现他是如此值得爱戴、赞美和尊敬。作为他的朋友，我感到很荣幸，我希望留给自己孩子的，跟他留给自己孩子的一样多，而不是大量的金钱。

　　"没错！简单、真诚、善意是人生中最好的资本。它不会随着名望和金钱的失去而消失，它是我们在这个世界上唯一可以带走的财富。记住，孩子们，如果你们想要赢得别人的尊重、信任和爱，就遵循约翰·布鲁克的脚步吧！"

第四卷

生命的加减法

The Four Ways of Good Life

Live Below Your Means. There will always be temptation to forsake the future for immediate gratification. Enjoy life's simple pleasures and save as much as you can. Expensive things don't create lasting happiness and security. Careful spending will bring you greater leisure and enjoyment in the long run.

Educate Yourself. To be happy we need continuous growth. The best way to grow is lifelong education. This doesn't mean you need to pursue a doctorate or spend two hours reading every day. Self-education can be anything that takes you out of your comfort zone. The important part is keeping an open mind and searching for fresh ideas and perspectives. Self-education builds over time. It might feel like the bits of wisdom you acquire don't mean much, but over the years they add up to form a wiser, kinder, more interesting person.

Develop Lasting Personal Relationships. Suppose you had everything you wanted. Would you be happy without anyone to share it with? The personal relationships we develop with friends and family members are the greatest source of happiness in our lives. Taking the time to cultivate and enjoy personal relationships is essential to long-term happiness. Without the people you care about you'll probably be miserable, no matter how successful you become.

Work Towards a Dream. Even if your life isn't perfect, you can always build towards a set goal. If you aren't building towards something, you're probably stagnating. The best way to reverse this is working towards a goal. We can't control everything about our lives, but working towards a goal gives us something positive to focus on and lays the foundation for future success. No matter what your goal is, get out there and start doing something. As Lao Tzu said, "A journey of 1,000 miles begins with a single step."

美好生活的四种方式

量入为出。世界总是充满诱惑，使很多人因暂时的满足而放弃了未来。享受生活简单的快乐，并尽可能保持这种状态。奢侈的东西无法创造持久的快乐和安全。谨慎开销最终会给你带来更大的安逸和快乐。

自我培养。要快乐，我们需要不断成长。成长的最好方法是穷其一生学习。这并不意味着你需要获得博士头衔或每天看两小时书。自我培养是能让你从安逸环境中走出来的任何方式。重要的是保持思想开放，寻求崭新的想法和观点。自我培养是通过时间累积而成的。可能你学到的聪明才智目前意义不大，但许多年后，它们会渐渐累积，使你成为一位更睿智、更善良、更风趣的人。

持久关系。假如你已拥有想要的一切，如果无人分享，你会开心吗？我们和亲友间建立的人际关系是我们人生中最大的幸福源泉。花时间培养和享受人际关系是永久快乐必不可少的因素。如果你没有要关心的人，无论你多么成功，都可能会痛苦。

坚持梦想。即使生活并不完美，你也总能朝一个既定目标逐步前进。如果没有努力的目标，你可能会停滞不前。扭转这种状况的最好方法就是朝一个目标前进。我们无法掌控生活中的一切，但不断朝一个目标努力，可以使我们聚精会神、积极行动，为未来的成功奠定基础。无论你的目标是什么，只要开始行动就成。老子曰："千里之行，始于足下。"

39 Laws of Life

When falling in love, some lose their head while others lose their heart.

Happiness is good health and a bad memory.

Love is the only thing that holds the dark at bay.

Love is a game that two can play and both win.

Life has taught us that love does not consist in gazing at each other but in looking outward together in the same direction.

The most important thing a father can do for his children is to love their mother.

Love is an act of endless forgiveness, a tender look which becomes a habit.

To be in love is to surpass oneself.

Love enters a man through his eyes; a woman through her ears.

Women are meant to be loved, not to be understood.

There are no ugly women; there are only women who not know how to look pretty.

If you would be loved, love and be lovable.

If you be loved, be worthy of love.

Ignorance and bungling with love are better than wisdom and skill without love.

Immature love says, "I love you because I need you." Mature love says, "I need you because I love you."

Love me little, love me long.

Where there is no trust, there is no love.

Learn from the past, look to the future. Live in the present.

Be happy. It is a way of being wise.

Comedy is tragedy plus time.

Love is springtime plant that perfumes everything with its hope, even the ruins to which it clings.

Do not scorn the person who is perpetually happy. He does know something you don't.

I'm an idealist. I don't know where I'm going, but I'm on my way.

I know of only one duty, and that is to love.

Love is the only satisfactory answer to the problem of human existence.

People who are sensible about love are incapable of it.

Contention is better than loneliness.

Good friends stab you in the front.

If there is anything better than being loved, it's loving.

Marriage is the alliance of two people, one of whom never remembers birthdays and the other who never forgets.

Love is like an hourglass, with the heart filling up as the brain empties.

Absence extinguishes small passions and increases great ones, as the wind blows out a candle and fans a bonfire.

My advice to you is to get married. If you find a good wife, you'll be happy; if not, you'll become a philosopher.

When love turns into dust, money becomes the substitution.

Romance is built on illusion, and when we love someone, we love the illusion they have created for us.

Love and a cough can't be hidden.

Love is wealth.

Imagination is more important than knowledge.

When you were born, you cried and the world rejoiced. Live your life so that when you die, the world cries and you rejoice.

39条人生定律

陷入情网时，有些人丢了头，另一些人丢了心。

幸福是良好的健康和糟糕的记性。

唯有爱可以把黑暗囚在海湾。

爱是可以两个人玩的双赢游戏。

人生教导我们，爱不在于相互凝视，而在于一起朝一个方向眺望。

一位父亲能为子女们做的最重要的事就是爱他们的母亲。

爱是一种无尽的宽恕行为，是一种成为习惯的温柔目光。

在爱中超越自我。

爱从男人的眼睛进入，从女人的耳朵进入。

女人是要让人爱，而不是让人理解。

没有丑女人，只有不懂得如何使自己美丽的女人。

想要别人爱你，就要去爱别人，做一个可爱的人。

要想被人爱，你要值得人爱。

具有爱的无知和笨拙，胜过缺乏爱的智慧和技巧。

不成熟的爱说："我爱你，因为我需要你。"成熟的爱说："我需要你，因为我爱你。"

爱不在深而在长。

没有信任就没有爱。

学习过去，放眼未来，活在当下。

快乐起来！这是一种明智的方法。

喜剧是悲剧和时间。

爱是春天的植物，它用希望使一切散发芬芳，即使身处废墟。

不要嘲笑总是快乐的人，有些事情你不懂，而他懂。

我是理想主义者。我不知何往，但正在路上。

我只晓得一个职责，那就是去爱。

对于人类生存的问题，唯一满意的答案是爱。

对爱保持清醒的人无法去爱。

争论比寂寞好。

好朋友当面刺痛你。

如果有什么事是比被爱着更好的话，那就是爱着。

结婚是两个人的结合：其中一个总是忘了生日而另一个从来不会忘记。

爱情就像沙漏，当脑子倒空时心就被填满了。

匮乏熄灭小欲望、增强大欲望，就像风吹灭蜡烛、煽旺篝火。

我给你的忠告是：结婚吧！如果你找到一个好妻子，你就会幸福；如果妻子不贤，你则会成为哲学家。

当爱沾染尘埃时，金钱成了替代品。

浪漫基于幻觉；爱上某个人时，我们也爱上他为我们营造的幻觉。

恋爱和咳嗽都无法掩藏。

爱是一笔财富。

想象力比知识更重要。

出生时，你啼哭，世界欣喜。享受你的一生，这样你离世时，世界哭泣，你欣喜。

Experience Life

I have known desire, struggle, anxiety and despair. I have always had to work beyond the limits of my strength. As I look back upon my life, I see it as a battlefield strewn with the wrecks of broken hopes and shattered dreams—a battle which has left me scarred and old before my time.

Yet I have no pity for myself; no tears to shed over the past and gone sorrows; no envy for the women who have been spared all I have gone through. For I have lived. They only existed.

I have drunk the cup of life to its very dregs. They have only sipped the bubbles on top of it. I know things they will never know. I see things to which they are blind.

It is only the women whose eyes have been washed clear with tears who get the broad vision that makes them sisters to all the world.

In the social university of hardships I have learned a philosophy that no woman who has had an easy life ever acquires. I have learned to live each day as it comes and not to borrow trouble by dreading the morrow because experience has taught me that when the time comes that I so fear, the strength and wisdom to meet it will be given me. Little annoyances no longer have the power to affect me. After you have seen your whole edifice of happiness topple and crash in ruins about you, it never matters to you again that a servant forgets to put the doilies under the finger bowls, or the cook spills the soup.

I have learned not to expect too much of people, and so I can still get happiness out of the friend who isn't quite true to me or the acquaintance who gossips.

Above all, I have acquired a sense of humor because there were so many things over which I had either to cry or laugh. And when a woman can joke over her troubles instead of having hysterics, nothing can ever hurt her much again.

I don't regret the hardships I have known because through them I have touched life at every point I have lived. And it was worth the price I had to pay.

体 验 人 生

我已经明白了欲望、奋斗、忧虑和绝望。我总是超极限工作。我回首过去的生活，常常把它看作到处充满破灭希望和梦想的战场。这场战斗使我伤痕累累、未老先衰。

然而，我从不怜悯自己。我没有为过去的忧伤流过泪，也没有嫉妒过那些从未经历过我这样痛苦的女人，因为我曾生活过，她们仅仅是生存过。

我喝干了生命之酒，她们只是呷了一口上面的泡沫。我明白她们从未知道的事情，我看到了她们不曾看到的东西。

女人的眼睛只有被泪水清洗过，才能看得更广，才能使她们成为世人的姐妹。

在充满艰辛的社会大学中，我学到了生活安逸的女人无法学到的一条哲理。我学会了顺其自然过好每一天，而不去害怕明天自找烦恼，因为经验教会我，每当非常害怕时，我就会被赋予对付它的力量和智慧。那些小烦恼再也无力影响我。当你看到整座幸福大厦在你身边轰然坍塌后，仆人忘记在热碗下放小布垫或厨师弄洒菜汤这类事对你绝不再重要。

我学会了不对人们寄予过多的期望，所以我仍能从那些对我并不真心的朋友和说三道四的熟人那里获得快乐。

尤其是我还获得了幽默感，因为有许多事曾使我悲喜交加。当一个女人能对自己的烦恼一笑而过不再歇斯底里时，任何事情都无法再过多地伤害她。

我不会为曾经历过的艰辛后悔，因为通过这些艰辛，我接触到了生活的点点滴滴。而且我为此付出的一切都物有所值。

Youth

Youth is not a time of life, it is a state of mind, it is not a matter of rosy cheeks, red lips and supple knees, it is a matter of the will, a quality of the imagination, a vigor of the emotions, it is the freshness of the deep spring of life.

Youth means a temperamental predominance of courage over timidity, of the appetite for adventure over the love of ease. This often exists in a man of 60 more than a boy of 20. Nobody grows merely by a number of years, we grow old by deserting our ideas.

Years may wrinkle the skin, but to give up enthusiasm wrinkles the soul. Worry, fear, self-distrust bows the heart and turns the spirit back to dust.

Whether 60 or 16, there is every human being's heart the lure of wonders, the unfailing childlike appetite of what's next and the joy of the game of living. In the center of your heart and my heart there is a wireless station: so long as it receives messages of beauty, hope, cheer, courage and power from men and from the infinite, so long as you are young.

When the aerials are down, and your spirit is covered with snows of cynicism and the ice of pessimism, then you've grown old, even at 20, but as long as your aerials are up, to catch waves of optimism, there's hope you may die young at 80.

青　春

青春不是生命的一段时光，不是指粉面、红唇和柔膝。它是一种精神状态，是指不懈的干劲、丰富的想象和滚烫的情怀。它是生命春意正浓时鲜活的记忆。

青春意味着战胜懦弱的阳刚之气和摒弃安逸的冒险精神。往往一个60岁的老者比一个20岁的青年更多一点这种劲头。人老不仅仅是岁月流逝所致，更主要的是不思进取懒惰的结果。

光阴可以在颜面上留下印记，而热情之火的熄灭则在心灵上刻下皱纹。忧虑、恐惧、缺乏自信，会扭曲人的灵魂，并将青年化为灰烬。

无论是60岁还是16岁，你需要保持永不衰竭的好奇心，永不熄灭的孩提般求知的渴望和追求事业的欢乐与热情。你我的心底都有一座无线电台，它能接收到人间万物传来的美好、希望、欢乐、鼓舞和力量信息多久，你就会年轻多久。

当天线倒塌时，如果你的精神被玩世不恭和悲观厌世的冰雪覆盖，你就会衰老下去，即使你只有20岁；而当你的天线巍然矗立时，凭着高昂的乐观主义，你就有希望在80岁死去时仍然青春不老。

Living Life over

If I had my life to live over, I would have talked less and listened more.

I would have invited friends over to dinner even if the carpet was stained and the sofa faded.

I would have taken the time to listen to my grandfather ramble about his youth.

I would never have insisted the car windows be rolled up on a summer day because my hair had just been teased and sprayed.

I would have burned the pink candle sculpted like a rose before it melted in storage.

I would have sat on the lawn with my children and not worried about grass stains.

I would have cried and laughed less while watching television—and more while watching life.

I would have gone to bed when I was sick instead of pretending the earth would go into a holding patter if I were not there for the day.

I would never have bought anything just because it was practical, would not show soil or was guaranteed to last a lifetime.

There would have been more "I love yous," more "I'm sorrys," but the most important is, given another shot at life, I would seize every minute, look at it and see it, live it and never give it back.

如果有来生

如果有来生，我会少说多听。

我会请朋友们来家吃饭，即使弄脏地毯、沙发褪色。

我会腾出时间听爷爷闲聊他的青年时代。

我绝不会因为刚刚梳过头发、定过型而坚持在夏天摇上车窗。

我会点燃那支雕成玫瑰的粉红色蜡烛，而不让它在储存中熔化。

我会和孩子们坐在草地上，不去操心草地上的污迹。

我会在看电视时减少哭笑，会在观察人生时增加哭笑。

如果我生病，就上床休息，而不是自以为那天没有我，地球就停止运转。

我绝不会买仅仅因为实用、不显脏或保用一生的任何东西。

我会更多地说"我爱你""对不起"，但最重要的是，如果有来生，我会抓住每一分钟……观察人生，了解人生，体验人生，永不放手。

The Addition and Subtraction of Life

A new year begins. Some people say, "We've lost one year." Some people say, "We've gained one year." This is the addition and subtraction of life.

Some people use the thinking of subtraction, so it will be less when he subtract, making life crisis-ridden and filled with stress:

The 20-year-old people lost childhood;

The 30-year-old people lost romance;

The 40-year-old people lost youth;

The 50-year-old people lost illusion;

The 60-year-old people lost health.

Some people use the thinking of addition, making life full of vitality and joy:

The 20-year-old people are young;

The 30-year-old people are talented;

The 40-year-old people are mature;

The 50-year-old people are experienced;

The 60-year-old people are relaxed.

In the course of life, we have to use "subtraction." Man has only one life, so at the end and the beginning of a year, we have to challenge ourselves to count what we have lost and what we have gained, and to count "harvest" more than "payout" or vice versa.

In the course of life, we have to use "addition." Because life can't be presumed, we have known the innocence in childhood and the recklessness in youth, accumulated the experience of life and come to see how to be master of our own destiny.

"Subtraction" brings us the pressure, making us understand the fleeting of life and the mercilessness of years. We look around ourselves and find how many outstanding people have gone ahead, so can't we catch up with them?

"Addition" brings us hope, making us add the experience and accumulate the wealth. The Sage of Time is fair to everyone, even if you went through countless difficulties and setbacks, which were the accumulation of experience. This accumulation will make us more intelligent and rational. With this accumulation, in the New Year, we will be more vigorous, steadier and more self-confident.

生命的加减法

新的一年开始了。有人说："我们又少了一年。"有人说："我们又多了一年。"这就是生命的加减法。

有人用的是减法思维，所以越减越少，使人生充满危机，充满压力：

20岁的人失去童年；

30岁的人失去浪漫；

40岁的人失去青春；

50岁的人失去幻想；

60岁的人失去健康。

有人用的是加法思维，使人生充满生机，充满快乐：

20岁的人拥有青春；

30岁的人拥有才干；

40岁的人拥有成熟；

50岁的人拥有经验；

60岁的人拥有轻松。

在生命的进程中，我们不能不用"减法"。人的生命只有一次，在岁末年初时，我们不能不鞭策自己，算一算自己失去了什么，得到了什么，是"收获"大于"支出"，还是"支出"大于"收获"。

在生命的进程中，我们不能不用"加法"。因为人生不能假设，我们知道了儿时的天真，知道了年轻时的莽撞，积累了人生经验，知道了如何把握自己。

"减法"给我们带来了压力，使我们明白了人生的苦短、岁月的无情。我们看看周围，有多少佼佼者已经走到了前面，我们能不奋起直追？

"加法"给我们带来了希望，使我们增添了阅历，积累了财富。时光老人对每个人都是公平的，哪怕你历经坎坷，遭遇挫折，也都是一种经历的积累。这种积累令我们更加聪明、理智。有了这种积累，新的一年里，我们的步伐就会更矫健、更沉稳、更自信。

Changes for Life

First you make your habits，and then your habits make you.

Break those habits that can break you.Adopt those practices that will become the new habits that will help you achieve the success you desire.

Your habits are a form of exercise.The harder you work at something，the harder it is to quit.The easier it is to do，the harder it is to change.Your habits are either the best of servants or the worst of masters.

You are what you repeatedly do.

In every change that you experience in life，there will be times when you'll wonder if you can endure.

But you'll learn that facing each difficulty one by one isn't so hard.

Changes are sometimes very painful，but they teach us that we can endure and that we can become stronger.

Everything that comes into your life has a purpose，but the outcome is in your hands by the action you take.

Be wise with your life，be willing to endure，and always be willing to face life's challenges.

人生因改变而改变

首先是你把习惯养成，然后是习惯把你造就。

打破可能毁掉你的那些习惯。要采取行动，渐渐养成有助于你获得想要的成功的那些新习惯。

你的习惯是一种练习形式。你在某件事上做的努力越多，就越难放弃。越容易做的事情，就越难改变。你的习惯要么是最好的仆人，要么是最坏的主人。

你做什么，就成什么。

在经历人生中的每次改变时，你有时会怀疑是否能经受得住。

但是，你会认识到，面临一个又一个困难并不那么艰难。

改变有时非常痛苦，但它们教会我们，我们能经受得住改变，会变得更加坚强。

进入你生活的所有东西都有目的，但结果在你手里，需要你采取行动。

要智慧地生活，甘愿忍耐，始终甘愿面对生活中的改变。

Life Is like a Bowl of Vegetable Soup

All eagles build their nests on the treetops or cliffs. After observing carefully through the binoculars, the ecologists found that the mother eagle first held some thorns on the bottom, then put some small keen-edged stones on the thorns, and later held some dried grass, feathers or hides on the small stones to make a nest for incubation.

As the young eagle grew up, its feathers gradually fledged. The mother eagle thought it was time for the young eagle to learn to be self-independent. She began to stir the nest, making the dried grass and feathers drop off it and expose the sharp small stones and thorns. The young eagle was pricked into shrieking. But the mother eagle drove it away ruthlessly, so the young eagle had to flap its wings and fly out of the nest reluctantly.

Was the mother eagle cold-blooded? No! She deeply loved the young eagle she gave birth to! However, more eagerly, she longed her cherished young to soar all around. So she must relentlessly force her baby to fly away from the comfortable home and learn to be independent.

In fact, life is like a bowl of vegetable soup, whose delicious seasoning, if not stirred, will always sink in the bottom. Only you work hard to "stir yourself," can you show all your inherent talent and ability. Just like the young eagle, the mother eagle stirred the nest mercilessly and forced it to fly independently.

人生就像一碗菜汤

老鹰都把窝巢筑在树梢或悬崖陡壁上。生态学家们用望远镜仔细观察后发现，母鹰先叼来一些荆棘放在底层，再叼来些尖锐的小石子铺放在荆棘上面，后来又衔了些枯草、羽毛或兽皮盖在小石子上，做成一个孵蛋的窝。

小雏鹰慢慢长大，羽毛渐渐丰满。母鹰认为，该是小鹰学会自我独立的时候了。母鹰开始搅动窝巢，让巢上的枯草、羽毛掉落，露出尖锐的小石子和荆棘。小鹰被扎得嗷嗷直叫。可是，母鹰无情地驱赶，小鹰只好忍着痛振翅离巢。

母鹰残忍无情吗？不！母鹰深爱着它生养的小鹰！但是，母鹰更渴望它疼爱的小鹰能成为四处翱翔的飞鹰。因此，母鹰必须无情地逼着小鹰飞离舒适的家，勇敢地学习独立。

其实，人生就像一碗菜汤，如果没有搅动，鲜美调料就会一直沉在碗底。只有辛勤地"搅动自己"，才能让内在的才华与能力全部呈现，就像小鹰一样，母鹰无情地搅动鸟巢才逼得它必须展翅独立飞翔。

A Lesson in Life

Everything happens for a reason. Nothing happens by chance or by means of good or bad luck.

Illness, injury, love, lost moments of true greatness and sheer stupidity all occur to test your soul. Without these small tests, without illness or relationships, life would be like a smoothly paved, straight, flat road to nowhere.

If someone hurts you, betrays you, or break your heart, forgive them. For they have helped you learn about trust and the importance of being cautious to who you open your heart to.

If someone loves you, love them back unconditionally, not only because they love you, but because they are teaching you to love and opening your heart and eyes to things you would have never seen or felt without them.

Make every day count. Appreciate every moment and take from it everything that you possibly can, for you may never be able to experience it again.

Talk to people who you have never talked to before, and actually listen. Hold your head up because you have every right to.

Tell yourself you are a great individual and believe in yourself, for if you don't believe in yourself, no one else will believe in you, either.

You can make of your life anything you wish. Create your own life and then go out and live.

人生的课堂

所有事情的发生都有原因。什么事情也不会因为巧合或运气好坏而发生。

疾病、伤害、爱、真正伟大和愚不可及的失落时刻都是对你灵魂的考验。如果没有这些小小的考验，如果没有疾病和各种关系，生活就会像一条铺好却没有目标的平坦道路。

如果有人伤害你、出卖你或让你伤心，要原谅他们，因为他们曾帮你学会了如何信任他人，以及向他人敞开心扉时小心谨慎的重要性。

如果有人爱你，也要无条件地爱他们。不仅是因为他们爱你，更是因为他们教你如何去爱，敞开心扉去感受你从未有过的感受，睁开眼睛去看你从未见过的事物。

让每一天都有价值。感激生命中的每一个瞬间，尽可能从中吸取所有的一切，因为你绝不可能再体验一次。

和你以前从未交谈过的人聊聊天，其实你是去倾听。要抬起头，因为你完全有权这样做。

告诉自己是一个了不起的人，要相信自己，因为如果你不相信自己，别人也不会相信你。

你可以按照自己的愿望生活，创造自己的生活，然后去享受人生。

The Traffic Lights of Life

When John went out in the evening, Mom and Dad made a rule that he must be home before 10: 00.

But once, John didn't return home as a rule but did at the latter half of the night. Afraid of being discovered by his parents, he jumped into the house from the back window when he went back.

The next morning, seeing a stool under the window, Dad called up John and said, "It's dangerous for you to do so. I'm not afraid you hurt yourself, but when others discover someone is jumping into the window, they are likely to shoot." This is the most dangerous in the United States.

Then, Dad also reiterated the rule on time to go home and told him the reason to do so.

The old grandfather said meaningfully, "The bigger and bigger the children grow as the cattle, the bigger and bigger they need the ranch. But no matter how big or small, we still use the fence to enclose the ranch."

Life can't have the rules. The rules are the traffic lights of life. This appears to be restricting but in fact to be protecting. The traffic lights are the commanders of city traffic. Without control, the whole city will sink into a chaos. So is man: without the restriction of "traffic lights", he will be lawless and get into big trouble.

Therefore, respecting and obeying the rules is a cultivation, a demeanor, a civilization and the essential character of a modern person. Without these, he can't live and find a foothold in the society; without the rules, the society can't be harmonious and peaceful yet.

人生的红绿灯

约翰晚上出去，爸爸妈妈规定，必须在10点前回家。

但有一次，约翰没有按规定时间回家，是后半夜才回来的。回家时怕父母发现，就从后窗跳进屋子。

第二天早上，爸爸见窗下有一个凳子，就把约翰叫起，说："你这样做是很危险的，不是怕你会摔伤，而是说别人发现有人在跳窗户，就有可能开枪。"在美国，这是最危险的。

然后，爸爸又重申了按时回家的规定，并告诉他这样做的道理。

年老的祖父意味深长地说："孩子像牛一样长得越来越大，需要的牧场也越来越大。但不管牧场大小如何，我们还是用栅栏将牧场围起。"

生活不能没有规则。规则就是人生的红绿灯。这看起来是在限制，实质是在保护。红绿灯是城市交通的指挥官，如果没有控制，整座城市将陷入一片混乱之中。人也一样，如果没有"红绿灯"的限制，将会无法无天，闯下大祸。

因此，尊重和遵守规则是一种教养、一种风度、一种文明，是一个现代人必备的品格，没有这些，便无法在社会上生存和立足。没有规则，社会也无法得到和谐与安宁。

Early Autumn

When Bill was very young, they had been in love. Many nights they had spent walking, talking together. Then something not very important had come between them, and they didn't speak. Impulsively, she had married a man she thought she loved. Bill went away, bitter about women.

Yesterday, walking across Washington Square, she saw him for the first time in years.

"Bill Walkers," she said.

He stopped. At first he did not recognize her, to him she looked so old.

"Mary! Where did you come from?"

Unconsciously, she lifted her face as though wanting a kiss, but he held out his hand. She took it.

"I live in New York now," she said.

"Oh" —smiling politely, then a little frown came quickly between his eyes.

"Always wondered what happened to you, Bill."

"I'm a lawyer. Fine firm, way downtown."

"Married yet?"

"Sure. Two kids."

"Oh," she said.

A great many people went past them through the park. People they didn't know. It was late afternoon. Nearly sunset. Cold.

"And your husband?" he asked her.

"We have three children. I work in the bursar's office at Columbia."

"You're looking very…" he wanted to say old. "…well," he said.

She understood. Under the trees in Washington Square, she found herself desperately reaching back into the past. She had been older than he then in Ohio. Now she was not young at all. Bill was still young.

"We live on Central Park West," she said. "Come and see us sometime."

"Sure," he replied. "You and your husband must have dinner with my family some night. Any night. Lucille and I'd love to have you."

The leaves fell slowly from the trees in the Square. Fell without wind. Autumn dusk. She felt a little sick.

"We'd love it," she answered.

"You ought to see my kids." He grinned.

Suddenly the lights came on up the whole length of Fifth Avenue, chains of misty brilliance in the blue air.

"There's my bus," she said.

He held out his hand. "Good-bye."

"When…" she wanted to say, but the bus was ready to pull off. The lights on the avenue blurred, twinkled, blurred. And she was afraid to open her mouth as she entered the bus. Afraid it would be impossible to utter a word.

Suddenly she shrieked very loudly, "Good-bye!" But the bus door had closed.

The bus started. People came between them outside, people crossing the street, people they didn't know. Space and people. She lost sight of Bill. Then she remembered she had forgotten to give him her address—or to ask him for his—or tell him that her youngest boy was named Bill, too.

初　秋

比尔年轻时，他俩曾相爱过。许多夜晚，他们厮守在一起散步、聊天。后来，两人之间发生了一件无足轻重的小事，便互不理睬了。冲动之下，她嫁给了一个她以为自己爱恋的男人。比尔带着对女人的怨恨离去。

昨天，穿过华盛顿广场时，她又见到了他，这么多年了还是第一次。

"比尔·沃克斯。"她说。

他停下来，起初没有认出她。在他眼里，她是那样苍老。

"玛丽！你是从哪里来的？"

她下意识地抬起脸，好像是等着他亲吻，而他却伸出了手。她握了握。

"我现在住在纽约。"她说。

"噢。"他彬彬有礼，面带微笑，然后很快微微皱了皱眉。

"我总在想着你发生了什么事，比尔。"

"我现在是律师。事务所不错，在商业区。"

"你已经结婚了吗？"

"当然，我现在有两个孩子。"

"噢。"她说。

穿越公园的许多人从他们身边走过，那是一些素不相识的人。天近黄昏，夕阳将坠，冷风飕飕。

"你的丈夫怎么样？"他问她。

"我们有三个孩子。我在哥伦比亚大学财务室工作。"

"你看起来很……"他想说"老"，"……很好。"他说。

她心知肚明。在华盛顿广场的那些树下，她发现自己拼命想奔回过去。在俄亥俄州时，她就比他的年龄大。现在她已经不再年轻了，比尔却仍然朝气蓬勃。

"我们住在中央公园西边，"她说，"有空到我们家来吧。"

"当然可以，"他回答说，"你和丈夫一定要来我们家吃晚饭，哪天夜里都行。我和露西尔都欢迎你们。"

广场上的那些树叶慢慢飘落，无风自落，秋日黄昏。她有点儿心烦意乱。

"乐意奉陪。"她说。

"你应该来看看我的孩子们。"他咧嘴笑道。

第五大道上的街灯整个亮了起来，在蓝色的天空中组成一串串朦胧的光带。

"我的公共汽车来了。"她说。

他伸出手说："再见。"

"什么时候……"她想说，但公共汽车就要开走了。大街上的路灯忽暗忽明、忽明忽暗。走上公共汽车时，她不敢张口说话，怕自己连一个字都说不出来。

突然，她大声尖叫道："再见！"但是，车门已经关上。

汽车已经启动。车外的人走在了他们俩中间：那些穿过大街的人，那些素不相识的人。空间和人流。她看不见比尔的身影。随后，她想起忘记把自己的地址给他了，也忘了要他的地址，同时忘记对他说，她的小儿子也叫比尔。

Step backward and Watch Life

Hope and trust is the tail of a lizard, which can reproduce even after being cut off.

To be lost in something you love is better than to win in something you hate.

One is always on a strange road, watching strange scenery and listening to strange music. Then one day, you will find that the things you try hard to forget are already gone.

Happiness is neither about being immortal nor having food or rights in one's hand. It's about having each tiny wish come true, or having something to eat when you are hungry or having someone's love when you need love.

Love is a lamp, while friendship is the shadow. When the lamp is off, you will find the shadow everywhere. Friends are who can give you strength at last.

I love you not for who you are, but for who I am before you.

Love makes man grow up or sink down.

If you can hold something up and put it down, it is called weight lifting; if you can hold something up but can never put it down, it's called burden-bearing. Pitifully, most of people are bearing heavy burdens when they are in love.

Most of people are looking forward the crystal-like love—pure without any defect. However the truth is most people are having the glass-like love—same transparent but easily broken.

One may fall in love with many people during the lifetime. When you finally get your own happiness, you will understand the previous sadness is a kind of treasure, which makes you better to hold and cherish the people you love.

During the whole life, you will regret for two things: one is that you don't get the one you love and the other is the one you love is not happy.

I hide my storm-like love in my heart just not to give you any pressure. The more precious my love is, the more I cherish the love from others.

If you love a girl, it's better to fight for her happiness than to abandon her for the sake of her happiness.

To love someone in secret is like a seed in bottle waiting for growing up, though not sure whether the future will be more beautiful, still waiting it earnestly and eagerly.

The love world is big, which can hold hundreds of disappointments; the love world is small which is crowded even with three people inside. The love world is big, it still has space for more happiness; the love world is small which will be ruined after one tread.

Why to ask so much when you are in love? If you ask too much, maybe you no longer love. The mature never ask the past, the wise never ask the present and the open-minded never ask the future.

The life is not always full of multiple choices or the yes-or-no questions, but application questions which need us to prove little by little. During the process, we need to make choice to get or lose. It matters not even if we get wrong answers.

The heart of woman is a glass holding water. It is full but seems to have nothing inside.

If you leave me, please don't comfort me because each sewing has to meet stinging pain.

It's not easy to change friendship into love. But it's even harder to turn love into friendship. If I swallow my heart, can I regain the friendship once I had?

If it blossoms, I will love; if not, give up. I just accompany you merrily for the sake of scenery not for you.

I believe in the fairy story you wrote for me, and myself becomes the faint flower in the story.

The key for happiness is not to find a perfect person, but to find someone and build a perfect relationship with him.

If a woman is not sexy, she needs emotion; if she is not emotional, she needs reason; if she is not reasonable, she has to know herself clearly; if she doesn't, she will only be misfortunate.

It's often said that you will have the same life as the person you find. Therefore, different choices make different endings.

Every girl was once an angel without tears. When she meets the beloved boy, she gets the tears. And after she cries, she falls into the earth. Therefore, every boy shall be nice to his girl, coz she once gave up the whole heaven for the boy.

It's not us to choose the opportunity, but it's opportunity that decides us.

When the opportunity comes, all we can do is to take this challenge. Don't say that opportunities never come. It came but you just don't willing to give up the things you own.

Men love from overlooking while women love from looking up. If love is a mountain, then if men go up, more women they will see while women will see fewer men.

Good love makes you see the whole world from one person while bad love makes you abandon the whole world for one person.

Only few people know that life is beautiful for lacking something. The so-called turning-around is that you not only miss the sun in the daytime but also the stars at night.

Happiness is when the desolate soul meets love.

When every love comes to the end, if you look back, you will find flowers and sorrows.

To keep someone around you is not love; love is to let the one you love go freely.

To forgive is not to forget, nor remit, but let it go; to be lonely is not coz you have no friends, but no one is living in your heart.

People will always change. Some choose to change the environment; some choose to be changed by the environment. Most of the time when you can't change, you have to choose to find something to make yourself happy.

The fact is that the world is out of everyone's expectation. But some learn to forget, but others insist.

No matter how cruel the destiny treats one with tribulation and misfortune, it will correspondingly treat him with happiness and sweetness. Even if the happiness is short and false, it's enough to light up the whole future life.

In your life, there will at least one time that you forget yourself for someone, asking for no result, no company, no ownership nor love. Just ask for meeting you in my most beautiful years. Love you, think of you, love you secretly, eagerly love you, wait, feel disappointed, try hard, lose, and feel sad, go apart, and recall. All of these are for sake of you. And I will never regret for it.

The most fearful thing in the life is the darkness deep in your heart. But soul told us that you'll have courage as long as the heart beats.

Don't forget the things you once you owned. Treasure the things you can't get. Don't give up the things that belong to you and keep those lost things in memory.

I love and am used to keeping a distance with those changed things. Only in this way can I know what will not be abandoned by time. For example, when you love someone, changes are all around. Then I step backward and watch it silently until I see the true feelings.

退后一步看人生

希望和信任是蜥蜴的尾巴，即使切断，还能再长出来。

宁可败在你爱的事上，也不要赢在你恨的事上。

一个人总要走陌生的路，看陌生的风景，听陌生的歌，然后在某个不经意的瞬间，你会发现，原本是费尽心机想要忘记的事真的就那么忘了。

幸福不是长生不老，不是大鱼大肉，更不是权倾朝野。幸福是实现每一个小小的愿望。饿时有东西吃，需要爱时有人来爱你。

爱情是灯，友情是影。灯灭时，你会发现周围都是影。朋友是最后能给你力量的人。

我爱你不是因为你是谁，而是我在你面前可以是谁。

爱情要么让人成长，要么让人沉落。

举得起放得下的叫举重，举得起放不下的叫负重。可惜，大多数人相爱时都在负重。

许多人向往水晶般的爱情——晶莹剔透，毫无瑕疵。更多人拥有的却是玻璃般的爱情——同样透明，但易破碎。

一个人一生可以爱上很多的人，等你获得真正属于你的幸福之后，就会明白一起的伤痛其实是一种财富，它让你学会更好地去把握和珍惜你爱的人。

人的一生，会有两种遗憾最折磨人：一是得不到你心爱的人；二是心爱的人得不到幸福。

我将暴风般的爱情藏在心底，就是为了不给你任何压力。我的爱情越珍贵，就越珍惜别人的爱情。

爱一个女孩，与其为了她的幸福而放弃她，不如留住她，为她的幸福而努力。

暗恋一个人的心情，就像是瓶中等待发芽的种子，永远不能确定未来是否美丽，但仍真心而急切地等待着。

爱情的世界很大，大到可以装下100种委屈，爱情的世界很小，小到3个人就挤到窒息；爱情的世界很大，塞了多少幸福还是有空隙，爱情的世界很小，被一脚踩过就变成废墟。

爱，又何必多问？问得太多，只怕就不爱了。成熟的人不问过去；聪明的人不问现在；豁达的人不问未来。

人生并非总是选择题或是非题，大部分是应用题，需要我们一点一点地论证，在取舍过程中，做错了也没关系。

女人的心是一只盛水的玻璃杯，虽然已经装满，里面却又像什么都没有。

离开我就别安慰我，要知道每一次缝补也会遭遇穿刺的痛。

友情变成爱情不容易，但爱情变成友情更不容易。如果我吞没了自己的心，我能恢复往日的友情吗？

如果花开了，就喜欢；如果花落了，就放弃。陪你在路上满心欢喜是因为风景，不是因为你。

我相信了你编写的童话，自己就成了童话中幽蓝的花。

幸福的关键不在于找到一个完美的人，而在于找到一个人，和他建立一种完美的关系。

女人如果不性感，就要感性；如果没有感性，就要理性；如果没有理性，就要有自知之明；如果连这个都没有了，她只有不幸。

人常说，找到了什么样的人，就会有什么样的生活。因此，不同的选择，就有不同的结尾。

每个女孩都曾是一个无泪天使。当她遇上心爱的男孩时便有了泪，天使落泪，坠落凡间。因此，每个男孩都会善待他的女孩，因为她曾为了他放弃了整个天堂。

不是我们去选择机遇，而是机遇选择我们。当机遇来时，我们所能做的就是接受这个挑战。不要说机会从未出现，它曾出现过，但你舍不得放下自己拥有的东西。

男人的爱俯视而生，女人的爱仰视而生。如果爱情像一座山，男人越往上走可以俯视的女人就越多，女人越往上走可以仰视的男人就越少。

好的爱情是你通过一个人看到整个世界，坏的爱情是你为了一个人舍弃整个世界。

只有很少的人才懂得，人生是因为缺憾而美丽。而所谓的回头，只不过是错过了白天的太阳之后，又错过了夜晚的星星。

幸福是荒废的灵魂与爱邂逅。

每段爱情走向终结时，如果回首，你会发现鲜花与忧伤共存。

不是把对方留在自己身边才叫爱，能放手让所爱的人离开，也是爱的一种。

原谅不是忘记，也不是赦免，而是放手。孤单不是因为没有朋友，而是没有人住在你的心里。

人都会改变，有些人选择改变环境，有些人选择被环境改变。大多时候当你无法改变时，只好选择在里面找到让自己快乐的东西。

事实上，这个世界不符合所有人的梦想。只是有人可以学会遗忘，有人却坚持。

无论命运怎样无情地赐予一个人以磨难和不幸，仍会相应地赐予他幸福与甜蜜，即使这幸福是如此短暂与虚假，也足以照亮整个前程。

一生至少该有一次，为了某个人而忘了自己，不求有结果，不求同行，不求曾经拥有，甚至不求你爱我。只求在我最美的年华里，遇到你，钟情，相思，暗恋，渴慕，等待，失望，试探，患得患失，痛不欲生，天涯永隔，追忆似水流年……种种这些，都曾因你而经历，也就誓不言悔。

人生最可怕的事情是你内心深处的黑暗，但灵魂告诉我们，只要还有心跳，你就一定有勇气。

曾经拥有的，不要忘记。不能得到的，要珍惜。属于自己的，不要放弃。已经失去的，留作回忆。

我喜欢并习惯对变化的东西保持距离，这样才会知道什么是最不会被时间抛弃的准则。比如爱一个人，充满变数。于是，我后退一步，静静地看着，直到看见真情。

Ten Kinds of People You Should Treasure Most

When you meet the one you love truly, you should strive to win the chance to stay with him all your life because when he is off, all will be too late.

When you meet a friend who can be trusted, you should get along well with him because it is really not easy to meet a bosom friend.

When you meet an honorable person, remember to express your gratitude properly because he is a turning point in your life.

When you meet the one you loved, remember to thank him because he made you know love more clearly.

When you meet the one you hated, you should greet him with a smile because he made you stronger.

When you meet the one who betrayed you, you should chat with him properly because without him you won't read this world today.

When you meet the one you liked in private, you should bless him, because when you liked him, didn't you wish him happiness?

When you meet the one who hurries to leave, you should thank him through your life because he is part of your wonderful memories.

When you meet the one who misunderstood you, you should dispel the misunderstanding because you may only have such a chance to explain this clearly.

When you meet the one you accompany all your life, you should, wholeheartedly, thank him who love you because both of you get happiness and true love now.

一生最应珍惜的十种人

遇到真爱的人时，要努力争取和他相伴一生的机会，因为当他离开时，一切都来不及了。

遇到可以相信的朋友时，要好好和他相处下去，因为一生中遇到知己真的不易。

遇到贵人时，记得好好感激，因为他是你人生的转折点。

遇到曾经爱过的人时，要记得感激他，因为他让你更懂得爱。

遇到曾经恨过的人时，要微笑向他打招呼，因为他让你更加坚强。

遇到曾经背叛你的人时，要好好和他聊聊，因为要不是他，你今天会看不懂这个世界。

遇到曾经偷偷喜欢的人时，要祝他幸福，因为你喜欢他时，不就是希望他幸福吗？

遇到匆匆离开的人时，要谢谢他走过你的人生，因为他是你精彩回忆的一部分。

遇到曾经和你有误会的人时，要消除误会，因为你可能只有这一次机会解释清楚。

遇到和你相伴一生的人时，要全心全意地感谢他爱你，因为你们现在都得到了幸福和真爱。

Salvation

I stood on tiptoe and handed the card from my school's help-wanted board to the tall, ruddy-faced man behind the counter of Mort's Deli at Farmers Market in Los Angeles. He wore a starched chef's hat and a clean white apron. Even before I opened my mouth, he was frowning and shaking his head.

"This is a tough job for any high school kid," the man said. "I need somebody big and strong."

At 16, I looked younger and was barely five feet tall. "Really, we need someone bigger," he said, "You'll find something easier than this, kid."

It was September 1957, and my family had just arrived in California. Without seniority in the local union, my father, a sheet-metal worker, was lucky to get work two or three days a week. Our meager saving was gone, and as the oldest boy of what would soon be six children, I was the only one able to help. I'd applied at retail stores, but without local references shopkeepers were reluctant to let me handle cash.

"Tell you what," I said, "Let me work the rest of the week, and if you don't like the way I do the job, don't pay me."

The tall man stared at me, then nodded, "I'm Mort Rubin. What's your name?"

At Mort's, a river of soiled utensils, trays, pots and pans flowed into my sinks. I washed and rinsed and scoured. By the end of my first after-school shift, sharp pains were shooting up my legs from standing four hours without a break. As closing time approached on Saturday, I was in agony. I also had no idea whether Mort would pay me. Near the end of the day he called me up front. "How much did that card at school say this job paid?" he asked.

"Dollar an hour," I murmured, "The minimum wage." I was willing to take less.

"That's not enough for someone who works as hard as you," Mort said, "You start at $1. 25."

Over the next few weeks I learned a lot about Mort. A few years older than my dad, he was from Chicago and had a daughter my age. When things were slow, he often shared stories from his army days. Early in World War II, he was nearly killed in a savage battle in New Guinea. He'd spent some time recuperating from the terrible head wound he had suffered.

We were closed Sundays, so every Saturday evening Mort urged me to take home the leftover soup in a huge jar. A rich broth of turkey, rice and vegetables, it was a meal in itself, a treat for my struggling family.

My father usually picked me up after work those days because the soup was too hard to lug home on my bike. Then one Saturday he let me take the family car.

After work I drove home and parked. With the warm jar in my arms, I crossed the lawn and passed the living-room window. As I glanced inside, I almost dropped the jar. In my father's chair was a large bald man. He was cursing my father in a voice dripping with contempt. My brothers and sisters sat like status, Dad's face was stone, Mom wept.

I crept into the kitchen, set the soup on a counter and listened through the door. The man wanted to take our car. Dad offered to make the three payments that were in arrears, but the man demanded the entire sum—$325—or the car. I had been in Los Angeles just long enough to understand how essential a car is. I slipped out the door, pushed the car down to the corner, started the engine and circled the neighborhood, thinking furiously. Who might have $325? Who would even consider lending me such a princely sum?

The only person I could think of was Mort. I drove back to his deli, rapped on the rear door, then waited until the window shade went up. I found myself staring down the barrel of an army 0. 45. "What do you want?" Mort growled, lowering the gun.

I stammered out my tale: the bald man, his foul cursing, the outrageous demand. "So could you possibly loan my father $325?" I finished, realizing how absurd it sounded.

Mort's eyes bored holes in my face. His cheeks began purpling, and his lips quivered. Realizing he was still clutching the gun, I took a step backward. At that, he smiled. "I'm not going to shoot you," he said, placing the pistol on his tiny desk. Then he knelt, pried a worn red tile from the floor to reveal a safe, and began to twist the dial.

He counted the money twice and placed it in an old envelope. "This is $325," he said. "When school is not, you'll work full time. I'll take back half your wages until it's repaid."

"Thank you," I said, trembling. "Do you want my father to sign something?"

He shook his head. "No, son. I'm betting on you."

I went in the back door like the lord of the manor, and Dad came rushing into the kitchen, the bald man on his heels. "Quick!" my father cried, "Drive the car away!"

I calmly handed the man the envelope. "Count it, give my father a receipt and get out of our house," I said, a speech I'd rehearsed all the way home.

That night I was a hero to my family. But the real hero was Mort Robin, who not only saved us from certain penury, but also quietly raised my salary every month until, by summer, I was earning $2. 50 an hour, double the original wage. I worked for Mort until I graduated two years later and joined the Army. We stayed in touch for many decades, but I lost track of him several years ago and don't even know if he's still alive.

But this I do know: Mort Robin made the world a better place.

325美元的拯救

我踮起脚尖站在那里，将我们学校的求助证明卡递给了洛杉矶农贸市场的莫特熟食店柜台后面的那个身材魁伟、面色红润的人。他戴着一顶浆洗过的厨师帽，围着一条雪白干净的围裙。还没等我开口，他就皱起眉，摇了摇头。

"这项工作中学生可吃不消，"那个人说，"我需要一个身高力壮的人。"

16岁的我看上去比较瘦小，几乎还不到1.5米高。"我们的确需要一个大个子，"他说，"孩子，你要找一个比这轻松的工作。"

这是1957年9月，我们一家刚到加州。我的父亲是一名金属薄板工，在当地工会还没有资历，所以一周能工作两三天已经很幸运了。我们家微薄的储蓄已经用完。作为马上就有6个孩子的家庭的长子，我是唯一能帮上家里忙的人。我到一家零售商店去应聘，但没有当地人的推荐，店主不愿让我负责现金。

"告诉我干什么，"我说，"让我在这周剩下的时间打工，你要不喜欢我干的活，就别给我工钱。"

那个高个子的人盯着我，然后点了点头："我叫莫特·鲁宾，你叫什么名字？"

在莫特的熟食店，一大堆脏兮兮的器具、盘子、锅和平底锅源源不断地放进水池中，我又是洗又是冲又是擦。第一天放学后到那里上班我一直洗了4个小时，连喘口气的时间都没有，两条腿疼痛难忍，站都站不稳了。星期六，快要打烊时，我万分痛苦，不知道莫特是不是会给我工钱。在这一天接近尾声时，莫特将我叫到前台，问道："学校这张救助卡要求我支付多少工钱？"

"每小时一美元，"我咕哝道，"最低工资。"我愿意接受更少的工钱。

"像你这样拼命工作的人是不够的。"莫特先生说，"先给你开1.25美元。"

在接下来的几周中，我了解到了莫特先生的很多情况。他比我的爸爸大几岁，来自芝加哥，有一个跟我同龄的女儿。不太忙时，他经常给我讲他当兵时的一些故事。"二战"初期，他在新几内亚的一次恶战中差点儿阵亡，过了一段时间，他才养好头上可怕的伤口。

星期天，我们关门休息。所以，每到星期六傍晚，莫特先生就催我将大罐里剩下的汤带回家。罐里有可口的火鸡汤，还有大米和菜，其实那本身就是一顿饭。这对苦苦挣扎的我们一家人更是一顿盛宴。

下班后，爸爸经常顺路把我捎回家，因为汤放在我的自行车上很难带回家。后来，有个星期六，爸爸让我开起了家里的汽车。

下班后，我驱车回家，将车停好，然后怀里抱着那暖暖的罐子，穿过草坪，从我们家的起居室的窗下走过。我向屋里瞧了一眼，差点儿把罐子摔在地上，只见一个身材高大的秃子坐在爸爸的椅子里，他正在声色俱厉、盛气凌人地责骂我爸爸。弟弟妹妹呆立在那里，爸爸面色铁青，妈妈呜呜直哭。

我悄悄溜进厨房，慢慢地将汤放在台子上，然后透过门倾听。那个人想要我家的汽车。爸爸本打算3次付清应付的欠款，而那个人却坚持要一次付清325美元，否则就开走汽车。我们刚搬到洛杉矶没有多久，明白一辆汽车有多么必要。我悄悄地从屋里溜出来，将汽车推到拐角，发动引擎，绕过附近地区，怒火中烧，心里想着：谁可能会有325美元？谁又会借给我这么多钱呢？

我所能想到的唯一的人就是莫特。我将车开回到他的店里，轻轻叩响了店的后门，然后站在那里等着，直到窗户打开。只见一支0.45英寸口径的军用手枪正对着我。"你想要干什么？"莫特放下枪吼道。

我结结巴巴向他讲了事情经过：那个秃子，他恶毒地谩骂、他蛮横地要求。"您能借给我父亲325美元吗？"说完后，我意识到这个故事听起来是多么荒唐。

莫特的目光就像要在我的脸上钻几个洞似的。随后，他的脸开始发紫，嘴唇颤抖。我意识到他手里仍然攥着枪，就后退了一步。看到这种情形，他露出了微笑。"我不会向你开枪的。"说完，他将手枪放在了小桌子上。随后，他跪下来，从地板上撬起一块旧红瓷砖，露出了一只保险箱，然后开始转动密码盘。

他把钱数了两遍，然后放在一个旧信封里。"这是325美元，"他说，"等你不上学时，可以全日工作。我每月扣你一半工资直到你还清。"

"谢谢，"我声音颤抖着说，"您要我父亲的签字吗？"

他摇了摇头："不，孩子，我打赌你能还。"

我像一个庄园主般走进后门。爸爸冲进了厨房，那个秃顶人也跟了进来。"快，"我父亲喊道，"把车开走！"

我镇定自若地将手里的信封递给那个人。"把钱数一下，给我父亲开个收据，然后从我们家滚出去。"我说，这些话我早已在回家的路上排练好了。

那天夜里，我成了家里的英雄。但是，真正的英雄是莫特·鲁宾，他不仅使我家摆脱窘境，而且不动声色地每个月给我提高了薪水。到了那年夏天，我每小时的工资涨到了2.5美元，是我最初薪水的两倍。我为莫特打工，一直到两年后毕业参军。在以后的几十年中，我们始终保持联络，但几年前我和他失去了联系，不知道他现在是否还活着。

但是，我的确知道，是莫特·鲁宾使这个世界变成了一个更加美好的地方。

Blind Dad Watched Me Play Football

Bob Richard's, the former pole-vault champion, shares a moving story about a skinny young boy who loved football with all his heart. Practice after practice, he eagerly gave everything he had. But being half the size of the other boys he got absolutely nowhere. At all the games, this hopeful athlete sat on the bench and hardly ever played. This teenager lived alone with his father, and the two of them had a very special relationship. Even though the son was always on the bench, his father was always in the stands cheering. He never missed a game.

This young man was still the smallest of the class when he entered high school. But his father continued to encourage him, but also made it very clear that he did not have to play football if he didn't want to.

But the young man loved football and decided to hang in there. He was determined to try his best at every practice, and perhaps he'd get to play when he became a senior. All through high school he never missed a practice or a game, but remained a bench warmer all four years. His faithful father was always in the stands, always with words of encouragement for him.

When the young man went to collage, he decided to try out for the football team as a walk-on. Everyone was sure he could never make the cut, but he did. The coach admitted that he kept him on the roster because he always put his heart and soul into every practice, and at the same time, provided the other members with the spirit.

The news that he had survived the cut thrilled him so much that he rushed to the nearest phone and called his father. His father shared his excitement and was sent season tickets for all the college games. This persistent young athlete never missed practice during his four years at college, but he never got to play in a game.

It was the end of the senior football season, and as he trotted on to the practice field shortly before the big playoff game, the coach met him with a telegram and he became deathly silent.

Swallowing hard, he mumbled to the coach, "My father died this morning. Is it all right if I miss practice today?"

The coach put his arm gently around his shoulder and said, "Take the rest of the week off, son. And don't even plan to come to the game on Saturday."

Saturday arrived, and the game was not going well. In the third quarter, when the team was ten points behind, a silent young man quietly slipped into the empty locker room and put on his football gear. As he ran onto the sidelines, the coach and his players were astounded to see their faithful teammate back so soon.

"Coach, please let me play. I've just got to play today," said the young man.

The coach pretended not to hear him. There was no way he wanted his worst player in this close playoff game. But the young man persisted, and finally feeling sorry for the kid, the coach gave in.

"All right," he said. "You can go in."

Before long, the coach, the players, and everyone in the stands could not believe their eyes. This little unknown, who had never played before was doing everything right. The opposing team could not stop him. He ran, passed, blocked, and tackled like a star. The score was soon tied.

In the closing seconds of the game, this kid intercepted a pass and ran all the way for the winning touchdown. The fans broke loose. His teammates hoisted him onto their shoulders.

Finally, after the stands had emptied and the team had showered and left the locker room, the coach noticed that the young man was sitting quietly in the corner all alone.

The coach came to him and said, "Kid, I can't believe it. You were fantastic! Tell me what got into you? How did you do it?"

He looked at the coach, with tears in his eyes, and said, "Well, you know my dad died, but did you know that my dad was blind?" The young man swallowed hard and forced a smile, "Dad came to all my games, but today was the first time he could see me play, and I wanted to show him I could do it!"

盲爸爸看我比赛橄榄球

撑竿跳高前冠军鲍勃·理查德讲过这样一个动人的故事，故事的主人公是一个全心全意热爱橄榄球的瘦小男孩。他一场接一场训练，热心奉献所有的一切。但是，他的个头比其他男孩矮了很多，在赛场上他绝对一事无成。在所有比赛中，这位满怀希望的小运动员坐在长椅上，几乎从未参赛过。这少年和他的父亲相依为命，两人有一种非常特殊的关系。即使儿子总坐在长椅上，父亲也在看台上欢呼，从未错过一场比赛。

上中学时，这个少年的个子还是全班最小的。但是，他的父亲不仅继续鼓励他，而且非常清楚地表明，如果不愿意，他不必打橄榄球。

但是，小伙子热爱橄榄球，决定坚持不懈。在每次训练中，他都下定决心，竭尽全力，也许当他成为一名资深运动员时，他就可以参赛了。整个中学期间，他从未错过一次训练，也从未错过一次比赛，但整整4年他仍坐在长椅上。他忠实的父亲总是在看台上，总是鼓励他。

小伙子上大学时，决定试着在校橄榄球队里跑龙套。每个人都确信他会被刷下去，但他留了下来。教练承认把他留在队里，是因为他总是全心全意地投入每场训练，同时，他还以这种精神鼓舞了其他队员。

他没被刷下去的消息让他万分激动，他急匆匆跑到最近的地方给父亲打电话。他的父亲也和他一样激动，并收到了观看他们大学所有橄榄球比赛的季票。大学4年期间，这个百折不挠的年轻运动员从未错过一次训练，但他也没上过一场比赛。

到了大学最后一年橄榄球赛季快结束时，盛大的最后决赛开始前不久，他一路小跑来到了训练场，教练拿着一份电报迎向他，他顿时陷入了死一般的沉默。

他强咽着泪水，对教练喃喃说道：“我父亲今天早上去世了。我不参加今天的训练可以吗？”

教练轻轻抱住他的肩膀说：“孩子，这星期剩下的时间你可以请假。星期六也不用来比赛现场了。”

星期六到了，比赛形势不妙。在第三节比赛中，当球队落后10点时，一个沉默不语的年轻人悄悄溜进了空荡荡的衣帽间，穿上了橄榄球服。当他跑到球场边线上时，教练和队员们看到他们忠实的队友会这么快返回都大吃了一惊。

“教练，请让我上吧！今天我必须参赛。”年轻人说。

教练装作没有听见。在这场势均力敌的决赛里，他绝不想让自己最差的队员上场。但是，年轻人执意坚持，最后出于可怜小伙子，教练让步了。

“好吧，”教练说，“你可以参加。”

他上场不久，教练、队员们和看台上的每个人都无法相信自己的眼睛。这个鲜为人知、从未上过场的队员步步到位。对方谁也挡不住他，他像明星一样奔跑、传球、拦挡、擒抱。比分很快持平。

在比赛还剩下最后几秒钟时，小伙子拦截了对方的一次传球，一路冲向攻方，持球触地获胜。球迷们沸腾了，队友们把他举到了肩上。

最后，当看台上观众散尽、队员们洗完澡离开衣帽间后，教练注意到了那个年轻人，他独自静坐在角落里。

教练走到他跟前说：“年轻人，我简直无法相信。你真棒！告诉我你是怎么回事？你是怎么做的？”

他眼含热泪，望着教练说：“噢，你知道我爸爸去世了，可你知道他的眼睛看不见吗？”年轻人哽咽着，强装笑脸。“爸爸来看我所有的比赛，但今天是他第一次能看见我比赛，我想让他看到我能行！”

The Yellow Handkerchief on the Oak Tree

I first heard this story a few years ago from a girl I had met in New York's Greenwich Village. Probably the story is one of those mysterious bits of folklore that reappear every few years, to be told a new in one form or another. However, I still like to think that it really did happen, somewhere, sometime.

They were going to Fort Lauderdale—three boys and three girls—and when they boarded the bus, they were carrying sandwiches and wine in paper bags, dreaming of golden beaches as the gray cold of New York vanished behind them.

As the bus passed through New Jersey, they began to notice Vingo. He sat in front of them, dressed in a plain, ill-fitting suit, never moving, his dusty face masking his age. He kept chewing the inside of his lip a lot, frozen into some personal cocoon of silence.

Deep into the night, outside Washington, the bus pulled into Howard Johnson's, and everybody got off except Vingo. He sat rooted in his seat, and the young people began to wonder about him, trying to imagine his life: perhaps he was a sea captain, a runaway from his wife, an old soldier going home. When they went back to the bus, one of the girls sat beside him and introduced herself.

"We're going to Florida," she said brightly. "I hear it's really beautiful."

"It is," he said quietly, as if remembering something he had tried to forget.

"Want some wine?" she said. He smiled and took a swig. He thanked her and retreated again into his silence. After a while, she went back to the others, and Vingo nodded in sleep.

In the morning, they awoke outside another Howard Johnson's, and this time Vingo went in. The girl insisted that he join them. He seemed very shy, and ordered black coffee and smoked nervously as the young people chattered about sleeping on beaches. When they returned to the bus, the girl sat with Vingo again, and after a while, slowly and painfully, he told his story. He had been in jail in New York for the past four years, and now he was going home.

"Are you married?"

"I don't know."

"You don't know?" she said.

"Well, when I was in jail I wrote to my wife," he said. "I told her that I was going to be away a long time, and that if she couldn't stand it, if the kids kept asking questions, if it hurt too much, well, she could just forget me, I'd understand. Get a new guy, I said—she's a wonderful woman, really something—and forget about me. I told her she didn't have to write me for nothing. And she didn't. Not for three and a half years."

"And you're going home now, not knowing?"

"Yeah," he said shyly. "Well, last week, when I was sure the parole was coming through, I wrote her again. We used to live in Brunswick, just before Jacksonville, and there's a big oak tree just as you come into town. I told her that if she'd take me back, she should put a yellow handkerchief on the tree, and I'd get off and come home. If she didn't want me, forget it—no handkerchief, and I'd go on through."

"Wow," the girl exclaimed. "Wow."

She told the others, and soon all of them were in it, caught up in the approach of Brunswick, looking at the pictures Vingo showed them of his wife and three children. The woman was handsome in a plain way, the children still unformed in the much-handled snapshots.

Now they were 20 miles from Brunswick, and the young people took over window seats on the right side, waiting for the approach of the great oak tree. The bus acquired a dark, hushed mood, full of the silence of absence and lost years. Vingo stopped looking, tightening his face into the ex-con's mask, as if fortifying himself against still another disappointment.

Then Brunswick was ten miles, and then five. Then, suddenly, all of the young people were up out of their seats, screaming and shouting and crying, doing small dances of joy. All except Vingo.

Vingo sat there stunned, looking at the oak tree. It was covered with yellow handkerchiefs—20 of them, 30 of them, maybe hundreds, a tree that stood like a banner of welcome billowing in the wind. As the young people shouted, the old con rose and made his way to the front of the bus to go home.

橡树上的黄手帕

几年前，我在纽约市格林尼治村第一次从一位遇到的姑娘那里听到了这个故事。它也许是那种每隔几年就会改头换面重新传播一次的神秘的民间传说。然而，我仍认为它是一个某地某时真正发生过的事儿。

3个男孩和3个女孩带着纸袋装的三明治和葡萄酒，乘车去佛罗里达州洛德代尔堡，梦想着金色的海滩。灰蒙蒙、冷飕飕的纽约消失在了他们身后。

当他们穿过新泽西州时，坐在前排的一个叫文哥的男人引起了他们的注意。他穿着一套不合身的朴素衣服，一动不动，满面灰尘掩盖了他的年龄，他不停地咬着嘴唇，陷入了沉思。

夜深了，汽车停在华盛顿郊外的霍华德·约翰逊连锁店，除了文哥，其他人都下了车。他像扎了根似的坐在那里。现在年轻人开始猜想，尽力想象着他的生活：也许他是一名船长，也许是逃离妻子，也许是一名返乡的老兵。当他们又回到车上时，其中一个女孩坐到文哥身边，作了自我介绍。

"我们都是去佛罗里达，"她满面春风地说，"我听说那里确实很美。"

"是的。"他平静地说，似乎想起了过去曾试图忘却的往事。

"来点葡萄酒吧？"那个女孩说。他微笑着喝了一大口。谢过她后，他又陷入了沉默。过了一会儿，她回到那群人中，文哥打起了盹儿。

第二天早上，他们醒来时汽车停在另一个霍华德·约翰逊连锁店前，这次文哥也走了进去。那个女孩坚持请他加入他们的团体。他看上去很不好意思，当那群年轻人谈论着如何在海滨过夜时，他点了黑咖啡，不安地抽着烟。当他们回到车上时，那个女孩又坐到文哥身边。过了一会儿，文哥才慢慢地、痛苦地讲起了他的经历。他在纽约蹲了4年监狱，现在他要回家了。

"你结婚了吗？"

"我不知道。"

"你不知道？"女孩问。

"呃，我在狱中曾给妻子写过一封信，"他说，"我告诉她我要离开很长一段时间，如果她忍受不了，如果孩子们不断追问，如果这使她非常痛苦，那她可以忘了我，我会理解的。我叫她重新嫁人——她是个很不错的女人，真的很不错——忘了我。我让她不必给我写回信。她没回信，3年半没有回信。"

"那你现在一无所知就要回家？"

"是的，"他羞涩地说，"噢，上周，当我确信假释得到批准时，我又给她写过一封信。过去我们住在布伦斯威克，就在杰克逊维尔前面，在进城去的路上有一棵大橡树。我告诉她，如果她愿意我回来，就在树上挂一块黄手帕，我就下车回家。如果她不要我，就算了——看不见手帕，我就继续前行。"

"哇，"那女孩惊叫道，"哇。"

她把这事儿告诉了其他人。他们都兴致勃勃盼着快点到布伦斯威克。文哥给他们看了一张他妻子和3个孩子的照片。这是一张被摸了好多次的照片，照片上是一个面容端庄的女人和3个年幼的孩子。

现在他们离布伦斯威克只有20英里了，那些年轻人占据了右边靠窗的座位，等待着那棵大橡树的出现。汽车里的气氛压抑、肃静，充满了离开家乡、失去岁月的寂静。文哥像做囚犯时那样绷紧脸庞，不再往外看，好像是加强自己的意志，抵制又一次失望的打击。

这时，离布伦斯威克只有10英里了，随后是5英里。突然，所有的年轻人都尖叫着、呼喊着从座位上跳起来，高兴得手舞足蹈，除了文哥。

文哥呆坐在那里，望着那棵橡树，上面挂满了黄手帕。20块，30块，也许有好几百块，这棵树耸立在那里，像一面迎风飘扬的欢迎的旗帜。在年轻人的叫喊声中，先前的那个囚犯站起来，走到车前，向家走去。

Smiles

Poor lame Jennie sat at her window, looking out upon the dismal, narrow street, with a look of pain and weariness on her face. "Oh, dear," she said with a sigh, "what a long day this is going to be," and she looked wishfully up the street.

Suddenly she leaned forward and pressed her pale face against the glass, as a rosy-checked boy came racing down the street, swinging his schoolbooks by the strap. Looking up to the window, he took off his hat and bowed with a bright, pleasant smile.

"What a nice boy he is," said Jennie to herself, as he ran out of sight. "I am so glad he goes by here on his way to school. When he smiles, it seems like having the sun shine. I wish everybody who goes by would look up and smile."

"Mamma," said George West, as he came from school, "I can't help thinking about that poor little girl I told you of the other day. She looks so tired. I took off my hat and bowed to her to-day. I wish I could do something for her."

"Suppose you should carry her a handful of pretty flowers some time when you go to school," said Mrs. West. "I'll do that to-morrow morning," said George, "if I can find my way into that rickety old house."

The next morning, as Jennie sat leaning her head wearily against the window, watching the raindrops chasing one another down the glass, she spied George with a handful of beautiful flowers carefully picking his way across the street. He stopped in front of her window, and, smiling very pleasantly, said, "How shall I find the way to your room?"

Jennie pointed to an alley near by, where he turned in, and with some difficulty found his way to the dingy staircase. Opening the door to Jennie's gentle "Come in," he said, "I have brought you a handful of flowers to look at this rainy day."

"Are they for me?" exclaimed Jennie, clapping her hands in delight. "How kind you are," she continued, as George laid them in her lap. "I have not had a flower since we live in the city."

"Did you use to live in the country?" asked George. "Oh, yes," answered Jennie, "we used to live in a beautiful cottage, and there were trees and flowers and green grass, and the air was so sweet."

"Well, what made you move here?" "Oh," said Jennie, softly, "papa died, and mamma was sick so long that the money was all gone. Then mamma had to sell the cottage, and she moved here to try to get work to do."

"Do you have to sit here all day?" asked George, glancing around the bare room and out into the dismal street. "Yes," said Jennie, "because I am lame; but I would not care for that, if I could only help mamma."

"I declare, it's too bad!" said George, who dreaded nothing so much as being obliged to stay in the house. "Oh, no, it isn't," said Jennie, pleasantly; "mamma says maybe we should forget the Lord if we had everything we wanted, and He never forgets us, you know."

"Well, I must rush for school," said George, not knowing exactly what to say next; and he was soon out of Jennie's sight, but had a happy little corner in his heart, because he had tried to do a kind act. He did not know how much good he had done in making a pleasant day out of a dreary one for a little sick girl.

"Mamma," said George, that evening, after he had told her what Jennie said, "papa must give them some money, so they can go back to their home."

"No," said his mother; "he can not do that, and they would not wish him to do so; but perhaps he can help us contrive some way to assist them, so that they can live more comfortably."

"I am going to carry Jennie some of the grapes grandpa sent me, to-morrow," said George, turning over the leaves of his geography. "I will put some of my pears into your basket, and go with you," said his mother; "but there is one thing we can always give, and sometimes it does more good than nice things to eat, or even money."

"What is that, mamma, —smiles?" asked George, looking up. "Yes," answered his mother; "and it is a good plan to throw in a kind word or two with them when you can."

微　笑

可怜的跛脚珍妮坐在窗前，忧郁地望着狭长的街道，苍白的脸上布满痛苦和疲惫的神情。"哦，亲爱的，"她深深地叹了口气说，"又将是一个漫长的白天！"她一脸憧憬地看着街道。

突然，她的身体向前倾，苍白的脸颊贴在玻璃上。这时一个面色红润的小男孩从街的另一端走过来，他不时地晃动自己的书包。走到窗下时，他摘下帽子向珍妮致意，并露出了甜甜的微笑。

"多可爱的男孩啊！"当男孩从视线中消失之后，珍妮自言自语地说，"真高兴他在去学校的时候能经过我的窗前，他的笑容就像阳光一样灿烂。真希望每个人经过的时候都能向这儿望一眼，笑一笑。"

"妈妈，"乔治·威斯特放学回家后对妈妈说，"我总是会情不自禁地想起那天对您说的那个可怜的小女孩。她看起来非常疲惫，今天，在经过她窗前的时候，我摘下帽子向她致意，我希望能帮她做点什么。"

"改天去学校的时候，你可以买束漂亮的鲜花送给她。"威斯特夫人说。"明天早上我就去送，"乔治激动地说，"假如可以找到那所旧房子的入口！"

第二天早晨，珍妮无聊地把头靠在窗户上，看着雨滴一个接一个从玻璃上滑下来；正在这时，她看见乔治抱着一束鲜花，小心地从街边走过来。他走到她的窗边停下来，愉快地微笑着说："我怎么才可以进到你的房子里面去？"

珍妮指了指旁边的小道，乔治费劲地找到一条小道，那条小道通向阴暗的楼梯。到门口，他听见珍妮温柔地说："请进。"他说："我给你带了一束花，在这下雨天你可以看一看。"

"这是给我的吗？"珍妮惊讶地说，她高兴地拍着手，"你真是太好了。"她继续说道。当乔治把花放在她腿上的时候，她激动地说："自从搬到城里之后，我就没有见过鲜花。"

"你曾住在乡下吗？"乔治问。"嗯，是的，"珍妮回答，"我们曾住在一个漂亮的小屋里，那儿有高大的树、美丽的花、翠绿的草，空气非常清新。"

"那么，你们为什么要搬到城里来呢？""噢，"珍妮轻轻地说，"爸爸去世了，妈妈病了好久，所有的钱都花光了，妈妈只好卖了小屋，她要搬到城里来找工作。"

"你一整天都坐在这儿吗？"乔治瞥了一眼空荡荡的房子，望向阴沉沉的街道。"是的，"珍妮说，"因为我的腿跛了，所以我必须待在家里，但是我不在乎，我很想帮妈妈。"

"真是太糟糕了！"乔治得去学校上课了，他不能在这里再多待一分钟。"哦，不，我想没那么糟，"珍妮愉快地说，"妈妈说过，我们拥有一切的时候也许会忘记上帝，但是你知道，上帝是从来不会忘记我们的。"

"天啊，看来我得跑着去学校了。"乔治说，接下来他也不知道应该说什么。他很快就从珍妮的眼前消失了，但是他心里非常高兴，因为他现在可以真正帮助别人了。然而，他不知道他所做的一切，使一个生病的小女孩高高兴兴地度过了一天。

那天晚上，乔治把珍妮的故事都告诉了妈妈。"妈妈，"乔治说，"爸爸一定可以给珍妮家一些钱的，那样她们就可以回到自己的家了。"

"不，"妈妈说，"爸爸不能那样做，她们也不会希望爸爸那样做，但是他也许可以帮我们想到一些让她们生活得比较好的方法。"

"明天我给珍妮带一些爷爷送给我的葡萄。"乔治翻着自己的地理书说道。"那么，我在篮子里放一些家里的梨，明天你一起带去给她，"妈妈说，"但是有一件更好的东西可以经常送给她，它甚至比吃的东西和钱更有用。"

"那是什么，妈妈？是微笑吗？"乔治抬起头问道。"是的，"妈妈回答，"如果在微笑的同时再说一些鼓励的话，就更好了。"

第五卷

幸福的旅程

Joy or Happiness

Joy and happiness are often understood to be the same thing, but in fact they're very different. Happiness is an emotion that is aroused in us when we buy a new car or get a promotion at work. It depends on our circumstances satisfying our desires. Joy is an emotion that occurs within us when we develop an appreciation or thankfulness for the constants of life, such as nature, freedom, relationships with people, or through having faith in something larger than ourselves.

Discovering the difference between happiness and joy is not about seeing one as better than the other, but instead realizing they're just different. Being happy as a result of good circumstances taking place is natural; however, we can't rely on having good circumstances all the time. It's not realistic. Happiness is not an emotion that we learn; we automatically get it. Joy, on the other hand, is an emotion that can predominantly rule our daily lives. We must develop and teach ourselves joy, much like the process of getting physically fit.

When I was 14, I remember so clearly how determined I was to do whatever was necessary to find happiness. After 20 years of experiencing better cars, bigger houses and more adventures, I finally admitted to myself that happiness was like smoking marijuana: the highs are great at the beginning, but the longer you smoke it, the more thrill diminishes—to the point where it becomes an addiction.

Joy is a powerful emotion and the opposite of fear, our second most influential emotion. My observation is that these two emotions are in a constant battle.

Since I have been teaching myself how to be more joyful, I have started observing joyful people. They seem to have many commonalities. They are in good health. They value discipline and strong relationships. They're appreciative and thankful, and they don't allow themselves to have too happy highs when great things happen. Meanwhile, they resist major discouragements when bad things happen.

Teaching yourself to be joyful is the most effective thing you could do to enhance your health. Advancing medical technology is enabling us to learn how the human physiology and psyche are affected by negative and positive emotions. Our three primary negative emotions—fear, anger and sadness—have devastating effects on our bodies when experienced in a prolonged state. On the other hand, our two primary positive emotions—joy and excitement—are like medicine to the body.

Everyone has a choice to live in joy and excitement or in fear, anger and sadness—regardless of their circumstances. Some people, however, think that after their difficult circumstances change, these negative emotions will subside and that's an illusion that can be overcome, if desired. Because fear is more of an illusion than a reality, the probability of overcoming it or other negative emotions is very high. Now that's something to be joyful about.

快乐还是幸福

人们常常认为快乐和幸福是一回事，但事实上，两者截然不同。幸福是我们买一辆新车或在工作中得到提升时内心升起的一种情感，它取决于满足我们愿望的环境因素。快乐是我们对自然、自由和人际关系这些生活要素心存感激，或追求超越自我的更崇高的信仰时发自内心的一种情感。

发现幸福和快乐的差别并不能说明谁好谁坏，它们只是不同而已。因条件好而感觉幸福是顺理成章的事儿。然而，我们并不能始终依赖好的环境，这不现实。幸福不是我们可以学来的情感，而是一种自动获得的情感。从另一方面来说，快乐是能主宰我们日常生活的一种情感。我们必须逐步教自己快乐，这和健身过程非常相似。

我清楚记得14岁那年自己下定决心无论如何都要寻找幸福。20年来，我的汽车越来越好，房子越来越大，体验的精彩也越来越多，而我最终承认幸福就像抽烟一样：开始激情高涨，但抽的时间越长，刺激感就越弱，直到抽烟成瘾。

快乐是一种有力的情感。快乐的对立面是担心，是对我们第二大有影响的情感。通过观察，我发现这两种情绪一直在相互斗争。

我从教自己如何才能更快乐以来，就已经开始观察那些快乐的人。他们似乎有很多共同之处。他们身体健康，重视自律，有良好的人际关系。他们善于欣赏和感恩。顺心时，他们也不让自己过度兴奋。同时，不顺心时，他们也不会让自己情绪低落。

学会快乐是增强体质的最有效的方法。日新月异的医疗技术使我们能了解到人们的生理和心理怎样受到积极和消极的情绪影响。我们有3种主要的消极情绪——担心、生气和悲伤，它们长期滞留在体内，就会给身体带来致命的影响。另一方面，我们的两种主要的积极情绪——快乐和兴奋则是身体的良药。

每个人在生活中，无论处境怎样，都可以选择快乐和兴奋，也可以选择担心、生气和悲伤。然而，一些人认为只有自己的困境改变，这些消极情绪才会减弱。那是一种错误观念，如果你渴望，你就能够战胜这种错误观念。因为担心是一种幻觉，而不是现实，我们十有八九能战胜担心或其他消极情绪，这才是让我们快乐的事儿。

How to Be Happier

Happiness, like cholesterol level, is a genetically-influenced trait. Yet as cholesterol is also influenced by diet and exercise, our happiness is to some extent under our personal control.

Realize that enduring happiness doesn't come from financial success.
Take control of your time.
Act happy.
Seek work and leisure that engages your skills.
Sound minds reside in sound bodies.
Give your body the sleep it wants.
Give priority to close relationships.
Focus beyond self. Reach out to those in need.
Be grateful.
Nurture your spiritual self.

十点让你更幸福

幸福，像人体的胆固醇含量一样，是一个受基因影响的特性。不过，正如胆固醇含量受饮食和锻炼影响一样，我们的幸福在某种程度上受个人控制。

要认识到，持久的幸福并非来自金钱上的富有；
控制好自己的时间；
快乐行事；
从事能发挥你技能的工作和休闲活动；
健全的思想寓于健康的身体；
使自己的身体有充足的睡眠；
优先考虑亲密的朋友；
不要只关注自我，要对危难中的人伸出援手；
心存感激；
滋养灵魂的自我。

The Ways to Happiness

How many ways are there to reach the state of being happy?
Happiness is not an aim, but a journey. If you seek for happiness in the course of the journey, the course will become a destination, and what's more, it will be a

prolonged, boundlessly beneficial destination for all your life.

The happy place is this place, and the happy moment is this moment. Remain standing here, seize the present moment, and you will be happy.

Happiness is mental before it is physical. In order to be physically happy to the full, you must first feel at ease and be free of worry. It is better to eat without meat than to have a load on your mind.

Happiness is the opposite of unhappiness; the decline of the one means the growth of the other. Release yourself from the unhappy mood and you will be happy.

Happiness is a matter of five cakes of bread and two fishes; the more you give out the more you will get back. Share your happiness with others and you will enjoy it more.

If your heart's desire is easily satisfied, your happiness will soon come to an end. In order that your happiness may last, you have to leave some of your desires unfulfilled.

When you are happy, you feel contented. You should also feel contented when you are unhappy. Be always full of zest and happiness will become an inveterate habit.

Happiness is a very strange thing. It will not turn up when you beckon it, call it and solicit it. But when you feign complete indifference, it will fawn on you, lean close to you and live with you. In dealing with happiness, you should adopt the strategy of leaving it at large the better to apprehend it.

Happiness is drifting from place to place. It is unwise and futile to try to retain it. You have got to keep on making new happiness, so that one happiness follows in the wake of another.

幸福有多少种方法

有多少种方法可以达到幸福的境界呢？

幸福不是目标，而是一段旅程。如果你在旅程中寻找幸福，那过程就会变成终点，而且是你一生中受益匪浅、得到延伸的终点。

幸福的地方就在此地，幸福的时刻就在此刻。立足此地、抓住此刻，你就会幸福。

幸福是先精神、后身体。为了使身体上的幸福更充实，你必须首先做到自由自在、无忧无虑。宁可吃饭时没有肉，也不要有思想负担。

幸福和不幸相互对立，此消彼长。从不幸中解脱出来，你就会幸福。

幸福是5块面包和两条鱼。分发得越多，你得到的就越多。和他人分享你的幸福，你会更幸福。

如果你的心愿很容易得到满足，那你的幸福就会很快结束。为了能延长自己的幸福，你必须留一些未了的愿望。

你幸福时，会感到满足；你不幸时，也要感到心安。如果总是充满热情，幸福就会成为一种根深蒂固的习惯。

幸福是一件非常奇特的事情。当你召唤它、命令它、恳求它时，它不会出现。但是，当你假装无动于衷时，它又会靠近你，和你相处。和幸福打交道，你需要采用"欲擒故纵"的策略。

幸福四处飘来飘去。你试图留住它，既愚昧又无用。你得创造新的幸福，这样幸福就会接踵而至。

What's Happiness like?

I don't know from when I began to admire others' happiness. Marriage should by all means be the peak of happiness for a woman. Otherwise there would not be so many women dreaming to step into the palace of marriage. On my way to work, wedding cars happened to pass by for several times. Seeing the bride carried the groom on the arm happily and her sweet and happy smile, I felt marriage must be something good and nice! Surely!

Father phoned me to take good care of myself and not to put myself to great inconvenience. Mother said her daughter should be surely happy when she grew up! Brother said a woman should lead an easier life.

But what is happiness I'm longing for?

Before I was five, I didn't remember what had happened. I believe it must have been a time of happy days!

When I was six, I felt so happy to tiptoe and grab the candy held high by Father. To think it now, happiness was so simple at that time.

When I was seven, I could climb onto a high fruit tree to pick a green fruit. Then I felt so happy enjoying the jealous eyes of other children under the tree! At any rate, I could try to climb that high!

When I was eight, I felt so happy to wear the little red rain boots Grandpa bought for me. You know, other ordinary children generally walked with bare foot in rainy days! In those days, what I expected most was raining.

When I was nine, I felt so happy I could sit in the warm classroom to listen to my grandpa teaching me how to learn pinyin, for Mother told me when she was nine she had begun to make money and understand the hardship of life. So I thought I was happier than Mother.

When I was ten, wearing the pants with braces I felt very happy. Though Mother with her old clothes made them, I was the only child to wear trousers with braces in our village.

When I was eleven, my foot was bruised, but I have a brother to carry me back home. Staying on my brother's back, I felt so happy. At least I have a brother, who makes me proud till now.

At twelve when I woke up, I could see my brother's silly posture in his sleep. I soon slipped into his quilt quietly and put my little icy hands onto his back. I was tickled all along till Mother entered our bedroom to hurry us to get up. I was happy. I don't know from when we were set to sleep separately.

When I was thirteen, I felt happy to listen to the novelty stories told by the little boy in the neighborhood. Cities were the heaven in my dream, the places I could long for but could not reach.

When I was fourteen…

When I was fifteen…

When I was sixteen, I felt happy, for Father could walk into my room and give his angel a kiss before I slept. Just for that sweet kiss, never have I had nightmares!

When I was seventeen, I felt happy for receiving a note sent by the boy from the neighbor class. I felt my heart beat faster, for he chose me while at least many a girl liked him. After all, he was my first love, though at that time we liked each other in a so simple way, which could not be simpler any more!

When I was eighteen, I felt happy to enter the key senior high school. Because I finally realized Father's first dream! I felt happy for his happiness!

When I was nineteen and twenty, I felt so happy because I could continue my dream sitting in the spacious classroom to listen to my teacher teaching abc and xyz. You know, my peers have already started jobbing!

When I was twenty-one, I felt very happy to be admitted to a university and enter a city, for my childhood expectation and dream as well as the city life just presented before me. To have the chance of leaving that land, I felt very happy!

When I was twenty-two, I felt so happy for having known the now boyfriend, who at least made me deeply concerned and felt dearly loved.

Time flew by. Just when I glanced back, I found no wonder the happiness I expected was so simple—I had always been that simple.

When I was twenty-three, I began to feel little muddled. The sense of happiness became more tasteless and dazed.

When I was twenty-four, my sense of happiness continued getting fainter…

When I was twenty-five, I worked. Suddenly it dawned on me that my happiness, like soup bubbles glistening the beautiful luster in the sun, burst out and was evaporated with the passage of time.

What's left in my memory is the sense of longing for happiness!

So what's happiness in my future? I wish it would not be soup bubbles any more. I just simply wish someone would wrap a coat on me when it turns cold, and someone would wait for me to share dinner when I overwork. I simply wish my parents healthy and sound, and my life simpler and simpler…

幸福的感觉什么样

不知道什么时候，我开始喜欢仰望别人的幸福！结婚一定是一个女人幸福的极点吧，要不为什么很多女人想步入婚姻的殿堂呢？上班的路上，婚车好几次从我身边经过，看着新娘幸福地挽着新郎，新娘那幸福甜美的笑容，我想婚姻一定是个美好的东西！一定是！

爸爸打电话来说，要我照顾好自己，要我别委屈自己。妈妈说，女儿长大了一定要幸福！哥哥说，女人过得简单点吧！

可什么是我要的幸福呢？

5岁前，因为我不记得我5岁前发生过什么事！我想那一定是一段幸福的时光！

6岁时，踮起脚尖去抢被父亲高高举起的糖果，觉得很幸福！现在想想那时候的幸福真的很简单！

7岁时，可以爬到高高的果树上摘一个青色的果子，然后看着树下其他孩子羡慕的眼光，觉得很幸福！爬得这么高，至少我可以做得到！

8岁时，穿着爷爷给我买的红色小雨鞋觉得很幸福，要知道那时的孩子，下雨时都是光脚走路的！那时候，我最盼望的就是下雨。

9岁时，可以坐在暖和的教室里，听爷爷教给我那些原始的拼音字母，觉得很幸福！因为妈妈说，她9岁时已经开始赚钱并懂得生活的艰辛了，所以我觉得我比妈妈幸福！

10岁时，穿着妈妈做给我的背带裤，虽然裤子是妈妈的旧衣服改做的，但至少我是村里唯一能穿得上背带裤的孩子！我觉得很幸福！

11岁时，因为脚受伤，哥哥背我回家， 趴在哥哥的背上我觉得很幸福，至少有个哥哥让我至今都很自豪！

12岁时，清晨醒来时，可以看见哥哥那傻乎乎的睡相，然后悄悄地跑进他的被窝，用冰凉的小手放在他的背上，然后被哥哥使劲地挠痒痒，直到妈妈走进房间，说赶快起床！那时觉得很幸福，但不知道什么时候开始，我们已经分开睡了！

13岁时，我听邻家小男孩讲述城里的新鲜事，觉得很幸福，城市是我那时候梦里的天堂，是我可望而不可即的地方！

14岁……

15岁……

16岁，因为爸爸可以在我睡前走进房间，亲吻一下他的天使，我觉得很幸福，就因为那个甜甜的吻，我从来都不会做噩梦！

17岁时，因收到隔壁班男孩投递过来的小纸条而心跳不止，至少很多女孩子喜欢他，而他选中了我，我觉得很幸福！毕竟他是我的初恋，虽然那时候真的只是很简单的喜欢！简单得不能再简单！

18岁时，考进重点高中，我觉得很幸福！因为我终于完成了爸爸的第一个梦想！爸爸高兴，所以我幸福！

19岁、20岁时，因为自己还可以继续完成自己的梦想，可以坐在宽敞的教室里，听老师讲那些abc、xyz，我觉得很幸福，要知道和我同龄的孩子，早已开始打工了！

21岁考进大学，走进城市，觉得很幸福，因为儿时的期盼，儿时的梦想，都市的生活，就那么真实地在我眼前。有机会走出那片土地，我觉得很幸福！

22岁认识现在的男朋友我觉得很幸福，至少有人让我那么牵挂，而又被人疼爱的感觉让我很幸福！

时间在流逝，回眸间，才发现，原来我一直很简单，所要的幸福也很简单！

23岁我开始有点儿迷糊，幸福的感觉变得越来越淡，我越来越迷糊！

24岁让我幸福的感觉继续变淡……

25岁，当我工作了才突然间明白，原来我的幸福就像肥皂泡，曾在阳光下闪烁着美丽的光彩，会突然破裂，被时光蒸发得一干二净！

剩下的只是留在记忆里那些对幸福渴望的感觉！

那么，我以后的幸福是什么呢？不再希望是肥皂泡，只是简单地希望天冷时有人为自己披件外衣，加班时可以有人在等自己吃饭，希望爸爸妈妈的身体安康，希望我的生活简单点，再简单点……

The Knack of Chasing Happiness

We chase after happiness, when it is waiting all about us.

"Are you happy?" I asked my brother, Ian, one day.

"Yes. No. It depends on what you mean," he said.

"Then tell me," I asked, "when was the last time you think you were happy?"

"April 1967," he said.

It served me right for putting a serious question to someone who has joked his way through life. But Ian's answer reminded me that when we think about happiness, we usually think of something extraordinary, a pinnacle of sheer delight—and those pinnacles seem to get rarer the older we get.

For a child, happiness has a magical quality. I remember making hide-outs in newly-cut hay, playing cops and robbers in the woods, getting a speaking part in the school play. Of course, kids also experience lows, but their delight at such peaks of pleasure as winning a race or getting a new bike is unreserved.

In the teenage years the concept of happiness changes. Suddenly it's conditional on such things as excitement, love, popularity and whether zit will clear up before prom night. I can still feel the agony of not being invited to a party that almost everyone else was going to. But I also recall the ecstasy of being plucked from obscurity at another event to dance with a John Travolta look-alike.

In adulthood the things that bring profound joy—birth, love, marriage also—bring responsibility and the risk of loss. Love may not last, sex isn't always good, loved ones die. For adults, happiness is complicated.

My dictionary defines happy as "lucky" or "fortunate," but I think a better definition of happiness is "the capacity for enjoyment." The more we can enjoy what we have, the happier we are. It's easy to overlook the pleasure we get from loving and being loved, the company of friends, the freedom to live where we please, and even good health.

I added up my little moments of pleasure yesterday. First there was sheer bliss when I shut the last lunch-box and had the house to myself. Then I spent an uninterrupted morning writing, which I love. When the kids came home, I enjoyed their noise after the quiet of the day.

Later, peace descended again, and my husband and I enjoyed another pleasure—intimacy. Sometimes just the knowledge that he wants me can bring me joy.

You never know where happiness will turn up next. When I asked friends what made them happy, some mentioned seemingly insignificant moments. "I hate shopping," one friend said. "but there's a clerk who always chats and really cheers me up." Another friend loves the telephone, "Every time it rings, I know someone is thinking about me."

I get a thrill from driving. One day I stopped to let a school bus turn onto a side road. The driver grinned and gave me thumbs up sign. We were two allies in a world of mad motorists. It made smile.

We all experience moments like these. Too few of us register them as happiness.

Psychologists tell us that to be happy we need a blend of enjoyable leisure time and satisfying work. I doubt that my great-grandmother, who raised 14 children and took in washing, had much of either. She did have a network of close friends and family, and maybe this was what fulfilled her. If she was happy with what she had, perhaps it was because she didn't expect life to be very different.

We, on the other hand, with so many choices and such pressure to succeed in every area, have turned happiness into one more thing we "gotta have." We're so self-conscious about our "right" to it that it's making us miserable. So we chase it and equate it with wealth and success, without noticing that the people who have those things aren't necessarily happier.

While happier may be more complex for us, the solution is the same as ever. Happiness isn't about what happens to us—it's about how we perceive what happens to us. It's the knack of finding a positive for every negative, and viewing a setback as a challenge. It's not wishing for what we don't have, but enjoying what we do possess.

追求幸福的秘诀

我们追逐幸福，这时幸福在身边等着我们。

有一天，我问哥哥伊恩："你幸福吗？"

"幸福，也不幸福。这要看你指的是什么。"他说。

"那告诉我，"我说，"你认为最近一次感到幸福是什么时候？"

"1967年4月。"他说。

我不该对一个游戏人生的人提出严肃问题。但是，伊恩的回答提醒了我：我们想到幸福时，通常想到的是非同寻常的事儿，一种纯粹的快乐顶点，而随着我们年龄的增长，那些快乐顶点好像越来越少了。

对一个孩子来说，幸福具有一种魔力。我记得我曾在新割的干草中捉迷藏，在树林里玩"警察与强盗"，在校戏里扮演演讲的角色。当然，孩子们也会情绪低落。但是，因为赢得一场比赛或得了一辆新车，他们会毫不掩饰地快乐到极点。

十几岁时，幸福观发生了改变。突然间，幸福是以激动、爱情、名气和青春痘会不会在舞会前消失这些事情而定。我现在仍能感受到，大家都去参加一个舞会而我未被邀请时的极大痛苦。但是，我也记得，在另一次活动中，我和一个貌似约翰·特拉沃尔塔的人共舞时的狂喜。

成年时，带来极度快乐的事情——生育、爱情，还有婚姻——也会带来责任和失落。爱情也许不会持久，性爱也不总是如意，心爱的人会死去。对成年人来说，幸福错综复杂。

我的字典里对幸福的定义是"吉祥"或"幸运"，但我认为幸福更好的定义是"感受快乐的能力"。我们对拥有的一切享受得越多，就会越幸福。我们很容易对爱与被爱、朋友相伴、惬意自由的生活，甚至健康的体魄熟视无睹。

我合计了一下昨天小小的快乐时光。首先我盖上了最后一个午饭盒，独享整个房间，感觉幸福到了极点。然后，整个早上，我都在进行心爱的写作，无人打扰。孩子们回到家时，我又享受到了安静一天后的热闹。

随后，安静再次降临，我和丈夫享受到了另一种快乐——亲热。有时只要想到他需要我，就能给我带来快乐。

你根本不知道幸福下次什么时候出现。当我问起朋友们什么能让他们幸福时，有些人提到了看似微不足道的时刻。"我讨厌买东西，"一个朋友说，"但有一个喜欢聊天的售货员确实让我开心。"另一个朋友喜欢接电话："每次电话铃响，我就知道有人在想我了。"

我常常从开车中获得刺激。有一天，我停下来，让一辆校车拐到一条小路。那个司机咧嘴一笑，向我竖起了大拇指。我们都是飙车一族，这让我很高兴。

我们都有过类似这样的经历，但很少有人把这看成幸福。

心理学家告诉我们，要幸福，我们既需要愉快的休闲时间，也需要满意的工作。我对曾祖母感到疑惑，因为她养育了14个孩子，还要给别人洗衣服，却能两者兼之。她确实有一个密友和家庭网，也许让她满足的正是这个。如果说她对自己拥有的一切感到幸福的话，也许是因为她不希望生活是另一种样子。

因为有太多的选择和想在各个领域成功的压力，我们把幸福变成了"我们必须得到"的另一种东西。我们认为我们"有权"得到它，这正是我们痛苦的根源。所以，我们追求幸福，并把它和财富与成功相提并论，没有注意到拥有那些东西的人不一定更幸福。

尽管对我们来说幸福也许更复杂，但获得幸福的方式仍然一样。幸福不是发生在我们周围的事儿，而是我们怎样去感知周围发生的事儿。这是变消极为积极、把挫折看成挑战的秘诀。幸福并不是期望我们没有的东西，而是享受我们真正拥有的一切。

Happiness Is a Feeling

When a friend and I were standing in line at the grocery store the other day, I told her how lazy my children were. After I had come in from work that day, my house was in a mess like most times.

"I believe children nowadays are just out for what they can get. I bend over backwards for them, but they can't even help keep our house clean. Even if it doesn't bother me so, the other women will laugh at me when they find my house is in a mess.

"Do you know how blessed you are?" a woman behind us asked. "I'd love to go home and find my house a mess. I won't mind my carpet being ruined or the dishes left everywhere. I won't mind the dirty clothes being piled or many socks to match. I won't even mind anyone talking about my dirty home. As a matter of fact, I'd love it. I'd dearly love to tell my children how much I love them. You see, my two children were killed in a car accident and now it's just my husband and me. My house stays clean.

"There are no fingerprints on my walls, no mysterious spots on my carpets. There're no voices of arguing, no slamming doors, no laughter, no I love you Mom. So you see, you're very blessed. What you're disgusted about now is just what I wish to get. How I'd love to hold my kids, wipe away their tears and share their dreams. Or just to watch them play. If I had my children, I wouldn't care how my house looked. I'd be happy just to have them."

Now if you come into my house and see a big old mess, you can think bad thoughts if you want, but I feel greatly blessed.

幸福是一种感觉

前几天，我和一位朋友在食品杂货店排队买东西时，我对她说自己的孩子们是多么懒。那天我下班回家后，家里像大多数时候那样乱得不成样子。

"我认为现在的孩子只是伸手索取。我为他们竭尽全力，可他们连帮我保持房间干净都做不到。即便我不烦，别的女人看到我的家又脏又乱也会笑话我。"

"你知道自己有多幸福吗？"我们身后的一个女人说，"我真想回到家，看到家里乱得不成样子。我不会介意地毯被弄坏、碟子被乱放。我不会介意脏衣服成堆、好袜子不成对。就算什么人对我脏兮兮的家说三道四，我也不会介意。事实上，我喜欢这样。我真想告诉自己的孩子们，我是多么爱他们。

你明白吗？我的两个孩子在一次车祸中死了，现在就剩下我和丈夫了。我的家里总是很干净。

"墙上没有手指印，地毯上没有莫名其妙的污点。没有吵闹声，没有重重的关门声，没有笑声，也没有人说'我爱你，妈妈'。所以，你明白吗？你非常幸福。你现在讨厌的一切正是我渴望得到的啊。我多么希望能抱着自己的孩子，擦去他们的眼泪，分享他们的梦想。或者只是看着他们玩。如果我还有孩子，我是不会介意自己的家里是什么样子的。只要拥有他们，我就会幸福。"

现在，如果你来我家里，看到还是那么乱七八糟，你怎么往坏处想都可以，但我感觉非常幸福。

The Secrets of Happiness

Happiness is largely under our control. It is a battle to be fought and not a feeling to be awaited. To achieve a happy life, it's necessary to overcome some stumbling blocks, one of which is "Missing Tile" syndrome.

One effective way of destroying happiness is to look at something and focus on even the smallest flaw. It's like looking at the tiled ceiling and concentrating on the space where one tile is missing. Once you've determined what your missing tile is, explore whether acquiring it will really make you happy. Then do one of the three things: get it, replace it with a different tile, or forget about it and focus on the tiles in your life that are not missing.

We all know people who have had a relatively easy life yet are essentially unhappy. And we know people who have suffered a great deal but generally remain happy.

The first secret of happiness is gratitude. All happy people are grateful. Ungrateful people cannot be happy. We tend to think that being unhappy leads people to complain, but it's truer to say that complaint leads to people becoming unhappy.

The second secret is realizing that happiness is a byproduct of something else. The more passion we have, the more happiness we are likely to experience.

Finally, we need a spiritual faith, or a philosophy of life. Whatever your philosophy, it should include this truism: if you choose to find the positive, you will be blessed; if you choose to find the awful, you will be cursed. As with happiness itself, this is largely your decision to make.

幸福的秘诀

幸福很大程度上在我们的控制之下。它是一场要搏击的战斗，而不是一种要等待的感觉。要获得幸福的生活，就必须克服一些障碍，其中一个障碍就是"缺少瓷片"综合征。

破坏幸福的有效方法是看待事物时总是吹毛求疵。这就像看平铺的天花板，将注意力集中在缺失瓷片的地方。一旦你确定缺少的瓷片是什么，就要探究得到它是否会真正让你幸福。接下来，做以下3件事之一：得到它；用另一块瓷片代替它；要么忘记它，将注意力集中在生活中没有丢失的瓷片上。

我们都知道有些人过着相对安逸的生活，却在本质上并不幸福。我们还知道有些人遭受了很多磨难，却仍很幸福。

幸福的第一个秘诀就是感恩。所有幸福的人都心怀感激。不心怀感激的人不可能幸福。我们往往认为，不幸福就会引起人的抱怨，但抱怨会让人变得不幸福，更是事实。

幸福的第二个秘诀就是要意识到幸福是其他东西的一种副产品。我们的激情越多，我们体验的幸福就可能越多。

最后，我们需要一种精神信仰或人生观。无论你的人生观是什么，它应该包含这一真理：如果你选择积极的一面，就会得到祝福；如果你选择糟糕的一面，就会遭受诅咒。对幸福本身来说，这在很大程度上取决你自己的决定。

The Paradox of Happiness

What is the definition of happiness? Is it material wealth filled with fancy cars, a dream house, extravagant furs and jewelry? Or is happiness simply having a roof over your head? Food in the fridge? Having a child? A pet? A swimming pool? Parents? Love? Money? The perfect job? Winning a lottery?

In fact, happiness may be destined to happen.

Do you recall a time—let's say when you were about 5 years old—what defined happiness back then? Was it getting a puppy for Christmas? Or maybe, you were a child of divorce; and all you wanted was for Mom and Dad to get back together again? Then as you got older, you were hoping that someone would ask you to the prom that would have made your day, maybe your life for the moment. During college, good grades made you happy, but it was short-lived. Because in the real world, you had to look for a job, and competition was stark. It's an employer's world you thought. But then, you got the perfect job—now you could be happy—or could you?

Life requires more than just what we want. One must understand to truly find happiness, he must make his own happiness "happen." Sounds a bit redundant, but truthfully, there is not set guidelines that will bring happiness. There is no magic wand we can wave to bring joy into our lives. Human nature thrives on the thrill of the chase. We dream and we hope for the next big break.

We are hopeless creatures of comfort. We like having and accumulating things. Whether one admits to it or not, to a certain extent, we all try to keep up with "the Jones." We work so that we can pay our rents, mortgages, credit card debts, school loans, car payment…the list goes on and on. And at some point, we realize, that aside from having most of what we want, we still aren't happy. Now since we've learned to adapt to new standards which we've created for ourselves, we find that we have less time, less patience, less sleep, which equates to more stress, more worry and more aggravation. So, is happiness honestly just comprised of things?

Sometimes we virtually trade our lives for not only basic necessities, but for excessive items and services as well. We become so obsessed with finding happiness, that we lose sight of the fact that happiness is within—always. Certainly you've heard of individuals trying to find themselves, or rediscover themselves. The reason they are attempting these innovative approaches is because they are seeking inner happiness. But the point has been missed: happiness is already there.

Disappointments and tragedies in life will come and go, but happiness never leaves you. The human's capacity to be resilient to trials is unfathomable. We can lose our jobs, but be grateful for our spouses. We can lose our homes to nature, but be thankful to be alive.

Happiness is a perception of each individual. We are instinctively compelled to find fault in our lives. It is then that we lose sense of self-worth and the bigger picture of vitality altogether. Struck in the patterns of the happiness paradox, we simply cannot find where our happiness has gone.

It's not a matter of bargaining, it's not an issue of money or fame—instead, happiness is what you resolve to accept. If we live through optimistic hope, if we dare to dream, if we empower ourselves to fully live, we have regained our sense of happiness.

自相矛盾的幸福感

幸福的定义是什么？幸福是拥有豪华汽车、理想居室、名贵裘皮和珠光宝气这样的物质财富吗？还是幸福仅仅是有住所、冰箱里有食物、有孩子、有宠物、有游泳池、有父母、有爱情、有金钱、有理想工作、彩票中奖了呢？

事实上，幸福也许是命中注定要发生的事情。

你能回忆起你5岁时对幸福的解释吗？那时，幸福是为圣诞节买的一只小狗？或许是爸爸妈妈离婚后，你想要他们能重新生活在一起？随后，当你渐渐长大，你希望有人会请你参加舞会，希望自己的一天，也许一生都为那个时刻而活。大学期间，考试得了高分让你开心，但这很短暂。因为在现实世界里，你得找一份工作，而且竞争激烈。你就会想，这真是一个雇主的世界。随后，你找到了一份理想的工作，现在你可能会很开心，是吗？

生活要求得比我们想要的多。一个人必须明白，要想真正找到幸福，他就必须让自己幸福起来。尽管听起来有点多余，但的确如此，因为生活中没有能带来幸福的固定指南，也没有挥一挥就能给我们带来欢乐的魔棒。人性在追求幸福的刺激中不断成长，我们梦想、希望下一个大的突变。

我们是不可救药的享乐者，喜欢拥有和积攒东西。无论承认与否，在某种程度上，我们都在相互攀比。我们工作，这样就可以缴房租、还抵押贷款、信用卡透支、助学贷款、买车……这种清单源源不断。于是，我们意识到，除了拥有了想要的一切，我们仍不幸福。自从我们学会适应自己创造的新标准，我们发现时间少了，耐性少了，睡眠少了，但压力大了，忧虑多了，脾气大了。这样说来，幸福真的是由物质组成的吗？

有时我们其实不仅用生命交换基本必需品，还用生命交换多余的物质和服务。我们这样沉迷于寻找幸福，却忽略了一个事实——幸福总在我们心里。当然，你曾听说过有些人在尽力寻找自我或重新发现自我。他们创新尝试的理由是因为他们在寻找内在的幸福。但是，他们忽略了一点：幸福已在那里。

失望和悲伤在生命中来来往往，但幸福从来不会离开你。人类对磨难的适应能力无可限量。我们可以失去工作，但会为拥有爱人而感恩；我们可以失去家园，但会为活着而感激。

幸福是个人的一种感性认识。我们本能地被迫对自己的生活进行挑剔。就是在那时，我们对自我价值失去了理性判断，我们失去了生命活力，陷入对幸福的矛盾中，完全无法找到幸福的方向。

幸福不是可以讨价还价的事情，也不是金钱和名誉问题，而是你决定去接受的东西。如果生活在乐观希望中，如果敢于梦想，如果生活充实，那我们就重新找到了幸福的感觉。

Happiness Index

In term of happiness, your spouse—if you have one—is worth $100,000 a year.

That's the finding of two economists who have tried to put a monetary value on happiness, measuring the emotional value of everything from religion to racial discrimination in dollars.

Such a calculation, admits economist David Blanchflower, is "a little bit off the wall" and may prompt wry comments within some marriages on "cashing in."

The two economists are, of course, speaking of averages. They have used an unusual survey of some 1,500 Americans from 1972 to 1998 to measure self-reported happiness and the factors that go with it. "The happiness value of a stable marriage is incredibly high," says Dr. Blanchflower. "Don't give it up lightly."

Blanchflower and his partner Andrew Oswald begin with this question: "Take all together, how would you say things are these days—would you say that you are happy, pretty happy, or not so happy?"

The survey results include detailed characteristics of those surveyed—married, divorced, single, income level, race, gender, etc. With the data, they found which factors are associated with greater happiness.

Extra money does buy some happiness, but not as much as many would suspect. Constructing a sort of happy index assigning 3 to "very happy," 2 to "pretty happy," and 1 to "to not too happy," the two reckon that an extra dollar provides 0.00000409 in additional happiness. Or $10,000 would give you 0.04 units of extra happiness.

The two economists, using this index, assign a dollar value to other factors associated with more or less happiness.

Using that device, a lasting marriage is worth $100,000 per year compared with being widowed or divorced. Being "separated" is the greatest depressant of happiness, followed closely by the death of a spouse.

Second and subsequent marriages are less happy than first marriage on average.

A 16-year-old whose parents divorced has a lower level of well-being in adulthood.

"Marriage is believed by psychologists and psychiatrists to provide a protective effect to mental well-being," the authors note.

Blanchflower suspects the decline in the happiness level of Americans from the early 1970s to the late 1990s, despite rising incomes, may be attributed to the rise in divorce. Other findings include:

To bring African-Americans up to average happiness levels, they would need an extra $30,000 in annual income.

This, the authors speculate, may be the impact of racial discrimination. Over the past few decades, however, their happiness level has risen.

Unemployment is highly damaging to men's happiness. It would take $60,000 a year to offset being jobless.

Men's happiness has trended up. Women's sense of well-being, though higher than that of men, has fallen "noticeably."

Policies aimed at ending discrimination against women apparently have not boosted their happiness overall.

The educated tend to be happier than those less educated.

Happiness and life satisfaction are U-shaped according to age. In the United States, people's sense of well-being sinks to a low around 40 and then rises.

Perhaps, the author suggests, people adapt to their circumstances, relinquish some unfulfilled aspirations by the middle of their lives, and enjoy life more.

Being religious has a positive effect.

Overall, the number of children and siblings a person has doesn't have an impact on their happiness. But for those under 30, happiness decreases proportionately to the number of both children and siblings.

幸 福 指 数

就幸福感来说，你的配偶——如果有的话——一年的价值是10万美元。

这是两位经济学家试图制定幸福感的金钱价值得出的结论，以美元为单位，从宗教到种族歧视来测量每件事物的情感价值。

经济学家戴维·布兰奇弗劳尔承认，这样的计算"有点儿离奇"，可能使人产生曲解，认为有些婚姻是想"大捞一把"。

当然，这两位经济学家说的是一般人。他们利用从1972年到1998年对大约1500位美国人进行的不同寻常的调查，估量自行报告的幸福感和相关因素。布兰奇弗劳尔博士说："稳定婚姻的幸福价值高得惊人，不要轻易放弃。"

布兰奇弗劳尔和他的合作伙伴安德鲁·奥斯瓦尔德这样问道："从总体来说，你会怎样描述近况，是幸福、相当幸福还是不怎么幸福？"

调查对象的详情包括：已婚、离异、单身、收入水平、种族和性别等。根据这些数据，他们发现了与幸福感相关的更多因素。

某种幸福感确实可以用金钱买到，但并不像人们猜想的那样多。他们俩设计了一种幸福指数：对"非常幸福"赋值3，"相当幸福"赋值2，"不太幸福"赋值1。根据幸福指数，他们计算出，幸福感每增值0.00000409，就增加1美元，或者每增加10000美元，幸福感就增值0.04。

两位经济学家用这个指数以1美元的价值附值于与幸福感或多或少相关的

其他因素。

按这种方式，持久的婚姻与鳏寡或离异相比，其每年的价值为10万美元。对幸福感最大的抑制剂是"与配偶分离"，丧偶次之。

第一次婚姻会比第二次婚姻和以后的再婚幸福。

一个孩子16岁时父母就离异了，其成人期的幸福级别很低。

"心理学家和精神病专家相信，婚姻对精神健康起保护作用。"两位作者指出。

布兰奇弗劳尔怀疑，从20世纪70年代初至90年代末，虽然美国人的收入提高了，但他们的幸福级别却降低了，这也许归因于离婚率的上升。

其他的发现包括：

非洲裔美国人的年收入需要增加3万美元，才能使他们的幸福程度上升到平均级别。

两位作者推测，这样的结果也许和种族歧视的影响有关。然而，几十年过后，他们的幸福级别会有所上升。

失业正在严重损伤男人的幸福，一年需要6万美元才能弥补这种无业状况。

男人的幸福感已经呈上升趋势。女人的幸福感一向比男人的高，但已经"显著"下降。

反对歧视妇女的政策显然没有全面推进她们的幸福感。

受教育多的人往往比受教育少的人幸福。

幸福感与生活满意度根据年龄而呈U形变化。在美国，40岁左右，人们的幸福感降至低谷，之后又会上升。

两位作者建议，也许人们到中年时就适应了自己的环境，放弃一些不能实现的理想，更能享受生活。

宗教信仰可以产生积极影响。

总的来说，一个人的孩子和兄弟姐妹的多少并不影响其幸福感。但是，对30岁以下的人来说，其幸福感随着孩子和兄弟姐妹数量的增加而相应下降。

Look in from outside

I step out the back door and the blackness of night engulfs me. There is no moon to light my way to the clothesline and my forgotten wash. I'm piloted by the memory of a thousand trips along the familiar path: now up two flagstone steps, now past the giant pine whose branches overhang our cottage.

Past the corner of the woodshed, my outstretched hands become my scouts, groping for the lines, fumbling with the pins. Soon my arms are heaped with night-damp pants and shirts that have danced all day to the wind's compelling tunes.

The trip back is easier. As soon as I round the shed, the lights of the house guide me—great squares of amber light suspended in the darkness. The moment my gaze penetrates the glass, I become suspended too.

Everything inside the house appears transformed. The cherry-stained kitchen cabinets look warmer, richer; the shelves of mixing bowls, crocks and casseroles, the rows of spices and jars and bottles, are homier. Even the pine wall behind the stove, so utilitarian with hanging pots, glows with a new personality.

The clothes still weighing down my arms, I back up farther into the yard. From here I can see the living room. John's head is bent over a spelling book, his hair golden in the lamplight, his face set with a frown of concentration. Robert kneels by the sofa, pushing a wheeled Lego contraption along the cliff-edge of the cushion. The corner of a newspaper flaps into sight and disappears as Richard's invisible hands turn the pages. I can picture his absorbed face, studious-looking in new reading glasses.

Colored as they are with a rich topaz light, these ordinary scenes now seem imbued with vibrancy and charm, which flow not so much from the lamps as from the feelings of warmth and peace they inspire. For a split second I am a stranger peeking into a home I have never seen before.

I ask myself, what if I really became a stranger? What if I could never get back into these rooms? What if I could never again touch John's springy hair or see Robert's guileless smile?

Deep inside me, a door opens—that barrier we set up to guard our secret selves—and without conditions I let my family in. All the annoyances that families are prone to, all the kinks and stumbling blocks in our relationships, all the difficulties of living together in harmony become trivial—overwhelmed by the simple fact that we love one another.

Moments like this don't occur every day, and maybe that's the way it should be. It would be exhausting to live our lives weighed down by such intensity of feeling. But the memory sustains me, just as the smell of fresh air clings to the clothes in my arms. Tomorrow morning when I slip them on, my armor against the world, the lingering fragrance will remind me that they have danced in the darkness, under the pines, on the edge of a deep, golden light.

从外向里看

我一跨出后门，沉沉黑夜便将我淹没了。我去晾衣绳上收那些被遗忘衣服的途中，没有月光为我照路。好在那条熟悉的小路，我已经走过上千次了。

凭着记忆的引导，我迈上两级石板台阶，然后绕过那棵巨松，松枝悬垂在我们家的小屋上。

走过柴棚拐角，我伸出的手成了侦察员。我一边探寻晾衣绳，一边摸索衣夹。我的胳膊上很快便摆满了沾有夜露的衣裤。这些衣裤伴随着呼呼的风的旋律已经在那里整整舞动一天了。

返回的路途则比较容易。我一拐过柴棚，房子里的灯光便为我引路——硕大的、琥珀色的方形灯光悬在沉沉夜幕之中。在我的目光穿过玻璃窗的那一刻，我也一下子悬在了那里。

房子里的一切似乎都变了样：樱桃色的橱柜看上去越发温馨富丽；混放着碗、坛子和砂锅的隔板，几排香料瓶和瓶瓶罐罐看上去越发亲切舒适；甚至炉子后面的松板壁上悬挂的锅壶也是那样恰到好处，闪射出新的个性。

衣服仍搭在胳膊上，我站在院子里，又向后退了两步。从这里，我可以看见起居室，约翰的头正弯在识字书上，他的头发在灯光下金黄金黄的，只见他眉头紧皱、聚精会神。罗伯特跪在沙发边，沿着坐垫的最边沿推动一只带轮的拼装玩具。报纸角随着理查德那双看不见的手的翻动时隐时现。我可以想象出他拿着新买的阅读放大镜一脸沉思看报的认真劲儿。

在黄玉色的富丽光彩下，这些普普通通的场景现在好像充满了动感和魅力，这些动感和魅力不仅是从灯光中流溢而出的，而且是从灯光激发出的温馨与平和之感中流溢而出的。一时间，我变成了一个向某处从未问津的住宅窥探的陌生人。

我扪心自问：假如我真的成为陌生人会怎样呢？假如我再也不能返回这些房间会怎样呢？假如我再也不能抚摸约翰那富有弹性的头发，再也不能看到罗伯特天真无邪的笑容，又会怎样呢？

深入到自己的内心世界，一扇门洞然而开——打开了我们为了维护各自秘密而设置的障碍——随后，我无条件地让家人走了进来。一切烦心家事、相互间的是非恩怨和磕磕绊绊、和谐共处的所有困难，一下子都变得微不足道——都让位于一个简单的事实：我们相亲相爱。

像这样的时刻不是每天都会发生的，也许就该是这个样子。如果生活中常被这种强烈情感所压倒，那将令人筋疲力尽，但这种回忆会常常支撑着我，就像清新的空气紧紧地贴着我怀抱里的衣服一样。明天早晨当我穿上它们，抵御世界的盔甲时，上面的袅袅余香将会提醒我，它们曾在沉沉夜幕中、在巨松下、在深沉的金黄色灯光边翩翩舞动过。

Paradise of Happiness

A man was kind-hearted and ready to help others before his death, so after his death, he went up to heaven to be an angel. When he became an angel, he still often went down to the secular world to help people, hoping to savor the happiness.

One day he met a farmer, who was so worried, telling the angel, "My buffalo just died. If it doesn't help me plow, how can I work out in the field?" So the angel granted him a strong buffalo. The farmer was so pleased that the angel savored the happiness from him.

Another day he met a man, who was frustrated, telling the angel, "All my money was cheated, so I have no expense to return home." So the angel granted him money to be traveling expenses. The man was so happy that the angel savored the happiness from him.

Another day he met a poet, who was young, handsome, talented and rich and whose wife was beautiful and tender, but he lived unhappily.

The angel asked him, "Aren't you happy? Can I help you?" the angel told the poet. "I have everything, only lacking one thin. Can you give me?"

The angel answered, "Okay."

The poet looked at the angel and said, "What I want is happiness."

This baffled the angel. Thinking for a while, the angel said, "I see." Then he took away what the poet owned.

The angel took away the poet's talent, damaged his visage and divested his property and his wife's life.

After doing these, the angel left.

One month later, the angel returned to the poet, who was ragged and starved half to death, struggling on the ground.

So the angel gave back all he had and then left.

After half a month, the angel went to see the poet again.

This time, the poet hugged his wife and kept thanking the angel because he got the happiness.

幸福的天堂

一个人生前善良，热心助人，所以死后升上天堂，做了天使。他当了天使后，仍时常到凡间帮助人，希望感受到幸福的味道。

有一天，他遇见一个农夫，农夫的样子非常苦恼，他向天使诉说："我家的水牛刚死了，没它帮忙犁田，那我怎能下田作业呢？"于是，天使赐他一头健壮的水牛，农夫很高兴，天使在他身上感受到幸福的味道。

又一天，他遇见一个男人，男人非常沮丧，他向天使诉说："我的钱被骗光了，没盘缠回乡。"于是，天使给他银两做路费，男人很高兴，天使在他身上感受到了幸福的味道。

又过了一天，他遇见一个诗人，诗人年轻英俊、有才有钱，妻子漂亮温柔，但他却过得不快活。

天使问他："你不快乐吗？我能帮你吗？"

诗人对天使说："我什么都有，只欠一样东西，你能给我吗？"

天使回答："可以。"

诗人望着天使："我要的是幸福。"

这下子把天使难倒了，天使想了想，说："我明白了。"然后把诗人拥有的都拿走。

天使拿走诗人的才华，毁去他的容貌，夺去他的财产和他妻子的性命。

做完这些事后，天使便离去了。

一个月后，天使再回到诗人身边，他那时饿得半死，衣衫褴褛地躺在地上挣扎。

于是，天使把他的一切还给他，然后又离去了。

半个月后，天使再去看诗人。

这次，诗人搂着妻子，不住地向天使道谢，因为他得到了幸福。

A Pair of New Shoes

"Don't you just love my new shoes?"

Rebecca's eyes shine with delight as she places a pair of elegant high-heeled shoes in my lap. The shoes are impeccable in their simplicity, and nothing but my old knobby hands mar their sleek lines.

"Such fine leather! These are lovely."

"And only eighty-five dollars!"

"Heavens! I must be getting old, Rebecca. That seems a great deal of money for a pair of shoes."

"Oh, Nana, I knew you'd say that."

Rebecca's lustrous hair swings in a soft curl as she leans forward to touch my cheek with a kiss. Her perfume embodies the essence of spring and of youth. At twenty-three, she is the baby of the family.

"Now, don't fall asleep, Nana. Your party's about to begin," she whispers, and slips out of the room.

Sleep. It would be so easy to let my wrinkled eyelids droop and to fall asleep like a fat old cat in the sun. I blink several times to keep awake and turn my gaze to the dining room where a silver bowl of yellow roses graces the table in honor of my eighty-sixth birthday. The linen has been laid and soon I shall feel its crispness beneath my fingertips. The heavy silverware is in place and for a moment I wonder if my weak, old hands will handle it without embarrassing clatters on the delicate china. The comforting sound of voices and dinner preparations lulls me and I begin to caress the smooth, cool leather of Rebecca's new shoes, which lie in my lap. With each touch, I relax, I let go. With each touch I remember another pair of shoes so long ago. Was I only thirty-nine? Impossible! I can almost hear the voice that called to me as I stood in my garden on that scorching afternoon in that relentless summer of 1935.

"Missus, say, Missus!"

The husky voice startled me and I turned quickly. The man at the fence was young, hardly twenty, with blond hair tousled like a little boy's. His clothes were dusty and rumpled, and I eyed him warily. I often saw ragged, tired, solitary men pass by the house from the rail yards nearby, men off the freights, men moving about the country, looking for work. My Jack was out there somewhere, too.

"Missus, could I please have a drink of water?"

"Come into the yard," I called, and pointed to the enameled cup that hung over the outdoor tap. I had just filled three pails of water for my garden and had set them to warm in the sun. The tap still dripped.

He drank in great gulps, swallowing slowly, and then splashed water on his face and ran his hands over his dusty hair and along the back of his neck. "That feels good," he said, by way of thanks, and stood there, self-conscious and awkward, a sudden tenseness coming over him when he noticed the pails sitting in the sun.

"Have you any work I can do for you? Weed and water your garden?"

Some garden! The bean and tomato plants struggled to survive in ground that was hard and cracked, and the sparse patch of lawn was no better. What work could I offer him? The house required a coat of paint, but paint cost money, and I had none. I made a pretense of looking around, before shaking my head.

When he dropped to the grass and placed his head on folded arms, I felt his tiredness and despair. A sudden tightness caught at my throat. He could be my son, I thought. He looks as young as Alice. I knew he must be hungry. What could I give him? The icebox held so little: some milk, a knob of butter, and a few slices of bologna for Alice's supper.

"Come in out of the sun. Sit on the porch," I said, surprised at the frankness of my command. "I'll get you something to eat." Emotions had a way of getting mixed up these difficult days and I couldn't trust mine, just as I couldn't bear the shame-faced look of gratitude in his eyes. As I climbed the steps to the house, I became angry at myself, at my helplessness, at my empty cupboards, at the unrelenting drought, at the whole damned suffering country.

I sliced a loaf of bread with vicious swipes of the knife, jerked open the ice-box for milk, twisted the lid off a jar of home-made jam, as though my frenzied actions would wipe out the feeling of guilt at offering him so little. When I carried the food to the porch, I saw the boy near the garden, rinsing his shirt in one of the pails. I beckoned to him, left him my scanty offering, and returned indoors.

Despite the drawn blinds, the house had trapped the heat and had become an airless box of yellow light. My flowered print dress clung to me in wet patches. On each patch, the faded daisies dared to bloom. I dropped into an armchair and swung my swollen feet up on a hassock.

When the sharp slap of the screen door awakened me, I was startled.

"Mama, where are you?"

I struggled to my feet and found Alice sitting at the kitchen table, her head and shoulders bowed in dejection.

"Mama, Acme Stores are hiring next week." She raised her head and stared into my face. "The employment officer said girls would be hired only if they were properly dressed." Her brown eyes sought confirmation that I understood her statement. "That means stockings and a decent pair of shoes, Mama, and look at me!" She thrust out her feet in their dusty running shoes.

Instinctively, I glanced at the old felt slippers I wore. There were no shoes in the house that could meet Acme's standards, and there was no money to buy a new pair. My heart ached with the folly of having sent my young one to find work, and I stepped behind her chair to comfort her with a hug.

"Honey, we have a whole week to work on it." I kissed her soft hair, still warm from the sun. "Maybe something will come our way."

"That's what you always say, Mama. What's the use of hoping!"

It wasn't till I began to prepare our meager supper that I remembered the young man, and I went to the porch for my tray. Had I found him sitting at the old wicker table, as dejected as Alice, I suppose I would have kissed the top of his head, too, before sending him on his way. I sent him a silent wish, instead. Take care, young man.

All that week the sun continued to scorch the land. I watered my garden in the cool of the mornings, with each cupful willing the plants to grow and bear fruit. This morning ritual of mine became my morning prayer. As I stooped in the garden with my pitiful cups of water, I prayed for Jack and Alice to find work; I prayed for Jack's safety on the road; I prayed for the forlorn, beaten land, and for the young man who had come and gone and had asked for so little.

The week after his stop at my gate, I watered, as usual. A hot, fitful breeze sent sheets of torn and dirty newspapers scudding across the yard and into the caragana hedge. Trapped in the branches, the papers flapped and rustled like large alien birds.

As I crossed the yard to gather them up, a flash of white in the mailbox caught my eye. Jack, I thought immediately, and hurried to the box.

The envelope bore no stamp, no name, and no address, but contained a message penciled on a scrap of brown paper:

> *To the lady in the garden*:
> *I got a job at a warehouse after you fed me and let me rest.*
> *You helped me feel and look respectable. Now, let me help you.*

Folded within the paper were three one-dollar bills.

I stared at the money in my hand and saw again the young man with tousled hair and dusty shirt. My lips began to quiver, but this was not the time for crying. "Alice, honey, please hurry," I called, as I ran into the house. "You are going shopping for the best pair of shoes you can find. You will be the neatest girl in Acme's lineup tomorrow morning!"

"Mama, are you awake? Are you ready for your birthday dinner?"

I open my eyes and see I am surrounded by the people I love: gentle Alice, now gray and heavy; young Rebecca, vivacious and pretty, and all the others, old and young.

"You were telling yourself a story, weren't you, Mama?" Alice says, teasing. "It must have been a happy story, Mama. You had a smile on your face."

"It was a beautiful story."

As I struggle to my feet, Rebecca's new shoes slide off my lap and fall to the carpet with a soft thud.

一 双 新 鞋

　　"您不喜欢我的新鞋吗？"

　　丽贝卡将一双精美的高跟皮鞋放在我的膝上，目光闪闪喜形于色。那双鞋的确美观大方无可挑剔，只是我长满茧子的老手会破坏它们的光滑线条。

　　"多好的皮子！真是太美了。"

　　"而且才85块钱！"

　　"天哪！我一定是老了，丽贝卡。一双鞋竟要花那么多钱呀。"

　　"噢，奶奶，我就知道您会这样说。"

　　丽贝卡倾身向前吻我的脸颊时，光泽轻柔的卷发摇晃起来，香水透出春天和青春的气息。她23岁，是全家的宠儿。

　　"哎，别睡着了，奶奶。您的寿宴就要开始了。"她低声说着，悄悄溜出了房间。

睡觉吧。让我那有皱纹的眼皮垂下来，像太阳下的老肥猫那样倒头睡去，那太容易了。我连眨了几下眼，保持清醒，将目光转向餐室，那里庆贺我86岁生日的餐桌上点缀着一只插满黄玫瑰的银碗。台布已经铺好，我的手指尖触摸上去就会有一种爽适感。沉重的银餐具摆放得井然有序，我突然担心自己虚弱的老手会不会稳稳使用餐具，会不会磕碰那些精致的瓷器令人不快呢？听着人们说话和备餐的声音，我感到舒心，有点昏昏欲睡，开始抚摸放在我膝上的丽贝卡新鞋凉爽光滑的皮革。每摸一次，我就心情舒畅、轻松愉快。每摸一次，我就要想起很久以前的另一双鞋。那时我只有39岁吧？不可能！我仿佛又听到了对我喊叫的那个声音。那是1935年酷夏的一个赤日炎炎的下午，当时我正站在自己的菜园里。

"太太，嗨，太太！"

那沙哑的声音吓了我一跳，我迅速转过身来。篱笆边的那个人年纪轻轻，还不到20岁，金黄色的头发像小孩似的蓬松。他的衣服满是灰尘，皱皱巴巴。我警觉地注视着他。我时常看到衣衫褴褛、疲惫不堪、孤独无依的男人从附近的铁道车场过来，经过我们的门前——有从货车上下来的男人，有四处游荡、找活儿干的男人。我的杰克也这样出门在外，不知在什么地方。

"太太，能赏口水喝吗？"

"进院里来吧，"我大声说，伸手指向挂在门外水龙头上的搪瓷杯。我刚放满3桶水，放在太阳地晒着，准备用来浇园子。水龙头还在滴水。

他大口大口地喝着，但咽得很慢，随后将水洒在脸上，又抹湿了沾有尘土的头发和脖颈。"这样感到好多了，"他这样说，算是道谢，他站在那里，有点儿踌躇不安和尴尬的样子。他注意到放在太阳地的那些水桶时，神情突然紧张起来。

"您有什么活儿我可以给您干吗？给您的菜园锄草和浇水？"

这算是什么菜园啊！蚕豆和西红柿在板结和裂缝的土地上挣扎着勉强存活，稀疏的草地也是一样。我能为他提供什么呢？房子需要上漆，但油漆得花钱买，而我却没钱。我装模作样地向四周看了看，然后摇了摇头。

他两手抱头颓然倒在草地上，我感到他已经精疲力竭、心灰意懒。我的喉咙突然发紧。他可能会是我的儿子呢，我想。他看上去和艾丽丝一般年纪。我知道他一定是饿了。我能给他什么呢？冰箱里存的东西少得可怜：一点牛奶，一小块黄油，还有为艾丽丝晚饭准备的几片波洛尼亚香肠。

"离开太阳地，进来吧。坐在走廊上，"我说着，对自己突然发出的命令感到惊讶，"我给你拿点东西吃。"在那些困难的日子里，各种感情有时会混淆颠倒，我无法信赖自己的情绪，同样也无法忍受他眼神中流露出的羞怯的感激之情。我爬上台阶向房里走时，对自己怨恨起来，恨自己无能为力，恨我空空的橱柜，恨那无情的干旱，恨这整个多灾多难的国家。

我用刀狠狠切下一块面包，猛地打开冰箱取出牛奶，又拧掉一瓶自制果酱的盖子，似乎我的发狂似的行动可能抹去自己给他东西太少的负疚感。我拿着食物走到走廊时，那孩子正在菜园边的水桶里洗他的衬衣。我向他招手，将可怜巴巴的一点食品给他留下，就返回了屋里。

尽管拉上窗帘，屋里仍存着热气，成了一只充满黄光的闷箱。我的印花布衬衣紧贴在身上，湿一块干一块。每一块洇湿的地方，那褪色的雏菊花就显得好像盛开一样。我颓然坐进扶手椅，将虚肿的双脚翘放在一只垫子上。

正在这时，纱门的拍打声惊醒了我，我吓了一跳。

"妈妈，你在哪里？"

我挣扎着站起来，发现艾丽丝坐在厨房桌边，垂头缩肩，显得很沮丧。

"妈妈，艾克米商店下周要招人了。"她抬起头，直盯盯地望着我的脸，"雇主说只招衣着得体的女孩子。"她的褐色眼睛注视着我，看我是不是明白她的用意。"那就是说，得有长筒袜和一双体面的鞋子，妈妈，看看我！"她伸出穿着脏兮兮跑鞋的两只脚。

我本能地瞥了一眼自己脚上穿的旧绒拖鞋。家里没有符合艾克米商店标准的皮鞋，而且也没钱买一双新的。我一想到自己把孩子送出去找活干的愚蠢，心就痛起来。我走到她的椅子背后，抱住她，试图安慰她。

"宝贝，我们有一周的时间来想办法。"我吻了吻她柔软的头发，还带着阳光的热气，"我们也许会有好运气。"

"你总是这样说，妈妈，光希望有什么用呀？"

直到开始准备我们简单的晚饭时，我才想起那个年轻人，就走到廊下取我的托盘。倘若我发现他还坐在那张旧柳树桌旁，和艾丽丝一样沮丧，我想我也会吻他的头顶，把他送走的。可是，他已经走了，我只能默默地向他祝愿：一路保重，年轻人。

那个星期，太阳继续炙烤着大地。我趁着清晨凉快浇菜园，每浇一杯水都祝愿种的菜能生长结果。这种清晨的惯例成了我的晨祷。我端着可怜的一杯杯水弯腰浇菜时，祈祷杰克和艾丽丝能找到工作；我祈祷杰克一路平安；我为悲惨和贫乏的土地祈祷，也为那来了又走、要求得这样少的年轻人祈祷。

他在我家门前停留的一周后的一天，我仍像往常那样浇着菜园。一阵热风吹来，将几张脏烂的报纸刮过院子，刮进锦鸡草篱笆，卡在了枝杈间，纸片犹如奇异的大鸟般随风舞动。我穿过院子去捡报纸，这时信箱里一块白色东西引起了我的注意。是杰克的来信，我马上想道，急步向信箱奔去。

信封上没贴邮票，没写名字，也没有地址。不过，里边装着一张牛皮纸，上面用铅笔写道：

寄给菜园的太太：

　　您给我吃，让我休息，后来我在一家货栈找到了一份工作。

　　您帮了我，使我感到体面和显得体面。现在，让我来帮您吧。

折叠在纸里的是3张一元钱的钞票。

我望着手里的钱，仿佛又看到那个头发蓬乱、衬衫肮脏的年轻人。我的嘴唇开始颤抖，但眼下不是哭的时候。"艾丽丝，宝贝，你快来，"我跑进屋里大声叫道，"你去商店买一双你能找到的最漂亮的皮鞋。明天早上你将是艾克米商店里排队的最体面的姑娘！"

"妈妈，您醒了吗？准备参加您的生日宴了吗？"

我睁开眼睛，只见我的身边围着我所爱的人：温柔的艾丽丝，如今已经头发花白、体态发福；年轻的丽贝卡，活泼而美丽；还有老老少少好多人。

艾丽丝调侃道："您刚才在对自己说故事，对吗，妈妈？那想必是个快乐的故事吧，妈妈。您刚才脸上还在笑呢。"

"那是个美丽的故事。"

当我挣扎着站起来时，丽贝卡的新鞋从我的膝上滑落到地毯上，发出了轻柔的碰击声。

第六卷

春天的乐章

Butterfly in the Cloud

It was 1953, it was spring, and it was a great time to be a kid!

The boy and his friend had been thinking about all these things as they watched their kite soar gracefully above them in the sky over the large open field. The boy was ten and his friend was eleven, and although they were a grade apart in school, they were the best of buddies and did everything together.

It was getting late, and the two friends decided it was time to go.

The path out of the field went by an old apple tree, and for the past week or so they had been watching a large yellow caterpillar who had made his home on one of the branches. They didn't see the caterpillar today. Instead they noticed a large, grey, lifeless looking cocoon, and they wondered if their yellow friend had died. But it was getting very late, and the boy's friend said his stomach hurt, probably from hunger, so they didn't wonder about it too long, and continued their walk home.

The next morning the boy and his friend walked to school together as usual. They decided to start getting their bicycle-built-for-two back together. Neither of them had a great like, but when the rear wheel was removed from one, and the front fork of the other attached, it made a super fast and fun vehicle!

Noon came, and when the boy entered the cafeteria to find his friend, he was told that his friend had gotten sick.

The boy hurried home to see if his friend had returned from the hospital yet. When he was back at home, his grandmother told him that his friend had suffered an attack of acute appendicitis. By the time they got him to the hospital it was too late. He had died just a short while ago.

His best friend was gone.

There was no one to take him to the funeral, and so he decided to go to the field. He hadn't had much experience with death. He had seen dead squirrels and birds of course, but a person, that was different.

Why did things have to die?

Where did they go?

Why did his best friend have to leave him?

He walked slowly down the road to the field, carrying the kite. As he passed the apple tree he noticed the dull, grey cocoon was broken open. There was nothing inside, it was just a cold empty shell now, and there was no trace of the caterpillar.

There was a strong breeze, and the kite went up into the bright sky easily.

As he watched he thought about all the good times he and his friend had had. Times that they could never have again.

Never again!

The boy was very sad, but he didn't cry.

He stood and began to wind the kite string onto its holder.

He hadn't wound more than a half dozen turns when a beautiful yellow Swallowtail butterfly landed on the line no more than two feet from his hand.

The string went slack in his hands, and it seemed the butterfly was pulling on the line, trying to catch just one last gust of air under the kite. The line was taut in his hands again and the boy continued reeling it in. As he did, the Swallowtail let go his hold on the line and flew upwards, up past the kite and into the clear blue sky until it disappeared from the boy's sight.

Now the boy understood.

The caterpillar hadn't died. He had changed into something new and wonderful, leaving behind an empty shell.

The boy knew he would never see his friend again, not as he had been. But he knew his friend wasn't really gone. Instead, he too was off on a great new adventure, his spirit soaring among the clouds. And he knew that if he kept all the memories alive, the friendship and the good times, then his friend would never truly leave him.

His spirit would always be there.

云 间 风 蝶

那是1953年的春天，一个属于孩子的伟大春天！

男孩和他的伙伴站在辽阔的旷野上，目不转睛地望着在天空中优美飞翔的风筝。男孩10岁，他的伙伴11岁。尽管在学校相隔一个年级，但他们是最好的伙伴，干什么事都形影不离。

天色渐渐晚了，两个伙伴决定回家。

离开旷野的小路上有一棵老苹果树，一周以来，他们一直望着一条在树枝上安家的黄色大毛毛虫。今天，他们没有看到那只毛毛虫，只看到一只没有生命的灰色大茧。他们想着他们的黄色伙伴是不是已经死了。可是，天更黑了，男孩的伙伴说肚子疼，也许是因为饿，所以他们没有想太久，就继续向家走去。

第二天早上，男孩和伙伴照常一起去上学。他们决定一起组装一辆"双人自行车"。他们都没有这种了不起的自行车，但当他们其中一人把自己的自行车后轮卸下来，再把另一辆的前叉装上去时，就组装成了一辆速度特快、外观滑稽的自行车！

中午时分，男孩走进自助餐厅找小伙伴，有人说小伙伴病了。

男孩匆匆赶回家，看看他的伙伴是不是已经从医院回来了。回到家时，奶奶告诉他，他的伙伴得的是急性阑尾炎，送到医院时已经太晚了，没抢救回来。

他最好的伙伴就这么走了。

没有人带他去参加他的伙伴的葬礼，于是他决定独自到那片旷野去。男孩没有过太多与死有关的经历。当然，他见过死松鼠或死鸟。但是，这次是一个人，那不一样。

为什么好多东西都必须得死？

他们都去哪呀？

为什么他最好的伙伴要离开他？

他拿着风筝，慢慢走在通往旷野的路上。当他经过那棵苹果树时，他注意到原来那只暗灰色的茧已经破开，里面什么东西也没有，现在只是一个冰冷的空壳，没有毛毛虫的痕迹。

一股强风吹来，风筝顺利地飞上了明亮的天空。

男孩注视着风筝，追忆着他和伙伴在一起度过的所有美好时光——他们永远无法再拥有的时光。

永远不再！

男孩非常悲伤，但他没有哭。

他站在那里，开始把风筝线绕回线圈。

他刚绕了6圈，一只漂亮的黄色风蝶落在了离男孩的手不到半米的线上。

线在男孩的手中松弛下来，那只风蝶似乎在拉着线，试着捕捉风筝下的最后一阵风。线再次在他手里绷紧。男孩继续把线绕进线圈。这时，风蝶放开了风筝线，向上飞去，越过风筝，飞上了晴朗的蓝天，直到从男孩的视野里消失。

男孩幡然醒悟。

毛毛虫没有死，它已经变成了一个奇妙的新生命，留下了一个空壳。

男孩知道，他永远也无法像以前那样见到他的伙伴了。但是，男孩知道伙伴并没有真正离开。伙伴也要开始一段新的伟大旅程，他的灵魂会翱翔在云间。而且男孩知道，如果他能留住所有的记忆、昔日的友情和美好的时光，那么他的伙伴就永远不会真正离开。

伙伴的灵魂将永远长存。

The Girl Who Loved the Wind

Every year at about this time, when the air turns sharp, I think about my mother. She was always the first to point out the sign of autumn: the evening sky marbled with streaks of smoke; the sudden urgency of the sparrow's song; the pale, thinned-out morning light.

To mother, autumn was a great book that she'd make up a sea of stories. "You must remember," she would say, "that the leaves which die in the fall are born again in the spring."

Balance and counterbalance; harmony and disharmony; lose and renewal. These seemed to be the themes that ran through my mother's stories—and her life.

A memory: when I was seven, on the night of my mother's 40th birthday, she took me outside to stand beneath a moon so bright it lit up every corner of the garden. "Look through these," my mother said, handing me binoculars. "You see that reddish part? That's the Sea of Tranquility. And the blue shadow to the side? That's the Ocean of Storms." Then she said something about how in life it was necessary to learn to navigate both.

To be honest, I didn't see either the Sea or the Ocean. Staring through the binoculars at the moon, I saw only my mother's face swimming about me through pale stars in a dark blue sky.

I thought about this in the cool, hickory-scented evening air of my own garden. I watched the moon appear and disappear as it worked its way through the delicate tracery of trees outlined on the horizon.

Before I knew it, I was zipping into the past.

My mother loved the wind. And she would often recite this poem to me:

> Who has seen the wind?
> Neither you nor I,
> But when the trees bow down their heads,
> The wind is passing by.

She told me once about how when she was a little girl walking to church, the wind lifted her hat off her head and carried it to the bottom of a steep hill. It was her best hat, navy straw, and she was afraid she'd be scolded for losing it. So she climbed down through the underbrush. She retrieved the hat—along with an abandoned kitten that was to become her most beloved pet. She named Zephyr, she told me, because he was as light as a gentle breeze.

There's an old photograph of them in the family album. My mother, about ten years old, is holding the small gray cat which is struggling to jump out of her arms.

The wind is blowing a few loose strands of her long, dark hair across her eyes. This girl who loved the wind is smiling—perhaps at the feel of the breeze touching her face.

My mother told me that as a child she loved dogs but was not allowed to have one. So she invented a spotted, medium-size blood-hound named Morley. Every night before going to bed she would go to the back door and call him in.

Usually, at this point, my mother would begin acting out the story. I can picture it even now: my mother in a long nightgown, her black braid falling to her waist, standing at the door on a frosty night, called, "Morley, Morley. Here, Morley."

Finally, as I smiled at the child my mother was, I could think of her without deep feelings of sadness and loss. I could picture her, to the sound of bagpipe, practicing the Highland fling in front of a mirror.

And so I sat the other night on the floor of my room holding my mother's handbag. I had brought it home with me from the hospital on the day of her death, but had not been able to open it.

Inside, along with the lipstick, wallet and photos of her grandchildren, I found a folded piece of paper upon which my mother had written these lines from nature writer Wendel Berry:

"Always in the big woods when you step off alone into a new place there will be, along with curiosity and excitement, a little nagging of dread. It is the ancient fear of the unknown, your first bond with the wilderness you are going into."

Just the sort of thing Mother would say, who could still teach me after all these years.

I went downstairs and opened the kitchen door. And suddenly a breeze blew in. You've been six years out of the wind, I thought. Then I found myself saying, to no one in particular:

Who has seen the wind?
Neither you nor I,
But when the trees bow down their heads,
The wind is passing by.

爱风的女孩

每年天气转凉的时节，我就想起了母亲。母亲总是第一个指出秋天的迹象：晚空飘起的袅袅青烟；麻雀突然的惊叫；淡淡的、稀疏的晨光。

对母亲来说，秋天是一本大书，她常有讲不完的故事。她常说："你一定要记住，秋天坠落的树叶，春天还会重新萌芽。"

平衡与失衡、和谐与失调、丧失与获得，这些似乎永远是母亲的故事和她生活的主题。

记得我7岁那年，在母亲40岁生日那天夜里，她带着我走出门外站在月光下，只见月光皎洁，照亮了花园的每个角落。"你拿这个看看，"母亲将望远镜递给我说，"你看到那淡红色的部分了吗？那是宁静之海。你看到那蓝色的阴影了吗？那是风暴之洋。"之后，她又说，生活之中既有宁静也有风暴，我们有必要学会在两者之间航行。

说真心话，我没有看到什么宁静之海，也没有看到什么风暴之洋。我仅仅是透过望远镜望着月亮。在深蓝色的淡淡星空下，我仅仅看到母亲的脸在我眼前晃来晃去。

我站在凉风习习、弥漫着山胡桃气息的花园中回想着这幕情景。只见月亮穿过远处地平线上精美窗格一样的树林，时隐时现。

我的思绪飞扬，又回到了从前。

母亲爱风，她常常给我吟诵：

谁看到过风？
你没看到，我也没看到。
而当树枝晃动时，
风正在徐徐吹过。

有一次，母亲告诉我，小时候她上教堂时，风掀掉了她的帽子，将帽子刮到了一个陡峭的山坡下面。那是她最漂亮的帽子——一只深蓝色的草帽。她害怕自己回家挨骂，就爬下山穿过灌木丛，找到了草帽，还带回了一只被人遗弃的小猫。后来，这只小猫成了她最心爱的宠物。她给它起名叫"西风之神"，她告诉我，那只小猫轻飘飘，如柔风一般。

家里的相册中有一张她和小猫在一起的旧照片。当时，母亲才10岁左右，只见她搂着那只小猫，小猫却挣扎着想跳出她的怀抱。她的乌黑的长发随风拂动，飘洒在她的眼睛上面。这个爱风的女孩微微含笑——也许是感到轻风拂面，她才那样笑的吧。

母亲还对我说，小时候她很爱狗，但家里人不准她养。她日思夜想，好像真的养了一只中等个头的花警犬，她还给它起名叫"莫利"。每天夜里上床睡觉之前，她都要走到后门口叫它进来。

每当此时，母亲总是活灵活现地向我表演一番。甚至现在我还能想象出当时的情景：只见母亲穿着长长的睡袍，梳着垂至腰间的乌黑辫子，在霜花满地的夜色中站在门口叫道："莫利，莫利，过来，莫利。"

最后，我对着童年时的母亲笑了。我回忆起母亲，但没有深深的悲伤和惆怅。我仿佛看到母亲伴着风笛之声，在镜子前面跳起了热情奔放的苏格兰高地舞。

随后，我坐在自己房间的地板上，抱着母亲的手提包，这是我在母亲去世那天从医院带回家的，但我一直没有打开。

与唇膏、钱夹和外孙们的照片放在一起的是一张折叠着的纸，上面是她抄录的自然作家温德尔·贝利的文章片段：

"一味生活在茫茫丛林，一旦走出来，进入一个新天地，你就会有点好奇、兴奋，甚至还会有点恐惧——这是你对未知世界的古老恐惧，也就是你和即将进入的荒原的第一次联系。"

这和母亲所说的话如出一辙。正因为如此，我受益了这么多年。

我走下楼，打开厨房门，一阵轻风翩然入内。你已经和风隔绝了6年了啊，我暗自想道。同时，我发现自己在默默自语：

谁看到过风？
你没看到，我也没看到。
而当树枝晃动时，
风正在徐徐吹过。

The Crystal Spring

Up earlier than usual. The air is calling. Spring air is different from winter air. Tree branches are serrated with red bud teeth. Later, they grow chartreuse fuzz, making pale green auras in the sun. Summer leaves will be dark, shading, but spring leaves let the light through. Spring trees glow in the daytime, spreading translucent canopies.

The birds are out, racketing their news from bush to branch. Cats are still curled up on fire escapes. They are in no hurry to get up in the cool morning air and they know it will warm up later. They are watching the birds. They can wait.

The air is clear, clean cool. The smells are tiny smells, little whiffs of green, a ribbon of brown mud, the blue smell of the sky. Midday is mild enough for short sleeves. I eat my lunch outsider, sitting on a warm brick wall. The breeze lifts my hair and riffles the edge of my skirt. I have to squint. Everything tastes better.

Until today I had been too huddled in my winter coat to notice the quiet coming of flowers. Suddenly, daffodils smile in my face, parrot tulips wave their beaky petals, and fragrant white blossoms are pinned to dogwood trees like bows in a young girl's hair.

The evening is soft. I need my thin jacket. It's still light out when I walk home from the Metro. I could walk for hours. Like a kid playing street games with her friends, I don't want to go in.

When I went to work this morning, I left my windows open. Spring came in through the screens while I was gone. It's as if I had used a big sliver key and rolled back the roof like a lid on a sardine can. The indoors smell like the outdoors. It will be like lying down in the grass to sleep. The sheets are cool. The quilt is warm. The light fades outside my windows.

透明的春天

我比往常起得都早。空气在呼唤我，春天的空气和冬天的空气就是不一样。树枝上长满了锯齿状的红红的嫩芽，后来长出了绒绒的黄绿色的叶子，在阳光下映出淡绿色的光环。夏天的树叶色调阴沉发暗，春天的树叶则晶莹透亮。树木在春日下闪闪发光，张开了半透明的天篷。

小鸟纷纷飞出来，在矮树丛和枝丫间叽叽喳喳传递着消息。猫仍然蜷缩在防火梯上，它们在凉爽的空气中并不急着，它们知道过一会儿天就会暖和起来。它们目不转睛地看着那些小鸟。它们能等得起。

空气清新、洁净、凉爽。空气中有淡淡的气味，有阵阵青绿的气味，有一股泥土的味道，还有天空的蔚蓝气味。中午温煦，足以穿短袖。我坐在一堵暖暖的砖墙上吃午饭。微风掀起我的头发，拂动我的裙边，我得眯起眼睛看，现在吃什么都比较可口。

我直到今天都裹着冬装，没有注意到春花在悄悄来临。突然，水仙花向我迎面微笑，鹦鹉郁金香晃动着鸟嘴状花瓣，朵朵雪白的香花点缀在山茱萸树间，宛如少女头发上系的蝴蝶结。

夜色温柔，我需要穿上薄夹克。我从地铁出来步行回家，外面的天光还亮，我可以走上好几个小时。我像小孩子在街上和伙伴玩游戏那样，不想进屋。

今天早上去上班时，我让窗户都开着。我不在家时，春天穿过纱窗走了进来。它就像是我用一把大大的银钥匙打开沙丁鱼罐头盖那样打开了房顶，现在屋里散发着屋外的气味。睡觉就会像躺在草地上一样，床单凉爽，被子温暖，窗外的光渐渐淡去。

A Haven of Sunflowers

I grew up, like any well-trained child on the South Dakota prairie, knowing sunflowers were my natural enemies because they were not allowed in the garden. Hoeing these weeds, under my parents' watchful eyes, stood between me and a long horseback ride on the prairie, where I could explore every pile of rocks and wade in every trickle of cool water.

Any tiny sunflowers I missed would grow like Jack's beanstalk; by the next day, it seemed, they would reach my knees. The thick, tough stems couldn't be chopped by the hoe. They had to be pulled, one by one. Leave them a few weeks, and their hold on the earth was greater than my strength.

After I got married, however, I came to change my views on sunflowers. When my husband, George, and I built our home, construction bared the earth around it. As we planted native grass and pulled weeds, we left the sunflowers because they were a vivid green against the brown earth.

They grew tall, blossomed and began to attract goldfinches by the dozens. From our windows we watched the birds hang upside down, just visible among the golden blooms, digging seeds out of each brown head.

In the evening, George and I would sit on the deck as sunset dropped over the ranch, coyotes hunting the valley below, bats swooping for insects around the eaves. Sometimes we'd watch quietly for more than an hour, holding hands.

I'd see my husband's face as the sun made it glow with golden light, then hid it in shadow. His eyes narrowed as if he were looking far off into the mountains. Now I think he was looking into a much greater distance.

It was in April, seven years after we built the house, that doctors found a rare tumor growing near George's spine. Months of surgery, struggle and pain followed. He died early in the morning of September 7, at the age of 42. Two days later, we gathered on a bare hillside at sunset for the funeral. We covered his casket with wildflowers and found a granite slab in the Black Hills for a headstone.

I had known from the day we buried George that growing flowers there would be difficult. The layer of fertile soil is only an inch or two deep, and by midsummer the brown dust rolls up where bare ground meets sun and wind. Walking through the fields, I collected native plants and wildflowers to cover the grave.

One afternoon I sat down, my arm across the shoulder of the headstone, and watched the sun drop behind the Black Hills. That may have been the day I first noticed the sunflowers.

I cut or pulled some of them, but most remained. Their leaves were a deep green; one flower grew in the precise center of the grave. Some evenings I was surprised, after the day's heat, to find damp patches of earth where the huge sunflower leaves provided shade. One day I even saw two tiny frogs hopping about.

Whenever I passed the cemetery on the way to town, I'd look for the grave. I could always pick it out, even from a half-mile away. It was framed in the deep green, stunning the dusty brown countryside. In the precise center stood "my" sunflower, nearly eight feet tall, covered with yellow blooms that swayed in the slightest breeze. I smiled each time I drove by, seeing it as a sign of hope.

As the weeks passed, my visits to George's grave became the best part of my day, just as our evenings together on the deck had once been. But one day in early fall, as I turned toward the cemetery from the highway, I realized something was missing. It wasn't until I had parked and turned off the ignition that it hit me: the sunflower was gone. All the sunflowers were gone.

I got out of the car and walked closer. A power mower had cut the plants back to short, bare stalks. Footprints, kneeprints and jagged holes showed where someone had uprooted the sunflowers' tough stems. I wept.

The caretaker probably thought I was an elderly widow, too weak to pull the sunflowers—and too dumb to pull them while they were small. Surely he didn't mean to cause the pain in my heart.

It is March now. Each warm day I haul another block of stone to the cemetery. Slowly, week by week, I am laying down a low wall.

Inside it I will plant wild sunflowers. Then, stone and sunflower shade will protect ordinary prairie plants. And the weeds will cheerfully renew themselves—and give me strength to go on.

太阳花的避风港

我像南达科塔州大草原所有训练有素的孩子那样长大成人，知道太阳花是我们的天敌，因为人们不允许它们长在菜园里。父母亲站在我和大草原的长马道之间，监视着我锄掉这些太阳花，我在那里可以探测每一堆岩石、迈进每一涓凉爽的水里。

我漏掉的任何小小的太阳花都会像杰克家的豆秆一样成长。到第二天，它们好像会长到我的膝盖那样高。那粗壮的杆用锄是锄不掉的，我不得不把它们一个个拔掉。留它们几周，它们就会紧紧地扎在地里，力量比我的还要大。

然而，结婚后，我终于改变了对太阳花的看法。当我和丈夫乔治建立起我们自己的家时，建筑四周露出了地面。栽种当地的草拔起杂草时，我们留下了那些太阳花，因为在褐色土的陪衬下，它们呈现出生机勃勃的绿色。

它们长高，绽开花蕾，开始吸引成群成群的黄雀。我们从窗户看到那些小鸟倒挂金钟，在金黄色的花中清晰可见，从每个褐色花穗中掏着籽吃。

　　傍晚，夕阳的余晖洒在我们的牧场上，我和乔治常常坐在露天平台上，郊狼在下面的山谷寻猎，蝙蝠在屋檐四周寻找着虫子。有时，我们紧紧地拉着手，常常静望一个多小时。

　　我看到太阳的金光照亮丈夫的脸，随后又将他的脸藏在了阴影里。他的眼睛眯成了细缝，好像在眺望着远处的山脉。现在我想他当时看得要远得多。

　　时值4月，在我们建房7年后，医生们在乔治的脊椎边发现了一块罕见的肿瘤。接下来是几个月的治疗、挣扎和痛苦。他9月7日凌晨去世，享年42岁。两天后，夕阳西下时，我们聚集在一个光秃秃的山坡边为他举行葬礼。我们在他的棺木上摆满了野花，在黑山里找到了一块花岗岩板作为墓碑石。

　　从埋葬乔治那天起，我就知道在那里种花很难。肥土层只有一两英寸深，而且到仲夏时，褐色土就会卷起，裸露的地面就会遭受风吹日晒。穿过田地，我采撷当地的花草盖在坟墓上。

　　一天下午，我坐下来，手臂搭在墓碑肩上，望着太阳落在了黑山后面。也许就是那天我才第一次注意到太阳花。

　　我把它们割掉或拔掉了些，但大多数还都在那里。它们的叶子呈深绿色；坟墓正中央长着一朵花。好几天傍晚，我都感到吃惊，热了一天后，竟发现了湿土，那里硕大的太阳花叶子提供了庇荫。有一天，我甚至看到两只小青蛙在四周跳动。

　　在去镇子的路上，无论什么时候经过墓地，我都要寻找乔治的坟墓。我总是能一眼认出来，甚至从半里远就能认出来。它耸立在深绿色的氛围中，使灰尘满面的褐色乡下亮丽了起来。墓地正中央耸立着"我的"太阳花，差不多有两米高，覆盖着黄花，在微风中摇晃着。每次开车路过，我都要面带微笑，将它看成希望的象征。

　　几个星期过去了，拜谒乔治的墓地成了我一天中最美好的时光，就像先前我们傍晚一块坐在露天平台上那样。但是，初秋的一天，从公路转向墓地时，我意识到什么东西不见了。直到我停下车，关掉发动机，才想起：那朵太阳花不见了。所有的太阳花都不见了。

　　我从车里钻出来，向墓地走近了些。一个动力割草机已经将太阳花割成了又短又秃的秆。脚印、膝盖印和参差不齐的窟窿表明，有人已经将太阳花的粗茎连根拔起。我失声哭了起来。

　　关照太阳花的人也许认为我是一个上了年纪的寡妇，虚弱不堪拔不掉那些太阳花——而且在它们太小时麻痹大意没去拔它们。他肯定不是想惹我伤心的。

现在是3月份。每到天气暖和的时候，我就拖一块石头堆到墓地边。慢慢地，周复一周，我在那里垒起了一堵矮墙。

我在里边种上了野太阳花。随后，石头和太阳花庇荫就会保护普通的草原植物，而且那些杂草会欢天喜地获得重生，并给我前进的力量。

The Creek in My Childhood

The creek in my childhood wound between Grandfather's apricot orchard and a neighbor's hillside pasture. Its banks were shaded by cottonwoods and redwood trees and thick tangle of blackberries and wild grapevines. On hot summer days the quiet water flowed clear and cool over gravel bars where I fished for trout.

Nothing historic ever happens in these recollected creeks. But their persistence in memory suggests that creeks are bigger than they seem, more a part of our hearts and minds than mighty rivers.

Creek time is measured in the lives of strange creatures, in sandflecked caddis worms under the rocks, sudden gossamer clouds of mayflies in the afternoon, or minnows darting like slivers of inspiration into the dimness of creek fate. Mysteries float in creeks' riffles, crawl over their pebbled bottoms and slink under the roots of trees.

While rivers are heavy with sophistication and sediment, creeks are clear, innocent, boisterous, full of dream and promise. A child can wade across them without a parent's cautions. You can go to it alone, jig for crayfish, swing from ropes along the bank. Creeks belong to childhood, drawing you into the wider world, teaching you the curve of the earth.

Above all, a creek offers the mind a chance to penetrate the alien universe of water, of tadpoles and trout. What drifts in creek water is the possibility of other worlds inside and above our own. Poet Robert Frost wrote: "It flows between us, over us, and with us. And it is time, strength, tone, light, life, and love."

Creeks lead one on, like perfume on the wind. A creek is something that disappears around a bend, into the ground, into the next dimension. To follow a creek is to seek new acquaintance with life.

I still find myself following creeks. In high mountain meadows I'll trace their course into the lime green grass and deep glacial duff, marveling at the sparkle of quartz and mica. The pursuit liquefies my citified haste and lifts weight from my shoulders. Once, in the California desert, as hummingbirds darted from cactus blossoms, I heard the babble of rushing water. My ears led me over dusty hillsides and down scabrous ravines to an unexpected ribbon of clear, cold water, leaping from rock to rock, filling little pools. The discovery seemed Biblical. It filled me with joy.

My boyhood creek long ago fell victim to ground—water pumping, subdivision and channelization into San Francisco bay. Not a single one is left without at least some stretch straightened and enclosed in concrete. With the creeks went the intimacies of the valley, the song of thrushes, the cool shade of cottonwoods, inspiration.

But I keep yet another vision of creeks as consolation. In it, the water flows through a small alpine meadow in the sierra Nevada. It is summer, and the late afternoon sun lines the golden haze with long, blue forest shadows. My six-year-old son's blond hair catches the light as he stretches a fishing rod over the creek. The water fairly boils with leaping rainbow trout. They dart impulsively, trying to draw him into their world just as he tries to lure them to his. When one finally becomes snagged, the boy dances triumphantly, the silvery fish wriggling on his upheld leader. In that vision it is clear who has been caught.

童年的小溪

我童年的小溪在祖父的杏园和邻居的山坡草地之间蜿蜒流淌。两岸的三叶杨和红杉树遮天蔽日，黑草莓苗和野葡萄藤盘根错节、密不透风。在赤日炎炎的夏天，清凉的溪水静静地流过我钓鳟鱼的小沙堆。

记忆中的小溪里从来没有发生过有历史意义的大事。但是，能留在记忆里，表明小溪比它们看上去的更大，相比大江大河，更是我们心灵的一部分。

小溪是以奇特动物——岩石下带着斑斑沙粒的石蚕虫，午后如浮云般突然飘来的蜉蝣，或者是像点点灵感飞蹿进命运小溪的米诺鱼的生命来计算的。小溪里每个涟漪都浮动着神奇的浪花，爬过鹅卵石水底，潜行在树根下。

大江大河充满了世故和沉积，显得那样沉重，而小溪则清澈、纯真、活泼，充满梦想和希望。一个孩子没有父母的告诫，就可以涉过小溪。你也可以独自一人去小溪玩耍，在水中蹦来跳去捉小龙虾，在岸边拴上绳子荡秋千。小溪属于童年，将你引向更广阔的世界，教会你大地是怎样的曲曲弯弯。

最重要的是，小溪给心灵提供了洞察蝌蚪和鳟鱼的奇特的水中世界的机会。在溪水中漂流的可能是另外的世界，既在我们的世界之中，又在我们的世界之外。诗人罗伯特·弗罗斯特曾写道："它流在我们中间，流在我们之外，跟我们一路同行。它就是时间、力量、音调、光明、生命和爱。"

小溪就像迎风飘来的芳香引人前行。小溪会在拐弯处消失，钻进土里，钻进另一个空间。追随小溪就是寻求新的生活体验。

我现在仍然去追寻小溪。在高山的草原上，我循着它的足迹走进暗黄绿色的草丛中和冰冷的枯叶深处，总会对闪亮的云母和石英惊叹不已。这种追寻溶化了我都市生活的匆忙，卸去了我肩上的重负。有一次，在加州的沙漠中，当蜂鸟从仙人掌花间飞出时，我听到了潺潺的流水声。我循声穿过土山坡，走下陡峭的峡谷，想不到眼前竟是一条清冷的小溪，它跃过一块又一块岩石，注入了一个个小小的池中。这个发现好像是上帝的安排，这使我充满了快乐。

我少年时代的小溪早已被用来抽取地下水、分流和建造水渠，把水引入旧金山湾。如今，没有一条小溪不是用混凝土围起来，并加上了笔直的出口的。小溪已经不在，随之而去的是山谷的亲昵、画眉的鸣唱、三叶杨的荫凉，以及灵气。

但是，我一直将小溪的另一种景象作为安慰。在这景象中，有一条小溪流过内华达山脉上一个小小的高山草原。时值夏天，夕阳带着长长的蓝色林影，洒下金色的余晖。6岁的儿子将鱼竿伸在小溪之上，他的金黄色的头发波光闪闪。欢蹦乱跳的虹鳟鱼飞溅起朵朵浪花，它们冲动地蹦动，试图将他吸引到它们的世界中去，就像他试图将它们引诱到他的世界中一样。当有一条终于咬钩时，银亮的鱼在举起的鱼线上扭动着，儿子十分得意，手舞足蹈。在那种景象中，谁已被捉住，显而易见。

Moongazing

There is a hill near my house that I often climb at night. The noise of the city is a far-off murmur. In the hush of the dark I share the cheerfulness of crickets and confidence of owls. But it is the drama of the moonrise that I come to see. For that restores in me a quiet and clarity that the city spends too freely.

From this hill I have watched many moons rise. Each one has its own mood. There have been broad, confident harvest moons in autumn; shy, misty moons in spring; lonely, white winter moons rising into the utter silence of an ink-black sky and smoke-smudged orange moons over the dry fields of summer. Each, like fine music, excited my heart and then calmed my soul.

Moongazing is an ancient art. To prehistoric hunters the moon overhead was as unerring as heartbeat. They knew that every 29 days it became full-bellied and brilliant, then sickened and died, and then was reborn. They knew the waxing moon appeared larger and higher overhead after each succeeding sunset. They knew the waning moon rose later each night until it vanished in the sunrise. To have understood the moon's patterns from experience must have been a profound thing.

But we, who live indoors, have lost contact with the moon. The glare of streetlights and the dust of pollution veil the night sky. Though men have walked on the moon, it grows less familiar. Few of us can say what time the moon will rise tonight.

Still, it tugs at our minds. If we unexpectedly encounter the full moon, huge and yellow over the horizon, we are helpless to stare back at its commanding presence. And the moon has gifts to bestow upon those who watch.

I learned about its gifts one July evening in the mountains. My car had mysteriously stalled, and I was stranded and alone. The sun had set, and I was watching what seemed to be the bright-orange glow of a forest fire beyond a ridge to the east. Suddenly, the ridge itself seemed to burst into flame. Then, the rising moon, huge and red and grotesquely misshapen by the dust and sweat of the summer atmosphere loomed up out of the woods.

But as the moon lifted off the ridge it gathered firmness and authority. Its complexion changed from red to orange, to gold, to impassive yellow. It seemed to draw light out of the darkening earth, for as it rose, the hills and valleys below grew dimmer. By the time the moon stood clear of the horizon, full-chested and round and the color of ivory, the valleys were deep in shadows in the landscape. The dogs, reassured that this was the familiar moon, stopped barking. And all at once I felt a confidence and joy close to laughter.

The drama took an hour. Moonrise is slow and serried with subtleties. To watch it, we must slip into an older, more patient sense of time. To watch the moon move inexorably higher is to find an unusual stillness within ourselves. Our imaginations become aware of the vast distances of space, the immensity of the earth and the huge improbability of our own existence.

Moonlight shows us none of life's harder edges. Hillsides seem silken and silvery, the oceans still and blue in its light. In moonlight we become less calculating, more drawn to our feelings.

On that July night. I watched the moon for an hour or two, and then got back into the car, turned the key in the ignition and heard the engine start, just as mysteriously as it had stalled a few hours earlier. I drove down the mountains with the moon on my shoulder and peace in my heart.

I return often to the rising moon, especially in the fall. Then I go to my hill and await the hunter's moon, enormous and gold over the horizon, filling the night with vision.

An owl swoops from the ridge top, noiseless but bright as flame. A cricket shrills in the grass. I think of Beethoven's "Moonlight Sonata" and of Shakespeare, whose Lorenzo declaims in The Merchant of Venice, "How sweet the moonlight sleeps upon this bank! Here will we sit and let the sounds of music creep in our ears." I wonder if their verse and music, like the music of crickets, are the voices of the moon. With such thoughts, my citified confusions melt into the quiet of the night.

望　月

我家附近有一座小山，夜里我常爬上山去。这时，城市的喧闹成了一种遥远的低语。在黑暗的静谧中，我可以分享蛐蛐的快乐，感受猫头鹰的自信。我上山是来看月出的情景，因为这可以让我重新得到在城市中浪掷的闲适与明净。

我已经从这座小山上看过许多次月出。每一次月出各有千秋。秋天，月亮丰满自信；春天，月色朦胧，羞羞答答；冬天，月亮孤寂苍白，升起在漆黑寂静的夜空中；夏天，烟熏一样的橙月俯望着干燥的田野。每一种月景，犹如美妙的音乐，使我心潮澎湃，随后我的灵魂渐渐平静下来。

望月是一种古老的艺术。在远古的猎人看来，头顶的月亮像心跳一样准确无误。他们知道，月亮每29天都要变得饱满璀璨，然后黯淡、消逝，之后又起死回生；他们知道，月盈期间，每经一次日落，头顶的月亮就会显得更大更高；他们知道亏月每天夜里都要迟迟升起，直到日出才消失。他们从经验中悟到月盈月亏，造诣一定很深。

但是，生活在室内的我们已经与月亮失去了联系。炫目的街灯和污浊的烟尘遮蔽了夜空。虽然人类已在月亮上行走过，但我们对月亮却越发生疏。我们中能说出今晚月亮几时升起的寥寥无几。

然而，月亮仍然牵动着我们的心灵。如果偶然碰到一轮又黄又大的满月升起在地平线上，我们都会禁不住回望它居高临下的身影。而月亮也会向观看它的人馈赠礼物。

我领略它的馈赠是在山中7月的一个夜晚。车子莫名其妙地熄了火，我被困在了山中，孤零零的。太阳已经坠落，我望着东边山脊外露出一团鲜橙色的林火似的亮光。突然，山脊本身似乎也燃起了火焰。紧接着，那轮升月，大大的、红红的，从林中奇异地隐隐出现，夏天空气中的尘埃与湿气使它变得奇形怪状、面目全非。

但是，月亮升离山岭时，聚集了坚定与威严。它的面色也由红变成了橘红，又变成了金色，最后是静止的明黄色。它似乎从渐暗的大地中吸走了光明，随着它的升起，下面的丘陵山谷越发黯淡。待到皓月当空，丰盈圆润，闪耀着象牙般乳白的清辉，山谷便成了风景中一片片幽深的阴影。那些狗知道这团光原是熟悉的月亮，便放下心来，停止了吠叫。我突然感到有了信心，开心得快要笑起来。

这种景象持续了一个小时。月出缓慢，充满了微妙。观看月出，我们必须进入过去那种对时间的耐心。观月不动声色地升空会让我们找到内心异常的宁静。我们的想象力渐渐意识到宇宙的辽阔和大地的博大，让我们忘掉自己的存在。

月光给我们展现没有棱角的生活。山坡仿佛丝绸般银亮；大海在月光中静谧碧蓝；我们在月光下不再精于算计，而是沉醉于自然的情感中。

在那个7月之夜，我望月一两个小时之后，回到车中，转动钥匙点火，听到引擎启动，就像几个小时前熄火那样神秘。我驱车沿着山路回家，肩披明月，心灵宁静。

后来，我常回到山上观月，尤其是在秋天。这时，我来到那座小山，等候猎人的月亮，硕大金黄，升起在地平线上，为黑夜带来光明。

一只猫头鹰从山岭顶上飞扑下来，无声无息，亮如火焰。一只蛐蛐在草丛内尖鸣。我想起了贝多芬的《月光奏鸣曲》，以及莎士比亚的《威尼斯商人》中洛伦佐的诵读："月光沉睡在这岸边多么甜美！我们要坐在这里，让音乐之声潜入我们的耳内。"我不知道他们的诗句和乐曲是否像蛐蛐的歌声都是月语。想到这些，我那被闹市扰乱的心也融化在静夜之中。

The Old Man and the Durian Tree

An old man was over 80 years old. He was planting a durian tree when he was observed by a neighbor.

The neighbor asked the old man, "Do you expect to eat durian from that tree? You see, the durian tree takes about 8 to 10 years to bear fruit."

The old man rested on his spade and said with a smile, "No, at my age I know I won't. All my life I have been enjoying durians but never from a tree I have planted before. I wouldn't have had durians if other people have not done what I am doing now. I am just trying to pay other people who planted durians for me." No wonder he was so happy.

We should be givers first and getters second in everything we do. We will not only get what we want but will actually be really happy in the end because we need to sow first before we can reap.

老人和榴莲树

一位老人已经80多岁了，邻居注意到他正在种一棵榴莲树。

邻居问这位老人："你想吃到那棵树上结的榴莲果吗？你明白吗？榴莲树要等8到10年才结果。"

老人拄着铁锹，微笑着说："不，我知道我这种年纪是吃不上了。我这辈子一直在享用榴莲，但从来没有一个是我以前种的树上结的果子。如果别人没有做过我现在正在做的事儿，我就不会有榴莲。我只是在尽力偿还那些为我种榴莲的人。"难怪他如此开心。

无论做任何事情，我们都应该先舍再得。这样，我们不仅能得到我们想要的，而且最终会真正幸福，因为我们需要先播种，然后才能收获。

Plant Yourself a Trouble Tree

The carpenter I hired to help me restore an old farm house had just finished a rough first day on the job. A flat tire had caused him to miss an hour of work, his electric saw didn't work, and now his ancient truck refused to start.

As I drove him home, he sat in stony silence. When we arrived he invited me in to meet his family. As we walked to the front door, he paused briefly at a small tree, touching the tips of the branches with both hands. When opening the door he underwent an amazing transformation. His tanned face was wreathed in smiles; he hugged his two small children and gave his wife a kiss.

Afterward he walked me to the car. We passed by the tree and my curiosity got the better of me. I asked him about what I had seen him do earlier.

"Oh, that's my trouble tree," he replied. "I know I can't help having troubles on the job, but one thing's for sure, they don't belong to the house with my wife and children. So, I just hang them on the tree when I come home in the evening and then I just pick them up again in the morning."

"Funny thing, though," he smiled, "when I come out in the morning to pick them up, there isn't nearly as many as I remembered hanging there the night before."

为自己种一棵烦恼树

我雇用帮我修复旧农舍的木匠刚刚结束了第一天不愉快的工作。车胎漏气让他误了一小时的工，电锯也不转，这会儿他那辆老式货车也拒绝启动。

我驱车载他回家，他板着脸静静地坐着。我们到达时，他邀请我见见他的家人。我们走到前门，他在一棵小树前稍停了一下，用双手碰了碰枝条梢部。一打开门，他陡然一变，令人惊异。他那晒成褐色的脸堆满笑容，他拥抱了两个小孩，又给了妻子一个吻。

之后，他步行送我上车。我们经过那棵树时，我的好奇心占了上风。我问他有关我看到的他先前的做法。

"噢，那是我的烦恼树，"他回答，"我清楚工作上我总会有烦恼，但有一件事是肯定的，烦恼不属于有太太和孩子的这个家。于是，晚上到家时，我就把它们挂在这棵树上，清晨再把它们带走。"

"然而，奇怪的是，"他笑着说，"清晨我出来摘走它们时，烦恼就远不如前一天晚上我记得挂在那里的那么多了。"

Patience Is a Virtue

Last fall I hang outside my window a bird feeder. Now not knowing the first thing about wild birds, I assumed that as soon as I hung this bird feeder outside, a multitude of beautiful birds would be swooping to my new addition. Days, weeks and months went by, no birds!

I asked so many people what to do. What was I doing wrong? "Nothing" most of them replied. "Just wait." So I waited and waited and waited, trying everything possible to attract these birds.

I cleared off the deck, I changed the feed, I washed the feeders, and I even made the cat go out the other door! But nothing seemed to work. So I went on waiting with patience and hope.

Two months later, on a Saturday afternoon, I froze! On the bird feeder had appeared the most beautiful bird I have ever seen in my life! All of a sudden, hundreds upon hundreds of birds were appearing from everywhere.

What a beautiful lesson I learned from this little creature. Patience and hope and things will attract the beautiful things in life. I never realized how much patience I really do have and how much I do rely upon hope to sort out the questions in my heart.

So I keep on hoping and waiting, waiting and hoping. I will try to use this little lesson with so many other things in my life. I guess patience is a virtue after all.

耐心是一种美德

去年秋天，我在我家窗外悬挂了一个喂鸟器。不光是野鸟，我猜过不了多久，一大群美丽的小鸟就会聚在我家窗前争相竞食。可是，数天、数周，甚至数月过去了，一只鸟都没有飞来。

我咨询了很多人，我究竟哪一步做错了？"没错啊！"大多数人都这样回答。"耐心再等等吧！"因此，我等啊等，试尽了各种可能的办法来吸引鸟群。

我清扫了甲板，更换了食料，洗刷了喂鸟器，甚至把我的爱猫都赶到了另一间房里！但好像根本没用。因此，我只得继续耐着性子、心存希望地等下去。

两个月后，一个周六的下午，我被眼前的景象惊呆了！喂鸟器上立着一只我这辈子从未见过的漂亮的小鸟！突然间，成百上千的鸟群从各个角落飞了出来。

我从这种小动物身上学到了宝贵的一课：一生中，耐心、希望和物质总能吸引最美好的事物。我以前从未意识到自己究竟有多大耐心，还有对待任何事有多大希望能厘清心中的疑团。

因此，我继续心存希望、等待，等待、希望。我会让这堂小课改变自己人生中诸多其他事情和看法。归根结底，我想耐心是一种美德。

Two Pebbles

Many years ago in a small Indian village, a farmer had the misfortune of owing a large sum of money to a village moneylender. The moneylender, old and ugly, fancied the farmer's beautiful daughter. So he proposed a bargain.

He said he would forgo the farmer's debt if he could marry his daughter. Both the farmer and his daughter were horrified by the proposal.

So the cunning money-lender suggested that they let God decide the matter. He told them that he would put a black pebble and a white pebble into an empty money bag. Then the girl would have to pick one pebble from the bag. If she picked the black pebble, she would become his wife and her father's debt would be forgiven. If she picked the white pebble she need not marry him and her father's debt would still be forgiven. But if she refused to pick a pebble, her father would be thrown into prison.

They were standing on a pebble-strewn path in the farmer's field. As they walked, the moneylender bent over to pick up two pebbles. As he picked them up, the sharp-eyed girl noticed that he had picked up two black pebbles and put them into the bag. He then asked the girl to pick a pebble from the bag.

Now, imagine that you were standing in the field. What would you have done if you were the girl? If you had to advise her, what would you have told her? Careful analysis would produce three possibilities:

1. The girl should refuse to take a pebble. 2. The girl should show that there

were two black pebbles in the bag and expose the money-lender as a cheat. 3. The girl should pick a black pebble and sacrifice herself in order to save her father from his debt and imprisonment.

Take a moment to ponder over the story. The above story is used with the hope that it will make us appreciate the difference between lateral and logical thinking.

The girl's dilemma cannot be solved with traditional logical thinking. Think of the consequences if she chooses the above logical answers. What would you recommend to the girl to do? Well, here is what she did.

The girl put her hand into the bag and drew out a pebble. Without looking at it, she fumbled it onto the pebble-strewn path where it immediately became lost among all the other pebbles.

"Oh, how clumsy of me," she said. "But never mind, just look into the bag for the one that is left, then you will be able to tell which pebble I picked."

Since the remaining pebble is black, it must be assumed that she had picked the white one. And since the money-lender dared not admit his dishonestly, the girl changed what seemed an impossible situation into an extremely advantageous one.

Most complex problems do have a solution. It is only that we don't attempt to think. Don't work hard. Work smart.

两块鹅卵石

许多年前在一个印第安的小村落里，一位农夫不幸欠下村里一个放债者一笔巨款。这个放债者又老又丑，却看上了农夫的漂亮千金。因此，他便想做笔交易。

他对农夫说，如果让女儿嫁给他，农夫欠他的债就一笔勾销。农夫和他的女儿都被这个建议震惊了。

于是狡猾的放债者就建议让天意来决定。他说他会将一枚黑色鹅卵石和一枚白色鹅卵石放进一个空钱包里，让女孩从包里选出一块石头。她如果选到了黑色的，那她就要成为他的妻子，而她父亲的债也会一笔勾销；如果选到了白色的，她就不用和他结婚，她父亲的债仍会一笔勾销。但如果她拒绝这个办法，她的父亲就要蹲大狱。

他们站在农夫田地里的一条鹅卵石小道上。他们一边走，放债者弯腰捡了两块鹅卵石。就在捡起的那一瞬间，目光敏锐的女孩注意到他实际上捡了两块黑色石头并迅速丢进包里。然后，他让女孩从包里选一块出来。

现在想象一下你们站在一片开阔的田野，如果你是那个小女孩会怎么做？如果你想给她提些建议，你会怎么说？深思熟虑之后，一般会产生下列三种可能性：

一、女孩拒绝选石头；二、女孩一语道破包中是两块黑色的石头，以此揭穿放债者的阴谋；三、女孩直接选出一块黑色石头，牺牲自己的幸福，以此挽救父亲的债务和牢狱之灾。

仔细思考一下整个故事。故事的用意在于让我们用心理解并欣赏横向思维与逻辑思维的差异。

传统的逻辑思维无法解决女孩的窘境。想一下她选择上述任何一种可能性结果会怎样。你会建议她怎么做？那么，答案将马上揭晓！

女孩将手伸入包中迅速抓出一块石头，连看都不看就直接将它扔到了鹅卵石堆里，那块小石头立马消失得无影无踪。

"噢，看我多笨啊，"她说，"但不用紧张，看看包里剩下的那块石头，然后你就知道我刚才选了哪块。"

包里剩下的那块自然是黑色的，所以她刚选出的那块理所当然就是白色的了。放债者此时是哑巴吃黄连，有苦说不出。女孩最终将这件完全不可能办到的事情变成了可能，还让这件事处于对自己十分有利的形势。

即使最复杂的问题都有一个解决方案。只是我们没有用心思考。凡事别蛮干，要巧干。

I Heard a Cricket

A man and his friend were in a city, walking through the street. It was during the noon lunch hour and the streets were filled with people. Cars were honking their horns, taxis were squealing around corners, sirens were wailing, and the sounds of the city were almost deafening. Suddenly, the man said to his friend, "I heard a cricket."

His friend said, "What? You must be crazy. You couldn't possibly hear a cricket in all of this noise!"

"No, I'm sure of it," the man said, "I heard a cricket."

"That's crazy," said the friend.

The man listened carefully for a moment, and then walked across the street to a big cement planter where some shrubs were growing. He looked into the bushes, and sure enough, beneath the branches, he located a small cricket. His friend was completely amazed. "That's incredible," said his friend. "You must have superman ears!"

"No," said the man. "My ears are no different from yours. It all depends on what you're listening for."

"But that can't be!" said the friend. "I could never hear a cricket in this noise."

"Yes, it's true," was the reply. "It depends on what is really important to you. Here, let me show you."

He reached into his pocket, pulled out a few coins, and carefully dropped them on the sidewalk. And then, with the noise of the crowded street still blaring in their ears, they noticed every head within twenty feet turn and look to see if the money that tinkled on the pavement was theirs.

"See what I mean?" asked the man.

"It all depends on what's important to you. So it's vital that you prioritize what you do."

我听到了蟋蟀的叫声

一名男子和他的朋友走在一座城市的街上。正值午餐时间，街上挤满了人。汽车不停地响着喇叭，出租车呼啸着转过弯，警报器在鸣叫，城市中的各种声音震耳欲聋。突然，那人对他的朋友说："我听到了蟋蟀的声音。"

他的朋友说："什么？你一定是疯了。你不可能在这所有的噪声中，还能听到蟋蟀的声音！"

"不，我确信，"那人说，"我听到了蟋蟀的叫声。"

"真是疯了。"他的朋友说。

这名男子仔细听了听，然后走到街对面一个大一些的水泥围边的种植灌木的地方。他观察树丛，千真万确，在灌木枝的下方，他发现了一只小蟋蟀。他的朋友感到十分吃惊。"真是难以置信，"朋友说，"你肯定有超人的耳朵！"

"不，"他说，"我的耳朵和你的没什么不同，这完全取决于你在听什么。"

"但这不可能！"这位朋友说，"我从来没有在这么嘈杂的环境中听到过蟋蟀的叫声。"

"是的，这是真的，"他回答说，"这要看什么对你是真正重要的。来，让我展示给你看。"

他把手伸进口袋，掏出几个硬币，小心地把它们扔在人行道上。尽管拥挤的街道上嘈杂的声音依然在耳畔回响，但他们很快发现五米内几乎每个人都转过头看，看人行道上叮叮当当响的是不是他们的钱。

"明白我说的意思了吗？"男子问。

"一切取决于什么对你是重要的。因此，将你的事情分个轻重缓急很重要。"

第七卷

坚持你的梦想

I Knew You'd Come

Horror gripped the heart of a World War I soldier, as he saw his lifelong friend fall in battle. The soldier asked his Lieutenant if he could go out to bring his fallen comrade back.

"You can go," said the Lieutenant, "but don't think it will be worth it. Your friend is probably dead and you may throw your life away." The Lieutenant's words didn't matter, and the soldier went anyway.

Miraculously, he managed to reach his friend, hoisted him onto his shoulder and brought him back to their company's trench. The officer checked the wounded soldier, and then looked kindly at his friend.

"I told you it wouldn't be worth it," he said. "Your friend is dead and you are mortally wounded."

"It was worth it, Sir," said the soldier.

"What do you mean by worth it?" responded the Lieutenant, "Your friend is dead."

"Yes, Sir," the soldier answered, "but it was worth it because when I got to him, he was still alive and I had the satisfaction of hearing him say, 'Jim, I knew you'd come.'"

Many times in life, whether a thing is worth doing or not, really depends on how you look at it. Take up all your courage and do something your heart tells you to do so that you may not regret not doing it later in your life.

我知道你会来的

"一战"中，一个战士看到好友倒在战场上时，内心充满了恐惧。这个战士向中尉请示他是否能去把倒下的战友背回来。

"你可以去，"中尉说，"但我认为这不值得。你的朋友可能已经死了，而且你也可能会丢掉性命。"战士没有听中尉的话，最后还是去了。

他居然奇迹般地找到了朋友，并把他背起来，带回了他们连队的战壕里。

"我告诉过你这样做不值，"中尉说，"你的朋友已经死了，而且你也因此受了重伤。"

"这样做值得，长官。"战士说。

"你说值得是什么意思？"中尉反问道，"你的朋友已经死了。"

"是的，长官，他是死了，"战士回答说，"但这样做是值得的，因为当我来到他身边时，他还活着。他说：'吉姆，我知道你会来的。'听到这句话，我就心满意足了。"

人生中很多时候，一件事情是否值得去做，完全取决于你如何看待它。只有鼓起勇气，去做内心指引你做的事情，这样你才不会在今后的生活中因没做它而遗憾。

Between Friends

There once was a milkman named Jack in the early 1900's. He and his horse, Pierre, did their job every day with joy in their hearts. Jack wasn't so bright and he couldn't read. When people needed extra milk, they would call to Jack as he left. They would yell, "I'll need some extra milk tomorrow!" which Jack would always reply, "To give your friends some pleasure!"

Jack and Pierre were great friends and did their job for years and years. After a while, Jack didn't have to do much any more, because Pierre knew where and when to stop. The friends continued their job until one sad morning.

Jack came into work one day to find his boss waiting for him.

"Jack," said his boss, "I have some sad news. This morning, Pierre died in his stall."

Tears started to run down Jack's face.

"It's OK, Jack," said his boss. "He was an old horse."

"I will never see my friend again," said Jack tearfully.

"Yes, you will. He's lying in his stall very peacefully right now. You can see him now if you'd like."

"You do not understand. I will never see Pierre again."

"I understand your sadness. You may have the day off if you'd like."

"No, I have a job to do," with that Jack walked off. He was given a new horse and carriage and he went off to do his job.

That day, Jack was in an accident. His carriage was hit by a car. When his boss heard this, he rushed down to where the accident happened. When he got there, he asked, "Is Jack OK?"

"No, he died in the accident," said the doctor.

"I don't understand," said the driver of the car. "It was like he didn't even see me!"

"That's because he didn't. This man has been blind for 5 years," said the doctor.

"I never knew!" said Jack's boss.

"He didn't tell you?" said the doctor.

Just then, Jack's boss remembered what Jack said about Pierre. "No, but someone else knew."

"Who?" asked the doctor.

"A friend of Jack's. His name was Pierre. I think that it was just a little secret between friends."

朋友间的小秘密

20世纪初，有一个名叫杰克的送奶工。他和他的马——皮埃尔每天都高高兴兴地一起工作。杰克有些愚笨，也不识字。当需要更多的牛奶时，人们会在杰克走时对他喊道："明天我需要更多的牛奶！"杰克总是回答说："给你的朋友带来些乐趣！"

杰克和皮埃尔这对好朋友年复一年地工作着。很快，杰克干起活来就省事多了，因为皮埃尔知道到哪里要停，也知道什么时候需要停。这对好朋友就这样一起工作着，直到一个让人悲伤的早晨到来。

这天，杰克来上班时发现老板正等着他。

"杰克，"老板对他说，"有个不幸的消息要告诉你。今天早上，皮埃尔在马厩里死了。"

眼泪顺着杰克的脸颊流了下来。

"这没什么，杰克，"老板安慰道，"它毕竟是一匹老马了。"

"我再也见不到我的朋友了。"杰克含泪说道。

"不，你能见到。它现在正安详地躺在马厩。如果你愿意，现在就能去看它。"

"你不明白。我再也见不到皮埃尔了。"

"我理解你的悲伤。如果你愿意，今天就休息一天吧。"

"不，我还有工作要做。"说完，杰克就走开了。他领了一套新马车，然后就去干活了。

那天，杰克发生了意外，他的马车被一辆汽车给撞了。老板听说后，赶紧跑到事发地点。到了那里后，他问："杰克还好吗？"

"不，他在事故中丧生了。"医生告诉他。

"我不明白，"汽车司机不解地说，"他好像根本没看见我！"

"那是因为他看不见，他的眼睛已经瞎了5年了。"医生说。

"他没有告诉过你吗？"医生问。

"我从来都不知道！"老板说。

就在那时，老板想起了杰克说的话。"他没有告诉我，但有人知道。"

"谁知道？"医生问。

"杰克的一个朋友，它的名字叫皮埃尔。我想那是朋友之间的一个小秘密。"

Experiencing Kindness

Some years ago, a tiny Korean orphan arrived in the United States to join her adoptive family. She was nine months old and weighed only 91/2 pounds. She grew and blossomed in her new home, but remained a diminutive size. Her new name was Edie.

One day when Edie was in second grade, she ran home from school, crying. She was frightened. That day, three new girls had been enrolled in her class. During the first recess, they picked the smallest girl in the class as the object of their anger and frustration. They pinched, poked, and pushed tiny Edie and threatened to beat her up. Edie had spent an hour in the principal's office with the three girls and was assured the teachers would be watching. The girls given a warning.

Edie's mother held her and comforted her. She learned later, after speaking with the principal, that the girls had been troublemakers at several other schools. They were being given one more chance at a new beginning.

"These girls must have been hurt in their young lives to be so angry. Her mother said. " The Bible tells us. A plan began to take shape. "I can't go to school with you every day, so you will need to stay close to a teacher when you are at recess or in line to go into school," said Edie's mom. "If the girls start to pick on you, tell them, I'd really like to be your friend. Are you brave enough to do that?" Edie's mother asked. The tiny girl perked up, and with a smile, looked at her mother and said, "Yes, Mom, I'll try."

The next morning, and every day before Edie left for school, she and her mom prayed for her to be safe and brave, and for the girls to be open to God's love. Everyday, the girls shoved into line behind Edie and called her names and tried to get in a poke or two.

Each time, Edie looked up at them and said, "I'd really like to be your friend." She did have to look up at them since they were so much taller than she was. The teachers kept an eye on them, but did not need to interfere as the girls were not hurting her.

After about two weeks, Edie came home looking so discouraged. She told her mother that she didn't think it was working. After they talked about it and prayed, she decided to keep trying and continued to faithfully tell them, "I'd really like to be your friend."

One day the following week, Edie ran home as fast as she could and ran into the house, shouting, "Mom, Mom, guess what happened today? Just like I always did, I said I'd really like to be your friend, and one of the girls said, 'Okay, Edie, we give up, we'll be your friend.'"

A short time later, as the girls were trying to become friends, Edie asked the teacher if she could sit at a table with these girls in the classroom. She had noticed that they were disruptive because they didn't understand the lessons. Edie became their tutor.

Toward the end of the school year, when Edie's parents went to school for a parent teacher conference, the teacher told them, "Because of Edie's kindness, those girls have completely turned around and are productive members of the class." She felt she had witnessed a miracle. And so did Edie's mom and dad.

How many people go through life never experiencing kindness? They don't see it in strangers, and some don't even find it in their own families. Without experiencing kindness, it becomes impossible to express kindness toward others. The result of this tragic lack is seen everywhere. What a difference society this would be if everyone who has received kindness would be kind to others, especially the unlovely.

体 验 友 善

许多年前，一个韩国的小孤儿被美国的一家人领养。当时她9个月大，体重只有9.5磅（1磅约合0.45千克）。她在新环境中成长起来，但还是身材瘦小。她的名字叫伊迪。

伊迪上二年级时，有一天，她从学校哭着跑回来。她感到很害怕，因为那天她的班上新来了三个女同学。下课休息时，她们就拿班上最弱小的学生来当她们的出气筒。她们对伊迪又是掐又是捅，并把她推翻在地，恐吓说要揍她。伊迪和那三个女生在校长办公室待了一个小时，校长让老师们留心盯着她们。三个女孩被学校给予了警告处分。

母亲抱着伊迪安慰她。后来，她在和校长谈过话之后才知道，这几位新来的学生原来在其他学校是出了名的捣蛋生。学校又给了她们一次在新环境中改过的机会。

"这些女孩小时候一定是受过伤害，才变得这么怒气冲天。"母亲说。母女俩有了办法。"我不能每天都陪你上学，所以课间休息或排队入校时你要待在老师身边。"母亲说，"如果她们要找你的麻烦，就告诉她们，你想和她们成为朋友。你有勇气那样做吗？"母亲问道。小伊迪抬起头，面带微笑地看着母亲说："好的，妈妈，我试试吧。"

　　在这之后，每天伊迪上学前，都和母亲一起祈求上帝保佑她平安和勇敢，也祈求这些女孩能接受上帝赐予的爱。但是，这些女孩每天都挤到伊迪后面去骂她，还要捅她一两下。

　　每次，伊迪都抬头看着她们说："我真的想成为你们的朋友。"她得抬着头看她们，因为她们比伊迪要高得多。老师留心看着她们，但并没有干预，因为她们并没有伤害她。

　　大概过了两周，一天伊迪心情沮丧地回到家，告诉母亲，她觉得这个办法并不奏效。后来经过母女俩的谈论和祈祷，她决定继续试着诚心诚意地告诉她们："我真的想成为你们的朋友。"

　　在接下来的那周里，一天伊迪从学校飞跑回家，大声叫道："妈妈，妈妈，猜猜今天发生了什么事？我坚持以往的做法，我说我愿意成为她们的朋友。其中一个女生说：'好吧，伊迪，我们不再欺负你了，我们将成为你的朋友。'"

　　很快，她们就成为朋友，伊迪要求老师让她和这几个女孩坐在一起。伊迪发现她们因为听不懂老师讲的课才经常捣乱。于是，伊迪就成了她们的辅导员。

　　当那个学年快要结束时，伊迪的父母去学校参加家长会，老师告诉他们："因为伊迪的善良，这些女孩已经彻底改好了，她们现在是好学生了。"老师和伊迪的父母都觉得他们见证了一个奇迹的发生。

　　有多少人一生中都没有尝过友善的滋味？他们在陌生人中找不到友情，有些人甚至在家庭中也没有尝试过友善的滋味。没有经历过友善，就不可能对别人友善。今天，缺乏友情的悲惨结果随处可见。如果每个曾接受过别人爱心的人都能对别人，尤其是对那些讨厌的人充满爱心的话，那么社会将大为改观。

Kiss a Stranger

　　The subway train sways back and forth, its wheels screeching more fiendishly than ever against the tracks. Outside the window, the freezing cold of winter rules and the dreary bay looks like an abyss as the train rumbles across it. The carriage is filled with frozen self-centered, bored passengers. Good morning!

　　Suddenly a little boy pushed his way in between discourteous grown-up legs—the kind that only grudging make room for you. While his father stays by the door, the boy sits next to the window, surrounded by unfriendly, weary adults. What a brave child, I think. As the train enters a tunnel, something totally unexpected and peculiar happens. The little boy slides down from his seat and puts his hand on my knee. For a moment, I think that he wants to go past me and return to his father, so I shift a bit. But instead of moving on, the boy leans forward and stretches his head up towards me. He wants to tell me something, I think. Kids! So I bend down to listen to what he has to say. Wrong again! He kisses me softly on the cheek.

Then he returns to his seat, leans back and cheerfully starts looking out of the window. But I'm shocked. What happened? A kid kissing unknown grown-ups on the train? To my amazement, the kid goes on to kiss my neighbors.

Nervous and bewildered, we look at his father questioningly, "He's so happy to be alive," the father says. "He's been very sick."

The train stops and father and son get down and disappear into the crowd. The doors close. On my cheek I can still feel the child's kiss—a kiss that has triggered some soul-searching. How many grown-ups go around kissing each other for the sheer joy of being alive? How many even give much thought to the privilege of living? What would happen if we all just started being ourselves?

The little boy had given us a sweet but serious slap in the face: Don't let yourself die before your heart stops!

亲吻陌生人

地铁的列车来回摇晃，轮子碾过铁轨，发出比以往更尖利的啸叫。窗外，冬日的严寒肆虐，随着列车呼啸而过，沉闷阴郁的海湾看起来像是裂开口子的深渊。车厢里挤满了冷漠、自私、无聊的乘客。早上好！

突然，一个小男孩从大人们横七竖八的腿中间挤进来——这些人的腿极不情愿地给他让出些地方。小男孩的父亲待在车门旁边，小男孩在窗边的位子坐下来，周围都是并不友好、疲惫不堪的大人们。多么勇敢的孩子，我想。随着列车驶入隧道里，令人完全想不到的怪事发生了。小男孩从他自己的座位上下来，把手放到我的膝盖上。那会儿，我以为他想从我这里过去，回到他父亲那里，所以我往边上挪了一下。但是，小男孩并没有继续往前走，他向前斜着身子，把头尽力抬起来对着我。他想跟我说什么，我想。真是个孩子！于是，我弯下腰听他要说什么。我又错了！他轻轻地在我的脸颊上亲了一下。

之后，他回到了座位上，靠在座位后背上高兴地看着窗外。但是，我很震惊。这到底是怎么回事？一个孩子在火车上亲吻一个素不相识的大人。更让我吃惊的是，这个小孩又接着亲吻我旁边的人。

我们既不安又疑惑，都看着他的父亲。"他为自己活着而高兴，"这位父亲说，"他已经是重病缠身了。"

列车到站了，父子俩下了火车，消失在人群中。车门又关上了。我依然能感觉到孩子在我脸上留下的亲吻——一个发人深省的吻。有多少大人只为自己还活着而开心亲吻彼此？有多少人好好想过活着也是一种特权？如果我们每个人都做回自我，又会是什么样呢？

小男孩给了我们一记甜美而沉重的耳光：不要让自己在心脏停止跳动之前就死去。

The Rescue of a Seagull

Imagine this scene: you are on the Florida coast. The sun is setting like a gigantic orange ball. It's the cool evening on an isolated stretch of beach. The water is lapping at the shore, the breeze is blowing slightly. There are one or two joggers and a couple of fisherman. Most people have gone home for the day.

You look up and see an old man with curved shoulders, bushy eyebrows, and bony features hobbling down the beach carrying a bucket. He carries the bucket up to the pier, a dock that goes out into the water. He stands on the dock and you notice he is looking up into the sky and all of a sudden you see a mass of dancing dots. You soon recognize that they are seagulls. They are coming out of nowhere. The man takes out of his bucket handfuls of shrimp and begins to throw them on the dock. The seagulls come and land all around him. Some land on his shoulders, some land on his hat, and they eat the shrimp. Long after the shrimp are gone his feathered friends linger. The old man and the birds.

What is going on here? Why is this man feeling seagulls? What could compel him to do this as he does week after week?

The man in that scene was Eddie Rickenbacher, a famous World War II pilot. His plane, the Flying Fortress, went down in 1942 and no one thought he would be rescued. Perhaps you have read or heard how he and his eight passengers escaped death by climbing into two rafts for thirty days. They fought thirst, the sun, and sharks. Some of the sharks were nine feet long. The boats were only eight feet long. But what nearly killed them was starvation. Their rations were gone within eight days and they didn't have anything left.

Rickenbacher wrote that even on those rafts, every day they would have a daily afternoon prayer time. One day after the prayer, Rickenbacher leaned back and put his hat over his eyes and tried to get some sleep. Within a few moments he felt something on his head. He knew in an instant it was a seagull which had perched on his raft. But he knew that they were hundreds of miles out to sea. Where did this seagull come from? He was also certain that if he didn't get that seagull he would die. Soon all the others on the two boats noticed the seagull. No one spoke, no one moved. Rickenbacher quickly grabbed the seagull and with thanksgiving, they ate the flesh of the bird. They used the intestines for fish bait and survived.

Rickenbacher never forgot that visitor who came from a foreign place. That sacrificial guest. Every week, he went out on the pier with a bucket of shrimp and said thank you, thank you, thank you.

海鸥的救援

想象一下这样的场景：你正站在佛罗里达海岸，太阳像一只橙色大球一样在慢慢降落。这是一个孤寂海滩上的凉爽之夜，海水拍打着海岸，微风轻轻吹着，沙滩上有一两个慢跑者和几个渔民，大多数人已经回家去了。

你抬起头，可以看见一位后背微驼、眉毛浓密的老人提着一只大桶在沙滩上蹒跚前行。他提着桶走到码头上，码头是一个伸进水里的船坞。他站在码头上，你可以注意到他正仰望着天空，突然你看到了许多飞舞的小点点。很快，你就认出这些小点点原来是一些海鸥。不知道它们是从哪里飞来的。老人从桶里抓起一把一把小虾撒在码头上来喂它们。那些海鸥飞过来落在他周围，有些落了他的肩上，有些落在了他的帽子上，然后开始吃这些小虾。吃完这些小虾后，这群海鸥和老人待在一起，久久不肯离去。

这到底是怎么回事？老人为什么要给海鸥喂食？是什么能让他这样一周又一周地做呢？

那一幕中的老人叫艾迪·瑞肯巴彻——"二战"期间的一位著名飞行员。他驾驶的名叫空中堡垒的飞机在1942年坠毁，人们都没想到他会获救。也许你曾经读到过或听到过他是怎样和8名乘客死里逃生的，他们爬进两个救生艇里，在上面待了整整一个月。他们战胜了口渴、烈日和鲨鱼，有些鲨鱼长达两米多。但是，让他们最忍受不了的是饥饿。他们的食物8天后就吃光了，什么吃的都没有了。

瑞肯巴彻记录说，待在救生艇上时，他们每天下午都会祈祷。一天祈祷后，他斜靠在船上，把帽子搭在眼睛上，想要睡会儿。过了一会儿，他感觉到头上有什么东西，很快就发现是一只海鸥落在了他的船上。但是，他知道他们是在几百英里（1英里约合1.6千米）以外的海上。那么，这只海鸥是从哪里飞来的呢？他也明白，如果不吃掉这只海鸥，他就会饿死。很快，其他人也注意到了那只海鸥。他们都一言不发，一动不动。瑞肯巴彻赶紧抓住那只海鸥，满怀感激地吃了它的肉，他们用剩下的肠子做成鱼饵来钓鱼，就这样他们活了下来。

瑞肯巴彻永远不会忘记那个远道而来的客人，那个献出自己生命的来客。每周，他都会提着一桶虾来到码头上，一边喂着海鸥，一边说着"谢谢，谢谢，谢谢你们"。

A Pillow and a Blanket

A long time ago, a young, wealthy girl was getting ready for bed. She was saying her prayers when she heard a muffled coming through her window. A little frightened, she went over to the window and leaned out.

Another girl, who seemed to be about her age and homeless, was standing in the alley by the rich girl's house. Her heart went out to the homeless girl, for it was the dead of winter, and the girl had no blanket, only old newspapers someone had thrown out.

The rich girl was suddenly struck with a brilliant idea. She called to the other girl and said, "You there, come to my front door, please." The homeless girl was so startled she could only manage to nod.

The young girl ran down the hall to her mother's closet, and picked out an old quilt and a beat-up pillow. She had to walk slowly down to the front door so as not to trip over the quilt which was hanging down, but she made it eventually. Dropping both the articles, she opened the door. Standing there was the homeless girl, looking quite scared.

The rich girl smiled warmly and handed both articles to the other girl. Her smile grew wider as she watched the true amazement and happiness alight upon the other girl's face. She went to bed incredibly satisfied.

In mid-morning the next day, a knock came to the door. The rich girl flew to the door, hoping it was the other little girl there. She opened the large door and looked outside. It was the other little girl. Her face looked happy, and she smiled. "I suppose you want these back." The rich little girl opened her mouth to say that she could keep them when another idea popped into her head. "No, I want them back."

The homeless girl's face fell. This was obviously not the answer she had hoped for. She reluctantly laid down the beat-up things, and turned to leave when the rich girl yelled, "Wait! Stay right there."

She turned in time to see the rich girl running up the stairs and down a long corridor. Deciding whatever the rich little girl was doing wasn't worth waiting for, she turned around and walked away. As her foot hit the first step, she felt someone tap her on the shoulder. Turning around, she saw the rich little girl, thrusting a new blanket and pillow at her. "Have these." She said quietly.

These were her personal belongings made of silk and down feather.

As the two grew older they didn't see each other much, but they were never far from each other's minds. One day, the rich girl, now a rich woman, got a telephone call from a lawyer, saying that she was requested to see him.

When she arrived at the office, he told her what had happened. Forty years ago, when she was nine years old, she had helped a little girl in need. She grew into a middle-class woman with a husband and two children. She had recently died and left something for her in her will. "Though," the lawyer said, "it's the most peculiar thing. She left you a pillow and a blanket."

枕头和毛毯

很久以前，一个年轻的富家女孩正准备上床睡觉。她在做睡前祷告时，听到从窗户那里传来一阵低沉的声音。她有些害怕，走到窗前，把身子探出窗外查看。

一个看起来和她年龄相仿的无家可归的女孩正站在房子附近的过道上。她非常同情这个无家可归的女孩。此时正值隆冬，女孩身上没有毯子，只有别人扔掉的旧报纸。

那个富家女孩突然想到一个绝妙的主意。她向那个女孩喊道："请你到我的前门来。"那个无家可归的女孩非常吃惊，勉强点了点头。

这个年轻女孩顺着走廊跑到母亲的壁柜前，翻出一条旧被子和一只破枕头，她不得不慢慢走下来到前门处，以免被散落下来的被子绊倒。富家女孩来到了前门，放下被子和枕头，打开了门，门前站着那个无家可归的女孩，她看起来一脸恐慌。

富家女孩亲切地笑了笑，把这两样东西交给了那个女孩，当她看到那个女孩脸上露出又惊又喜的神情时，她笑得更开心了，然后心满意足地去睡了。

第二天早上，外面响起了敲门声。那个富家女孩飞奔到门前，她希望是那个女孩。富家女孩打开大门向外看看，确实是那个女孩，她看起来很开心，笑着说："我猜你想要回这些东西。"富家女孩正要开口说她可以留着这些东西，突然富家女孩想到了一个好主意，于是说道："是的，我想要回它们。"

那个无家可归的女孩脸色阴沉下来，显然这并不是她想要的回答。她不情愿地放下这些破旧东西，正要转身离开时，那个富家女孩喊道："等等！就待在那里别走。"

她转过身，看见那个富家女孩跑上楼，沿着一条长走廊跑过去。她想，不管那个富家女孩做什么，都不值得她再等下去。想到这里，她转身就走。正当她抬脚要走时，感觉有人拍她的肩膀。她转过身，看到了那个富家女孩。富家女孩塞给她一条新被子和一个新枕头，轻声说："拿着吧。"

这是富家女孩自己用的蚕丝被子和羽绒枕头。

随着年龄的增长，她们彼此并未经常见面，但她们的心却连在一起。一天，那个富家女孩——现在已经是贵夫人了——接到一个电话，是一位律师打来的，说要见她。

她来到律师的办公室后，律师告诉她，她9岁时，曾经帮助过一个身处困境的女孩。那个女孩后来生活殷实，有了丈夫和两个孩子。最近，那个女孩去世了，遗嘱中说有些东西要留给她。"可是，"律师说，"奇怪的是，她留给你一条被子和一只枕头。"

The Undeserved Gift

I grew up in a small town in Ohio. There was a man in town that everyone seemed to know. Bob was uneducated and couldn't talk plain. It seemed that because he was good-natured and not very smart, every one teased him. I guess he was an easy mark.

One day when I was sitting on the porch, he came walking by. I was about 12 years old and thought it would make me feel grown up to tease him like some adults did in the town.

He asked how I was doing. I told him that my father had lost his job, and that we were short of money. I could see my friends laughing in the background so I went on with the lie. I had him fooled so completely that every time he asked me a question, I would make the situation seem worse and worse.

I knew he made a meager living doing odd jobs, so it seemed funny when he asked me if we needed anything. I told him that we didn't know if we would have enough to eat. He replied, "You poor thing. I will pray for you."

That night I heard the door rattle softly. I thought it was the wind whipping against the door so I didn't pay much attention to it. Later when I opened the door to go outside, I found a box of groceries. I knew who had given the food. I looked through the small box of canned food with tears in my eyes. I felt ashamed, and wanted to return the groceries.

My father would not let me take the box back. He said it would hurt Bob's feelings. Each day when we would have dinner my father would ask, "What side dish are we having from the gift box today?"

It was hard for me to eat the food. I knew Bob had given sacrificially. I did not deserve the gift, but he gave the best he had.

受之有愧的礼物

我从小在俄亥俄州的一个小镇上长大，那里有一个大家似乎都熟悉的人。鲍勃。鲍勃没有上过学，而且笨言拙语。因为他脾气好，又不怎么聪明，大家都欺负他，我觉得他就是一个智障。

一天，我正坐在家门口，他走过来。我当时大概12岁，我想如果我能像镇上的一些大人那样戏弄他一番的话，就会觉得自己长大了。

他问我过得怎么样，我告诉他父亲丢了工作，我们正缺钱。这时，我看到伙伴们正藏在后面狂笑，于是就继续编造谎言。我完全愚弄了他，每次他问我一个问题，我就会把我们的状况说得越来越糟。

我知道他平时打些零工，生活拮据，因此当他问我们是否需要些什么时，听起来很可笑。我告诉他，我们不知道是否能有足够的东西吃。他回答："你真可怜。我会为你祈祷。"

那天夜里，我听到门轻轻地响了一下。我以为是风吹动了门，就没太在意。后来，我打开门走到外面时，发现了一盒食品。我明白是谁送的。我含泪看着这个小盒子里的罐头食品，感到很羞愧，想把它们还回去。

父亲不让我把它们还回去，他说那样会伤害鲍勃的感情。每天当我们要吃晚饭时，父亲就会问："看看今天礼物盒里有什么小菜？"

对我来说，我很难咽下这些食物。我知道鲍伯已经倾其所有，我不配得到他的礼物，但他却给出了他最好的东西。

I Wish You Enough

At an airport I overheard a father and daughter in their last moments together. Her plane's departure had been announced. Standing near the door, he said to his daughter, "I love you, I wish you enough."

She said, "Daddy, our life together has been more than enough. Your love is all I ever needed. I wish you enough, too, Daddy." They kissed goodbye and she left.

He walked over toward the window where I was seating. Standing there I could see he wanted and needed to cry. I tried not to intrude on his privacy, but he welcomed me in by asking, "Did you ever say goodbye to someone knowing it would be forever?" "Yes, I have," I replied.

Saying that brought back memories I had of expressing my love and appreciation for all that my Dad had done for me. Recognizing that his days were limited, I took the time to tell him face to face how much he meant to me. So I knew what this man was experiencing.

"Forgive me for asking, but why is a forever goodbye?" I asked.

"I am old and she lives much too far away. I have challenges ahead and the reality is, her next trip back will be for my funeral," he said.

"When you were saying goodbye I heard you say, 'I wish you enough. 'may I ask what that means?"

He began to smile. "That's a wish that has been handed down from other generations. My parents used to say it to everyone." He paused for a moment and looking up as if trying to remember it in detail, he smiled even more.

"When we said 'I wish you enough, ' we wanted the other person to have a life filled with enough good things to sustain them," he continued and turning toward me he shared the following as if he were reciting it from memory.

"I wish you enough sun to keep your attitude bright. I wish you enough rain to appreciate the sun more. I wish you enough happiness to keep your spirit alive. I wish you enough pain so that the smallest joys in life appear much bigger. I wish you enough gain to satisfy your wanting. I wish you enough loss to appreciate all that you possess. I wish enough 'Hellos' to get you through the final 'Goodbye'."

He then began to sob and walked away.

It is said that "It takes a minute to find a special person, an hour to appreciate them, a day to love them, but then an entire life to forget them."

愿 你 足 够

我曾在一个机场里无意中听到一位父亲和女儿离别时的谈话。广播里传来女儿所乘的飞机即将起飞的信息。父亲站在入口附近，对女儿说："我爱你，愿你拥有足够的一切。"

女儿说："爸爸，我们曾在一起生活，这就足够了。您的爱永远是我需要的一切，我希望您也拥有足够的一切，爸爸。"他们吻别后，女儿就离开了。

那位父亲走向我座位旁边的那个窗户，站在那里，我看得出他想哭，他也需要哭。我不想侵犯别人的隐私，但他却主动问我："你曾经在诀别时对谁说过再见吗？""是的，我说过。"我答道。

这话使我想起我曾对爸爸为我所做的一切表达过我的爱和感激之情。我知道他将不久于人世，于是就面对面地告诉他，他对我有多重要。所以，我理解这位父亲的感受。

"恕我冒昧，为什么这是永别呢？"我问道。

"我已经老了，而且她住得离我非常远。我以后的日子会很难。事实上，她下次回来将会是因为我的葬礼。"他说。

"当你们道别时，我听到你说'愿你拥有足够的一切'，能告诉我这是什么意思吗？"

他笑起来。"那是从老辈们传下来的一种祝愿。我的父母过去对每个人都这么说。"他停了一会儿，仰起头，似乎在回忆细节，他笑得更开心了。

"当我说'愿你拥有足够的一切'时，我希望对方的生活幸福美满，并且能长久下去。"他接着说，然后转向我，像根据记忆背诵一样：

"我希望你拥有足够的阳光让你乐观。我希望你拥有足够的雨水，更加感激阳光。我希望你拥有足够的幸福，神清气爽。我希望你拥有足够的痛苦，放大你生命中最小的快乐。我希望你拥有足够的收获，满足你的需要。我希望你拥有足够的失去，珍惜所有。我希望你拥有足够的简单问候，跨越最终的离别。"

说完，他呜咽着走开了。

据说，发现一个特别的人需要一分钟，理解他们需要一小时，爱上他们需要一天，忘记他们却要用整整一生的时间。

Fly like a Bird

Once upon a time, there was a little boy who was raised in an orphanage.

The little boy had always wished that he could fly like a bird. It was very difficult for him to understand why he could not fly. There were birds at the zoo that were much bigger than he, and they could fly.

"Why can't I?" he thought. "Is there something wrong with me?" he wondered.

There was another little boy who was crippled. He had always wished that he could walk and run like other little boys and girls.

"Why can't I be like them?" he thought.

One day the little orphan boy who had wanted to fly like a bird ran away from the orphanage. He came upon a park where he saw the little boy who could not walk or run playing in the sandbox.

He ran over to the little boy and asked him if he had ever wanted to fly like a bird.

"No," said the little boy who could not walk or run. "But I have wondered what it would be like to walk and run like other boys and girls."

"That is very sad," said the little boy who wanted to fly. "Do you think we could be friends?" he said to the little boy in the sandbox.

"Sure." said the little boy.

The two little boys played for hours. They made sand castles and made really funny sounds with their mouths. Sounds which made them laugh real hard. Then the little boy's father came with a wheelchair to pick up his son. The little boy who had always wanted to fly ran over to the boy's father and whispered something into his ear.

"That would be OK," said the man.

The little boy who had always wanted to fly like a bird ran over to his new friend and said, "You are my only friend and I wish that there was something that I could do to make you walk and run like other little boys and girls. But I can't. But there is something that I can do for you."

The little orphan boy turned around and told his new friend to slide up onto his back. He then began to run across the grass. Faster and faster he ran, carrying the little crippled boy on his back. Faster and harder he ran across the park. Harder and harder he made his legs travel. Soon the wind just whistled across the two little boys' faces.

The little boy's father began to cry as he watched his beautiful little crippled son flapping his arms up and down in the wind, all the while yelling at the top of his voice. "I'm flying, daddy, I'm flying!"

像小鸟那样飞翔

从前，有一个小男孩在孤儿院里长大。

他总希望自己能像一只小鸟那样飞。他很难理解自己为什么不会飞。动物园里有许多鸟比他大得多，它们就会飞。

"为什么我不会飞？"他心想。"我有什么问题吗？"他感到疑惑。

另一个小男孩是个跛脚。他一直希望自己能像其他孩子一样能走能跑。

"为什么我不能像他们一样？"他心想。

一天，那个想要像鸟儿一样飞翔的小男孩离开了孤儿院，来到一个公园里，看到了那个既不会走又不会跑的男孩正在玩沙子。

他跑过去问那个男孩是否想过能像鸟儿那样飞翔。

"没有，"那个男孩回答，"但我想知道能像其他孩子那样走路跑步会是什么样。"

"太让人难过了。"想要飞的男孩说，"你觉得我们能做朋友吗？"他对那个玩沙子的男孩说。

"当然可以。"小男孩回答。

这两个小男孩在一起玩了好几个小时。他们一起用沙子垒城堡，用嘴巴发出有趣的声音。那种声音令他们大笑。然后，跛脚的小男孩的父亲推着轮椅走过来接儿子。那个总想飞的小男孩跑到跛脚的男孩的父亲那里，在他耳边低声说了几句话。

"那敢情好。"父亲答道。

然后，总想飞的男孩跑到他的新朋友跟前说："你是我唯一的朋友，我希望自己能做点什么，让你像别的孩子那样能走能跑，可我做不到，而有的事情我能为你做。"

孤儿院的小男孩转过身，让他的新朋友爬到他的背上，然后在草地上奔跑起来。他背着这个跛脚的男孩，越跑越快。他摆动双腿，穿过公园，跑得越来越快。很快，他们就感觉到风呼呼吹过他们的脸颊。

小男孩的父亲哭了起来，他看着自己可爱的跛脚儿子在风中上下拍打着胳膊，扯着嗓子喊着："我在飞，爸爸，我在飞呢！"

God Is Here Working through Me to Give You Hope

I am a mother of three (ages 14,12,3) and have recently completed my college degree. The last class I had to take was Sociology. The teacher was absolutely inspiring with the qualities that I wish every human being had been graced with. Her last project of the term was called "Smile."

The class was asked to go out and smile at three people and document their reactions. I am a very friendly person and always smile at everyone and say hello, so I thought this would be easy.

Soon after we were given the project, my husband, youngest son, and I went out to McDonald's on a crisp March morning. It was just our way of sharing special play time with our son. We were standing in line, waiting to be served, when suddenly everyone around us began to back away, and then even my husband did! I didn't move an inch...an overwhelming feeling of panic welled up inside me as I turned to see why they had moved.

As I turned around I smelled a horrible "dirty body" smell, and there standing behind me were two poor homeless men. As I looked down at the short gentleman, he was "smiling." His beautiful sky blue eyes were full of light. He said, "Good day" as he counted the few coins he had been clutching. The second man fumbled with his hands as he stood behind his friend. I realized the second man was mentally deficient and the blue-eyed gentleman was his salvation.

I held my tears as I stood there with them. The young lady at the counter asked him what they wanted. He said, "Coffee is all, Miss" because that was all they could afford.

Then I really felt it—the compulsion was so great I almost reached out and hugged the little man. That is when I noticed all eyes in the restaurant were set on me, judging my every action. I smiled and asked the young lady behind the counter to give me two more breakfast meals on a separate tray. I then walked around the corner to the table that the men had chosen as resting spot. I put the tray on the table and laid my hand on the blue-eyed gentleman's cold hand. He looked up at me, with tears in his eyes, and said, "Thank you." I leaned over, began to pat his hand and said, "I did not do this for you. God is here working through me to give you hope." I started to cry as I walked away to join my husband and son.

When I sat down my husband smiled at me and said, "That is why God gave you to me, honey—to give me hope."

I returned to college with this story in hand. I turned in "my project" and the instructor read it. Then she looked up at me and said, "Can I share this?" I slowly nodded as she got the attention of the class. She began to read.

上帝让我给你希望

我是三位孩子的母亲（年龄分别是14岁、12岁、3岁），最近刚刚修完了大学课程。我的最后一门必修课是社会学，教这门课的老师非常优秀，她留给我们的最后学期课题作业叫作"微笑"。

学生们被要求走出去对三个人微笑并对他们的反应做详尽的记录。我是一个非常友好的人，总是对每个人微笑致意，所以我觉得这并不难。

布置了这个课题不久，清新的3月的一天早上，我和丈夫带着我们最小的儿子去麦当劳吃饭。我们经常以这种方式和儿子分享快乐时光。我们正在排队等候，这时突然间周围所有的人都开始后退，接着连我的丈夫也这样！我一动不动……内心涌上一种强烈的恐慌感，我转过身去看他们为什么后退。

就在转身时，我闻到了一股难闻的"体臭"味，只见身后正站着两个无家可归的流浪者。我看了一眼那个个子矮的，他正在"微笑"。他的蓝眼睛非常漂亮，充满光芒。他数着一直攥在手里的几枚硬币说道："早上好。"另一个人站在他身后，笨拙地拉着他的手。我意识到他是智障，那个蓝眼睛的人就是他的救星。

我和他们站在那里，我强忍住眼泪。站在柜台里的年轻女服务生问他需要买什么，他说："只要咖啡，小姐。"因为他们只买得起那个。

当时，我真感觉到——我如此冲动，几乎就要伸出胳膊拥抱那个小个子的流浪汉。就在那时，我注意到餐馆里所有的人都在看我，打量着我的一举一动。我微笑着向站在柜台后面的服务生多要了两份早餐，放在另一只托盘里，然后绕过拐角处，走到那个流浪汉的桌前，把盘子放在桌子上，握住他的手。他抬起头看着我，热泪盈眶地说："谢谢你！"我弯下腰拍着他的手说："我并没有为你做这个，是上帝正在这里通过我给你希望。"我走开，回到丈夫和儿子那里时，哭了起来。

我坐下时，丈夫对我微笑着说："亲爱的，上帝把你交给我，是为了给我带来希望。"

我带着这个故事回到了学校，把"作业"交上去。老师看了看，然后，她抬起头对我说："我能分享它吗？"我微微点了点头。她让大家注意听，然后就读了起来。

The Horsemen

It was bitter cold evening in northern Virginia many years ago. The old man's beard was glazed by winter's frost while he waited for a ride across the river. The wait seemed endless. His body became numb and stiff from the frigid north wind. He heard the faint, steady rhythm of approaching hooves galloping along the frozen path.

Anxiously, he watched as several horsemen rounded the bend. He let the first one pass by without an effort to get his attention. Then another passed by…and another. Finally, the last rider neared the spot where the old man sat like a snow statue.

As this one drew near, the old man caught the rider's eye and said, "Sir, would you mind giving an old man a ride to the other side? There doesn't appear to be a passageway by foot."

Reining his horse, the rider replied, "Sure thing. Hop aboard."

Seeing the old man was unable to lift his half-frozen body from the ground, the horseman dismounted and helped the old man onto the horse. The horseman took the old man not just across the river, but to his destination, which was just a few miles away.

As they neared the tiny but cozy cottage, the horseman's curiosity caused him to inquire, "Sir, I notice that you let several other riders pass by without making an effort to ask for a ride. Then I came up and you immediately asked me for a ride. I'm curious why on such a bitter winter night, you would wait and ask the last rider. What if I had refused and left you there?"

The old man lowered himself slowly down from the horse, looking the rider straight in the eyes, and replied, "I've been around here for some time. I think I know people pretty good."

The old man continued, "I looked into the eyes of the other riders and immediately saw there was no concern for my situation. It would have been useless even to ask them for a ride. But when I looked into your eyes, kindness and compassion were evident. I knew, then and there, that your gentle spirit would welcome the opportunity to give me assistance in my time of need."

Those heartwarming comments touched the horseman deeply.

"I'm most grateful for what you have said," he told the old man. "May I never get too busy in my own affairs that I fail to respond to the needs of others with kindness and compassion."

With that, Thomas Jefferson turned his horse around and made his way back to the White House.

同是骑马人

那是多年前弗吉尼亚州北部一个寒冷的晚上。一位老人站在河边等待搭乘过路人的马过河。天气寒冷，他的胡须蒙上了一层冰霜。这样的等待似乎漫无尽头，刺骨的北风把他的身体都冻僵了。这时，他听见从上冻的小路上传来了由远及近的马蹄声。

老人焦急不安地眼看着几个骑马人绕过河湾处。当第一个过去时，他没有作声，然后第二个也过去了……接着是第三个。老人坐在那里，已经像雪雕一样了。这时，最后一个骑马的人走过来。

当最后一个骑马人走近时，老人看着他说："先生，你愿意把一位老人带到河对面去吗？这里看起来没有什么步行的通道。"

那个骑马人勒住缰绳，回答道："当然可以，上马吧。"

当看见老人身体僵硬，站不起来时，那个骑马人就跳下马，把老人搀扶到马背上。他不仅将老人带过了河，还把他送到了仅有几英里远的目的地。

当他们快要到达老人那座舒适的小屋时，骑手忍不住好奇地问道："先生，我注意到你无意搭乘前面好几位骑马人的马过河，可当我走过来时，你却立刻要我带你过河。"

老人慢慢地下了马，直视着他的眼睛答道："我在这里已经等了有一段时间了，我想我看人是很准的。"

老人接着说："我仔细观察了那几个骑马人的眼神，很快就发现他们对我的处境漠不关心。即使我向他们求助，也无济于事。但当我看见你的眼睛时，你的眼神中明显带着仁慈和同情。那时我就知道，你会在我需要时给我帮助。"

这些感人的话深深地打动了这位骑马人的心。

"我很感激你说的一切，"他告诉老人，"但愿我永远不会因为自己事务繁忙而不去用善良和怜悯之心帮助别人。"

说完这些，托马斯·杰斐逊调转马头，踏上了去白宫的路。

A Simple Gesture That Changed Life

A little boy selling magazines for school walked up to a house that people rarely visited. The house was very old and the owner hardly ever came out. When he did come out he would not say hello to neighbors or passers-by but simply just glare at them.

The boy knocked on the door and waited, sweating for fear of the old man. The boy's parents told him to stay away from the house, a lot of the other neighborhood children were told the same from their parents.

As he was ready to walk away, the door slowly opened. "What do you want?" the old man said. The little boy was very afraid but he had a quota to meet for school with selling the magazine.

"Uh, sir, I am selling these magazines and uh…I was wondering if you would like to buy one." The old man just stared at the boy. The boy could see inside the old man's house and saw that he had dog figurines on the fireplace mantle. "Do you collect dogs?" the little boy asked. "Yes, I have many collectibles in my house, they are my family here. They are all I have." The boy then felt sorry for the man, as it seemed that he was a very lonely soul. "Well, I do have a magazine here for collectors, it is perfect for you. I also have one about dogs since you like dogs so much." The old man was ready to close the door on the boy and said, "No, boy, I don't need any magazines of any kind, now goodbye."

The little boy was sad that he was not going to make his quota with the sale. He was also sad for the old man being so alone in the big house that he owned. The boy went home and then had an idea. He had a little dog figure that he got some years ago from an aunt. The figurine did not mean nearly as much to him since he had a real live dog and a large family. The boy headed back down to the old man's house with the figurine. He knocked on the door again and this time the old man came right to the door. "Boy, I thought I told you no magazines."

"No, sir. I know that, I wanted to bring you a gift." The boy handed him the figurine and the old man's face lit up. "It is a Golden Retriever, I have one at home. This one is for you." The old man was simply stunned; no one had ever given him such a gift and shown him so much kindness. "Boy, you have a big heart. Why are you doing this?" The boy smiled at the man and said, "Because you like dogs."

From that day on, the old man started coming out of the house and acknowledging people. He and the boy became friends. The boy even brought his dog to see the man weekly.

This simple gesture changed both of their lives forever.

改变生活的简单举动

一个为学校代卖杂志的小男孩走到一座人们很少光顾的房子前。房子很破旧，房子的主人很少出来，就是出来，他也不会和邻居们或路人打招呼，一般只是瞪他们一眼。

小男孩敲了敲门，在那里等着，因为害怕那个老人，他吓得身上出汗。小男孩的父母告诉过他让他离那座房子远点，许多邻居的孩子也都从父母那里受到过这样的警告。

他正要走开，这时门慢慢地打开了。"你干什么？"老人问。小男孩很害怕，但他得完成为学校销售杂志的任务。

"呃，先生，我在卖杂志，呃……我不知道你是否需要买一份。"老人只是盯着那个男孩。男孩可以看到老人房子里面的壁炉架上放了一些小狗雕像。"你收集狗的雕像吗？"男孩问。"是的，我家里收藏了许多，它们是我的家人，是我的全部。"男孩为老人感到难过，因为老人似乎是一个很孤独的人。"嗯，我这里有一本收藏者看的杂志，很适合你看。既然你那么喜欢狗，我这里也有一本关于狗的杂志。"这时，老人准备关门，就对男孩说："不，孩子，我不需要任何一种杂志，再见。"

小男孩很难过，他完不成销售任务了。他也为老人感到难过，老人在自己的大房子里孤孤单单的。男孩回到家里，然后想出了一个好主意。几年前，他的姑妈曾送给他一只小狗雕像。因为他有一只真正的小狗和一个大家庭，这个小雕像对他来说并不算什么。于是，他拿着这个雕像返回老人的房子，他又一次敲了敲门。这次老人径直走到门口说："小伙子，我想我已经告诉过你了，我不需要杂志。"

"是的，先生。我知道你不需要杂志，我想送给你一件礼物。"男孩把雕像递给老人，老人一下子面露喜色。"这是一只金毛猎犬，我家里有一个，这个给你吧。"老人完全不知所措，从来没有人送给他这样的礼物，也从来没有人对他这么好。"孩子，你有一颗伟大的心。你为什么要这样做？"男孩对他微微一笑说："因为你喜欢狗。"

从那天起，老人开始走出屋子和人们打交道。老人和男孩成了朋友，这个男孩甚至每星期都带着他的狗去看望老人。

这个简单的举动永远改变了两个人的生活。

The Grass Will Come Back

When Mike was two he wanted a sandbox, and his father said, "There goes the yard. We'll have kids over here day and night, and they'll throw sand into the flowerbeds, and cats will make a mess in it, and it'll sure kill the grass."

And Mike's mother said, "It'll come back."

When Mike was five, he wanted a jungle gym with swings that would take his breath away and bars to take him to the summit, and his father said, "Good grief, I've seen those things in back yards, and do you know what they look like? Mud holes in a pasture. Kids digging their gym shoes in the ground. It'll kill the grass."

And Mike's mother said, "It'll come back."

Between breaths, when Daddy was blowing up the plastic swimming pool, he warned, "You know what they're going to do to this place? They're going to use it for a missile site. I hope you know what you're doing. They'll track water everywhere and have a million water fights, and you won't be able to take out the garbage without stepping in mud up to your neck. When we take this down, we'll have the only brown lawn on the block."

"It'll come back," Mike's mother said.

When Mike was 12, he volunteered his yard for a camp out. As they hoisted the tents and drove in the spikes, his father stood at the window and observed, "Why don't just put the grass seed out in bowls for the birds and save myself the trouble of spreading it around? You know those tents and all those big feet are going to trample down every single blade of grass, don't you? Don't bother to answer. I know what you're going to say, 'It'll come back.'"

The basketball hoop on the side of the garage attracted more crowds than the Olympics. And a small patch of lawn that started with a barren spot which was the size of a garbage can lid soon drew to encompass the entire side yard.

Just when it looked as if the new seed might take root, the winter came and the sled runner beat it into ridges. Mike's father shook his head and said, "I never asked for much in this life—only a patch of grass."

And his wife smiled and said, "It'll come back."

The lawn this fall was beautiful. It was green and alive and rolled out like a sponge carpet along the drive where gym shoes had trod…along the garage where bicycles used to fall…and around the flower beds where little boys used to dig with iced-tea spoons.

But Mike's father never saw it. He anxiously looked beyond the yard and asked, "He will come back, won't he?"

草还会长出来的

麦克两岁时想要一个沙箱，但他的父亲说："我们的草坪会被毁掉，孩子们每天都会到这里玩，他们会把沙子扔进花圃里，猫也会进到里面把它搞得一团糟，这些草肯定会死掉的。"

麦克的母亲却说："草还会长出来的。"

麦克五岁时，他想要一个带有秋千的攀爬游戏架和一些横杆，这样，他就可以把秋千荡得高高的，还可以爬上游戏架的最高处。但是，父亲说："老天，我见到过有些家的后院里放有那些东西，你知道那成什么样子吗？草坪上都是泥坑，孩子们穿着球鞋在地上踩来踩去，那些草准会被踩死的。"

麦克的母亲却说："草还会长出来的。"

爸爸正在给塑料游泳池充气，赶紧警告麦克的母亲："你知道他们要拿院子里这块地方干什么吗？他们要把它用做一个导弹发射场。我希望你清楚自己在做什么。他们会经常在这里打水仗，把水弄得到处都是。你得伸到很深的泥里才能把那些垃圾清理出来。我们把这个搞定后，留给我们的就只有一片褐色的草坪了。"

麦克的母亲却说："草还会长出来的。"

麦克12岁时，他主动提出要把他们家的院子作为一个露营地。当他正在打桩、定钉子、支帐篷时，父亲站在窗边看着母亲说："我还不如把草籽放到碗里出去喂鸟，也省得我再麻烦去撒播草籽。你知道那些帐篷和他们的大脚会把每一片草都踩死的，难道你不明白吗？别提了。我知道你还是那句话：'草还会长出来的。'"

车库旁的篮球框架比奥运会还吸引人。这一小块草坪刚开始只是一个像垃圾桶那么大的一小块贫瘠之地，现在却很快就要包围住整个院子的一侧了。

正当新的草籽看起来要发芽时，冬天到了，孩子们穿的冰鞋的冰刀又把草坪划成了一道一道的。麦克的父亲摇着头说："我这辈子没什么奢求——只是想要一块草坪。"

他的妻子却笑着说："草还会长出来的。"

今年秋天的草坪非常漂亮。在院子里的小道边，在车库旁边，以及在花坛周围，都长满了郁郁葱葱、生机勃勃的青草，就像一片海绵地毯一样绵延铺开……而过去孩子们经常穿着运动鞋在那些小道上踩来踩去，他们把自行车扔在车库边……还经常用小勺在那个花坛上挖来挖去。

但是，麦克的父亲却从来都不理会这些，他总是焦急地望着院子外面问道："麦克还会回来，不是吗？"

The Mustard Seed and Sorrow

Once there was a woman whose only son had died. In her sorrow she went to ask a wise holy man if there was a way to bring her son back to life.

"Fetch me a mustard seed from a home that has never known sorrow. We will use it to bring your son back to life." He said to her instead of trying to reason with her.

At once she set off looking for that elusive mustard seed. The first place she came to was a huge mansion. Knocking on the door, she asked, "I am looking for a house that has never known suffering. Is this the place? It is very important to me."

"You have come to the wrong place," they told her. They began to pour out all the tragic things that had befallen upon them.

"Who is better to be able to help these poor unfortunate souls than I who have experienced sadness and can understand them?" she thought. Therefore she stayed behind and consoled and comforted them before going to another house that had never known sorrow before.

However, where she went, from huts to palaces, there was never without tales of sadness and misfortunes. In time to come, she became so involved in listening to other people's sad stories that she forgot about her quest for that elusive mustard seed. By listening to other people, she had actually driven the grieving out of her life.

Someone once said that one of our strangest traits lie in the fact that it takes a tragedy, failure or some form of misfortune to make us realize the power of a positive mental attitude.

芥菜籽和悲伤

曾经有一个女人失去了唯一的儿子。悲伤之余，她去询问一位圣明之人是否有办法使儿子起死回生。

"拿给我一粒芥菜籽，要取自一个从来不知悲伤滋味的家里。我会用它使你的儿子起死回生。"圣明之人没有劝她而是这样说道。

她马上出发去寻找那粒莫名其妙的芥菜籽。她来到的第一个地方是一个大宅院。她敲敲门，问道："我在寻找从来不知痛苦滋味的一家，是这个地方吗？这对我非常重要。"

"你找错了地方。"他们告诉她，然后把发生在他们身上的悲惨事情统统说了出来。

"还有谁能比我更适合去帮助这些可怜不幸的人呢？我经历过悲伤，能够理解他们的痛苦。"她想。于是，她就留下来安慰他们，然后又接着去找另一个从来没有伤心事的家庭。

然而，不管她走到哪里，从茅草小屋到豪华宅邸，每家都有悲伤和不幸之事。很快，她变得非常热衷倾听别人的伤心事，把她自己寻找那粒芥菜籽的事情忘到了脑后。通过倾听别人的伤心事，她已经赶走了自己的痛苦。

有人曾经说过，我们最奇特的品质在于一个悲剧、一场失败或某种不幸能使我们意识到一种积极心态的力量。

My Mother Is Not a Belt

I had wandered into a small Indian shop in the foothills of the Sierras in Northern California and struck up a conversation with the Native American woman who owned the shop. My own Modoc Indian heritage and love of Indian jewelry prompted me to tell her of the pain I suffered when my mother's silver Navajo belt was stolen. My mother had worn it almost every day of her life. It has passed on to me when she had passed through the arch of life to the other side.

I remembered as a small girl putting my arms around my mother's waist and feeling the warmth of her body through the silver platelets. Having her belt gave me great comfort after her death.

As I talked with the Indian woman, I could sense her empathy. But when I finished expressing my grief at having lost the belt, her message was not the one of sympathy I expected. What she gave me was a new beginning and an insight into my mother.

"Remember," she said, "the true gift you were given was things of the spirit. Don't ever cry over things that can't cry over you."

My mother is not a belt. My mother is reflected in the woman who now stands in her place—me. My true heritage is the talents and strength that she left to me. I no longer cry over things that can't cry over me. I cherish the fortitude and the love the woman left to me.

母亲不是一条腰带

我走进位于加利福尼亚州北部内华达山脚下的一家印第安人小店，跟这个小店的主人——一个印第安女人攀谈起来。我的莫多克人的血统和我对印第安珠宝的喜爱，促使我向她倾诉了母亲的银色纳瓦霍腰带被人偷走后我遭受的痛苦。我的母亲在世时几乎每天都戴着它，母亲去世时把它留给了我。

我记得自己还是一个小女孩时常常搂着母亲的腰，透过那银色的薄片感觉到母亲身体的温暖。母亲去世后，我能拥有它对我来说是莫大的安慰。

和这个人印第安女人交谈时，我觉得她能理解我的感情。但是，当我把我失去这条腰带的痛苦倾诉完后，她并没有表现出我意料中的同情。她给了我一个人生新起点和对母亲的理解。

"记住，"她说，"你收到的真正礼物是心灵的礼物，不要为那些不能为你哭泣的东西而哭泣。"

母亲不是一条腰带，我的母亲能够通过这个和她一样已为人母的女人——我而表现出来。我得到的真正遗产是她留给我的才能和力量，我不再为那些不能为我哭泣的东西哭泣，我珍惜她留给我的坚毅和爱。

A Coward and a Beggar

A very wealthy man was standing thoughtfully on a bridge. Despite of all his riches, he could feel none of happiness but sorrow and emptiness in his heart. He intended to commit suicide by jumping into the raging water.

When he was about to do it, a filthy beggar approached him. "Sir, please give me some money to buy some food. I will pray for your health and long life."

Hearing this, he took out the wallet from his pocket and gave all the money inside to the beggar. "Take all of this," he said.

"All of this?" the beggar repeated. He could not believe his good luck.

"Yes, take it all. I am going to a place where I won't need it anymore," said the man. He looked back at the river below.

The beggar became suspicious of the man's attitude. Looking at the money, and holding it for a while, he hurriedly returned it and said, "No, thank you. I won't take it. I may be a beggar but I'm not a coward and I'm not going to receive any money from a coward! Bring that money with you to the river, sir!"

Hearing his response, the man was very shocked. The satisfaction and happiness of him giving his money to the beggar vanished instantly. He was not even able to make the beggar receive his sincere soon-to-be-useless money.

At that moment, he suddenly realized that the feeling that he felt just now, that good feeling and satisfaction from giving others happiness, had indeed in turn became his own true happiness. By this he was enlightened, and had found what would make his life worth living.

Happiness is only real when shared.

懦夫和乞丐

一个非常富有的人站在一座桥上，陷入深思。尽管家财万贯，他却毫无幸福感，内心充满了忧伤和空虚。他打算跳入湍急的河水中，一死了之。

正当他要跳河时，一个脏兮兮的乞丐向他走过来："先生，请给我点钱买些吃的吧，我会为你的健康和长寿祈祷的。"

听到这话，他从口袋里掏出钱夹，把里面所有的钱都给了乞丐。"都拿去吧。"他说。

"所有的吗？"乞丐连声问道。他不相信自己竟有如此好运。

"是的，都拿走吧。我将要去一个不再需要钱的地方了。"这个人说，他回头看着桥下的河。

乞丐感到这个人的神态很可疑，看着这些钱，在手里握了一会儿，匆忙把钱还给他说："不，谢谢你。这钱我不能要。我可以做乞丐，但我不是懦夫，我不会接受一个懦夫的钱！你带着那些钱一起跳河吧，先生。"

听到乞丐的话，富人非常震惊，把钱施舍给乞丐带给他的满足感和幸福感瞬间消失了。他甚至无法使这个乞丐接受他真诚给予的这些很快就没用的钱。

就在那一刻，他突然意识到他刚才有的那种感觉，那种给予他人快乐的美好感觉和满足感，反过来事实上已成为他自己真正的快乐。这下他明白了，并且知道了什么才能使自己的人生有价值。

当与人分享时，快乐才是真正的快乐。

The Revelation of the Lagoon

On one tour, a traveler asked the guide an interesting question, "I noticed that the lagoon side the reef looks pale and lifeless, while the ocean side is vibrant and colorful," the traveler observed. "Why is this?"

The guide gave an interesting answer, "The coral around the lagoon side is in still water with no challenge for its survival. It dies early. The coral on the ocean side is constantly being tested by wind, waves, and storms. It has to fight for survival every day of its life. As it is challenged and tested, it changed and adapts. It grows healthy. It grows strong. And it reproduces."

Then he added, "That's the way it is with every living organism."

That's how it is with people. Challenged and tested, we come alive! Like coral pounded by the sea, we grow. Physical demands can cause us to grow stronger. Mental and emotional street can produce tough-mindedness and resiliency. Spiritual testing can produce strength of character and faithfulness. So, you have problems? No problem! Just tell yourself, "There I grow again!"

Remember, "A smooth sea never made a skilled mariner."

环礁湖的启示

一次旅游中，一名游客问了导游一个有趣的问题："我注意到环礁湖这边的礁石看起来颜色苍白、毫无生气，而海洋那边的礁石却生机勃勃、五颜六色，"游客说，"这是为什么？"

导游给出了有趣的回答："环礁湖周围的珊瑚礁处于静止的水中，很容易存活，死得也早。海洋那边的珊瑚礁不断受到风、浪和暴雨的考验，它们每天都必须要挣扎着活下来。随着它们不断受到挑战和考验，它们也不断改变自己，适应环境。它们茁壮成长，长得结实，所以才能繁衍下去。"

然后，他又加了一句："所有的生物体都是那样的。"

人就是那样的。受到挑战和考验，我们就能活过来！就像被大海冲刷的珊瑚礁一样，我们能够成长。外界环境的要求可以使我们长得更强壮。心理和情绪上的压力可以使我们产生坚强的意志和适应力。精神上的考验能带来品格的力量和信念。因此，你有问题吗？没问题！那就告诉自己："那种情况下我又一次成长！"

记住："平静的大海永远造就不出熟练的水手。"

The Master's Lesson on Gratitude

While roaming the desert, a young man came across a spring of delicious crystal-clear water. The water was so sweet that he filled his leather canteen so he could bring some back to a tribal elder who had been his teacher.

After a four-day journey he presented the water to the old man who took a deep drink, smiled warmly and thanked his student lavishly for the sweet water. The young man returned to his village with a happy heart.

Later, the teacher let another student taste the water. He spat it out, saying it was awful. It apparently had become stale because of the old leather container.

The student challenged his teacher, "Master, the water was stale. Why did you pretend to like it?"

The teacher replied, "You only tasted the water. I tasted the gift. The water was simply the container for an act of loving-kindness and nothing could be sweeter."

Gratitude doesn't always come naturally. Unfortunately, most children and many adults value only the thing given rather than the feeling included in it. We should remind ourselves and teach our children about the beauty and purity of feelings and expressions of gratitude. After all, gifts from the heart are really gifts of the heart! Also, when we express our gratitude, we must never forget that the highest of appreciation is not to utter mere words, but to live by them.

The next time you receive any gifts from anyone, no matter however small it may be, remember the love behind and don't judge the gift by its appearance! Have a deep sense of gratitude for whatever you receive in life in whatever from it may be!

老师的一堂感恩课

一个年轻人在沙漠中行走时偶然碰到了一眼甘甜可口、清澈透明的泉。这水如此甘甜，于是他把皮革水壶装得满满的，这样就可以带一些回去，给一个部落的老族长喝，这个人曾经做过他的老师。

经过4天的跋涉，他把水呈给了这位老人。老人痛饮一口，满脸堆笑，为这甘甜的水对他的学生大为感谢。年轻人满心欢喜地回到自己的村子。

后来，老师让他的另一位学生尝了一下这水。学生把水吐了出来，说这水太难喝了。显然，装在这个皮革水壶里，水已经变味了。

这个学生不服气地问老师："老师，水已经变味了，你为什么还要假装喜欢喝呢？"

老师回答说："你只尝到了水的味道，我却尝到了礼物的味道。这水只是一种仁爱之举的载体，没有什么比这更甜的了。"

感恩并不总是自然地来到。不幸的是，大多数孩子和许多成年人看重的只是被给予之物而不是包含在其中的感情。我们应该提醒自己并教给我们的孩子感情的美丽纯洁和表达感恩之情。毕竟，来自内心的礼物才是真心实意的礼物！而且，我们表达感激时，永远不能忘记感激的最高境界不仅仅是说出感激的话语，而是践行感激之语。

下次你无论从任何人那里收到任何礼物，不管礼物有多小，请记住它包含的爱，不要以貌取物。你要有一颗感恩之心，不管你在生活中收到了什么礼物，也不管它来自哪里！

Put the Glass down

A professor began his class by holding up a glass with some water in it. He held it up for all to see, and asked the students, "How much do you think this glass weighs?"

"50g!"…"100g!"…"125g!…" the students answered.

"I really don't know unless I weigh it," said the professor, "but my question is what would happen if I held it up like this for a few minutes?"

"Nothing," the students said.

"Ok. What would happen if I held it up like this for an hour?" the professor asked.

"Your arm would begin to ache," said one of the students.

"You're right. Now what would happen if I held it for a day?"

"Your arm could go numb. You might have severe muscles stress, or paralysis. Have to go to hospital for sure!" said another student. All the students laughed.

"Very good. But during all this, did the weight of the glass change?" asked the professor.

"No," the students said.

"Then what caused the arm ache and the muscle stress?" The students were puzzled.

"Put the glass down!" said one of the students.

"Exactly!" said the professor. "The problems of life are something like this. Hold it for a few minutes in your head, they seem OK. Think of them for a long time and they begin to ache. Hold it even longer and they begin to paralyze you. You will not be able to do anything. It's important to think of the challenges in your life, but it's even more important to 'put them down' at the end of every day before you go to sleep. That way, you are not stressed, you wake up every day fresh and strong and can handle any issue, any challenge that comes your way!"

Remember to put the glass down today.

放下玻璃杯

一名教授举起一只装有水的玻璃杯开始上课，他把杯子举起来，让大家都看到，然后问学生们："你们认为这个玻璃杯有多重？"

"50克！""100克！""125克！"学生们答道。

"我真不知道它有多重，除非我称一下它，"教授说，"但我的问题是，如果我就这样举着它过几分钟，将会发生什么？"

"什么也不会发生。"学生们说。

"好的，如果我像这样举着它一个小时，将会发生什么？"教授问。

"你的胳膊将会感觉疼。"其中一个学生说。

"你说得对，如果我举一天，将会是什么结果？"

"你的胳膊会变麻，你的胳膊可能会有严重的肌肉紧张或完全麻痹，肯定得去医院了！"另一个学生说。所有的学生都笑了起来。

"很好。但在这整个期间，玻璃杯的重量改变了吗？"教授问道。

"没有。"大家说。

"那是什么导致了胳膊疼痛和肌肉紧张？"学生们都疑惑不解。

"放下玻璃杯！"一个学生说。

"正是这样！"教授说。"生活中的问题和这个颇为相似。你思考几分钟，它们似乎没什么。如果想很长时间，它们就开始疼痛起来。思考的时间更长些，它们就开始使你瘫痪，你将会无力做任何事情。思考生活中的挑战固然重要，但在每天结束时，你临睡前'放下它们'更重要。那样就不会有压力，你每天早上醒来，神清气爽，精力充沛，可以应对任何事情，应对你面前的任何挑战。"

记住今天要放下玻璃杯！

Lao Tzu and One Big Tree

Lao Tzu was traveling with his disciples and they came to a forest where hundreds of woodcutters were cutting the trees. The whole forest had been cut except for one big tree with thousands of branches. It was so big that 10,000 persons could sit in its shade.

Lao Tzu asked his disciples to go and inquire why this tree had not been cut. They went and asked the woodcutter and they said, "This tree is totally useless. You cannot make anything out of it because every branch has so many knots in it—nothing is straight. You cannot use it as fuel because the smoke is dangerous to the eyes. This tree is absolutely useless, that's why we haven't cut it."

The disciples came back and told Lao Tzu. He laughed and said, "Be like this tree. If you are useful you will be cut and you will become furniture in somebody's house. If you are beautiful you will be sold in the market, you will become a commodity. Be like this tree, absolutely useless, and then you will grow big and vast and thousands of people will find shade under you."

老子和一棵大树

老子和他的弟子们正在旅行，这时他们来到了一片森林里，森林里有几百名伐木者正在伐木，整个森林里的树除了一棵枝杈繁茂的大树，其余的全都被砍掉了。这棵树如此之大，能容纳上万人坐在树荫下乘凉。

老子就让弟子们去询问一下这棵树没有被砍掉的原因，弟子们就问了伐木者，他们回答说："这棵树一点用也没有，用它什么也做不了，因为它的每一根树枝上都生有太多的硬结——没有一根是直的。你也不能用它当柴烧，因为它冒出的烟会伤害眼睛。这棵树完全无用，所以我们才不砍它。"

弟子们回来告诉了老子，老子大笑着说："像这棵树一样，如果你是有用之才，你就会被砍掉，然后成为别人家里的家具。如果你漂亮美观，你就会变成一件商品在市场上被出售。如果像这棵树一样，完全无用，你将会长得高大粗壮、枝繁叶茂，许多人都能在你这里找到乘凉之地。"

Keep Your Dream

I have a friend named Monty Roberts who owns a horse ranch in San Ysidro. He has let me use his house to put on fund-raising events to raise money for youth at risk programs.

The last time I was there he introduced me by saying, "I want to tell you why I let Jack use my house. It all goes back to a story about a young man who was the son of an itinerant horse trainer who would go from stable to stable, rack track to rack track, farm to farm and ranch to ranch, training horses. As a result, the boy's high school career was continually interrupted. When he was a senior, he was asked to write a paper about what he wanted to be and do when he grew up.

That night he wrote a seven-page paper describing his goal of owning a horse ranch someday. He wrote about his dream in great detail and he even drew a diagram of a 200-acre ranch, showing the location of all the buildings, the stables and the track. Then he drew a detailed floor plan for a 4,000-square-foot house that would sit on a 200-acre dream ranch.

He put a great deal of his heart into the project and the next day he handed it in to his teacher. Two days later he received his paper back. On the front page was a large red F with a note that read, "See me after class."

The boy with the dream went to see the teacher after class and asked, "Why did I receive an F?"

The teacher said, "This is an unrealistic dream for a boy like you. You have no money. You come from an itinerant family. You have no resources. Owning a horse ranch requires a lot of money. You have to buy the land. You have to pay for the original breeding stock and later you'll have to pay large stud fees. There's no way you could ever do it. Then the teacher added, "If you rewrite this paper with a more realistic goal, I will reconsider your grade."

The boy went home and thought about it long and hard. He asked his father what he should do. His father said, "Look, son, you have to make up your own mind on this. However, I think it is a very important decision for you."

Finally, after sitting with it for a week, the boy turned in the same paper, making no changes at all. He stated, "You can keep the F and I'll keep my dream."

Monty then turned to the assembled group and said, "I tell you this story because you are sitting in my 4,000-square-foot house in the middle of my 200-acre horse ranch. I still have that school paper framed over the fireplace." He added, "The best part of the story is that two summers ago that same schoolteacher brought 30 kids to camp out on my ranch for a week." When the teacher was leaving, he said, "Look, Monty, I can tell you this now. When I was your teacher, I was something of a dream stealer. During those years I stole a lot of kids' dreams. Fortunately you had enough gumption not to give up on yours."

"Don't let anyone steal your dreams. Follow your heart, no matter what."

坚持你的梦想

我有个朋友，叫蒙蒂·罗伯茨，他在圣西多有个马场。我常借用他宽敞的住宅举办募款活动，以便为帮助青少年的计划筹备基金。

上次我在他家做客时，他告诉我："你知道我为何会让杰克借用我的住宅吗？我给你讲个故事吧——曾经有个年轻人，他是一位经常巡回表演的驯马师的儿子。他们经常在不同的马厩、棚架、农场和马场之间穿梭，驯养了很多优良马匹。可是，因为家族生意，这个小伙子荒废了高中学业。当他升入大四时，有一次老师布置了一项作业，要求每个人写一篇关于自己未来事业的文章。

"那天夜里，他写了一篇长达7页的文章，讲述的是他将来如何拥有一家私人马场的目标和志向。他详细描述了自己的梦想，甚至在纸上画了一幅200英亩大的马场的示意图，详细描绘了所有的内部建筑结构、马厩和道路规划，然后又画了一幅详细的平面图，就是有关4000平方英尺的大宅如何坐落在这座梦幻般的200英亩大的马场里的。

"他在这篇文章里投入了大量心血，第二天他将自己的作品交给老师。两天后，他收到了自己的作业，只见首页上标着一个醒目的红色F（表示不及格），另外附注了一条信息：下课后来找我。

"充满梦想的男孩下课后径直找到了老师并问道：'为什么给了我个不及格？'

"老师回复：'对于一个像你这样年纪的男孩来说，这是一个不现实的梦想，因为你没有钱。你来自一个靠巡回演出赚钱而仅能糊口的穷困家庭，也就是说你没有任何可利用资源。你要知道，拥有一家马场需要很多钱，比如说你要买地，你要花钱为起步阶段驯养的牲口买饲料，然后还要花大量金钱为马匹配种。总之，你绝不可能成功！'然后，老师又补充道，'如果你能带着一个更切合实际的目标重写这份作业，我会重新考虑你的分数。'

"男孩回家后冥思苦想，但想破了头，也想不出一个更好的主题。他就问父亲该怎么办。父亲告诉他：'听着，孩子，在这件事上，你要有自己的主见。无论如何，我都认为这对你来讲将是一个非常重要的决定！'

"苦想了一周后，最终男孩还是交上了相同的文章，一点也没有改动，他还说道：'你可以保留你的F，但我仍要坚持我的梦想！'"

蒙蒂缓缓转过身，面对所有的听众说道："我之所以告诉你们这个故事，就是因为此时此刻，你们大家正坐在我的200英亩大马场正中央的4000平方英尺的大豪宅里。我仍保留着当年写的那篇文章，就装裱在壁炉的正上方。"顿了一下，他又补充道："这个故事最精彩的部分是在前年夏天，还是那个老师，曾带着30个小孩来我的农场露营了一周时间。临行之际，他对我说：'蒙蒂，我想告诉你一件事。我还是你的老师时，曾是个偷梦者。那些年我曾偷过很多孩子的梦想。幸运的是，你拥有了进取心，不会放弃自己的梦想。'"

"不要让任何人偷走你的梦想。无论如何，都要坚持你的梦想！"

Don't Abandon Your Dream

There were once two brothers who lived on the 80th level. On coming home one day, they realized to their dismay that the lifts were not working and that they had to climb the stairs home.

After struggling to the 20th level, panting and tired, they decided to abandon their bags and come back for them the next day. They left their bags then and climbed on. When they had struggled to the 40th level, the younger brother started to grumble and they began to quarrel. They continued to climb the flights of steps, quarreling all the way to the 60th floor.

They then realized that they have only 20 levels more to climb and decided to stop quarreling and continue climbing in peace. They silently climbed on and reached their home at long last. Each stood calmly before the door and waited for the other to open the door.

And then they realized that the key was in their bags which were left on the 20th floor.

This story is a reflection on our life. Many of us live under the expectations of our parents, teachers and friends when young. We seldom get to do the things that we really love and are under so much pressure and stress that by the age of 20, we get tired and decide to dump this load.

Being free of the stress and pressure, we work enthusiastically and dream ambitious wishes. But by the time we reach 40 years old, we start to lose our vision and dreams. We began to feel unsatisfied and start to complain and criticize. We live a miserable life as we are never satisfied. Reaching 60, we realize that we have little left for complaining anymore, and we begin to walk the final episode in peace and calmness.

We think that there is nothing left to disappoint us, only to realize that we could not rest in peace because we have an unfulfilled dream—a dream we abandoned 60 years ago.

So what is your dream? Follow your dreams, so that you will not live with regrets.

不要放弃你的梦想

曾有两兄弟一起住在一栋公寓楼的80层。有一天回家时，他们突然非常沮丧，因为所有的电梯都坏了，这也就意味着他们要爬80层楼梯进到家。

勉强爬到第20层时，二人都气喘吁吁、疲惫不堪。于是，他们决定扔下身上所有的背包，轻装前进，等第二天再来取。扔掉背包后，他们继续向上爬。当他们爬到第40层时，弟弟开始抱怨，于是二人产生了口角。他们就这样不停地边吵边爬，不知不觉中已爬到了第60层。

此刻，他们意识到只需再爬20层就可以到家了，于是便停止争吵，平静地继续向上爬。爬啊爬，他们终于爬到了家门口。此时，两人都镇定地立于门前，等着对方拿钥匙开门。

他们意识到：家门钥匙留在了20层楼梯处的背包里。

这个故事反映了我们的人生。我们中许多人年轻时都曾处于父母、老师和朋友们的过高期望值下，因此20岁时我们很少有机会去做我们真正想要做的事情，并面临着诸多压力和压迫，于是我们身心俱疲，决定扔掉这个包袱。

摆脱压力和压迫，我们就会热情工作，梦想自己的雄心壮志。但当我们上了40岁时，便开始逐步丧失自己的宏伟抱负，开始觉得不知足，牢骚满腹，愤世嫉俗。我们痛苦地活了一辈子，因为我们从不会满足。到60岁时，我们认识到自己这辈子稀里糊涂地过去了，也没什么可再抱怨的了，然后就开始安逸地走完这人生的最后一段路。

我们意识到没什么可失望的了，只是我们无法安息，因为没有完成毕生的心愿和梦想——一个我们早在60年前就放弃的梦想。

那你的梦想又是什么呢？追随自己的梦想，你就会此生无憾。

The Courage of His Convictions

Abraham Lincoln made the great speech of his famous senatorial campaign at Springfield, Illinois. The convention before which he spoke consisted of a thousand delegates together with the crowd that had gathered with them.

His speech was carefully prepared. Every sentence was guarded and emphatic. It has since become famous as "The Divided House" speech. Before entering the hall where it was to be delivered, he stepped into the office of his law-partner Mr. Herndon, and, locking the door, so that their interview might be private, took his manuscript from his pocket, and read one of the opening sentences: "I believe this government cannot endure permanently, half slave and half free."

Mr. Herndon remarked that the sentiment was true, but suggested that it not be good policy to utter it at that time. Mr. Lincoln replied with great firmness, "No matter about the policy. It is true, and the nation was entitled to it. The proposition has been true for six thousand years, and I will deliver it as it is written."

Hope is like a dream-fire burning in the background of our minds. We start with hope. Where there is even a spark of hope, faith lives and dream-fires burn. We keep visualizing a brighter future. And when our desire can burn no brighter, we do the most important thing: begin turning our dreams into reality.

信念的勇气

亚伯拉罕·林肯曾在伊利诺伊州春田市参加过参议员竞选活动，并在大会上发表了一篇著名演讲。这次集会聚齐了1000位会议代表，还有选民和群众。

他精心准备了演讲稿，字里行间充满了谨慎和强调，这就是美国历史上有名的"分裂之家"演说词。在即将进入进行演说的大厅之前，林肯先进了他的法律合伙人赫恩登先生的办公室，随手锁上门，这样他们的会面就保证了隐私。然后，林肯从口袋中掏出手稿，读了一句开场白："我相信这个政府维持不了多久了——一半奴隶，一半自由。"

赫恩登先生评论说，尽管情感真实，但当时宣读这句话不是一个明智的策略。林肯却斩钉截铁地回复道："这和策略无关。我说的都是实话，全国也都是这样定性的。6000年来的时间见证了提案的真实性，而我也会按照稿上所写的来宣读！"

希望就像是我们大脑中在燃烧的梦想之火，我们从希望开始，只要我们有一点希望的火种，信念就会存活，梦想之火就会燃烧。

Where There Is a Will There Is a Way

Henry Bond was about ten years old when his father died. His mother found it difficult to provide for the support of a large family, thus left entirely in her care. By good management, however, she contrived to do so, and also to send Henry, the oldest, to school, and to supply him, for the most part, with such books as he needed.

At one time, however, Henry wanted a grammar, in order to join a class in that study, and his mother could not furnish him with the money to buy it. He was very much troubled about it, and went to bed with a heavy heart, thinking what could be done.

On waking in the morning, he found that a deep snow had fallen, and the cold wind was blowing furiously. "Ah," said he, "it is an ill wind that blows nobody good."

He rose, ran to the house of a neighbor, and offered his service to clear a path around his premises. The offer was accepted. Having completed this work, and received his pay, he went to another place for the same purpose, and then to another, until he had earned enough to buy a grammar.

When school commenced, Henry was in his seat, the happiest boy there, ready to begin the Lessonin his new book.

From that time, Henry, was always the first in all his classes. He knew no such word as fail, but always succeeded in all he attempted. Having the will, he always found the way.

有志者事竟成

亨利·邦德10岁左右的时候，他的父亲去世了。他的母亲发现自己很难维持一个大家庭，因为所有的事情都要她来操心。但是，通过苦心经营，她支撑起了这个家，她把最大的孩子亨利送进了学校，并尽可能支持他，为他提供需要的书。

有一次，亨利需要买一本语法书，母亲却拿不出钱来。他感到很烦心，便心情不安地上床睡觉了，他心想自己应该做点什么来改变困境。

他早上醒来的时候，发现天上下起了大雪，寒风猛烈地吹着。"啊，"他说，"这风吹得太猛烈，对任何人都没有好处。"

于是，亨利站起身，跑到邻居的房子前，说自己能够为他清除周围道路的积雪。他的这一提议被邻居接受了。于是他扫完积雪，得到了一笔收入，然后他挨家挨户为人清扫积雪，直到赚够了买一本语法书的钱。

开学的时候，亨利是他们班里最幸福的男孩，他快乐地坐在座位上，开始准备学习新的课程。

从那时起，亨利总在班级名列前茅。在他的字典里没有"失败"这个词，因为他总是想方设法取得成功。带着这种信念，他总是能够如愿以偿。

Annie's Dream

It was a clear, cold, winter evening, and all the Sinclairs but Annie had gone out for a neighborly visit. She had resolved to stay at home and study a long, difficult Lesson in Natural Philosophy.

Left to herself, the evening passed quickly, but the Lesson was learned a full half hour before the time set for the family to come home.

Closing her book, she leaned back in the soft armchair in which she was sitting, soon fell asleep, and began to dream. She dreamed that it was a very cold morning, and that she was standing by the dining-room stove, looking into the glass basin which was every day filled with water for evaporation.

"Oh, dear," she sighed, "it is nearly school time. I don't want to go out in the cold this morning. Then there is that long lesson. I wonder if I can say it. Let me see—it takes two hundred and twelve degrees of heat, I believe, for water to evaporate—"

"Nonsense!" "Ridiculous!" shouted a chorus of strange little voices near by; "Look here! is this water boiling?What an idea; two hundred and twelve degrees before we can fly, ha, ha!"

"Who are you?" asked Annie, in amazement. "Where must I look?" "In the basin, of course."

Annie looked, and saw a multitude of tiny forms moving swiftly around, their numbers increasing as the heat of the fire increased. "Why you dear little things!" said she, "what are you doing down there?"

"We are water sprites," answered one, in the clearest voice that can be imagined, "and when this delightful warmth comes all about us, we become so light that we fly off, as you see."

In another moment he had joined a crowd of his companions that were spreading their wings and flying off in curling, white clouds over Annie's head. But they were so light and thin that they soon disappeared in the air.

She could not see where they went, so she again turned to the basin. "Doesn't it hurt you," she asked one, "to be heated—?" "Not always to two hundred and twelve," said the sprite, mischievously.

"No, no," replied Annie, half-vexed; "I remember, that is boiling point—but I mean, to be heated as you all are, and then to fly off in the cold?"

"Oh, no," laughed the little sprite; "we like it. We are made to change by God's wise laws, and so it can't hurt us. We are all the time at work, in our way, taking different shapes. It is good for us. If you will go to the window, you will find some of my brothers and sisters on the glass."

Annie went to the window, and at first could see nothing but some beautiful frostwork on it. Soon, however, the panes seemed to swarm with little folks. Their wings were as white as snow, and sparkled with ice jewels.

"Oh," cried Annie, "this is the prettiest sight I ever saw. What is your name, darling?" she asked one that wore a crown of snow roses. The little voice that replied was so sharp and fine that Annie thought it seemed like a needle point of sound, and she began to laugh.

"Fine Frost is our family name," it said. "I have a first name of my own, but I shall not tell you what it is, for you are so impolite as to laugh at me."

"I beg your pardon, dear," said Annie; "I could not help it. I will not laugh at you any more if you will tell me how you came here. I have been talking with one of your brothers over there in the basin."

The little sprite then folded her wings in a dignified manner, and said, "I will tell you all I know about it, since you promise to be polite. It is a very short story, however.

"Last evening we all escaped from the glass basin, as you have seen our companions do this morning. Oh, how light and free we felt! But we were so very delicate and thin that no one saw us as we flew about in the air of the room.

"After a while I flew with these others to this window, and, as we alighted on the glass, the cold changed us from water sprites into sprites of the Fine Frost family." "It is very wonderful," said Annie. "Is it nice to be a sprite?"

"Oh, yes, we are very gay. All last night we had a fine time sparkling in the moonlight. I wore a long wreath full of ice pearls and diamonds. Here is a piece of it. Before long we shall be water sprites again. I see the sun is coming this way."

"Shall you dread to be melted?" inquired Annie. "No, indeed," answered the sprite. "I like to change my form now and then."

A thought flashed across Annie's brain. What if she should breathe on the frost and not wait for the sun to melt it. In a moment more she had done so. Down fell a great number of the tiny mountains and castles, carrying with them a multitude of frost sprites, and all that could be seen was a drop of water on the window sill.

"Oh, dear! have I hurt them?" she exclaimed. "No, no," replied a chorus of many small voices from the drop of water, "we are only water sprites again. Nothing hurts us; we merely change." "But you are always pretty little things," said Annie. "I wish—"

Here a ring at the doorbell woke Annie. She started up to find the family had returned from their visit, which all declared was a delightful one. But Annie said she did not believe they had enjoyed their visit better than she had her half hour's dream.

安 妮 的 梦

这是冬天的一个寒冷的晚上，辛克莱家的人都去邻居家串门了，但是安妮决定留下来，好好学习那又长又难的自然哲学课。

一个人在家里，夜晚过得很快，离家人回来还有半小时的时候，她才弄明白。

于是，她合上书，躺在柔软的扶手椅上，很快进入了梦乡。她梦见在一个寒冷的清晨，她站在餐厅的火炉旁，看那个每天都盛满水的玻璃盆，它散发的蒸汽能让屋里空气潮湿。

"哦，天啊，"她叹口气说，"快到上课的时间了。但是我不想在这么冷的天出门。还要上那么长一节课。不知道我是否能答上来所学的东西。我认为把水蒸发掉，需要至少212华氏度（100摄氏度）。"

"胡扯！" "真荒谬！"从她旁边传来了古怪的声音。"看看这儿！这水没有沸腾吗？有212华氏度的话，我们都能飞了，哈哈！"

"你们是谁？"安妮惊讶地问道，"我朝哪儿看？" "当然是水盆里。"

于是安妮看向脸盆，她发现脸盆里面有许多细小的东西在来回游动，随着温度的上升，它们的数量在不断激增。"你们怎么这么小啊！"安妮说，"你们在这里做什么？"

"我们是水精灵，"它们中的一个用最清晰的声音回答道，"你能够看到，当水的温度足够高时，我们就会飞起来。"

刹那间，它和同伴们一起展开翅膀，飞向了空中，在安妮的头顶形成了一团白色的烟雾。但是它们太轻、太薄，所以很快就消失在了空气中。

安妮不知道它们去哪儿了，于是她问脸盆："这样疼吗？加热到这样——""温度并不总是要加热到212华氏度。"水精灵开玩笑似地答道。

"不，不，"安妮回答道，"我记得沸点。不，我的意思是，你们被加热，然后飞到寒冷的空气中？"

"哦，不疼，"水精灵笑着说，"我们喜欢这样。伟大的自然定律能够保证我们不受到伤害。我们无时无刻不在用自己的方式忙碌着，变换各种形态。这对我们来说，是有好处的。如果你去窗户那儿，就能在玻璃上找到好多我的兄弟姐妹。"

于是安妮去了窗户那儿，起初她除了看到一些窗花之外，什么也看不到。但是很快，玻璃上聚集起了许多小东西。它们的翅膀和雪一样洁白，像珠宝一样闪耀。

"噢，"安妮叫道，"这是我见过的最漂亮的东西。你叫什么名字，小可爱？"她冲其中一个带着白雪皇冠的小家伙问道。那个小家伙回答的声音就像针尖一样尖利，安妮开始笑起来。

"霜是我们的姓，"它说，"我有自己的名字，但是我不想告诉你，因为你竟然嘲笑我，这是很不礼貌的。"

"非常抱歉，小可爱，"安妮说，"我实在没忍住。如果你能告诉我你是怎么来到这里的，我就不会再笑你了。我刚才和你的一个兄弟聊过天，它就在那个水盆里。"

于是，小精灵用非常优雅的姿势伸展开自己的翅膀，然后说道："既然你承诺了会对我礼貌，那么我就把我所知道的告诉你。但是，这个故事很短。

"昨天晚上我们从玻璃盆里逃了出来，就像你今天早上在盆里看见的那些水精灵那样。我们觉得非常轻松自由！但是，我们又轻又小，当我们飞向空中之后，没人能看见我们。

"之后，我和一些同伴飞到这个窗户上，当我们附着在窗户上之后，严寒把我们从水精灵变成了霜精灵。""这多奇妙啊，"安妮说，"当精灵有意思吗？"

"噢，当然，我们非常快乐。在月光的照射下，我们浑身都是亮闪闪的。我有一个大花环，上面有冰珍珠和钻石。但是我们就快要变成水精灵了，因为太阳快出来了。"

"你怕被融化掉吗？"安妮问。"不怕，"精灵答道，"我喜欢随时变换形态。"

这时，一个想法闪过安妮的脑海，如果她冲精灵哈气的话，那么在太阳到来之前，精灵就能被融化掉。于是她吹了一口气，只见细小的山和城堡连同那些精灵一起掉落下来，而这所有的一切都发生在从窗户上落下来的一滴水珠里。

"噢，天啊，我伤着它们了吧？"安妮大叫道。"没有，没有，"从水滴里传来了欢快的声音，"我们不过是又变回了水精灵而已。我们没有受伤，只是改变了外形。""但愿你们永远是小精灵。"安妮说。

这时，门铃的响声把安妮吵醒了。她站起来，发现家人都回来了，他们都很开心。但是，安妮心想，你们度过的时光再愉快，也没有我刚才做的那半小时的梦美好。

第八卷

看不见的小奇迹

"No Depression" Cake

It was the depths of the Great Depression. Several families on our block were receiving food from the welfare people. Hard times for everyone. But it was my birthday, and I was just a little girl.

My mother said there was no money for a girl or a cake. I sat forlornly on the front stoop and felt sorry for myself. Then Mama came out. "Remember, there is always hope. Come and see. I have a surprise inside for your birthday!" I ran in to find inside was the most adorable kitten with huge blue eyes. I immediately fell in love with it and called it "Fluffy."

Then I noticed a cake on the table with a candle on the top. "How did you do it, Mama?" I asked curiously. "The kitten came from nice Mrs. Jones. She gave us the recipe for this 'no Depression' Cake. When you bake it, you can't be sad! Mrs. Jones said we must think of what we have on hand, not what we don't have. We can always create something new and useful if we think positively. That is why it is called the 'no Depression' Cake!"

Mama was right. I will never forget the happiness of that day. I took a piece of my birthday cake to Mrs. Jones to thank her.

I remembered the "No Depression" Cake when my own babies were little and my husband's dry-cleaning business failed. To help him, I began a tiny advertising business on foot, pushing our children ahead of me on a broken baby stroller in the rural town of Baldwin Park, California.

Because there were no jobs, I asked the weekly newspaper to sell me space at a wholesale rate. Then I went out and resold the space in the form of a shopper's column to merchants. Soon I had the house payment covered.

Then I spoke to service club luncheons to promote my advertising column. I had no car or baby sitter, so I made a deal with my neighbor. I traded baby sitting for the use of her car. Another helping of "No Depression" Cake! All of the business I run today, world-wide, began with that "No Depression" system.

As the children grew up we had many ups and downs. I especially remember one time when we had no money for groceries. I sat down with them and said, "Let's make a 'no Depression' Cake! Let's see what we have on hand." My son said, "Mom, the avocado tree is full of fruit. I'll sell them today by the curb."

"There aren't enough oranges on our tree to sell," my daughter said. "I'll pick them, keep some for us, and take a bag to our neighbor to see if they'll trade for some of their great tasting plums!" We all got busy. With the first avocado sales, I ran to the grocery store and bought day-old bread, a big bag of beans, some brown sugar and powdered milk. Then I baked a "No Depression" Cake. We had a grand lunch, counting all of our blessings and thinking of all the good things we could do together.

By the end of the afternoon, my son had sold many more of the avocados, and I had a big bowl of beans baking in the oven. Then the phone rang. It was one of my advertisers asking me to come over and pick up a big ad and a check.

Next time you're feeling low, trying counting the good things you have on hand. Do with what you have. Bake up a positive-thinking "No Depression" Cake!

"没有萧条" 的蛋糕

那是大萧条的最低点，我们楼的好几个家庭都接受到福利机构的食物，每个人都处于困难时期，但那时是我的生日，我只是一个小女孩。

妈妈对我说："没有钱给你，也没有钱买蛋糕。"我可怜巴巴地坐在前门廊上，弯着腰，替自己感到伤心，一会儿妈妈出来对我说："记着，希望总在。来，看一下，里面有个你意想不到的生日礼物。"我跑进去一看，是一只有着蓝色大眼睛的小猫，我立刻就喜欢上了它，并叫它"毛毛"。

然后，我发现桌子上有一个蛋糕，顶部插了一根蜡烛。"你怎么做的，妈妈？"我好奇地问。"猫是善良的琼斯阿姨给的，她给了我们这个'没有萧条'蛋糕的秘方，你烘烤它时，就不会悲伤，琼斯说我们必须关心我们手头有什么，而不是没有什么，如果积极思考，我们就会创造出新奇有用的东西。这就是它为什么叫作'没有萧条'蛋糕的原因。"

妈妈说得对。我永远不会忘记那天我有多开心，我拿了一块蛋糕给琼斯阿姨，表示感谢。

当我的孩子尚小、丈夫的干洗生意又失败时，我想起了"没有萧条"的蛋糕。为了帮他，我用破旧的小推车推着我们的孩子，在加州鲍德温公园的乡镇上到处张贴广告。

因为没有工作，所以我请求周报把版面以批发价卖给我。然后，我出去再以购物指南专栏的形式转售这个版面。很快，我就付清了房款。

我刊登了同行福利俱乐部午饭的广告，宣传我的广告专栏。我没有车，也没有保姆，于是和邻居们做了笔交易，我以替他们照看婴儿为代价使用他们的车。又是"没有萧条"蛋糕帮的忙！我今天经营的生意闻名世界，都始于"没有萧条"这个系统。

在孩子成长的过程中，我们经历了许多动荡起伏。我尤其记得有一次，我们没钱买食品。我跟他们一块坐下来说："让我们做一个'没有萧条'的蛋糕吧！让我们看看手边都有什么。"儿子说："妈妈，鳄梨树挂满了果。我决定今天在路边把它们卖了。"

"树上没有足够多的橘子来卖。"女儿说，"我要把它们摘下来，给我们留一些，再背一袋子到邻居那里，看看能不能换他们一点可口的李子！"我们全都忙碌起来。我首先用卖鳄梨赚来的钱跑到食品杂货店买了放了一天的面包、一大袋豌豆、一些红糖和奶粉。然后，我烤了一个"没有萧条"蛋糕。我们吃了一顿丰盛的午餐，清点着我们所有的幸福，想着我们一起所能做的一切好吃的东西。

下午结束时，儿子又卖出了好多鳄梨，我又在烤箱里烤了一大碗豌豆。然后，电话响了，是我的一个广告商让我过去接一大单广告并拿支票。

下次你感到失落时，试着回想一下你手头拥有的好东西，用你现有的材料烤一个积极思维的"没有萧条"蛋糕！

Find Our Starfish

The old man awoke just before sunrise, as he often did, to walk by the ocean's edge and greet the new day. As he moved through the morning dawn, he focused on a faint, far away motion.

He saw a youth, bending and reaching and flailing arms, dancing on the beach, no doubt in celebration of the perfect day soon to begin. As he approached, he realized that the youth was not dancing to the day, but rather bending to sift through the debris left by the night's tide, stopping now and then to pick up starfish and then standing, to heave it back into the sea.

He asked the youth the purpose of the effort. "The tide has washed the starfish onto the beach and they cannot return to the sea by themselves," the youth replied. "When the sun rises, they will die, unless I throw them back into the sea."

As the youth explained, the old man surveyed the vast expanse of beach, stretching in both directions beyond eyesight. Starfish littered the shore in numbers beyond calculation.

The hopelessness of the youth's plan became clear and the old man countered, "But there are more starfishes on this beach than you can ever save before the sun is up. Surely you cannot expect to make a difference."

The young man listened politely. Then bent down, picked up another starfish and threw it into the sea, past the breaking waves and said, "It made a difference for that one."

There is something very special in each and every one of us. We have all been gifted with the ability to make a difference, and if we can become aware of that gift, we gain through the strength of our visions the power to shape the future.

We must each find our starfish. And if we throw our stars wisely and well, the world might be different.

找到自己的海星

天没亮，老人就醒了，他通常都这样，在海边走走，迎接新的一天。他借着黎明的曙光往前走时，眼神集中在一个微弱遥远的动作上。

他看到一个年轻人弯腰捡起东西，甩着胳膊，在海滩上跳舞，毫无疑问是在庆祝新一天的开始。他走近时，意识到年轻人不是在向新一天跳舞，而是弯腰从海滩上捡一些东西。这些东西是晚上的潮水带过来的。年轻人时不时地捡起一些海星，然后站起来，把它们尽力朝海中扔去。

他问年轻人这样做的目的是什么。"潮水把海星冲到海面上，它们自己回不了大海，"年轻人回答，"太阳出来时，它们就会死的，除非我现在把它们扔进大海。"

年轻人说着，老人看了看广阔的海滩，一眼望不到边，海滩上散落的海星不计其数。

年轻人的计划显而易见是不可实现的，老人反驳道："可是，海滩上这么多海星，太阳升起来了，你也不能把它们全部扔进海里。你肯定不可能产生多大影响。"

年轻人很有礼貌地听着，弯下腰，捡起另一条海星，扔进大海，海星擦过碎落的浪花。年轻人说："对那只来说产生了影响。"

我们每个人都有特殊之处，都被赋予了对他人产生影响的能力。如果能意识到这种天赋，我们从远见中就会获得能量，塑造未来。

我们每个人必须找到自己的海星。如果我们能重新把它们扔进海里，世界将因此产生变化。

Kindness Is a Strength

In a small village there lived a man who was always happy, kind, and well-disposed to everyone he met. People knew they could depend on him, and regarded him as a great friend.

One of the villagers was curious to know what his secret was, how could he be always so kind and helpful? How is it that he held no grudge towards anyone and was always happy?

Once upon meeting him in the street he asked him: "Most people are selfish and unsatisfied. They do not smile as often as you do; neither are they as helpful or kind as you are. How do you explain it?"

"When you make peace with yourself, then you can be in peace with the rest of the world. If you can recognize the spirit in yourself, you can recognize the spirit in everyone, and then you find it natural to be kind and well-disposed to all. If your thoughts are under your control, you become strong and firm."

"But there are many walls that need to be climbed. It is not an easy task," lamented the villager.

"Do not think about the difficulties, otherwise that's what you will see and experience. Just quiet your feelings and thoughts and try to stay in this peace. All the abilities and powers awake spontaneously."

"Is that all?" asked the villager.

"Try to watch your thoughts and see how they come and go. Stay in the quietness that arises. The moments of peace will be brief at first, but in time they will get longer. This peace is also strength, power, kindness, and love."

"I will try to memorize your words," said the villager and continued, "There is another thing that I am curious about. You do not seem to be influenced by the environment. You have a kind word to everyone and are helpful. Yet people do not exploit your goodness, and they treat you well."

"Goodness and being kind do not necessarily point to weakness. When you are good you can also be strong. People sense your strength and do not impose on you. You then act from strength and not from weakness. Goodness can also go with power and strength; it is not a sign of weakness as some people erroneously think."

"Thank you very much for your advice," said the villager and went away happy and satisfied.

友善是一种力量

小山村里住着一个人，他总是快乐友善，并对他遇见的每个人都有好感。人们都知道他可信，就把他当成好朋友。

一个村民好奇，想知道他的秘密是什么，他是怎样做到友好和乐于助人的？他是怎样做到对任何人都没有私心，总是乐乐呵呵的呢？

有一次，村民在街上遇到了他，便问：“大多数人都非常自私，欲壑难填，他们不像你那么经常笑，也不像你那么友好、乐于助人。你是怎么做到的？”

“你能和自己和平相处时，就能和世界上的其余一切和平相处。如果能认识到这点，你就能认清自己的内心。然后，你就会发现你能够自然地对所有人友好。如果你能控制自己的思想，你就会变得坚强。”

"可是，有很多障碍要攀越。这并不是一件简单的事儿。"村民悲叹道。

"别想那些困难，否则那会是你该看到的和经历的，只要你安定情绪，尽力保持平静，所有的能力和力量都会不由自主焕发出来。"

"完了吗？"村民问。

"尽力观察你的思想，看看它们是怎样产生和消逝的，和'静'待在一起，安静的瞬间起初很短暂，但随着时间流逝，它会慢慢变长。这种'静'也是一种力量、友善和爱。"

"我会记住你的话，"村民继续说道，"还有一件事我很好奇，你似乎不会被环境影响，你与每个人都友善交谈并乐于帮助他们。他们没有利用你，对你很好。"

"善良和友善并不一定指脆弱。你友善时，也可能会变得强大，人们感到你的强大，就不会强加于你，然后你就可以自由行事，而不是变得脆弱。善意伴着力量和能力同行，它不是人们那种错误的认识：那是一种错误的标志。"

"多谢你的建议。"村民说完，快乐而满足地走了。

Patience to Learn

A young man presented himself to the local expert on gems and said he wanted to become a gemologist. The expert brushed him off because he feared that the youth would not have the patience to learn. The young man pleaded for a chance. Finally the expert consented and told the youth, "Be here tomorrow."

The next morning the expert put a jade stone in the boy's hand and told him to hold it. The expert then went about his work, cutting, weighing, and setting gems. The boy sat quietly and waited.

The following morning the expert again placed the jade stone in the youth's hand and told him to hold it. On the third, forth, and fifth day the expert repeated the exercise and the instructions.

On the sixth day the youth held the jade stone, but could no longer stand the silence. "Master," he asked, "when am I going to learn something?"

"You'll learn," the expert replied and went about his business.

Several more days went by and the youth's frustration increased. One morning as the expert approached and beckoned for him to hold out his hand, he was about to blurt out that he could go on no longer. But as the master placed the stone in the youth's hand, the young man exclaimed without looking at his hand, "This is not the same jade stone!"

"You have begun to learn," said the master.

学 会 耐 心

一个年轻人到当地一位研究宝石的师傅那里，说他想成为一位宝石专家。师傅没有同意，担心年轻人学习没有耐性，年轻人恳求给他一次机会。最后，师傅终于同意了，告诉年轻人："明天到这里来。"

第二天上午，师傅在男孩手中放了一块玉石，告诉他拿好，然后继续工作，切削，称重，摆放宝石，年轻人静静地坐在那里等着。

第二天早上，师傅同样在男孩手中放了一块玉石，告诉他让他握着。第三天、第四天、第五天，师傅一直重复这样的动作和指令。

第六天，男孩依然握着宝石，但无法再静静地坐在那里了。"师傅，"他问道，"我什么时候开始学东西啊？"

"你会学到的。"师傅边回答边继续工作。

几天过去了，年轻人越来越沮丧。一天早晨，师傅来后召唤他，让他伸出手，他打算说他不能再继续……但当师傅再次把宝石放在年轻人手中时，年轻人看都没看，便大叫起来："这不是原来那块宝石。"

"你已经开始学习了。"师傅说。

Live and Laugh

This is the day I learned that my life is coming to an end, and that's all right. Eighty-eight years is more than most people get.

My daughter and I sat in Dr. Barbara's office. "I have done everything I can do for you," she said, kindness in her voice. "Would you like me to contact hospice?"

Surprised, I didn't know how to react. The doctor was looking into my eyes, waiting for a sign of understanding. "They can take care of your needs, enabling you to stay home." She paused, and then said, "Do you know about hospice?"

I said, "Yes, I had known hospice when Mia's dad died." I was remembering the flurry of activity, almost eight years ago, when a registered nurse and two aides arrived at our home, along with a delivery of a hospital bed, a bedside potty, a wheelchair, and a walker. In no time the bed was made up and standing in the living room, the potty was hidden behind a screen, the wheelchair was out of the line of traffic, and the walker was folded and leaned against a wall. Yes, I was acquainted with hospice.

Mia asked, "Are you telling me my mother has six months to live?"

The doctor transferred her attention to Mia. "No. We don't say that now." She looked back at me, "You may live several months or a year…" I sensed hesitation in her. I stood, ready to leave; I needed to go home and talk this over with God.

However, before I could go home, I had to keep an appointment made last week with a beautician, a stranger, since retirement had claimed the operator I was in the habit of using. Maybe the hair-do would make me feel better. Yet I felt a strong need to talk about what I was thinking of my new status. Until I was better acquainted with it myself, I didn't want to discuss the obvious change in my relationship with Mia; she needed time, too.

Back in the car an unfamiliar silence lay between us. By the time Mia stopped the car to let me out at the beauty shop, I knew what I was going to do. Suddenly I was glad I didn't know the hairdresser.

Her name was Melody. After introductions, I was seated in an adjustable chair, leaned back against a sink, and felt water and shampoo fingered onto my scalp. Then, before I could change my mind, I said, "I've just been told that I'm going to die." Her fingers stilled immediately. She said nothing for a moment, so I added, "I'll have to call in hospice." Then I sat quietly, waiting. When her fingers started working again, I felt the muscles in my neck become tense. What was she going to say?

"Hospice, huh? You're telling me you've got six months to live?" I opened my mouth to speak but didn't have time before she continued. "You can't have six months. That's mine. You can have three months or five or nine, but you can't have six."

For the second time that day, I was too surprised to speak. She finished rinsing my hair and pushed a knob on the chair that allowed me to sit up—and just kept talking…I began to laugh.

"I get lots of free lunches out of that six-month prognosis. My kids treat me great too. The other day my granddaughter said, 'Don't say that, Grandma. It might be bad luck.' I said, 'Well, someday it's going to be true. Then won't you be glad you were nice to me all those years?" I was laughing out loudly now, and it felt wonderful.

"I tell anybody who needs to know," she added. "One day I parked in a hard-to-find-space, and a woman in a Mercedes stopped behind my car as I got out. She yelled at me, 'I've been waiting to park there. I had to turn around first.' The teenage boy sitting in the passenger seat looked embarrassed—as well he should. I told her, 'You want this parking place? Okay. You can have it. I've got six months to live, so a parking place is the least of my worries. I'll just get in my car and pull out. You can have it.' The teenager said, 'M-o-m-m-m?' and the lady left without further chatter. It comes in handy, you know?" I continued to laugh.

Only God has the wisdom and the knowledge to choreograph that particular afternoon in my life, with all the right people in all the right places at the right time. As I got ready to go home, I faced the back of the shop where Melody was shampooing her next client and talking a mile a minute. Smiling, I said in my head, "Thank you, God."

Occasionally, when I sense a dark mood, waiting to pounce, I think of Melody and laugh. Oh, I'll still going to die, but I won't die in six months. I wouldn't dare!

活到老，笑到老

这一天，我知道我的生命即将结束，那没关系。大多数人都没活88岁。

我和女儿坐在芭芭拉医生的办公室。"我可以为你做一切，"医生善良地说，"你愿意我联系安养院吗?"

我很惊讶，不知道如何应对。医生直盯着我的眼睛，等待我理解。"他们能使你在家里得到照顾并满足你的需求，"她顿了一下，然后说，"你知道安养院吗?"

我说："是的，我知道安养院是在米娅的爸爸逝世的时候。"我回忆起来一连串的活动：8年前，一名注册护士和两个助手来到我们家，连同医院的一张病床、一个床边的便壶、一把轮椅和一个拐杖。很快床便支好了，摆在起居室里，便壶放在屏风后面，轮椅搁在不挡道的地方，拐杖合着靠在墙上。是的，我很熟悉安养院。

米娅问道："你是说我妈妈只剩6个月活头了吗?"

医生把她的注意力转向了米娅。"不，我并没有这样说。"她回头看了看我说，"你可以再活几个月或一年……"我感到了她语气中的犹豫。我站起来，准备离开，我需要回家和上帝好好聊聊。

然而，回家之前，我不得不遵守上周和一个陌生美容师的约定，因为我习惯用的那位行家退休了。也许换个发型会让我感觉好些，但我感到强烈需要谈谈新形势下我的想法。直到我更了解时，我才想讨论我和米娅关系的明显变化，她也需要时间。

回到车里，我和米娅之间充斥着一种陌生的沉默。米娅停下车来，让我上美容院，我知道我将要做什么。突然，我很高兴我不认识这个理发师。

理发师的名字叫梅洛迪。介绍之后，我坐在一个可调整的椅子上，椅子靠着一个水池，我感到水和香波在我的头皮上被手指揉搓着。然后，我还没来得及改变想法，话就说出了口："我刚刚被告知，我快死了。"理发师的手指马上停止不动了，一时间她什么也没说。于是我又说道："我将不得不来安养院。"然后，我静静地坐着，等待着。当她的手指重新开始工作时，我感觉自己脖子上的肌肉变得紧张起来。她会说什么呢？

"安养院，嗯？你是在说你还有6个月的存活时间吗？"我张嘴准备说话，但是我没来得及，她又继续说道，"你不可能有6个月的时间，那是我的。你可以有3个月、5个月或9个月，但你不能有6个月。"

那天，我第二次惊讶得说不出话来。她冲洗完我的头发，按了一下椅子上的旋钮，让我坐起来——只是继续说着……我开始笑了。

"我从预测的这6个月里得到许多免费的午餐。我的孩子们对我也很好。那天，我的孙女说：'别这样说，奶奶，那也许是不走运。'我说：'很好，总有一天它将会是真实的。然后，你会不会为你们这些年对我那么好而感到高兴？'"我大声地笑了，那感觉特棒。

"我告诉需要知道的任何人，"她接着说道，"有一天，我把车停在一个很难找到的停车位，我下车时，一个开着一辆梅赛德斯的女人在我的车后停下。她冲我大叫：'我一直都在等停在那里。现在我不得不掉头。'坐在乘客座位上的那个男孩看起来很尴尬——他还是尴尬的好。我告诉她：'你想要这个停车位？好吧，给你，我只有6个月活头了，所以一个停车位对我而言根本不算什么。我上车，把车开出来。你就可以停在这里。'少年说：'妈妈？'然后，那位女士没有再唠叨离开了。""这迟早派得上用场，是吧？"我继续笑着。

唯有上帝的智慧和学问能设计我生命中的那个特殊的下午。天时地利人和。我准备回家了，朝着美容店的后面看去，梅洛迪正在那里给她的下一位顾客洗头，说得很快，没有停顿。"谢谢你，上帝。"我微笑着在脑海里说。

有时，当我感觉一种悲观情绪等要袭来时，我就会想起梅洛迪而笑。噢，我还是会去死，但我不会在6个月后死去。我不敢！

Dad Is Taking Me Home

The story is told by a man who had been on a long flight. The first warning of the approaching problems came when the sign on the airplane flashed on: "Fasten your seat belts."

Then, after a while, a calm voice said, "We shall not be serving the beverages at this time as we are expecting a little turbulence. Please be sure your seat belt is fastened."

As he looked around the aircraft, it became obvious that many of the passengers were becoming apprehensive. Later, the voice of the announcer said, "We are so sorry that we are unable to serve the meal at this time. The turbulence is still ahead of us."

And then the storm broke out. The ominous cracks of thunder could be heard even above the roar of the engines. Lightening lit up the darkening skies and within moments the great plane was like a cork tossed around on a celestial ocean. One moment the airplane was lifted on terrific currents of air; the next; it dropped as if it were about to crash.

The man confessed that he shared the discomfort and fear with those around him. He said, "As I looked around the plane, I could see that nearly all the passengers were upset and alarmed. Some were praying. The future seemed ominous and many were wondering if they would make it through the storm. And then, I suddenly saw a girl to whom the storm meant nothing. She had tucked her feet beneath her as she sat on her seat and was reading a book. Everything within her small world was calm and orderly. Sometimes she closed her eyes, then she would read again; then she would straighten her legs, but worry and fear were not in her world. When the plane was being buffeted by the terrible storm, when it lurched this way and that, as it rose and fell with frightening severity, when all the adults were scared half to death, that marvelous child was completely composed and unafraid."

The man could hardly believe his eyes. It was not surprising therefore, that when the plane finally reached its destination and all the passengers were hurrying to disembark, he lingered to speak to the girl whom he had watched for such a long time. Having commented on the storm and behavior of the plane, he asked why she had not been afraid.

The sweet child replied, "Sir, my dad is the pilot and he is taking me home."

爸爸正带我回家

这个故事是一个乘飞机长途旅行的人告诉我的。当飞机上这样一个信号闪烁："系好你的安全带！"那就是对将要遇到的问题的第一次警告。

接着，过了一会儿，一个平静的声音说："我们不在这个时候提供饮料了，因为我们认为要遇上一小股湍流。请确保你们的安全带系好了。"

他环扫了一下整个飞机，显然许多乘客都变得越来越恐惧。稍后，广播员的声音响起："我们很抱歉不能在这个时候提供食物，因为湍流还在我们的前方。"

此时，暴风雨开始了，不祥的噼啪雷声在引擎上面咆哮，闪电照亮了夜空，瞬间飞机像软木塞一样在大海般的天空被抛来抛去。一时间，飞机被一股可怕的气流抬起，接着又像要坠落似的跌下去。

这个人坦言，他跟他周边的人一样感到不安和恐惧。他说："我环顾了一圈飞机，我看到几乎所有的乘客都心烦意乱、惊慌失措，一些人在祈祷。未来似乎凶多吉少，许多人都在纳闷他们是否能顺利挺过这场暴风雨。突然，我看到一个女孩，只见她对暴风雨一副无所谓的样子。她蜷着脚坐在位子上，正在读一本书。在她小小的世界里，所有的一切都是那么平静有序。有时她闭上眼睛，然后又开始阅读；接着她伸直腿，似乎担心和恐惧从来没有出现在她的世界里。当飞机遭遇暴风雨时，当它突然向这边或那边倾斜时，当它以骇人的严峻态势上下颠簸时，当所有的成年人都吓得半死时，那个非凡的女孩镇定自若、毫不畏惧。"

这个男人简直无法相信自己的眼睛。所以，当飞机终于到达目的地，所有的乘客都慌忙下机就不足为怪了。他待了一会儿，想跟那个他注视了很久的女孩说话。评论过这场暴风雨和飞机的壮举后，他问她当时为什么一点都不害怕。

这个可爱的小女孩回答："先生，我爸爸是这次的飞行员，他正带我回家呢。"

The Tale of Two Businessmen

There were once two businessmen who lived in a thriving city somewhere in the northeastern United States. Both were highly successful and both were very wealthy. One day they heard of a man who had lost his ability to earn a living because of disability. Both businessmen decided they would help him.

The first businessman sent his assistant to the grocery store to buy a month's worth of provisions. He sent another assistant to a department store to buy new clothes. When they returned, he had all the purchases set up and displayed in the company's conference room. Then the businessman sent a third assistant to fetch the man and his family, and a fourth to call the media.

Amid flashing strobe lights, video cameras, and shouting reporters, the first businessman explained that the man's plight had touched his heart and, out of compassion, had generously supplied the bounty displayed in the room. Strangely enough, the man and his family seemed embarrassed by all the sudden publicity and the endless demands by the press to pose with the businessman and mountain of his gifts.

The second businessman saw the coverage on TV and in the newspapers, but his plan to help the man and his family was different. Instead of going to the grocery store or to the department store—or the press—he quietly visited the man's home.

"I'd like to offer you a job," said the second businessman as he sat in the unemployed man's living room, sipping a cup of coffee.

"But, sir," the jobless man protested. "I work a lathe and my legs have suddenly given out. I cannot stand in one place for more than a minute or two."

The businessman smiled. "We have already made provision for your disability down at the shop," he answered. "Besides, you are an excellent lathe operator and the kind of man I am looking for. Do you want to work?"

"Oh, yes sir. I want to be able to provide for my family without having to accept charity."

"I thought that might be the case," the businessman replied. "I will give you a good job at a fair wage—and no one needs to know how you got it except you and me. In fact, I would rather you not tell anyone about our arrangement."

"But," the jobless man said, still unsure, "I don't want you to go to any special bother just to accommodate me. There are many lathe operators out there that can stand."

The businessman stood up to leave. "It was a small price to pay, I assure you. I would rather have an excellent lathe operator that sits down than a poor one that stands up. By hiring you, both of us are blessed."

两个商人的故事

从前有两个商人住在美国东北部一座繁荣的城市里，他们都功成名就、腰缠万贯。有一天，他们听说了一个因残疾而失去谋生能力的人，都想帮助他。

第一个商人派助手到水果店买了足够一个月吃的水果，派另一个人去商店买了衣服。他们回来后，第一个商人把所有买来的东西收好，放在公司会议室，然后派第三个助手去请那个残疾人和他的家人，又派第四个助手去请记者。

在闪烁的灯光、无数的摄像机和叫嚷的记者中，第一个商人说："这个残疾人的不幸触动了我的心。出于爱心，我把会议室里的这些东西全给他。"很奇怪，这个残疾人和他的家人对这种突然摆在别人面前。商人施舍如山的礼物，感到特别尴尬。

第二位商人在电视和报纸上看到了这篇报道，他帮助那个人和他的家人的方法不同。他没有去水果店、商店，也没有去请记者，而是悄悄拜访了这个人的家。

第二位商人坐在残疾人的家里，一边喝咖啡一边说："我很乐意给你提供一份工作。"

"可是，先生，"这个失业的人吃惊地说，"我做车床工时，腿受了重伤。我现在几乎不能在一个地方持续站一两分钟。"

这位商人微微一笑。"我们已经在车间为你的不便预先做好了准备，"他说，"此外，你是一位非常出色的车床操作工，正是我们想找的那类。你想去工作吗？"

"噢，是的，先生。我想我能养活全家人，不必接受慈善机构的帮助。"

"我想也是这样，"商人回答，"我将给你提供一份好工作，工资也很公平。除了你和我，没人知道你是如何获得这份工作的；事实上，我希望你不要告诉任何人我们之间的约定。"

"可是，"这个没有工作的残疾人仍然没有自信地说，"我不想你为了照应我而增添任何麻烦。毕竟，能站立的车床操作工有很多。"

商人起身准备离开。"这只是小小的代价，请放心。我宁愿要一个坐着的优秀车床操作员，也不愿要一个站立而差劲的车床操作工。雇用你，我们俩都开心。"

I Am with You, Darling

A boy was born to a couple after eleven years of marriage. They were a loving couple and the boy was a gem of their eyes.

When the boy was around two years old, one morning the husband saw a medicine bottle open. He was late for work, so he asked his wife to cap the bottle and keep it in the cupboard. His wife, preoccupied in the kitchen, totally forgot the matter.

The boy saw the bottle, playfully went to the bottle, was fascinated by its color and drank it all. It happened to be a poisonous medicine meant for adults in small dosages. When the child collapsed, the mother took him to the hospital in a hurry, where he died. The mother was stunned. She was terrified at how to face her husband.

When the distraught father came to the hospital and saw the dead child, he looked at his wife and uttered just five words. What do you think the five words were?

The husband just said, "I am with you, Darling."

The husband's totally unexpected reaction is a proactive behavior. The child is dead. He can never be brought back to life. There is no point in finding fault with the mother. Besides, if only he had taken time to keep the bottle away, this would not have happened. No one is to blame. She had also lost her only child. What she needed at that moment was consolation and sympathy from the husband. That is exactly what he gave her.

Sometimes we spent too much time in asking who is responsible or whom to blame, By this way we miss out some warmth in human relationship. "A journey of a thousand miles begins with a single step." Take off all your envies, jealousies, complaint, selfishness, and fears. And you will find things are actually not as difficult as you think.

亲爱的，我和你在一起

一对夫妇结婚11年后，生了一个男孩。他们十分恩爱，把孩子视若掌上明珠。

孩子两岁时，一天早上，丈夫看到了一个药瓶没盖，但因为上班快迟到了，所以他让妻子盖好瓶盖，放在橱柜里。他的妻子一直在厨房里忙，完全忘了这件事。

孩子非常淘气，看到瓶子后走了过去，被它的颜色深深地吸引住了，就把药全吃了。碰巧，那是一种毒药，成人吃很少就会中毒。孩子突然倒下了，妈妈匆忙把他送到医院，但孩子还是死了。妈妈惊呆了，她恐惧万分，不知道如何面对丈夫。

发狂的父亲赶到医院，看到死去的孩子，又看了看妻子，只说了一句话。你能猜出这句话是什么吗？

丈夫只说了句："亲爱的，我和你在一起。"

丈夫这种反应完全出乎人们的意料。孩子死了，他永远也回不来了。找孩子母亲的错已经没有任何意义。此外，要是丈夫当初花时间把瓶子拿开，一切都不会发生。不要责备任何人。她已经失去了她唯一的孩子。此刻，她需要的就是来自丈夫的同情和安慰。丈夫给她的正是这些。

有时，我们花费太多的时间责问谁该负责或谁该受责备，这使我们遗漏了人际关系中的一些温暖。"千里之行，始于足下。"甩掉你所有的嫉妒、抱怨、自私和恐惧，你会发现，事实上事情并不像你想象的那么难。

The Red and Blue Coat

Once there were two boys who were great friends, and they were determined to remain that way forever. When they grew up and got married, they built their houses facing one another. There was a small path that formed a border between their farms.

One day, a trickster from the village decided to play a trick on them. He dressed himself in a two-color coat that was divided down the middle. So, one side of the coat was red, and the other side was blue.

The trickster wore this coat and walked along the narrow path between the houses of the two friends. They were each working opposite each other in their fields. The trickster made enough noise as he passed them to make sure that each of them would look up and see him passing.

At the end of the day, one friend said to the other, "Wasn't that a beautiful red coat that man was wearing today?"

"No," the other replied. "It was a blue coat."

"I saw the man clearly as he walked between us!" said the first, "His coat was red."

"You are wrong!" said the other man, "I saw it too, and it was blue."

"I know what I saw!" insisted the first man. "The coat was red!"

"You don't know anything," the second man replied angrily. "It was blue!" They kept arguing about this over and over, insulted each other, and eventually, they began to beat each other and roll around on the ground.

Just then, the trickster returned and faced the two men, who were punching and kicking each and shouting, "Our friendship is OVER!"

The trickster walked directly in front of them, and showed them his coat. He laughed at their silly fight. The two friends saw that his coat was red on one side and blue on the other.

The two friends stopped fighting and screamed at the trickster, saying, "We have lived side by side like brothers all our lives, and it is totally your fault that we are fighting. You have started a war between us."

"Don't blame me for the battle," replied the trickster. "I did not make you fight. Both of you are wrong, and both of you are right. Yes, what each one saw was true. You were fighting because you only looked at my coat from your own point of view."

红外套，蓝外套

从前有两个男孩，他们是非常要好的朋友，决定做一辈子的好朋友。他们长大后结了婚，各自也盖了房子，而且门对门。他们的农田之间只隔着一条小路。

一天，村里的魔术师想捉弄他们一下。他穿了一件两种颜色的外套，两种颜色从中间分开，因此，外套一侧红一侧蓝。

魔术师穿着这件外套，从这两个朋友家中间那条窄窄的小路上走过。他们俩彼此相对在各自的田里干活。魔术师从他们身边走过，故意弄出很大声响，目的是确保他们两个都抬起头看见他经过。

这天结束时，一个朋友对另一个朋友说："今天那个人穿的红外套是不是很漂亮？"

"不对，"朋友反驳道，"那是一件蓝色外套。"

"他从我们中间穿过时，我看得很清楚！"第一个说，"他的外套是红色的。"

"你错了，"另一位说，"我也看见了，那是蓝色的。"

"我知道我看见了什么！"第一个人坚持说，"那个外套是红色的。"

"你知道什么？"第二个人生气地回答，"那是蓝色的！"他们对此不停地争辩起来，并相互侮辱对方，最后彼此打起架来，在地上来回翻滚。

就在那时，魔术师返了回来，面对着这两个人。他们又踢又打，还叫嚷着："我们不再是朋友了！"

魔术师径直走到他们面前，把外套拿给他们看。他们都笑了，感觉他们刚才那场打斗好蠢。两个朋友看到那件外套是一面红一面蓝。

这两个朋友停止了打斗，冲魔术师大叫："我们住在一块，一直都亲如兄弟。我们打斗全是你的错，你挑起了我们之间的战争。"

"这场打斗别责怪我，"魔术师说，"我并没有让你们俩打架。你们都对，也都错。对，你们每个人看到的都是真实的。你们之所以打架，是因为你们都只是从自己的观点来看我的外套。"

Small Unseen Miracle

Life's a little thing! Robert Browning once wrote. But a little thing can mean a life. Even two lives. How well I remember! Two years ago in downtown Denver, my friend, Scott Reasoner and I saw a tiny and insignificant thing change the world, but no one else even seemed to notice.

It was one of those beautiful Denver days, crystal clear and no humidity, not a cloud in the sky. We decided to walk the ten blocks to the Sixteenth Street Mall. The restaurant, in the shape of a baseball diamond, was called The Blake Street Baseball Club. Tables were set appropriately on the grass infield. Many colorful pennants and flags hung limply overhead.

As we sat outside, the sun continued to beat down on us, and it became increasingly hot. There wasn't a hint of a breeze, and the heat radiated up from the tabletop. Nothing moved, except the waiters, of course.

After lunch Scott and I started to walk back up the mall. We both noticed a young mother and her daughter walking out of a card shop toward the street. She was holding her daughter by the hand while reading a greeting card. It was immediately apparent to us that she was so engrossed in the card that she did not notice a bus moving toward her at a fast speed. She and her daughter were one step away from disaster when Scott started to yell. He hadn't even got a word out when a breeze blew the card out of her hand and over her shoulder. She spun around and grabbed the card nearly knocking her daughter over. By the time she picked up the card from the ground and turned back to cross the street, the bus had whizzed by her. She never knew what almost happened.

To this day, two things continue to perplex me about this event. Where did that one spurt of wind come from to blow the card out of that young mother's hand? There had not been a whisper of wind at lunch, or during our long walk back up the mall. Secondly, if Scott had been able to get his words out, the young mother might have looked up at us as they continued to walk into the bus. It was the wind that made her turn back to the card—in the direction that saved her life and that of her daughter. The passing bus did not create the wind. On the contrary, the wind came from the opposite direction.

Miracles often blow unseen through our lives!

看不见的小奇迹

罗伯特·布朗宁曾经写道：生活乃小事！但是，一件小事就能反映生活，甚至两个人的生活。我记得非常清楚！两年前在丹佛闹市区，我和朋友斯科特·里森纳看到了一件极其微小、无关紧要，却改变了整个世界的事情，好像其他任何人都没有注意到。

那天，丹佛的天很美：清澈透明，没有潮气，晴朗无云。我们决定步行十个街区到第16街购物商场。我们吃饭的家餐馆形状像棒球内场，名叫布莱克街棒球俱乐部，桌子井井有条地摆在绿茵内场，许多五彩小旗和旗帜毫无生气地悬挂在头顶。

我们在外面坐下，太阳继续火辣辣地照在我们身上，我们感觉越来越热。没有一丝风，热气从桌面上直往上冒，一切都纹丝不动，当然除了服务生。

午饭后，我和斯科特开始步行回购物商场。我们都注意到一个年轻妈妈和她的女儿从卡片店出来，正朝路上走。她一手拉着女儿，一边在看一张祝福卡片。显而易见，她太专注于看那张卡，竟没有注意到一辆公共汽车正急速向她驶来。斯科特准备要叫时，她们母女离灾难只剩一步之遥。甚至他一个字还没出口，一阵微风就把卡片从她手上吹过了她的肩膀。她转身去抓那张卡片，差点儿把女儿撞翻。等她从地上捡起卡片，转身再去横穿马路时，那辆公共汽车从她身边飕地开了过去，她根本不知道差点儿发生了什么事。

直到今天，这件事仍有两点让我迷惑。吹走那位年轻妈妈手中卡片的那股风是从哪里来的呢？无论午餐时候，还是我们返回购物商场走的那一大段路期间，始终一点风都没有。其次，即使斯科特把话喊出了口，这位妈妈很可能会抬头冲我们这边看，那样她们就会继续往前撞上那辆公共汽车。是那阵风使她转离汽车去追卡片——朝的正是救了她和女儿生命的那个方向。那辆驶过来的汽车并没有带风。相反，那风是从对面吹过来的。

奇迹在我们的生活中无处不在，却难觅其踪！

The Ripple Effect

The Master was walking through the fields one day when a young man, a troubled look upon his face, approached him.

"On such a beautiful day, it must be difficult to say so serious," the Master said.

"Is it? I haven't noticed," the young man said, turning to look around and notice his surroundings. His eyes scanned the landscape, but nothing seemed to register, his mind elsewhere. Watching intently, the Master continued to walk.

"Join me if you like." The Master walked to the edge of a still pond, framed by sycamore trees, with their leaves golden orange and about to fall.

"Please sit down," the Master invited, patting the ground next to him. Looking carefully before sitting, the young man brushed the ground to clear a space for himself.

"Now, find a small stone, please," the Master instructed.

"What?"

"A stone. Please find a small stone and throw it in the pond."

Searching around him, the young man grabbed a pebble and threw it as far as he could.

"Tell me what you see," the Master asked.

Straining his eyes not to miss a single detail, the man looked at the water's surface.

"I see ripples."

"Where did the ripples come from?"

"From the stone I threw in the pond, Master."

"Please reach your hand into the water and stop the ripples," the Master asked.

Not understanding, the young man stuck his hand in the water as a ripple neared, only to cause more ripples. The young man was now completely baffled.

"Were you able to stop the ripples with your hands?" the Master asked.

"No, of course not. I only caused more ripples."

"What if you had stopped the stone from entering the water to begin with?" The Master smiled such a beautiful smile that the young man could not be upset.

"Next time you are unhappy with your life, catch the stone before it hits the water. Do not spend time trying to undo what you have done. Rather, change what you are going to do before you do it." The Master looked kindly upon the young man.

"But Master, how will I know what I am going to do before I do it?"

"Take the responsibility for living your own life. If you're working with a doctor to treat an illness, ask the doctor to help you understand what caused the illness. Do not just treat the ripples. Keep asking questions." The young man stopped, his mind reeling.

"But I came to you to ask you for answers. Are you saying that I know the answers?"

"You may not know the answers right now, but if you ask the right questions, you will discover the answers."

"But what are the right questions, Master?"

"There are no wrong questions, only unasked ones. We must ask, for without asking, we cannot receive answers. But it is your responsibility to ask. No one else can do that for you."

波 纹 效 应

一天，一位大师在田野里走着，这时一个年轻人满面愁容地向他走来。

大师说："这么美好的一天，不要那么严肃。"

"是吗？我没有注意到，"说着，年轻人看了看周围，注意到了周边环境。他扫视了一下风景，但似乎没有留下任何印象，他的思想在别处。大师认真地看着，继续往前走。

"如果愿意，和我一块吧。"大师朝着一片宁静的池塘走去，池塘周围栽满了小无花果树，叶子呈橘黄色，好像快要落下来了。

"请坐吧，"大师拍了拍他旁边的地面邀请道。年轻人仔细看了看，给自己清了一块地面才坐下来。

"现在，请你找一小块石头。"大师指示道。

"什么？"

"一块石头。请找一块小石头，把它扔进池塘里。"

年轻人在周围搜索了一下，随即抓起一块小鹅卵石，尽力把它向远处扔去。

"告诉我，你看到了什么。"大师问。

他朝水面看去，眼睛睁大，不准备错过任何一个细节。

"我看到了波纹。"

"波纹从哪里来？"

"从我扔进池塘里的那块石头来的，大师。"

"请把你的手伸进池塘里阻止这些波纹。"大师说。

年轻人不理解，当波纹靠近时，他把手伸进水里，但引起了更多的波纹。这时，年轻人完全困惑了。

"你能用手阻止这些波纹吗？"大师问。

"不能，当然不能。我只是造成了更多的波纹。"

"要是你一开始就阻止那块石头进入水中会怎样？"大师笑得很灿烂，这使年轻人更加迷惑了。

"下次你生活得不开心时，请在它还没有落入水中之前抓住它。不要把时间浪费在试图挽回你做过的事情上。在你做之前改变你要做的。"大师和蔼地看着年轻人。

"可是，大师，我怎样才知道我做之前要做的事呢？"

"对你自己的生命负责。当你和一位医生共同去治疗一种疾病时，让医生帮助你了解疾病的原因。不要像对待波纹一样，要不断提出问题。"年轻人头脑眩晕，停住了。

"可我当初来，就是要问你要答案。你是说我知道答案吗？"

"现在你可能还不知道答案，但如果你问对了问题，你就会发现答案。"

"可什么才是问对问题，大师？"

"只有没有提出的问题，没有错误的问题。我们必须问，因为不问，我们就得不到答案。不过，问是你的责任，没人可以帮你做。"

The Golden Rule

To act with integrity and good faith was such a habit with Susan that she had never before thought of examining the Golden Rule: "All things whatsoever ye would that men should do to you, do ye even so to them." But the longer she reflected upon it, the stronger was her conviction that she did not always obey the precept; at length, she appealed to her mother for its meaning.

"It implies," said her mother, "in the first place, a total destruction of all selfishness: for a man who loves himself better than his neighbors, can never do to others as he would have others do to him. We are bound not only to do, but to feel, toward others as we would have others feel toward us. Remember, it is much easier to reprove the sin of others than to overcome temptation when it assails ourselves.

"A man may be perfectly honest and yet very selfish; but the command implies something more than mere honesty; it requires charity as well as integrity. The meaning of the command is fully explained in the parable of the Good Samaritan. The Levite, who passed by the wounded man without offering him assistance, may have been a man of great honesty; but he did not do unto the poor stranger as he would have wished others to do unto him."

Susan pondered carefully and seriously on what her mother had said. When she thought over her past conduct, a blush of shame crept to her cheeks, and a look of sorrow into her eyes, as many little acts of selfishness and unkindness came back to her memory. She resolved that for the future, both in great things and small, she would remember and follow the Golden Rule.

It was not long after this that an opportunity occurred of trying Susan's principles. One Saturday evening when she went, as usual, to farmer Thompson's inn, to receive the price of her mother's washing for the boarders, which amounted to five dollars, she found the farmer in the stable yard.

He was apparently in a terrible rage with some horse dealers with whom he had been bargaining. He held in his hand an open pocketbook, full of bills; and scarcely noticing the child as she made her request, except to swear at her, as usual, for troubling him when he was busy, he handed her a bank note.

Glad to escape so easily, Susan hurried out of the gate, and then, pausing to pin the money safely in the folds of her shawl, she discovered that he had given her two bills instead of one. She looked around; nobody was near to share her discovery; and her first impulse was joy at the unexpected prize.

"It is mine, all mine," said she to herself; "I will buy mother a new cloak with it, and she can give her old one to sister Mary, and then Mary can go to the Sunday school with me next winter. I wonder if it will not buy a pair of shoes for brother Tom, too."

At that moment she remembered that he must have given it to her by mistake; and therefore she had no right to it. But again the voice of the tempter whispered, "He gave it, and how do you know that he did not intend to make you a present of it?Keep it; he will never know it, even if it should be a mistake; for he had too many such bills in that great pocketbook to miss one."

While this conflict was going on in her mind between good and evil, she was hurrying homeward as fast as possible. Yet, before she came in sight of her home, she had repeatedly balanced the comforts which the money would buy against the sin of wronging her neighbor.

As she crossed the little bridge over the narrow creek before her mother's door, her eye fell upon a rustic seat which they had occupied during the conversation I have before narrated. Instantly the words of Scripture, "Whatsoever ye would that men should do to you, do ye even so to them," sounded in her ears like a trumpet.

Turning suddenly round, as if flying from some unseen peril, the child hastened along the road with breathless speed until she found herself once more at farmer Thompson's gate. "What do you want now?" asked the gruff old fellow, as he saw her again at his side.

"Sir, you paid me two bills, instead of one," said she, trembling in every limb. "Two bills?did I?let me see; well, so I did; but did you just find it out?Why did you not bring it back sooner?" Susan blushed and hung her head.

"You wanted to keep it, I suppose," said he. "Well, I am glad your mother was more honest than you, or I should have been five dollars poorer and none the wiser." "My mother knows nothing about it, sir," said Susan; "I brought it back before I went home."

The old man looked at the child, and, as he saw the tears rolling down her cheeks, he seemed touched by her distress. Putting his band in his pocket, he drew out a shilling and offered it to her.

"No, sir, I thank you," sobbed she; "I do not want to be paid for doing right; I only wish you would not think me dishonest, for, indeed, it was a sore temptation. Oh! sir, if you had ever seen those you love best wanting the common comforts of life, you would know how hard it is for us always to do unto others as we would have others do unto us,"

The heart of the selfish man was touched. "There be things which are little upon the earth, but they are exceeding wise," murmured he, as he bade the little girl good night, and entered his house a sadder, and, it is to be hoped, a better man. Susan returned to her humble home with a lightened heart, and through the course of a long and useful life she never forgot her first temptation.

黄 金 法 则

做事正直，具有崇高的信仰，是苏珊的习惯，所以她在此之前从未想过去检验这条黄金法则："你想别人怎么待你，你就要怎么待别人。"不过她对这句话思考的时间越长，就越觉得自己并没有遵从这一法则。最后，她问妈妈这句话是什么意思。

妈妈说："这句话的意思是，首先要彻底摧毁一切自私的心理。当一个人爱自己胜过爱他的邻居，就不会像自己希望别人对待他一样去对待别人。我们不仅要去做，还应该去体会，只有体会别人的感受，别人才会用同样的方式体会我们的感受。记住，我们总是更容易指责别人的错误，却很难抵挡自己面临的诱惑。

"一个人可以既诚实又自私，不过这一法则指的不仅仅是诚实这么简单，还有宽容和正直。那个善良的撒马利亚人的故事就很好地诠释了这一点。故事里讲到的那个利未人从受伤的人身边走过时，却没有提供任何帮助，或许他是个诚实的人，但却不会为可怜的陌生人做他希望别人会为他做的事。"

苏珊仔细思考着妈妈的话，当她想到过去的所作所为时，不禁羞愧得脸庞通红，露出了懊悔的神色。她又回想起之前做过的许多自私而又粗鲁的事。她下定决心，从今以后，不管大事小事，她都会尽力做好。她会遵循黄金法则，并把它铭记在心。

在这之后不久，出现了一个考验苏珊的机会。一个周六的晚上，苏珊像往常一样去汤普森农场旅店，收取妈妈给旅店客人洗衣服应得的报酬，一共是5美元。她在马圈里看到了汤普森。

很显然，农场主正在对那些和他讨价还价的马贩子大发雷霆。他手上拿着一个钱包，里面有好多钱。当苏珊找他要钱的时候，他都几乎没注意到，只是像以往一样骂她几句，嫌她在忙的时候打搅他，然后随手递给她一张纸币。

苏珊很庆幸这么快就拿到了钱，快速跑出门，然后，她停下来，把钱放到折好的围巾里。这时，她发现农场主给了她两张钞票，而不是一张。苏珊环顾一下四周，发现没有人看到这一幕，她的第一反应就是对这个天上掉下的馅饼喜出望外。

"是我的，都是我的了，"她对自己说，"我要给妈妈买一件新斗篷，这样就能把那件旧斗篷送给妹妹玛丽，明年冬天玛丽就能和我一起去主日学校了。不知道还够不够再给弟弟汤姆买双鞋。"

苏珊当时心想，农场主一定是多给她钱了，因此她没有权利花这笔钱。不过诱惑的声音在她耳边轻诉道："这是他给你的，你怎么知道这不是他送给你买礼物的呢？拿着吧，他不会知道的；即使是他的失误，但是他的钱包里有那么多钱，丢一张也不会被发现的。"

在苏珊的脑子里，善与恶在不停地斗争，她用最快的速度向家跑去。快要到家的时候，她反复权衡是用金钱买来的享受重要还是诚实重要。

当她穿过门前小桥的时候，看到了她和妈妈聊天时坐过的锈迹斑斑的凳子。这时，那项黄金法则在她耳边响起来："你想别人怎么待你，你就要怎么待别人。"

她突然转过身跑起来，速度快得让她喘不过气来，像是要逃离什么危险似的。她再次来到汤普森农场门前。"你还想干什么？"那个粗鲁的汤普森问。

"先生，您刚才给了我两张钞票，"她颤抖着说，"两张？是吗？让我看看，确实是这样，你怎么发现的？干吗还要送回来？"农场主说。苏珊红着脸，低下了头，没有吱声。

"我想，你一定想留着它，"他说，"我很高兴，你的母亲比你诚实，要不然我就会跟个傻子一样，丢了5美元。""我妈妈不知道这事，"苏珊说，"我回家之前，就决定把它送回来了。"

老人看着苏珊，只见苏珊在流泪，他被苏珊的行为感动了，从钱包里拿出1先令，送给苏珊。

"不，我不要，谢谢，"苏珊啜泣道，"今天这种事不值得受到嘉奖，我只是希望您能够把我当作诚实的孩子，因为那是一种极大的诱惑。先生，如果您看到您最爱的人连最基本的生活用品都没有的话，你就会明白对待别人就像别人对待自己一样是多么的困难。"

这个自私的农场主被打动了，他向苏珊道了晚安，回到屋里，嘟囔道："这个世上有的事情看似很小，实则充满了智慧。"他为自己感到惭愧，但他坚信他会变得更好。苏珊如释重负地回了家。在今后漫长的人生道路上，她一直铭记着这最初的诱惑。

第九卷

飞向我的爱

Love Is like a Flower

I'm aware that happiness may be tied in the ribbon of New Year,but I put my yearning for you into the necklace close to my heart.

Resting in the sun, listening to the billows, lying on the grass and in your arms, I embrace the dream of love in my heart.

Your glance like glittering spring lingers in my heart, more profound than poetry, more elegant than painting, making the start of a new era for me.

It was very late last night when I managed to get into sleep. My yearning for you was boundless like the vast sky.

It is said that dews are tears that stars shed, but I will tell you they are my love tears.

I long for the coming of a rainy night. I'll never forget those pledges of love given on those rainy nights. Under the shelter of my umbrella, the seeds of love have begun to sprout.

I miss you more at night than in the daytime. The flashing stars cover my sky once and again. I can only count the sparkling ones silently, thinking of those sunny days with you.

I saw you off in that flowering season, the path spreading quietly under our feet with occasional sunny rain floating about.

I'm a drifting little boat, longing for a warm harbor. I'll sail forward, however hard the voyage, however tempestuous the sea, to your heart, to pour out to you my endless yearning.

You can take away my soul, everything of mine. But leave me my eyes with which to see you.

If thoughts have wings, today you'd hear the sound of songbird fly near. If wishes bloomed, I'd bring you the sweetest flower that ever grows.

爱 的 花 季

我明白，幸福可以系在新年的丝带上，但现在我却把对你的思念挂在项链上，贴在心口。

枕着阳光，听着涛声，躺在草上，倚在你的怀里，我把爱之梦抱在心里。

你的匆匆一瞥像波光闪闪的泉水流在我的心里，它比诗还深刻，比画还优美，对我来说就像新世纪的一个起点。

昨夜，我很晚才设法进入梦乡。我对你的思念就像茫茫苍天没有尽头。

据说露珠是星星流下的眼泪，但我要告诉你那是我的相思泪。

我渴望雨夜的来临。我永远不会忘记那些在雨夜发的爱的誓言。在我的伞的保护下，那些爱情的种子已经开始发芽。

我夜里想你比白天多。繁星闪闪一次次覆盖我的天空，我只能默默地数着那些闪闪发光的星星，想起了我和你在一起的那些阳光灿烂的日子。

我在那个花季为你送行，小路静静地在我们脚下伸展，偶尔也有太阳雨在四处飘动。

我是一叶漂流的小船，渴望停靠在一个温暖的港湾。无论航程多么艰难，海上风暴多么汹涌，我都会驶向你的心灵，向你倾诉我无尽的思念。

我的心灵，我的一切，你都可以拿去，但要把眼睛留给我，让我能看到你。

如果思念能有翅膀，今天你就会听到小鸟的歌声飞近。如果心愿能开花，我会把最美的鲜花献给你。

I Am the Wind

I am the wind, the gentle wind;

I am the cloud, the slow, drifting clouds;

I am the water, the silent water;

I am the mountain, the boundless mountain…

If you wish, I will be the gentle wind that will ease your lonely spirit!

If you wish, I will be the slow, drifting clouds that will be your support at leisure!

If you wish, I will be that silent water, without a murmur, protecting you by your side!

If you wish, I will love you, just like those boundless, unbroken mountain ranges and valleys!

But I regret I am not the wind and not able to take care of you.

I hate that I am not the clouds and not able to bring you warmth.

I pity myself that I am not the water and not able to be so pure.

I am angry that I am not the mountain and not able to have my love as immovable as I would like.

I can only be myself this time, my mortal, earthly self, my only self, the only self that I can ever hope to be.

I thirst for love but I do not understand her deep mystery.

I strive for transcendence but I would rather be silent and nameless.

I want to be mature but I would rather remain innocent.

I would like that she love me, but I do not know even if I truly love her!

Endless searching, thirsting, striving, pursuing—where are my goals? Where is my future?

In this mundane world, I am one lonely speck;

In this universe I am a powerless particle of dust.

My love, though beautiful, is nothing great in itself.

And so, I ask only to live as well as I can.

In truth, there is no need to live one's life basking in glory, rising above men—so long as one's life has some value and some security…my love will be more radiant!

我 是 风

我是风，轻轻的风；

我是云，缓缓的云；

我是水，静静的水；

我是山，连绵的山……

如果你愿意，我愿做轻轻的风，抚慰你寂寞的心灵！

如果你愿意，我就是缓缓的云，从容悠闲让你依偎！

如果你愿意，我愿做你身边静静的水，默默守护着你！

如果你愿意，我将会爱你，就像那连绵不断的山脉深谷！

可是，我悔自己不是风，不能照顾你。

我恨自己不是云，不能带给你温暖。

我怜自己不是水，不能那样的纯净。

我气自己不是山，不能让爱像我喜欢的那样岿然不动。

我这次只能做自己，平凡的自己，唯一的自己，希望中的自己。

我渴望爱情，却不懂她的深奥。

我争取超越，却甘愿默默无闻。

我想要成熟，但我宁愿单纯。

我但愿她能爱我，但我又不知道，即使我真的爱她！

无尽地寻找、渴望、奋斗、追求，哪里是我的目标？哪里是我的未来？

在这尘世间，我是一颗孤独的微粒；

在这宇宙中，我是无力的尘埃。

尽管我的爱美好，但并不伟大。

所以，我只求好好活着。

其实，人生不必轰轰烈烈，出人头地——只要人生有价值，平安踏实……我的爱就会更加璀璨！

When Love Beckons You

When love beckons you, follow him, though his ways are hard and steep. And when his wings enfold you, yield to him, though the sword hidden among his pinions may wound you. And when he speaks to you, believe in him, though his voice may shatter your dreams as the north wind lays waste the garden.

For even as love crowns you so shall he crucify you. Even as he is for your growth so is he for your pruning.

Even as he ascends to your height and caresses your tenderest branches that quiver in the sun, so shall he descend to your roots and shake them in their clinging to the earth.

All these things shall love do unto you that you may know the secrets of your heart, and in that knowledge become a fragment of life's heart.

But if, in your fear, you would seek only love's peace and love's pleasure, then it is better for you that you…pass…into the seasonless world where you shall laugh, but not all of your laughter, and weep, but not all of your tears.

Love gives naught but itself and takes naught but from itself. Love possesses not nor would it be possessed, for love is sufficient unto love.

When you love, think not you can direct the course for love; if it finds your worth, it will direct your course. Love has no other desire but to fulfill itself. But if you love and must have desires, let these be your desires:

To melt and be like a running brook that sings its melody to the night.

To know the pain of too much tenderness.

To be wounded by your own understanding of love. And to bleed willingly and joyfully.

To wake at dawn with a winged heart and give thanks for another day of loving;

To rest at the noon hour and meditate love's ecstasy;

To return home at eventide with gratitude;

And then to sleep with a prayer for the beloved in your heart and a song of praise upon your lips.

爱 的 召 唤

当爱召唤你时，你跟随他去，尽管爱的道路艰难险峻。当爱的翅膀拥抱你时，你要向他让步，尽管藏在爱的翅膀里的剑会击伤你。当爱向你倾诉时，你要相信他，尽管他的声音会打碎你的美梦，就像北风吹荒花园一样。

因为爱给你戴上王冠时，也会把你钉上十字架。爱让你成长时，也会修剪你的心性。

爱登上你的枝头，爱抚你在阳光下颤抖的最柔嫩的枝条时，也会下到你的根部，摇晃你依附大地的根须。

所有这一切都是爱为你做的，就是让你了解自己内心的秘密，也让它们变成你生命中心的片段。

但如果出于恐惧，你只想寻求爱的平和与爱的快乐，那你最好进入一个没有季节的世界——你在那里可以欢笑，但并不是一直欢笑；你可以哭泣，但不是一直流泪。

爱只奉献本身，也只从自身索取。爱不会占有，也不会被占有，因为爱对爱已经足够。

你爱时，不要去想你可以为爱引导方向；如果爱发现你值得爱，它会指引你的方向。爱没有别的心愿，只会充实自己。但如果你爱，一定会有欲望，就让这些成为你的心愿：

将自己融化为涓涓溪流，对夜晚唱着自己的旋律。

明白太多柔情带来的痛苦。

因为对爱领悟而受伤，心甘情愿、喜笑颜开地流着血。

黎明醒来时心像长了翅膀，感激又迎来了爱的一天。

中午休息时沉思爱的迷醉。

黄昏时心怀感激回到家里。

然后，为心上人祈祷，进入梦乡，唇间吟诵着赞美的歌。

Mother Love Is like a Circle

"M" is for the million things she gave me.

"O" means that she's growing old.

"T" is for the tears she shed to foster me.

"H" is for her heart of purest gold.

"E" is for her eyes, with the love-light shining.

"R" means right, and right she'll always be.

Put them together and they'll spell "MOTHER," a word that means the world to me.

A mother's love is like a circle, it has no beginning and ending.

It keeps going around and around, ever expanding, touching everyone who comes in touch with it, enveloping them like the morning's mist, warming them like the noontime sun and covering them like a blanket of evening stars.

A mother's love is like a circle, it has no beginning and ending.

母 爱 像 圆

"M"是她给予我的无数东西。

"O"意味着她越来越老。

"T"是她在养育我时流的眼泪。

"H"指她的心像金子般纯洁。

"E"指她闪着爱的光芒的眼睛。

"R"是正确的意思，而且她总是正确的。

如果把这几个字母放在一起，就会拼成"MOTHER（母亲）"，这个词对我意味着整个世界。

母爱像圆，没有始终。

它周而复始，不断扩展，感动着每个接触它的人，像晨雾一样包围着他们，像正午的阳光一样温暖着他们，又像满天的繁星一样覆盖着他们。

母爱像圆，没有始终。

The Wedding Band

My mother's wedding band may not have been fancy or expensive, but to me, it was a priceless jewel.

When I was growing up, my mother had a ring she never took off. It was the only ring I ever saw her wear during my childhood. It was made of a shiny silvery metal with an oblong penny-brown metallic piece upon which two hearts were attached in the center.

She wore it when she swept, when she mopped, when she made her large mound of golden flour tortillas, when she sewed on her treadle Singer sewing machine and when she washed clothes on the rub-board.

She didn't really have any other jewelry, and, in fact, I remember my father saying that he didn't even buy her a ring when they were married. He hadn't thought about it, and during the ceremony, they had borrowed her brother Charlie's ring.

The years passed. My father, who had come from Mexico in the 1920s to try to earn a living, worked long, long hours at the service station he operated. And my mother, who was also from Mexico, toiled at home, keeping house for her husband

and eight youngsters. With his hard work and her thriftiness, they sent their first son off to college, then another child and then another. The older children helped with the expenses of the younger ones.

Just as the last two children were graduating from college, my father died suddenly of a heart attack, but my mother lived on for another twenty-three years. Their children had become lawyers, businessmen and teachers. In the last years of her life, my mother was finally able to enjoy the luxuries that had always been denied her. She was even able to buy some jewelry, which, I was surprised to learn, she really loved.

A few years before she died, she told me that she wanted her jewelry to go to her granddaughters. And when she died, it was done. A diamond ring to this one, a pearl ring to that one, an opal ring to another, and so it went.

Then I discovered it: her first ring. Now I could identify the metal. The ring was a thin, fragile thing by now, a small strip of stainless steel attached to two small hearts on either side of an oblong-shaped piece of copper. It had been worn so long that the copper had become unattached to the circle. Its value was naught.

I took the ring, polished it with a cloth and carried it to the bank to place in a safety-deposit box. To me, it was a gem that symbolized the sacrifices my mother had made for us and the values that she lived. How many years had she worn it? How many times had she denied herself so that we might succeed? Why did she save this ring when it seemed worthless? Was it a symbol to her, too?

The rest of my family doesn't quite understand this, but when I look at that ring, I see the priceless jewel of my mother's strength and the brilliance of the love that she showed us every day of her life.

结 婚 戒 指

母亲的结婚戒指也许不别致，也不贵重，对我来说却是无价之宝。

我从小到大，母亲手上的戒指从未摘下过。那是我小时候看到她戴的仅有的一枚。这戒指是闪亮的银色金属打造的，便士铜色的长方形金属底座中间镶着两颗连在一起的心。

无论是打扫房间、拖地、擀大摞大摞金黄的玉米饼，还是用脚踏缝纫机做针线活、在洗衣板上洗衣服，她都戴着这枚戒指。

她的确没有其他首饰，而且，事实上，我记得爸爸说过他们结婚时他根本没给母亲买婚戒，也没考虑过这事儿。婚礼期间用的婚戒还是借她弟弟查理的。

时光荏苒。20世纪20年代，来自墨西哥的爸爸为了谋生在自己开的加油站长时间工作。妈妈也是墨西哥人，在家里操劳，为丈夫和8个孩子持家。在爸爸的辛苦劳作和妈妈的勤俭节约下，他们供第一个儿子上了大学，然后供一个又一个孩子上了大学。哥哥姐姐们也在弟弟妹妹的花费上帮了一把。

就在家里最小的两个孩子马上要大学毕业时，爸爸因心脏病发作突然离去，但妈妈又继续生活了23年。他们的孩子当上了律师、商人和老师。在生命的最后几年，妈妈终于过上了多年没有享受过的舒适生活。她甚至能买一些首饰，得知她真正喜欢首饰，我吃了一惊。

去世前的几年，妈妈告诉我她要把自己的首饰都留给孙女们。她去世时也是这么做的。钻戒给这个孙女，珍珠的给那个，猫眼石的给另一个，就这样都送了出去。

后来，我才发现了她的第一枚戒指。现在，我才看清它是金属的。这枚戒指现在又薄又脆；长方形铜片两边镶着两颗由一个小不锈钢条连在一起的小小的心。戴得已经很久了，铜片和戒指圈之间已不连接，毫无价值。

我拿起这枚戒指，用布擦亮，把它放到了银行的保险柜中存放了起来。对我来说，这枚戒指是一块宝石，它象征着妈妈为我们奉献的一切和她一生存在的价值。她曾戴了多少年？为了我们能功成名就，她曾多少次为难自己？为什么这枚戒指看似毫无价值而妈妈还要保留？这对她也有象征意义吗？

尽管家里其他人并不是很理解这一点，但每当我看那枚戒指时，都会看到母亲在生命的每一天展示给我们的力量和爱的光辉。

If You Have Enough Love

Recently, John lost his wife Janet. For eight years she fought against cancer, but in the end her sickness had the last word.

One day John told me, when he tidied up some drawers at home, he found a small love letter Janet had written. He took out a folded piece of paper from his wallet.

It was a beautiful recipe for how to keep a marriage together.

Janet's description of her husband begins thus, "Loved me. Took care of me. Worried about me."

Even though John always had a ready answer, he never joked about cancer. Sometimes he came home in the evening to find Janet in the middle of one of those depressions. In no time he drove her to her favorite's restaurant.

"Helped me when I was ill," the next line reads. Perhaps Janet wrote this while the cancer was in one of the horrible and wonderful lulls.

"Forgave me a lot."

"Stood by my side."

"Always praising." "Made sure I had everything I needed," she goes on to write.

After that she has turned over the paper and added, "Warmth. Humor. Kindness. Thoughtfulness." And then she writes, "Always there for me when I needed you."

"John," I ask. "How do you stick together with someone through 38 years—not to mention the sickness? How do I know if I can bear to stand by my wife's side if she becomes sick one day?"

"You can," he says quietly. "If you have enough love, you can."

如果你有足够的爱

最近，约翰失去了妻子珍妮特。她和癌症抗争了8年，最终疾病还是夺去了她的生命。

有一天，约翰告诉我说，他在收拾家里的一些抽屉时发现了珍妮特写的一封小情书。他从钱夹里拿出一张折叠的纸。

对维系婚姻来说，这封情书是灵丹妙药。

珍妮特开头这样描写自己的丈夫："你爱过我，照顾过我，关心过我。"

尽管约翰总是对答如流，但他从来不对癌症开玩笑。有时他傍晚回家时发现珍妮特情绪低落，就会马上开车带她去她最喜欢的餐馆。

接下来的一行写道："我生病时帮助过我。"也许写这文字时，珍妮特正处在可怕而奇妙的平静期。

"总是原谅我。"

"支持我。"

她接着写道："总是称赞我。""确保我拥有所需要的一切。"

之后，她又在纸的背面补充道："热心，幽默，善良，周到。"然后，她又写道："我需要时，你总是在我身边。"

"约翰，"我问，"你和一个人生活了38年，却没有提过她的病情，你是怎么做到的呢？如果有一天我的妻子病了，我怎么知道自己能否坚守在妻子身边呢？"

"你能，"他平静地说，"如果有足够的爱，你就能。"

Words from the Heart

Most people need to hear these three little words "I love you." Once in a while, they hear them just in time.

I met Connie the day she was admitted to the hospital ward, where I worked as a volunteer. Her husband, Bill, stood nervously nearby as she was transferred from the gurney to the hospital bed. Although Connie was in the final stages of her fight against cancer, she was alert and cheerful. We got her settled in. I finished marking her name on all the hospital supplies she would be using, then asked if she needed anything.

"Oh, yes," she said, "would you please show me how to use the TV? I enjoy the soaps so much and I don't want to get behind on what's happening." Connie was a romantic. She loved soap operas, romance novels and movies with a good love story. As we became acquainted, she confided how frustrating it was to be married 32 years to a man who often called her "a silly woman."

"Oh, I know Bill loves me," she said, "but he has never been one to say he loves me, or send cards to me." She sighed and looked out the window at the trees in the courtyard. "I'd give anything if he'd say 'I love you, ' but it's just not in his nature."

Bill visited Connie every day. In the beginning, he sat next to the bed while she watched the soaps. Later, when she began sleeping more, he paced up and down the hallway outside her room. Soon, when she no longer watched television and had fewer waking moments, I began spending more of my volunteer time with Bill.

He talked about having worked as a carpenter and how he liked to go fishing. He and Connie had no children, but they'd been enjoying retirement by traveling, until Connie got sick. Bill could not express his feelings about the fact that his wife was dying.

One day, over coffee in the cafeteria, I got him on the subject of women and how we need romance in our lives; how we love to get sentimental cards and love letters.

"Do you tell Connie you love her?" I asked, knowing his answer, and he looked at me as if I was crazy.

"I don't have to," he said. "She knows I do!"

"I'm sure she knows," I said. "but she needs to hear it, Bill. She needs to hear what she has meant to you all these years. Please think about it."

We walked back to Connie's room. Bill disappeared inside, and I left to visit another patient. Later, I saw Bill sitting by the bed. He was holding Connie's hand as she slept. The date was February 12.

Two days later I walked down the hospital ward at noon. There stood Bill, leaning up against the wall in the hallway, staring at the floor. I already knew from the head nurse that Connie had died at 11 a. m.

When Bill saw me, he allowed himself to come into my arms for a long time. His face was wet with tears and he was trembling. Finally, he leaned back against the wall and took a deep breath.

"I have to say something," he said. "I have to say how good I feel about telling her. I thought a lot about what you said, and this morning I told her how much I loved her…and loved being married to her. You should have seen her smile!"

I went into the room to say my own good-bye to Connie. There, on the bedside table, was a large Valentine card from Bill. You know, the sentimental kind that says, "To my wonderful wife…I love you."

爱，就要说出来

大多数人都需要听到"我爱你"这三个微不足道的字。偶尔，他们听到的会非常及时。

我看到康妮那天，她刚被送到医院的病房，我在那里做志愿者。她被从装有轮子的金属担架移到病床上时，她的丈夫比尔不安地站在旁边。尽管康妮已到了与癌症对抗的最后阶段，但她仍然活泼开心。我们把她安顿好，我在她要用的所有东西上都标上她的名字，又问她是否还需要什么东西。

"噢，是的，"她说，"请你告诉我怎么使用这部电视好吗？我喜欢看肥皂剧，不想错过任何情节。"康妮是一个浪漫主义者，爱看肥皂剧、言情小说和带有精彩爱情故事情节的电影。随着我们渐渐熟悉，她吐露说，她真失望，竟然和一个常称她"傻女人"的男人生活了32年。

"噢，我知道比尔爱我，"她说，"但他从来没有说过他爱我，也从来没有给我寄过贺卡。"她叹了口气，望着窗外庭院里的那些树。"如果他说'我爱你'，我愿意付出一切，但那恰恰不是他的本性。"

每天比尔都来看望康妮。开始，康妮看肥皂剧时，他坐在床边。后来，她睡觉的时间越来越多，他就在病房外的走廊上踱来踱去。不久，康妮不再看电视，清醒的时刻越来越少，我开始有了更多时间和比尔在一起。

他说他是做木工的，很爱钓鱼。他和康妮没有孩子，便以旅行来享受退休时光，直至康妮病倒。面对妻子病危的这个事实，比尔无法表达这种感受。

有一天，在自助餐厅喝咖啡时，我和他谈起了女人的话题，谈起了生活中我们如何需要浪漫，谈起了我们如何喜欢收到柔情的贺卡和情书。

"你告诉康妮你爱她了吗？"我明知故问。他看着我，好像我疯了一样。

"没必要，"他说，"她知道我爱她！"

"我确信她知道，"我说，"可是，她需要听到，比尔。她需要听到这些年她对你意味着什么。请想一下这件事。"

我们走回康妮的病房。比尔走了进去，我离开去看望另一个病人。随后，我看到比尔坐在床边，握着入睡的康妮的一只手。那天是2月12日。

两天后的中午，我顺着医院病房走廊走着，看到比尔靠墙站在那里，盯着地板。我已经从护士长那里得知，康妮上午11点已经去世。

比尔看见我，久久地伏在我的怀里，泪流满面，浑身颤抖，最后靠回墙上，深深地吸了口气。

"我必须说点什么，"他说，"我必须说把那句话告诉她感觉真好啊。我对你说的话想了很多。今天早上我告诉她我是多么爱她……非常喜欢和她结为夫妻。你真该看看她听到这句话后的微笑！"

我走进病房，和康妮告别。只见床头桌上放着比尔送的一张大大的情人节贺卡。你知道的，贺卡上写着一句情意绵绵的话语："献给我的爱妻……我爱你。"

You Are My Life

There was a boy who was sent to a boarding school. He used to be the brightest student in his class. He was at the top in every competition. But things changed after that. His grades started dropping. He hated being in a group. He was lonely all the time. He felt worthless and that no one loved him.

His parents began to worry. But even they did not know what was wrong. So his dad decided to visit the school and talked with him.

They sat on the bank of the lake near the school. The father started asking him casual questions about his classes, teachers and sports. Then he asked, "Do you know why I am here today, son?"

The boy said, "To check my grades?"

"No, no," his dad replied. "I am here to tell you that you are the most important person for me. I want to see you happy. I don't care about grades. I care about you. I care about your happiness. You are my life."

Now the boy had everything he wanted. He knew there was someone on this earth who cared for him deeply. He meant the world to someone.

Thanks a lot, Dad. You are my life.

你是我的生命

一个男孩被送到寄宿学校。他曾是班里最聪明的学生，他在每次竞赛中总是名列前茅。但到了寄宿学校后，情况发生了变化。他的成绩开始下滑，他讨厌参加团体活动，总是感到孤独。他觉得自己毫无价值，也没有人爱他。

他的父母亲开始担心，但就连他们也不知道这是怎么回事。于是，他的爸爸决定到学校跟他谈谈。

他们坐在学校附近的湖岸上。父亲开始漫不经心地问他上课、老师和运动这样的问题。然后，他又问："儿子，你知道我今天为什么来这里吗？"

男孩说："来查看我的分数？"

"不，不是的，"他的爸爸回答说，"我是来这里告诉你，你对我来说是最重要的人。我想看到你开心。我在乎的不是成绩，我在乎的是你，我在乎的是你开心。你是我的生命啊。"

现在，这个男孩拥有了他想要的一切。他知道在这个世界上有人深深地爱他，他就是这个人的一切。

非常感谢，爸爸。你是我的生命。

Seagulls and Tears

I sat on the wet sand at the seaside, so that only the ocean could see my sadness. The beach was deserted, the salted wind caressed my cheeks, drying my bitter tears of loneliness. I sat like this for a long time, thinking that my bitter tears had driven away every living creature around. Only the sea witnessed my immense sadness. I brought my despair to her, like always, to swing it in her waves, the steady, peaceful crashing waves, until it fell asleep within me, into oblivion. Then I would feel no pain for a time, no loneliness…

Suddenly, a rustle startled me and I fought my way up through the gloom of my thoughts and the despair of my feelings. Suddenly, I was not alone any longer. A seagull was slowly coming towards me, seeming to search some food among the dead shells. He stopped next to me and for one moment we looked at each other in silence. I was expecting him to fly away, frightened by my teary eyes, but he came a step closer to me, unafraid.

Then I asked him, "Why don't you run away? My sadness has scared all the creatures of the earth from here and from everywhere I look. The shells have closed inside themselves and the sea birds, with translucent slumber, have flown away frightened. Even the sea, if she had been able to, would have gone from this place. My tears have chased away every living creature. Why are you not afraid of tears?"

The seagull answered me, "Because tears don't last. Once they reach here, by the sea, they disappear like they have never existed. Nobody remembers them any longer. The good sea embraces all sadness, caresses the weary and the broken against her chest and brings them back to the shore, replacing the heavy-hearted with her song of love and eternity. The same will happen to you. You only have to look around and you will find it."

The seagull lifted his wings and flew away over my shoulder. I wanted to call him back, to ask him to stay with me a little longer. I wanted to ask him to caress away my teary loneliness. I wanted to beg him to stay, not to go away, not yet. But as I turned my head over my shoulder to plead with him, I understood he had been right.

There, on the other side of the tracks that he had left in the sand, two eyes were watching me. The bitterness of my tears was slowly disappearing, taking on the sweetness of the happy tears of love.

海鸥和眼泪

我坐在海边潮湿的沙滩上，这样只有大海才能看见我的悲伤。海滩上空无一人，咸咸的海风亲吻着我的脸颊，吹干了我孤独苦涩的泪水。我这样坐了很久，心想我苦涩的泪水已经吓走了周围的每一个生物，只有大海目睹我无尽的痛苦，我把痛苦带给她，在她一如既往的平静波浪里漂荡，直到那痛苦的感觉在我的体内安睡，直至遗忘。随后，一时间，我不再感到痛苦和孤独⋯⋯

突然，一阵沙沙声惊动了我。我努力从忧郁的思考和绝望的感觉中挣脱出来，蓦然发现，我不再是单独一人。一只海鸥慢慢地向我走来，似乎在死去的贝壳中寻找着食物。它挨着我停下来，我们静静地对视了一会儿，我期待它会被我的眼泪吓得飞走，但它却又向我走近了一步，毫不害怕。

我问他："你为什么不逃走？我的悲哀已经吓走了我看到的所有生物，贝壳吓得把它们自己关在壳里，海鸟带着朦胧的睡意被吓得飞走了，甚至大海也会离开这个地方，如果她能的话。我的眼泪已经驱走了所有的人，你为什么不害怕？"

海鸥对我说："因为眼泪不会持久。一旦它们随着大海到了这里，就会消失，仿佛从未存在过一样，没有人再记起它们。善良的大海包容了所有的悲伤，用她的胸怀抚慰着疲倦和伤心，并把它们带到岸上，用爱和永恒的歌取代沉重的心灵。同样的事情也会发生在你身上，你只要环顾四周，就会找到。"

海鸥抬起翅膀，从我的肩上掠过，飞走了。我想喊它回来，请求它和我多待一会儿。我想请求它抚慰我充满泪水的孤独。我想乞求它留下来，不要走。但当我扭头去恳求它时，我明白它是对的。

在那里，在海鸥留下足印的沙滩的另一边，一双眼睛正在注视着我。我痛苦的眼泪正在慢慢消失，甜蜜幸福的爱的泪水开始涌了出来。

Butterfly and Shell

Once upon a time there was a very sad and lonely butterfly. He was so sad and lonely that he did not want to live anymore. One day, when he was sitting very depressed on the seashore, thinking about the life's uselessness, he heard near him a small and clear voice: "Good morning. Who are you?"

"I'm a butterfly, but who are you? A speaking stone? I can't believe it!"

"But I'm not a stone, I'm a shell and I'm a living creature just as you are. Would you like to be my friend?"

"I have no friends. I'm very unhappy because nobody loves me and for this reason I wanted to die in the sea…"

"I don't want you to die. I have been just as lonely and sad as you. I have never known what love was. But now you're here and none of us is alone. Stay with me, be my wingy prince and tell me about all you have ever seen in the world, about all that could never be seen by the salted eyes of a sea's daughter."

And the butterfly kept staying by the shell's side and they loved each other more than one could imagine. The butterfly was gathering on his wings the colors of the world to give them as a bouquet to his sweetheart and the shell was bringing as gift to her wingy prince all the mysterious whispers of the sea depths.

But as butterflies usually have shorter life than the shells, one day the butterfly died. The shell buried him in the sand and cried much over him, so much that she died of sadness, getting melted in her own tears till she totally disappeared. But the next morning, around the empty shell embracing a sand pile guarded by a coral cross, a pearly snowfall seemed having fallen down. Because the pearl is nothing else but shell tear and butterfly powder mixed with much, with very much love.

蝴蝶和贝壳

很久以前，有一只非常悲伤和孤独的蝴蝶。他是那样悲伤和孤独，再也不想活下去了。一天，他垂头丧气地坐在海边，想着这无助的生活，听到身边传来一个小而清晰的声音："早上好。你是谁？"

"我是一只蝴蝶，可你是谁？是一个正在说话的石头吗？我无法相信！"

"我不是石头，我是一只贝壳，我是像你一样的生物。你想做我的朋友吗？"

"我没有朋友。我很不幸，因为没有人爱我，为此，我想死在大海里……"

"我不想让你死。我也和你一样孤独，从不知道爱是什么。但现在，你在这里，我们俩就不孤单了。留下来跟我在一起，做我的飞翔王子吧，告诉我你看到的所有事情，海的女儿看不见的所有事情。"

蝴蝶继续留在贝壳身边，他们相亲相爱，超出了任何人的想象。蝴蝶在他的翅膀上聚集了世界上所有的颜色，作为花束送给心爱的人，贝壳也将深海里所有的神秘低语作为礼物送给她的飞翔王子。

但因为蝴蝶的寿命通常比贝壳的寿命短，所以有一天蝴蝶死了。贝壳把他埋在沙子里，为他痛哭不已，伤心而死，渐渐融化在她自己的眼泪里，直到她完全消失。但第二天早晨，在这个沙堆拥抱、珊瑚十字架守卫的空贝壳周围，仿佛一颗珍珠般晶莹的雪花飘落了下来。这枚雪花是贝壳的眼泪和蝴蝶身上的粉末混合而成的，凝结着融融爱意。

The Day I Met My Mother

Mine was, at times, a lonely childhood. Born in Chungking, China, of missionary parents, I lost my mother at birth. I was two months old when my father sent me to Mother's favorite sister in Morgantown, West Virginia. There I grew up in the house where Mother had spent her girlhood.

When Aunt Ruth was at home, I was surrounded by love. But she was our sole breadwinner and worked in an office six days a week. Left with a procession of hired girls, I felt the loneliness of the big, old house.

In the evening, before Aunt Ruth came home, I often sat on the floor beneath a picture of my mother—a sweet-faced young woman of 20, with dark eyes and black curly hair.

Sometimes I talked to the picture, but I could never bear to look at it when I'd been naughty. There was one question always in my mind: What was my mother like? If only I could have known her!

Twenty years passed. I had grown up, married and had a baby, named Lucy for her grandmother—the mother I'd so longed to know.

One spring morning, 18-month-old Lucy and I boarded a train for Morgantown to visit Aunt Ruth. A woman offered me half her seat in the crowded car. I thanked her and busied myself with Lucy, while the woman turned her attention to the landscape speeding by.

After settling my baby in my arms for a nap, I started to talk with the woman. She said she was going to Morgantown to see her daughter and brand-new grandson. "Surely you know my aunt, Ruth Wood," I said. "She's had a real-estate office in Morgantown for years."

"No," she answered. "I've been away a long time, and that name is not familiar to me."

For several minutes, the woman looked out the window. Then, without turning her head, she began to speak.

"There was a Miss Lucy Wood, a teacher, in Morgantown years ago. She probably left there before you were born. You said the name Wood, and, suddenly, I can't stop thinking about her. I haven't thought of her for years, but once I loved her very much. She was my teacher. My parents owned a bakery on Watts Street. They were on the verge of divorce. They fought and quarreled all the time. I had to work very hard at home and in the bakery, too.

"I loved school, though I didn't make good grades. Miss Wood's room was a happy place; it seemed like heaven to me. One day, after my folks had a big fight at breakfast, I came to school late, holding back the tears. Miss Wood kept me after school. I thought she would scold me but, instead, she let me tell her my troubles. She made me feel how much my brothers and sisters, and even my parents, needed me and from that day on, my life was worth living.

"A few months later, I heard a little girl say: 'Miss Wood's going to marry a missionary and go live in China!' I went home crying. My parents stopped in the middle of a fight to ask me what was wrong, but they could not know how great a light was going out in my life. I couldn't sleep that night.

"The next day, Miss Wood again kept me after school to see what was wrong. When I told her, she looked surprised and tender. 'Please don't go way off to China!' I begged.

"'Viola, ' she answered, 'I can't give up China. I'm going where my heart calls me, with the man I love. But I'll think of you often, and I'll send you a postcard. '

"I'd never had any mail of my own, so that made me feel better. When I told my mother, she shook her head, saying, 'Don't feel too bad, Viola, if she forgets; she'll have so many folks to write to. '

"Two months later, I got a postcard with a picture of the Yangtze River, postmarked Chungking, China. 'Are you still making me proud of you, my little brave one?' it asked. If anyone had given me a million dollars, it couldn't have made me more proud.

"Right after that, my parents broke up and we moved away from Morgantown. I raised my five brothers and sisters, married, and raised four children of my own.

"Goodness, we are almost there! I've talked too much. I do hope I haven't bored you."

Then, for the first time, she turned to me and saw the tears in my eyes.

"Would you like to see Lucy Wood's granddaughter?" I asked.

My baby was waking from her nap. My heart was singing. The burning question of my childhood had been richly answered.

At long last, I knew exactly what my mother had been like.

我见到母亲那天

我的童年有时非常孤独。我出生于中国重庆的一个传教士家庭，我一生下来就失去了母亲。我两个月大时，父亲把我送到了西弗吉尼亚州摩根城妈妈最爱的妹妹那里。我在那里长大成人，母亲曾在那个房子里度过了少女时代。

当鲁思姨妈在家里时，我被爱包围着。但她是我们中唯一养家糊口的人，每周要上6天班。我跟一群女用人待在一起，在大大的老房子里感到非常孤独。

傍晚时分，鲁思姨妈回家前，我常常坐在母亲照片下面的地板上。照片上是一个脸蛋甜美、年方20岁的年轻女人，有着乌黑的眼睛、卷曲的黑发。

有时我和那张照片说话，但当我调皮时永远不敢看它。我脑海里总有一个问题：我的母亲是什么样子？要是我能认识她该多好！

20年过去了。我已经长大、结婚，并有了一个宝宝，名叫露西，和她的外婆（我曾渴望认识的母亲）同名。

一个春天的早晨，我抱着18个月大的露西登上了开往摩根城的一列火车，去看望鲁思姨妈。在拥挤的车厢里，一名妇女为我让了半个座位。我谢过她，就忙着照看起露西，那名妇女将目光转向了飞驰而过的风景。

我把宝宝安顿在怀里睡觉后，开始和那名妇女攀谈起来。她说她要去摩根城看望女儿和刚出生不久的外孙。"你肯定认识我的姨妈鲁思·伍德吧，"我说，"她在摩根城房地产办公室上班有好几年了。"

"不认识，"她回答说，"我已经离开那里好久了，那个名字我不熟悉。"

那名妇女向窗外望了好几分钟。随后，她没有回头，又开始说了起来。

"有一位露西·伍德小姐，很多年前在摩根城当过老师。她可能在你出生前就离开了。你刚才说起伍德这个姓氏，我突然情不自禁想起了她。我好多年没有想起她了，但我曾非常爱她。她是我的老师。我的父母在瓦特街开有一间面包店。他们快要分道扬镳了，他们天天打架争吵，我不得不在家里和面包店内拼命干活。

"我喜欢学校，尽管我的成绩不好。伍德小姐的房间是一个快乐的地方，那对我来说就像天堂一样。有一天早饭时，父母大吵一场后，我上学迟到了，强忍着眼泪。放学后，伍德小姐把我留了下来。我以为她会训我，相反她却让我告诉她我有什么麻烦。她让我感到她是我的兄弟姐妹，甚至是我的父母，是多么需要我，从那天起，我的生活就过得有价值了。

"几个月后，我听到一个小女孩说：'伍德小姐准备嫁给一名传教士，要到中国去生活了！'我哭着回到家里。我的父母正打着，停了下来，问我出了什么事儿，但他们可能不知道我人生中一盏多么伟大的灯就要熄灭了。那天我彻夜难眠。

"第二天放学后，伍德小姐又把我留了下来，问我有什么心事。当我告诉她时，她既吃惊又温柔。'请不要去中国！'我恳求说。

"'维奥拉，'她回答说，'我不能放弃中国。我要到心灵召唤我的地方，和我的意中人厮守在一起。但是，我会常常想起你，我会给你寄明信片的。'

"我从未有过自己的任何邮件，所以这让我感觉好了些。当我告诉母亲时，她摇摇头说：'维奥拉，如果她忘了，不要感觉太糟。她会给好多好多亲人写信。'

"两个月后，我收到了一张明信片，上面有一幅长江的照片，邮戳上写着'中国重庆'。'你仍然让我为你感到骄傲吗，我的小勇敢？'明信片上问道。就是有人给我100万元，也不能让我如此自豪。

"紧接着，我的父母就分手了，我们搬出了摩根城。我把兄弟姐妹5个抚养成人，然后结婚成家，并抚养自己的4个孩子。

"天啊！我们快到了！我说得太多了。我真希望没有让你厌烦。"

随后，她第一次转向我，看到了我眼里的泪花。

"你想见露西·伍德的外孙女吗？"我问。

我的宝宝刚好睡醒，我的心在歌唱，我童年时渴望的那个问题已经得到了圆满的回答。

我终于确切知道自己的母亲是什么样子的了。

Father Oak

I don't remember when I was born. All I know is that my first cradle has been an oak leaf and that the light filtered through the branches has tenderly caressed me. I was only a little acorn but the light was my mother. I was living wrapped up in a leaf near the heart of my father, the old oak.

My parents loved me very much: my mother was waking me up each morning with sunrays and my father was singing to me each evening leaf lullabies and I was falling asleep in the leaf's cradle, dreaming of angels.

But one morning when I woke up, all forest had been covered by gold. I was so happy that I wanted to sing, but my father's sadness has broken my joy.

"The fall is already here, little girl," he said. "And now we have to pass away. But don't be afraid; next spring we'll be back again for the earth to rejoice."

And I still have lived like this for some time, each day in more light, each day between fewer leaves, until one day when my father dropped me down from his old and tired arms. And very soon it has snowed from the angels' wings and all my sleep has become angel wing and silver moon until one morning when I woke up gently touched by a snail's horns.

"Good morning, dad!" I said.

"Good spring, little girl!" answered the old oak.

"But what's this? All winter long I have dreamed of millions of angels and now I woke up with millions of eyes. What happened, dad?"

My father didn't answer me, but I found the answer in the infinitely multiplied echo of my words. I wasn't anymore the little acorn who had sadly entered the winter's sleep. I was a rustling forest.

橡 树 爸 爸

我不记得我何时出生。我所知道的是我的第一个摇篮曾是一片橡树叶,阳光从树枝间透过来,温柔地爱抚着我。我只是一颗小小的橡子,但阳光是我的母亲。我被一片叶子包裹着,生活在我父亲——那棵老橡树的心的旁边。

我的父母非常爱我:每天早晨母亲用阳光把我唤醒,每天晚上父亲用沙沙的树叶声给我唱催眠曲,我在树叶摇篮里进入了梦乡,梦见了天使。

但有一天早晨,我醒来时,整个树林一片金黄。我快乐得想放声歌唱,但父亲的悲伤打断了我的欢乐。

"秋天已经来了,小女孩,"他说,"现在我们必须离去,但不要害怕,明年春天,我们还会回来,和大地一起欢庆。"

而我仍像这样生活了一段时间，每天的阳光越来越多，每天树间的叶子越来越少，直到有一天，父亲将我从衰老而疲惫的双臂上放下去。没过多久，雪从天使的翅膀上落了下来，我所有的睡眠都变成了天使的翅膀和银色的月光，直到一天早晨，我被一只蜗牛的触角温柔地触醒。

"早安，爸爸！"我说。

"春天好，小女孩！"老橡树回答说。

"可这是怎么回事？整个漫长的冬天，我曾梦到了数百万的天使，现在我醒来却带着数百万的眼睛。发生了什么事，爸爸？"

父亲没有回答我，但我从我话音的众多回声中找到了答案。我不再是那颗悲伤地进入冬眠的小橡子，而是一片沙沙作响的橡树林。

True Love

It was a busy morning, approximately 8 : 30 a. m. , when an elderly gentleman in his 80s, arrived to have stitches removed from his thumb. He stated that he was in a hurry as he had an appointment at 9 : 00 a. m.

I took his vital signs and had him take a seat, knowing it would be over an hour before someone would be able to see him. I saw him looking at his watch and decided, since I was not busy with another patient, I would evaluate his wound.

On exam it was well healed, so I talked to one of the doctors, got the needed supplies to remove his sutures and redress his wound.

While taking care of his wound, we began to engage in conversation. I asked him if he had a doctor's appointment this morning, as he was in such a hurry. The gentleman told me no, that he needed to go to the nursing home to eat breakfast with his wife.

I then inquired about her health. He told me that she had been there for a while and that she was a patient of Alzheimer Disease. As we talked, and I finished dressing his wound, I asked if she would be worried if he was a bit late. He replied that she no longer knew who he was, that she had not recognized him in five years till now.

I was surprised, and asked him, "And you still go every morning, even though she doesn't know who you are?"

He smiled as he patted my hand and said, "She doesn't know me, but I still know what she is." I had to hold back tears as he left, and thought, "That is the kind of love I want in my life."

True love is neither physical nor romantic. True love is an acceptance of all that, has been, will be, and will not be. The happiest people don't necessarily have the best of everything; they just make the best of everything they have.

真　爱

那是一个忙碌的早晨，大约清晨8点30分，一位80来岁的老先生跑来要拆他拇指上缝合的针线。他说他时间很紧，因为他早晨9点有个约会。

我领会了他急切的心情，让他坐下，告诉他这需要一个多小时后，别人才能见他。我发现他看了看表后表示同意，由于我没有忙于其他病人，因此就检查了他的伤口。

检查发现伤口已经痊愈，于是我对一个医生说，准备药具给他拆线，然后重新敷裹伤口。

处理伤口时，我们聊了起来。我问他早晨是否预约过医生，因为他这么匆忙。老先生告诉我他没有预约，他又说要去疗养院陪妻子吃早饭。

我接着询问起他妻子的健康状况。他告诉我说，她在那里已经有一段时间了，她是老年痴呆症患者。我们聊天的同时，我敷好了他的伤口，我问如果他迟到的话，她会不会担心。他回答说，她再也不会知道他是谁了，而且到现在为止，她已经有5年时间认不得他了。

我很吃惊，又问他：“即便她都不认得你是谁，那你每天早晨仍然去吗？”

他笑了笑，拍拍我的手说：“她认不得我了，但我仍然清楚地知道她是谁。”他离开时我强忍着眼泪，心里想道：“这就是我这一生期望的爱情。”

真爱既非肉欲也非情欲。真爱是接纳一切之一切，既定事实，可能之事，以及不能之事。最谐幸福之人无须享万事之幸，他们唯善己之所能。

I'll Fly to My Beloved

Once upon a time, there was a bird in a cage who sang for her merchant owner. He took delight in her song day and night, and was so fond of her that he served her water in a golden dish. Before he left for a business trip, he asked the bird if she had a wish, "I will go through the forest where you were born, past the birds of your old neighborhood. What message should I take for them?"

The bird said, "Tell them I sit full of sorrow in a cage singing my captive song. Day and night, my heart is full of grief. I hope it will not be long before I see my friends again and fly freely. Bring me a message from the lovely forest. I long for my beloved, to fly with him, and spread my wings."

The merchant traveled on his donkey through the forest. He listened to the melodies of many birds. When the merchant reached the forest where his bird came from, he stopped, pushed his hood back, and said, "Oh you birds! Greetings to you all from my pretty bird in her cage. She sends her love to you. She asks for a reply that will ease her heart. She wants to join her beloved and sing her songs through the air with a free heart, but I would miss her beautiful songs and cannot let her go."

All the birds listened to the merchant's words. Suddenly one bird shrieked and fell to the ground. The merchant froze to the spot where he stood. Nothing could shock him more than this did. One bird had fallen down dead!

The merchant wend on his way to the city and traded his goods. At last he returned to his home. He did not know what to tell his bird. He stood before her cage and said, "Oh, nothing to speak of."

"No, no," the bird cried, "I must know at once."

"I do not know what happened," said the merchant. "I told them your message. Then, one of them fell down dead."

Suddenly the merchant's bird let out a terrible shriek and fell on her head to the bottom of the cage. The merchant was horrified. "Oh, what have I done?" He cried, "Now my life means nothing."

He opened the cage door, reached in, and cupped took her in his hands gently and carefully. "I will have to bury her now," he said, "the poor thing is dead."

The moment he lifted the bird out of the cage, she flapped up, flew out of the window and landed on the nearest roof. She turned to him and said gratefully, "Thank you for delivering my plea. I fly to my beloved who waits for me. To my beloved I'll fly. Goodbye, my master."

"My bird was wise. She taught me secret of life," the merchant reflected.

飞向我的爱

从前有一只笼中鸟，总是为从商的主人歌唱。商人整天以她的歌声为乐，是那样喜爱她，居然用一只金碟为她盛水喝。他外出经商前，问鸟儿有没有心愿："我要穿越你出生的那片森林，遇到你以前居住地的那些鸟儿，我该为他们带去什么口信呢？"

鸟儿说："告诉他们，我卧在笼子里，充满忧伤，唱着囚歌。我的心整天充满哀伤。我希望再见到朋友们，但愿离自由飞翔的日子不会太久。从那片可爱的森林给我带个口信，我渴望见到心上人，同他一起展翅飞翔。"

商人骑驴穿越森林，倾听鸟儿们优美的歌声。商人走到那只鸟生长的树林时，停下来，把帽子推到脑后，说："噢，你们这些鸟儿！我那只漂亮的笼中鸟向你们问好，把爱送给你们。她请求你们的答复来安抚她的心灵。她想和心上人在一起，自由自在把歌声送入云霄，但我常常想念她美妙的歌声，所以不能放她走。"

所有的鸟儿都在倾听商人说的话。突然，一只鸟尖叫一声，落在了地上。商人僵立在原地。再没有什么能比这更让他震惊的了，一只鸟落地而亡！

商人继续赶路，到城里卖掉了货物，最后回到了家里。他不知道该告诉鸟儿什么。他立在鸟笼前说："噢，没什么可说的。"

"不，不，"鸟儿大声说道，"我必须马上知道。"

"我不知道发生了什么事儿，"商人说，"我把你的口信告诉了他们，接着，其中一只鸟就落地而亡了。"

突然，商人的鸟儿发出一声可怕的尖叫，一头栽落在笼底。商人大惊失色。"噢，我都做了些什么啊？"他哭道，"现在我的生活毫无意义。"

他打开笼门，伸进手，轻轻地、小心地把她捧在手里。"我现在不得不把她埋葬，"他说，"这个可怜的东西死了。"

就在他把鸟儿捧出笼子的那一刻，她振翅而起，飞出窗外，落在了最近的屋顶上。她转向他，感激地说："谢谢你送去了我的请求，我要飞向我的爱。再见，主人。"

"我的鸟儿非常聪明，是她教给了我人生的秘诀。"商人细想道。

The Butterfly-shaped Brooch

He, a gentleman, was regarded to be the most handsome man in the world, wonderfully urbane, extremely agreeable. His pure eyes and charming smile always quivered a network of ripples in the hearts of his fans. He was the charming prince in the dreams of tens of thousands of women and adored crazily by them in the last half of the century. His name was Gregory Peck.

She, an angel of blue-blood birth, could speak in five languages. Refined and elegant, noble and good-natured. Her enchanting smiles and communicative eyes kept countless admirers spell-bound at her feet. Her elegance and style will always be remembered in film history. She was an angel that fell onto the earth with her unique nobility and grace. Her name was Audrey Hepburn.

When angel met gentleman in that romantic *Rome Holiday*, the purest and most beautiful love in the world began.

He liked to see into her big and liquid eyes, which were full of the tender affection that melted him away.

Her heart lost a beat with a different feeling rising within her every time she met his gaze, like the beach sand kissed by the sea wave, soft and moist.

He was in secret love with her. However, he had been in marriage and was the father of three kids. He, who was not good at putting his feelings across, had his love buried deep in the heart.

In that summer, her love, melt in his smile, bloomed in despair over and over again. She dared not declare her love because the education she received and the shadow of her broken family since young prevented her from getting close to the husband of another lady.

Soon after that unforgettable summer, she got her love and got married with Mel Ferrer, a famous director, actor and writer in Hollywood.

He attended her wedding ceremony with his usual good nature and magnanimity. No one knew under his peaceful look there was something called resigning to destiny.

As a present, he sent her a butterfly-shaped brooch. That was the year of 1954. Love to him and her was a beginning and an end in the meanwhile.

She, at that time, was ingenuous to believe that a turn could help her escape from millions of heartbreaks. What she couldn't expect was she, in that way, had missed the scenery for all her life there.

He parted with his wife after her wedding, and then got married again.

Her marriage didn't actually bring her any happiness. Mel's betrayal was a fatal blow on her thirst for an everlasting love. She got married a second time, then divorced again, in that way one after another man came into and went out of her life. The only company at her side, during the 40 years, was that brooch, the butterfly-shaped brooch.

Again and again, she made him a phone call, pouring her sob stories to him with tears rolling down. He tried to console her in soft voice. Like a falling comet, her every tear pierced into his heart of the ocean which looked calm, billowing inside, however.

Perhaps, the contact between males and females is pretty occult. There seems to be just one step away from friendship to love, a long journey of thousands of mountains and rivers from love back to friendship. They, whereas, make it on the basis of respect for destiny and belief in friendship. They two brought distant love into near friendship by concealing all their love and affection deep in that summer *Roman Holiday*.

She didn't know to her death that from the day when he met her, she was always his life-long moonlight, day and night, shining brightly in his innermost soul.

In January, 1993, the angel flied back to her heaven. He came for a last sight and sent her off. He had been an old man of 77 with a walking stick, unsteady in gait.

She, with her eyes closed lightly among the flowers, looked pure and quiet like a pond lily after the summer rain.

He called her softly with response of silence. She couldn't hear him, couldn't forever. The white-haired old man gazed at her with tears running down the aged face.

The moment came when he had to say goodbye to her. Looking down at her, gently he kissed her coffin and murmured, "You are the woman I love most in my life."

He eventually bared his heart to her, for which she had been waiting all her life. But it was too late, late for the whole 40 years.

Ten years later, her former clothes and jewelry were sold at the famous Sotheby's. Once again, he came, just for that butterfly-shaped brooch and in the end he got what he wanted. With that butterfly-shaped brooch held in his palm, he was taken back to those long past old days. He seemed to see once again that girl in *Roman Holiday*, that beautiful and kind, pure and noble girl walking briskly towards him…

For 40 years, he had never told her the wedding present he sent was not an ordinary brooch, but one handed down from his grandmother.

49 days later, he closed his eyes with a smile, a butterfly-shaped brooch held in his hand as if he was holding her heart that would never beat, the past days that would never return, the true love that would never come back…

蝴 蝶 胸 针

　　他，是一位绅士，被认为是世界上最英俊的男人。他举止优雅，和蔼可亲，纯真的眼睛和迷人的微笑总能在粉丝们心里荡起阵阵涟漪。他是那个世纪下半叶成千上万女人梦中的白马王子，受到她们的疯狂追捧。他的名字叫格雷戈里·派克。

　　她，是一个拥有贵族血统的天使，会讲五国语言。她优雅端正，高贵善良，迷人的笑靥和两只会说话的大眼睛让无数爱慕者迷醉，典雅的举止和仪表将被铭记在电影史中。她是一个降临世间的天使，兼具无与伦比的高贵和典雅。她的名字叫奥黛丽·赫本。

　　当天使在那个浪漫的《罗马假日》里遇到绅士，尘世间一段最纯洁、最美丽的爱情便悄然而生。

　　他喜欢看她那双清澈的大眼睛，它们蕴含着将他融化的无限柔情。

　　每当她遇到他凝视的眼神——就像海水吻过的沙滩一样柔软温润——她的内心便会顿一下，陡然升起一股异样的情愫。

他暗恋上了她。然而,他已经结婚,而且是三个孩子的父亲。他不善表达自己的感情,于是将对她的爱深深地埋在了心底。

那个夏天,她的爱在他的笑容里融化,绝望地开了一次又一次。她不敢表达自己的爱,因为她受的教育和幼年时破裂的家庭阴影阻止她靠近另一个女人的丈夫。

那个难忘的夏天过后,她很快获得了自己的爱情,跟好莱坞一位著名导演、演员兼剧作家梅尔·费勒结了婚。

他参加了她的婚礼,他依然温厚宽宏。没人知道他平静的外表下掩藏着某种叫作认命的东西。

他送给她一枚蝴蝶胸针,作为礼物。那是1954年,爱情于他和她,既是开始同时也是结束。

那个时候的她天真地以为,一转身便可以逃脱千万次的伤心。她想不到的是,她也错失了她整个人生的那道风景。

她结婚后不久,他就和妻子离了婚,然后又结了婚。

她的婚姻实际上并没有给她带来任何幸福。梅尔的移情别恋给渴望拥有一份永恒爱情的她一个致命的打击。她第二次又结了婚,然后又离了婚,就这样一个又一个男人在她的生命里走来又走去。40年的岁月里,唯一一成不变陪伴在她身边的只有那枚胸针——蝴蝶胸针。

她多次给他打电话,说到伤心处忍不住泪如雨下。他轻声努力安慰她。她的每一滴眼泪就像一颗滑落的流星刺在他的心头,他的心犹如大海,表面风平浪静,底下却波涛汹涌。

也许男女之间的交往确实微妙。从友情到爱情似乎仅有一步之遥,但从爱情回到友情仿佛得翻越千山万水。然而,凭借着对缘分的尊重和对友情的信任,他们做到了。他们把所有的爱与情深深埋藏在那个夏天的《罗马假日》里,他们俩将远在天涯的爱情转化成了咫尺的友情。

她到死都不知道,从他遇见她的第一天起,她就一直是他生命里的月光,日日夜夜照亮他心灵的最深处。

1993年1月,天使飞回了天堂。他来,是为看她最后一眼,给她送行。他已是77岁的老人,拄着拐杖,步履蹒跚。

她微合双眼躺在花丛中,看上去就像夏日雨后的一株睡莲,纯洁而宁静。

他轻声呼唤她,却不见回答。她听不到他的声音了,永远也听不到了。

这位白发苍苍的老人凝视着她，不禁老泪纵横。

他不得不跟她说再见的时刻到了。他低下头看着她，轻轻地吻了一下她的棺木，喃喃说道："你是我一生最爱的女人。"

他终于向她袒露了自己的心声，为此她等待了整整一生。可是，它来得太晚，晚了整整40年。

10年后，苏富比拍卖行举行赫本生前衣物首饰的义卖活动。再一次，他来了，只为那枚蝴蝶胸针。最终，他如愿以偿拿回了它。手里捧着那枚蝴蝶胸针，他被带回了久远的往日。他仿佛再一次看到了《罗马假日》里那个女孩，那个美丽善良、纯洁高贵的女孩正轻盈地向他走来……

40年里，他从来没有告诉过她，自己送她的这件结婚礼物并不是一枚普通的胸针，而是他祖母的家传之物。

49天后，他微笑着合上了双眼，手里握着一枚蝴蝶胸针，仿佛他握着的是她那颗永不再跳动的心，是那些永不复返的往昔岁月，是那份永不回来的真爱……

The Good Son

There was once a jeweler, noted for many virtues. One day, the Jewish elders came to him to buy some diamonds, to put upon that part of the dress of their high priest.

They told him what they wanted, and offered him a fair price for the diamonds. He replied that he could not let them see the jewels at that moment, and requested them to call again.

As they wanted them without delay, and thought that the object of the jeweler was only to increase the price of the diamonds, the elders offered him twice, then three times, as much as they were worth. But he still refused, and they went away in very bad humor.

Some hours after, he went to them, and placed before them the diamonds, for which they again offered him the last price they had named; but he said, "I will only accept the first one you offered to me this morning."

"Why, then, did you not close with us at once?" asked they in surprise. "When you came," replied he, "my father had the key of the chest, in which the diamonds were kept, and as he was asleep, I should have been obliged to wake him to obtain them.

"At his age, a short hour of sleep does him a great deal of good; and for all the gold in the world, I would not be wanting in respect to my father, or take from him a single comfort."

The elders, affected by these feeling words, spread their hands upon the jeweler's head, and said, "Thou shalt be blessed of Him who has said, 'Honor thy father and thy mother'; and thy children shall one day pay thee the same respect and love thou hast shown to thy father."

孝顺的儿子

曾经有一个珠宝商，他因品行端正而受人爱戴。一天，几个年纪较大的犹太人到他的珠宝店买珠宝，他们想把珠宝镶在代表他们最高权力的长袍上。

他们向珠宝商描述了他们想要的珠宝的样子，并给出了合适的价位。但珠宝商说，他们不能立刻看到想要的珠宝，他们还得再来一趟。

但是那几位犹太老人急需珠宝，不想耽搁。他们以为珠宝商是想要更高的价钱，就出了两倍、三倍，甚至更高的价钱，但珠宝商依然拒绝了，几位老者情绪低落地离开了。

过了几个小时，珠宝商去拜访几位老者。到了之后，他将他们想要的珠宝放在他们面前。老人们要支付最后答应的价格，可珠宝商却说："我只要早上你们第一次出的价格。"

"为什么？最初你为什么不和我们做这笔生意呢？"老人们惊奇地问，"你们来的时候，存放珠宝的柜子是锁着的，我的父亲拿着钥匙，但那时候他正在睡觉，我不能打扰他休息。

"到了父亲这个年龄，睡一小时的觉对他是有很大好处的。就算给我世界上所有的金钱，我也不会去打扰他休息。"

几位老者被他的话深深地打动了，他们伸出手轻拍着珠宝商的头说："孝敬你的父亲和母亲，以后你的儿女也会像你孝敬父母一样孝敬你。"

The Gentle Hand

When and where it matters not now to relate—but once upon a time, as I was passing through a thinly peopled district of country, night came down upon me almost unawares. Being on foot, I could not hope to gain the village toward which my steps were directed, until a late hour; and I therefore preferred seeking shelter and a night's lodging at the first humble dwelling that presented itself.

Dusky twilight was giving place to deeper shadows, when I found myself in the vicinity of a dwelling, from the small uncurtained windows of which the light shone with a pleasant promise of good cheer and comfort. The house stood within an inclosure, and a short distance from the road along which I was moving with wearied feet.

Turning aside, and passing through the ill-hung gate, I approached the dwelling. Slowly the gate swung on its wooden hinges, and the rattle of its latch, in closing, did not disturb the air until I had nearly reached the porch in front of the house, in which a slender girl, who had noticed my entrance, stood awaiting my arrival.

A deep, quick bark answered, almost like an echo, the sound of the shutting gate, and, sudden as an apparition, the form of an immense dog loomed in the doorway. At the instant when he was about to spring, a light hand was laid upon his shaggy neck, and a low word spoken.

"Go in, Tiger," said the girl, not in a voice of authority, yet in her gentle tones was the consciousness that she would be obeyed; and, as she spoke, she lightly bore upon the animal with her hand, and he turned away and disappeared within the dwelling.

"Who's that?" A rough voice asked the question; and now a heavy-looking man took the dog's place in the door.

"How far is it to G—?" I asked, not deeming it best to say, in the beginning, that I sought a resting place for the night.

"To G—!" growled the man, but not so harshly as at first. "It's good six miles from here."

"A long distance; and I'm a stranger and on foot," said I. "If you can make room for me until morning, I will be very thankful."

I saw the girl's hand move quickly up his arm, until it rested on his shoulder, and now she leaned to him still closer.

"Come in. We'll try what can be done for you." There was a change in the man's voice that made me wonder. I entered a large room, in which blazed a brisk fire. Before the fire sat two stout lads, who turned upon me their heavy eyes, with no very welcome greeting. A middle-aged woman was standing at a table, and two children were amusing themselves with a kitten on the floor.

"A stranger, mother," said the man who had given me so rude a greeting at the door; "and he wants us to let him stay all night."

The woman looked at me doubtingly for a few moments, and then replied coldly, "We don't keep a public house."

"I'm aware of that, ma'am," said I; "but night has overtaken me, and it's a long way yet to G—."

"Too far for a tired man to go on foot," said the master of the house, kindly, "so it's no use talking about it, mother; we must give him a bed."

So unobtrusively that I scarce noticed the movement, the girl had drawn to her mother's side. What she said to her I did not hear, for the brief words were uttered in a low voice; but I noticed, as she spoke, one small, fair hand rested on the woman's hand.

Was there magic in that touch? The woman's repulsive aspect changed into one of kindly welcome, and she said, "Yes, it's a long way to G——. I guess we can find a place for him."

Many times more during that evening, did I observe the magic power of that hand and voice—the one gentle yet potent as the other. On the next morning, breakfast being over, I was preparing to take my departure when my host informed me that if I would wait for half an hour he would give me a ride in his wagon to G——, as business required him to go there. I was very well pleased to accept of the invitation.

In due time, the farmer's wagon was driven into the road before the house, and I was invited to get in. I noticed the horse as a rough-looking Canadian pony, with a certain air of stubborn endurance. As the farmer took his seat by my side, the family came to the door to see us off.

"Dick!" said the farmer in a peremptory voice, giving the rein a quick jerk as he spoke. But Dick moved not a step. "Dick! you vagabond! get up." And the farmer's whip cracked sharply by the pony's ear.

It availed not, however, this second appeal. Dick stood firmly disobedient. Next the whip was brought down upon him with an impatient hand; but the pony only reared up a little. Fast and sharp the strokes were next dealt to the number of half a dozen. The man might as well have beaten the wagon, for all his end was gained.

A stout lad now came out into the road, and, catching Dick by the bridle, jerked him forward, using, at the same time, the customary language on such occasions, but Dick met this new ally with increased stubbornness, planting his fore feet more firmly and at a sharper angle with the ground.

The impatient boy now struck the pony on the side of the head with his clinched hand, and jerked cruelly at his bridle. It availed nothing, however; Dick was not to be wrought upon by any such arguments.

"Don't do so, John!" I turned my head as the maiden's sweet voice reached my ear. She was passing through the gate into the road, and in the next moment had taken hold of the lad and drawn him away from the animal. No strength was exerted in this; she took hold of his arm, and he obeyed her wish as readily as if he had no thought beyond her gratification.

And now that soft hand was laid gently on the pony's neck, and a single low word spoken. How instantly were the tense muscles relaxed—how quickly the stubborn air vanished!

"Poor Dick!" said the maiden, as she stroked his neck lightly, or softly patted it with a childlike hand. "Now, go along, you provoking fellow!" she added, in a half-chiding, yet affectionate voice, as she drew up the bridle.

The pony turned toward her, and rubbed his head against her arm for an instant or two; then, pricking up his ears, he started off at a light, cheerful trot, and went on his way as freely as if no silly crotchet had ever entered his stubborn brain.

"What a wonderful power that hand possesses!" said I, speaking to my companion, as we rode away.

He looked at me for a moment, as if my remark had occasioned surprise. Then a light came into his countenance, and he said briefly, "She's good! Everybody and everything loves her."

Was that, indeed, the secret of her power? Was the quality of her soul perceived in the impression of her hand, even by brute beasts! The father's explanation was doubtless the true one. Yet have I ever since wondered, and still do wonder, at the potency which lay in that maiden's magic touch. I have seen something of the same power, showing itself in the loving and the good, but never to the extent as instanced in her, whom, for want of a better name, I must still call "Gentle Hand."

温 柔 的 手

这件事是在什么地方、什么时间发生的也许并不重要。曾经有一天，当我走过一个人烟稀少的村子时，不知不觉天快黑了。由于是步行，我估计还需至少一个小时才能到达要去的镇子，所以我决定在第一个遇到的房子里歇脚，对付一个晚上。

暮色使地上的影子越来越深，这时我发现自己走到了一所房子附近，房子的窗户上没有窗帘，灯光从窗户上照射出来，让人感到愉快而舒适。那房子坐落在一个院子里，离我站的道路不远。

我拐了过来，穿过歪斜的栅栏门，向小屋走去。那门摇来晃去，我进去之后，门闩锁上了，不过我没有注意这些。我一直走到房前的走廊，看见那儿站着一个瘦弱的女孩，她听到门口的响动，就站在那儿等我。

关门声刚落，一串低沉、急促的狗叫声就像大门关上时的回声一样响起来。一只大狗像幽灵一样突然出现在门口。就在它要跳起的时候，一只手轻轻地抚在它蓬松的脖颈上，同时一个声音轻声响起。

"进去，小虎。"女孩说道，不是用命令的口气，但她温柔的音调却非常坚定，似乎知道它一定会服从命令。她一边说，一边用手轻轻拍狗。狗转过头，从房间消失了。

"你是谁？"一个沙哑的声音问道，这时一个看起来很结实的男子出现在门口。

"请问这里离G镇还有多远？"我问道，我想找个地方过夜，所以一开始还是不要说太多。

"去G镇！"男子低哼一声，但语气不像开始那么严厉，"离这儿还有整整六英里。"

"还有那么远！我以前没去过那儿，而且我是步行来的，"我说，"您看我能不能在这儿住一夜，如果可以，我会不胜感激。"

我看到那个女孩的手很快移向他的手臂，伏在他的肩膀上。女孩紧紧地靠在他的身边。

"进来吧，我们会尽力帮你的。"男子的声音变了，这让我感到很奇怪。我走进一间大房子，房间里点着炉火。火堆前坐着两个粗壮的小伙子，他们睡眼蒙眬地看着我，并没表示欢迎。一位中年妇女站在桌子旁，两个孩子在和地板上的小猫玩。

"妈妈，是一个过路的。"刚才在门口很粗鲁地和我说话的男子说道，"他希望今晚可以在这儿过夜。"

那位妇女用怀疑的目光看了我一会儿，然后冷冷地回答："我们这里又不是旅店。"

"我知道，夫人，"我说，"天太黑了，而且这里离G镇还很远。"

"他很疲惫，而且步行，这儿离G镇又太远，"主人温和地说，"所以，妈妈，我们别再犹豫了，就留他住一晚吧！"

我都没注意到，那个女孩已经悄悄地走到她母亲的身边。她低声向母亲说了些什么，我没有听到，只是注意到，她在说话时把白皙的小手放在母亲的手上。这一抚摸是不是有什么魔法？妇女的态度瞬间从排斥转向欢迎，她说："是的，离那儿太远了，我想我们可以留他住一宿。"

那天晚上，我几次都注意到这双手和这个有魔力的声音——虽然轻柔，但是对别人却有一种力量。第二天早上吃过早餐后，我正准备离开，这时主人告诉我，如果我再等半个小时，就可以搭他的马车去G镇，因为他正好有事要去那儿。我非常高兴地接受了他的好意。

半个小时后，农夫驾着马车来到屋前的路上，并请我上去。我注意到拉车的马是一匹暴烈的加拿大矮种马，它看上去非常结实。农夫坐到我身边，家里人都出来和我们告别。

"迪克！"主人专横地吼了一声，同时迅速将缰绳拉了一下。但是迪克站着没动。"迪克，你这个无赖，走啊！"主人的鞭子抽在小马的耳朵上，发出响亮的声音。

尽管又喊了一声，但迪克还是不动，它站在那儿，毫不驯服。农夫又不耐烦地抽了它一鞭子，可迪克只是跳了跳。主人气急败坏地连着抽打了六七下，他的力气几乎用完了，可迪克仍站着不动。

这时，一个粗壮的小伙子站在路上，他抓住迪克的马辔头，将它往前拉，还对着迪克粗鲁地叫嚷，可这会儿迪克更加倔强，它的前蹄贴着地面，站得更稳了。

失去耐心的小伙子攥起拳头击打小马的头部，仍无济于事，看样子迪克是不会向这些方法屈服的。

"不要这样，约翰！"当女孩甜美的声音传入我的耳中时，我情不自禁地扭过头去看她。她穿过大门，走到马路上，拉住小伙子，把他拖到一边，但她并没用力，只是握着小伙子的胳膊，小伙子非常顺从，他似乎只想满足她的愿望而不再多想什么。

这会儿，那双温柔的手正抚摸小马的脖子，并对它低声说着什么，马儿紧绷的肌肉似乎突然放松下来，它那倔强的脾气也立刻消失得无影无踪。"可怜的迪克！"她说，一会儿抚摸着马的脖子，一会儿又像孩子一样轻拍着迪克。"现在，出发吧，你这个爱折腾人的家伙。"她抓起缰绳，半责备半怜爱地说。

小马转头看着女孩，它一遍又一遍地用头蹭着她的胳膊。然后，它竖起耳朵，轻快地小跑起来，就像从来没有过叛逆的情绪。

"那双手，拥有的力量真神奇！"路上我对同伴说。马车跑起来了。

他看着我，似乎我的话让他感到很惊讶。他的眼睛一亮，然后简单地说了句："她是个好孩子，我们都喜欢她。"

这就是她那神奇力量的秘密吗？她那双纤弱的小手所表现出来的精神力量，甚至可以感化粗野的牲畜。主人的解释毫无疑问是正确的，然而自始至终，我都被少女的魔力深深地感动着。我曾经见过同样充满爱意的力量，但它们都不如女孩的手那么神奇，我想不到更好的名字，只能称它为"温柔的手"。